rck

Shaw, Plato, and Euripides

THE FLORIDA BERNARD SHAW SERIES

UNIVERSITY PRESS OF FLORIDA

Florida A&M University, Tallahassee
Florida Atlantic University, Boca Raton
Florida Gulf Coast University, Ft. Myers
Florida International University, Miami
Florida State University, Tallahassee
New College of Florida, Sarasota
University of Central Florida, Orlando
University of Florida, Gainesville
University of North Florida, Jacksonville
University of South Florida, Tampa
University of West Florida, Pensacola

Shaw, Plato, and Euripides

Classical Currents in *Major Barbara*

Sidney P. Albert

FOREWORD BY R. F. DIETRICH

UNIVERSITY PRESS OF FLORIDA

Gainesville · Tallahassee · Tampa · Boca Raton

Pensacola · Orlando · Miami · Jacksonville · Ft. Myers · Sarasota

17 16 15 14 13 12   6 5 4 3 2 1

Library of Congress Cataloging-in-Publication Data
Albert, Sidney P.
Shaw, Plato, and Euripides : classical currents in Major Barbara / Sidney P. Albert ;
foreword by R. F. Dietrich.
p. cm.—(The Florida Bernard Shaw series)
Includes bibliographical references and index.
ISBN 978-0-8130-3764-6 (acid-free paper)
1. Shaw, Bernard, 1856–1950. Major Barbara. 2. English drama—Greek influences.
3. Euripides. Bacchae. 4. Plato. Republic. 5. Euripides—Influence. 6. Plato—Influence.
I. Title.
PR5363.M23A43 2012
822.'912—dc23   2011037499

The University Press of Florida is the scholarly publishing agency for the State University
System of Florida, comprising Florida A&M University, Florida Atlantic University,
Florida Gulf Coast University, Florida International University, Florida State University,
New College of Florida, University of Central Florida, University of Florida, University
of North Florida, University of South Florida, and University of West Florida.

University Press of Florida
15 Northwest 15th Street
Gainesville, FL 32611-2079
http://www.upf.com

Funding to assist in publication of this book
was generously provided by the
David and Rachel Howie Foundation.

To my lovely and loving sisters
Shirley Albert Luxenberg and
Beverly Albert Cooper Silvers

It is a natural law that wisdom and great power attract each other. They are always pursuing and seeking after each other and coming together . . . whether they are themselves discussing [this subject] in a private gathering, or are listening to the treatment of it by others in poems. . . . With much the same idea, I believe, primitive men brought together Prometheus and Zeus. The poets also show how in some such cases the two characters became enemies—in others, friends—how in some cases they were first friends and then enemies, and how in others they agreed in some things but differed on other points.

Plato, Second Letter, *Plato: Collected Dialogues*, trans. L. A. Post (1564)

Contents

Foreword

In "Shakespeare Studies" it is not unusual to find scholars who devote most of their published research and study to a single play, and that California State University, Los Angeles, Professor Emeritus of Philosophy Sidney Albert has taken that route with a Shaw play (here and in other publications) speaks to the increasing realization that there are Shaw plays every bit as intricate, complex, allusive, rich in historical context, and worthy of such focus as some of Shakespeare's plays. In *Major Barbara* Albert has certainly picked one of the richest of plays in meaning, as evidenced by its already being much written about and being embroiled in controversy. But it has not been written about from this specific angle with this degree of historical/philosophical contextualizing, and rarely has the general area of philosophical discourse been graced by such clarity of writing as will be found here.

The unique contribution of this work lies in the extensiveness and intensity of its focus on "classical currents," specifically from Plato and Euripides, which Albert's considerable expertise in both Greek and Greek philosophy makes him particularly qualified to elucidate. Shaw clearly invited this by making a central character in the play, Adolphus Cusins, a professor of Greek philosophy (modeled on a translator of Greek works of Shaw's acquaintance, Gilbert Murray, who had recently translated *The Bacchae*) and by a constant allusiveness to Greek antecedents. This text offers everything you always wanted to know about *Major Barbara*'s Greek roots.

This work makes significant contributions in at least three different areas. First, the frequency with which Albert finds clear echoes or "currents" of Greek thought in *Major Barbara*, mostly from Plato's *The Republic* and Euripides's *The Bacchae*, is truly remarkable and very convincing of an intertextual relationship of considerably more depth and exactitude than has been thought, constituting a dialectic within the play that must be grasped in order to fully grasp the play.

The second contribution is in Albert's enlightening us about the Greek works themselves, employing in this comparative study a sensitivity to problematics of translation and interpretation that perhaps even specialists would find revelatory.

And, third, and probably most important, in showing so specifically and concretely how Shaw has borrowed Greek thought but modernized it, Albert has indirectly delivered a marvelous critique of both Greek and modern thought in a way that reveals how the latter can be a growth from the former and, in Shaw's view, an improvement. He shows Shaw interacting with Greek thought in a way that both reconfirms ancient wisdom and yet goes beyond it, adapting it to the fresh perspectives of the modern world, perspectives not available to the classical authors. Albert convincingly presents *Major Barbara* as a step forward, an evolutionary growth, from ancient wisdom, while never losing sight of the fact that it is a play, not a philosophical disquisition, and that Shaw is not a philosopher but an "artist-philosopher." The appendix speaks eloquently to that last distinction, and you would not go wrong in starting there, especially if this has been a stumbling block in your appreciation of Shaw as a playwright.

R. F. Dietrich
Series Editor

Acknowledgments

At my present age (ninety-seven), many of the people I must thank—or wish I could thank—are no longer alive. I have worked on this manuscript intermittently for more than half a century, during which time I have benefited from collegial relations and friendships with Shavians and non-Shavians alike.

The Shaw scholar I am most indebted to is the late Dan H. Laurence, to whom I gave written expression of my gratitude as a participant in the "Tribute to Dan Laurence" at the 1992 Shaw conference in West Virginia. That tribute was later published in *SHAW: The Annual of Bernard Shaw Studies* 14 (1994). There is probably no Shaw scholar of merit who has not benefited substantially from Dan Laurence's knowledge and generous counsel. I feel sorry for those in future generations who will lack direct access to this fountainhead of Shavian erudition.

Another Shavian to whom I am deeply indebted is Bernard F. Dukore, Distinguished Emeritus Professor at Virginia Tech. Bernie and I first learned about Shaw together at the University of Illinois, Urbana-Champaign, and were later colleagues on the faculty of California State University, Los Angeles, at which institution I assisted him in his stage production of *Major Barbara*. He remains a longtime friend.

Yet another is Stanley Weintraub of Penn State University, prominent scholar, prolific writer, former editor of the *Shaw Review*, and founder of the Shaw Annual, who offered me numerous opportunities to publish in Shaw studies. Also to be gratefully acknowledged is Shaw bibliographer Charles (Al) Carpenter.

I wish to acknowledge my Yale roommate Gordon Alderman, who persuaded me to go to Yale graduate school where he surrounded me with theater and theater people. Of drama professors who led me in the direction of Shaw, I am indebted to the late Professor Allardyce Nicoll, then director of the Yale Drama School, for whom I worked as a graduate student assistant, and who became my adviser as a Ph.D. candidate. Later influences were Lawrence Carra of Carnegie Mellon University; Eric Bentley, Maurice Valency, and Margaret Bieber at Columbia University; and Charles Shattuck of University of Illinois, Urbana-Champaign. More recently, I wish to acknowledge the friendship of Donald R. Burrill and other colleagues with whom I worked closely in the philosophy department at California State University, Los Angeles, including Thomas Annese, Sharon Bishop, Ann Garry, and Joseph Prabhu. In connection with founding one of the largest emeriti organization in the country, Emeritus and Retired Faculty Association (ERFA), I had the pleasure of dealing with many college faculty leaders in the California State University system for many years.

Richard Dietrich, the series editor at University Press of Florida, has proved a steadfast and diligent supporter of this work on Shaw. An earlier version of the manuscript was directed toward publication in the late 1970s by John Pickering, then editor at Pennsylvania State University Press, abetted by a generous and painstaking evaluation submitted by the late Frederick P. W. McDowell of the University of Iowa, who provided his expert opinion and praise of the work; those comments many years ago have guided the form it has taken.

Lissa McCullough immersed herself in Shaw to become an indispensable literary editor of this project for more than two years (shades of Liza Doolittle!). Henry R. Mendell, my replacement in the philosophy department at California State University, Los Angeles, generously helped to refine the Greek terminology. Nettie Coleman, my amanuensis for many years, entered the manuscript into the computer from the copy that Lucy Albert had typed in the pre-computer era. The editors at the University Press of Florida, Amy Gorelick, Shannon McCarthy, Marthe Walters, and Jesse Arost, and freelance copyeditor Elizabeth Detwiler, have patiently seen it through to the printed page. Meanwhile the administration and staff of the Terraces at Park Marino in Pasadena, where I live, have supported this project in sundry practical ways.

•

Elaine Amromin has been a constant companion during my twilight years. As for the most personal debt of all, my three children Vivian and husband Moshani, Alan and wife Carolyn, Larry and wife Beth, have been and continue to be members of a stalwart family, progeny of my late father Simon Albert and mother Gertrude Dora Albert, née Siskin. My mother came to the United States alone as a thirteen-year-old immigrant child fleeing a wicked stepmother, and managed with remarkable tenacity and ingenuity to make sure that her son received an advanced education despite living in poverty at the height of the Great Depression. (It helped that Syracuse University, my alma mater, was within walking distance of our home.)

·

A few brief portions of this book have appeared previously in print. The appendix appeared more than half a century ago as "Bernard Shaw: The Artist as Philosopher," in *The Journal of Aesthetics and Art Criticism* 14, no. 4 (June 1956): 419–38. Approximately a sixth of the first essay appeared as "Shaw's *Republic*" in *SHAW: The Annual of Bernard Shaw Studies* 25, ed. MaryAnn K. Crawford (2005): 82–88. A brief excerpt has been borrowed and inserted into the second essay from "Barbara's Progress," *SHAW: The Annual of Bernard Shaw Studies* 21, ed. Gale K. Larson (2001): 81–93. I am grateful to these publications for their permission to publish revised versions here.

Jeremy Crow of The Society of Authors has given kind permission, on behalf of the Bernard Shaw Estate, to quote from numerous Shaw sources, published and unpublished; previously unpublished Shaw material copyright © 2011 The Trustees of the British Museum, the Governors and Guardians of the National Gallery of Ireland, and Royal Academy of Dramatic Art. Likewise has Oxford University Press kindly granted permission to quote from F. M. Cornford's translation of *The Republic of Plato*.

Introduction

THE WAY FROM ATHENS

Once, on being told he enjoyed a great reputation in America, Shaw asked, "Which? I am a philosopher, novelist, sociologist, critic, statesman, dramatist and theologian. I have therefore seven reputations."

Arthur H. Nethercot, "Bernard Shaw, Philosopher"

With a minimum of aid from others, [Shaw] taught himself how to write, sing, and speak in public. Later he acquired a broad knowledge of art, drama, literature, economics, and sociology; and developed his own spelling, punctuation, diet, mode of dress, manners, tact, committee personality, and literary style; so that by a prodigious effort he actually became the fabulous machine, and infinitely more than the machine, that he aspired to be.

William Irvine, The Universe of G.B.S.

Bernard Shaw's *Major Barbara* has on various occasions been called "a masterpiece" for which "nothing short of a cast of geniuses will be of the slightest use," and a drama that has "strained the resources of the stage to the breaking point: the acting requires three stars of the first magnitude." Indeed, "for plays of this class, the great question is whether the audience will be a failure or a success." As for its critics, "I have never met any expert who professed to get on easy terms with, say, *Major Barbara*, in less than four visits."

The author of these comments is none other than the playwright, Shaw himself.[1] Such assessments, whether proffered seriously or in jest, merit scrutiny if for no other reason than Shaw's own stature as a drama critic of remarkable perspicacity. It should not prove surprising that he could judge his own work discerningly. Yet after more than a century of critical inspection, this play still poses elusive problems for interpretation.

Shaw himself attested to the difficulty, writing on a postcard to actress and writer Elizabeth Robins in 1906: "There is a strong difference of opinion in my own mind about the last act; but pending its settlement I hereby certify that YOU are right."[2] Unfortunately my own thoroughgoing attempts to track down Robins's "right" interpretation have proved unsuccessful.

Shaw's preface to the play seeks to provide "First Aid to Critics," informing them what to say about it.[3] Despite this tender of assistance from the dramatist, which discusses its central ideas, the drama has continued to disturb audiences and critics, and for scholars at least the task of grasping and interpreting the drama remains a persistent challenge. What Shaw remarked about it after its first production in 1905 is still to some extent true: "—and now nobody understands" (*The Fabric of Memory*, 51).

Intricacies of the Drama

William Irvine, an early discerning biographer of Shaw, referred to *Major Barbara* as "the most widely misunderstood of all Shaw's dramas" (*Universe of G.B.S.*, 174). Evidence for this misunderstanding abounds in the varying, even contradictory, interpretations it has evoked. Successive scholars have undertaken to construe it in Nietzschean, Marxian, and Comtian terms; it has been viewed by socialist and communist critics as marking a Shavian compromise with capitalism, and by others as a surrender of his Fabian socialism to Marxist revolution by force. Still others have stressed its religious nature; one interpreter has seen it to be a Dante-like religious allegory dealing with sin, repentance, and salvation.[4] Comparing *Major Barbara* to *Hamlet*, Irvine was led to predict that, "as the clarifications of the critics accumulate, it threatens to become equally perplexing" (259).

Such a prediction need not preclude an alternative judgment: that this play, which provokes such diversity in its reception, may well have an inherent complexity of meaning that eludes partial and partisan approaches. If this be the case, then something may be said for forgoing, at least initially, attempts at a single definitive account, and instead undertaking the mining of separate veins of meaning detectable in the drama. From such individual explorations a comprehensive intricate design of the work may eventually emerge, for there is more to *Major Barbara* than greets the casual eye.

It is my hope that this book will contribute to achieving such an end. The present book conjoins two complementary essays that explore in depth the classical currents in Shaw's controversial drama. The first essay, "Shaw's *Republic*," traces in analytic detail the social and political views dramatized in *Major Barbara* in relation to those of Plato in his classic work, *The Republic*. The second, much longer essay, "Shaw's *Bacchae*," elaborates the social, economic, mythic, ritual, and musical dimensions employed by Shaw in striking parallel with Euripides's drama, *The Bacchae*. The argument uses these Greek sources—Plato's *Republic* and Euripides's *Bacchae*—as lenses to reveal significant and subtle aspects of Shaw's play that remain difficult to interpret. Through examining the central characters in their social settings and interrelations, these essays search out unexplored depths of meaning in the drama and seek to challenge certain prevailing conceptions.

The book includes an appendix, "Bernard Shaw: The Artist as Philosopher," which provides philosophical context for the classical ties traced in the body of the book. Those readers who have less familiarity with the wide-ranging philosophical influences on Shaw, from ancient to modern, may benefit from reading the appendix in advance, before commencing the two major essays. This concise tracing of Shaw's views on the interrelations between art, philosophy, and religion may help orient the reader for the sustained close analysis of *Major Barbara* undertaken here.

Major Barbara and Plato's *Republic*

Shaw readily expressed his admiration for the rich legacy of the ancient Greek world. His lifelong friendship with Gilbert Murray, Regius Professor of Greek at Oxford University, undoubtedly helped fuel his classical Hellenic interests, but those interests appear to have traversed a fairly independent course of their own.[5] Indeed, acknowledgments of his indebtedness to that world are spread throughout his writings. He frequently sang the praises of Aeschylus, Aristophanes, and Aristotle, while holding Sophocles in much lower esteem. But the Greeks for whom he felt a special affinity were the dramatist Euripides and the philosopher Plato, along with Plato's teacher, Socrates.

G. K. Chesterton once wrote that "Plato was only a Bernard Shaw who unfortunately made his jokes in Greek" (*Eugenics and Other Evils*, 10). Shaw's rejoinder was that he could not guess at the reason for the allegation, "for it is impossible to understand what the word 'only' means in this sentence" (*Pen Portraits and Reviews*, 97). Much earlier Chesterton had observed that "Shaw found his nearest kinsman in remote Athens." Specifically, he located Shaw's affinity to Plato "in his instinctive elevation of temper, his courageous pursuit of ideas as far as they will go, his civic idealism; and also it must be confessed in his dislike of poets and a touch of delicate inhumanity" (*George Bernard Shaw*, 205, 203). One after another of Shavian critics have come to endorse this judgment of kinship between Shaw and Plato.[6] Shaw himself—whose family arms bore the Socratic motto, "Know thyself"—made his high regard for Plato evident throughout his writings.[7] What is more, he left us a comment on his long-term reading of the Athenian philosopher: "There is no foundation for the suggestion that I read Plato *first* at fifty. I have read him at all ages, and there is a sense in which I have not read him at all. That is to say, I have never been right slap through him (see Wegg on Gibbon *passim*); but I have dipped into him at all sorts of times and ages, and have always managed to keep awake and interested until it was time to stop under the pressure of external circumstances."[8]

In the belief that an inquiry into the Platonic aspects of Shaw's work would contribute to a better understanding of his plays, I propose to consider one of these, *Major Barbara*, as a Shavian *Republic* comparable in significant respects to Plato's *Republic*. My intention is to demonstrate that in this drama Shaw was preoccupied with many of the same basic problems of human life that Plato explored in his *Republic*; that in some measure he was influenced by Plato's efforts to solve these problems; that like Plato he was engaged in moral criticism of the society of his time; that he cherished a similar vision of a community life in which people could devote themselves to higher pursuits more worthy of their potentialities; and that he shared Plato's belief that questions of individual morality are inseparable from social, political, and economic issues, making lasting reform in personal morality impossible without fundamental social and institutional reform. Implicit in the relations of the key characters in Shaw's drama is a functional analysis of society akin to Plato's. In this work, as in Plato's, irony, wit, and humor operate as indispensable intellectual and dramatic instruments. Finally, as we shall see, the Shavian dramatic dialogue pointedly resembles the dialectic of Plato in its capacity to represent philosophy as a living expression of personality and drama germinating in the impact of mind upon mind.

The Platonic parallels provide a perspective that can illuminate much of the argument of *Major Barbara* as well as help to dispel some of the accumulated misunderstandings about the functions, interrelationships, and import of the principal characters. Perhaps they can also help rescue the play from excessively literal interpretation, a chronic weakness in Shavian criticism; for, as with Plato, Shaw's dramatic thinking frequently took figurative and mythical form. Above all, Shaw's persistent preoccupation with the ills of society and his stress upon the need for its reconstitution underlie the whole play, and both the criticism and proposed remedies have a Platonic coloration. To overlook these features is to miss much of the significance of the play.

Major Barbara and Euripides's *Bacchae*

"Perhaps the nearest modern parallel to the *Bacchae* (if one may compare great things with smaller) is Shaw's *Major Barbara*." That insightful observation was written in 1929 by E. R. Dodds, the distinguished Euripidean scholar and eventual successor to Gilbert Murray as Regius Professor of Greek at Oxford University. In a footnote he added, "Or rather, not a parallel but an echo; for it was Professor Murray's translation of the *Bacchae* which set Shaw exploring the truncated manifestations of orgiastic religion in our day" ("Euripides the Irrationalist," 102 n. 9). Dodds's underestimation of the modern work in this comparison need not detain us: what is noteworthy is the perceptive and highly suggestive pairing of those seemingly disparate dramas.

Yet another classical scholar, Gilbert Norwood, had captured a fleeting glimpse of the parallelism nearly two decades earlier in a 1911 lecture on Euripides and Shaw: "The comparison between Euripides and Mr. Shaw has often been made, and is, indeed, quaintly suggested to us by the delightful passage in *Major Barbara* where Shaw himself alludes to Euripides, and almost brings him upon the stage in the person of the Professor of Greek" ("Euripides and Shaw," 7). But even to casual inspection, the play imparts more than a "quaint" suggestion of Euripides—and of his *Bacchae*, which Norwood neglected to mention in this connection. For not only did Shaw model Adolphus Cusins, the play's professor of Greek, on his professor friend Gilbert Murray, and have him quote—as his own—passages from Murray's verse translation of the Euripidean tragedy, but this display of literary credentials, in turn, motivates Andrew Undershaft to address the poet-translator as "Euripides," a nickname retained to the very last line in the play. Cusins, for his part, repeatedly calls the millionaire armament manufacturer "Dionysos." In addition Shaw pays special tribute to the Murray version of the *Bacchae* in the introductory N.B. to the printed text of his play (13).

By themselves these instances amount to little more than bows in the direction of Euripides and his *Bacchae*, but they are explicit enough to warrant much closer scrutiny of *Major Barbara* as a possible modern counterpart to the Greek drama.[9] It is ironic indeed that the parallel should have first been detected by eminent classical scholars while generally escaping the critical attention of Shaw interpreters until decades later.[10] Dodds's likening of *Major Barbara* to the *Bacchae* is an encouraging place to start, but unfortunately his further commentary does not take us very far: "The difference of treatment in the two plays is as striking as the similarity of subject. Shaw approaches salvationism as a psychologist: Euripides studies Bacchism both as psychologist and poet. That is why he can deal faithfully alike with the surpassing beauty and the inhuman cruelty of irrationalist religion, where Shaw sees only its humour and its pathos" (103). But surely the two works exhibit a great deal more in common than a psychological interest in the religious phenomena under examination. For as Dodds himself acknowledges in the same essay, "Euripides happens to be, like Bernard Shaw and Pirandello, a philosophical dramatist" (97).

We have only to consider Thomas G. Rosenmeyer's observation on the philosophic thrust of the *Bacchae* in order to perceive an immediate basis for correlating it with *Major Barbara*. Maintaining that its ideas are what really count in the end, Rosenmeyer looks upon Euripides's drama as "a forerunner of the Platonic dialogues. The smiling god is another Socrates, bullying his listeners into a painful reconsideration of their thinking" (*Masks of Tragedy*, 127). That is the exact function of the Dionysian character in Shaw's play, namely Andrew Undershaft, who is likewise "cast in the philosophical mode," to use Rosenmeyer's phrase. That being the case, why not at least look beyond "the similarity of subject" and homology in psychological explorations to the broader philosophical questing and questioning that their dramatic creations so comparably—and incomparably—pursue?

On Translations from the Greek

Citations here of Plato's *Republic* are from *The Republic of Plato*, translated by Francis M. Cornford, unless otherwise indicated. The clarity of this translation commends its use in preference to earlier ones available to Shaw, since this study in no way presupposes that Shaw made direct and conscious use of the language of the *Republic*. In any event, I have tried to avoid undue reliance upon wording peculiar to this translation.

As for Euripides's *Bacchae*, quite apart from the textual uncertainties that all versions of the work inherit, there is the need to find a modus operandi among the array of variant and frequently discrepant translations from the Greek. Complicating the situation is the special and close relation that the Gilbert Murray translation of the *Bacchae* bears to *Major Barbara*. Since Shaw not only quoted from it in his play but knew Euripides and his playwriting mainly, if not only, by way of Murray, it might seem that the simplest and wisest approach would be to cleave to that scholar's version, and thereby obviate innumerable difficulties.

As defensible as such a decision might be, there are compelling reasons for rejecting the Procrustean bed of this particular rendering of Euripides's tragedy. For one thing, Murray's work is a highly individual and creative poetic effort, often straying imaginatively beyond the bounds of the language and thought of the original.[11] "The poetic renderings of Gilbert Murray are the most readable in English," asserted G.M.A. Grube: "They are always pleasant, frequently revealing even to those who know the Greek; but at times they only dimly reflect Euripides, especially in the lyrics. Moreover, and this is more insidious, Euripides is constantly romanticized, bowdlerized, as it were. Where the Greek is often colloquial, rhetorical, purposely harsh and even stilted, the English is uniformly smooth. Not infrequently the sentiments and the characters themselves are romanticized" (13–14). Much harsher than Grube was T. S. Eliot's criticism in "Euripides and Professor Murray" (1920). Eliot's acerbic assault on Murray accused him of "habitually [using] two words where the Greek language requires one, and where the English language will provide him with one." In Eliot's judgment Murray "interposed between Euripides and ourselves a barrier more impenetrable than the Greek language" (*The Sacred Wood*, 74–75).

Granted, as Grube further points out, Murray's transgressions were by no means unique among translators of Euripides; nevertheless it just will not do to consider the Shaw play solely in relation to this idiosyncratic translation. For however great his indebtedness to Murray's *Bacchae*, it is not just Shaw the dramatist, but his drama—in its own separate life-and-blood character as a work of art—that is being studied here. Mutatis mutandis the same holds true for Euripides and the *Bacchae*.

Lest any suspicion linger about the integrity of my methodology, or about its possible employment to slant the *Bacchae* toward language favorable to the theses of this study, let me add a word concerning the strict constraints I have imposed in making each translation choice. The object of the present analysis being to identify authentic—not specious or contrived—parallels between *Major Barbara* and Euripides's tragedy, purely coincidental or fortuitous phraseology peculiar to a single translator has been studiously avoided, no matter how advantageous or expedient it might be in the circumstances. Instead, I have opted only for renderings readily replaceable by substitutes whose use would entail no revision of argument or interpretation. This should not be taken to imply the absence of incompatible or conflicting versions of the Euripidean lines; in light of the myriad deciphering problems posed by the *Bacchae*, that would be unreasonable to expect. Nevertheless, the guiding principle has been to shun dubious or aberrant language. On the constructive side, variant readings abound in the text and notes, especially in grappling with key or thorny passages.

In his own critical writings on Ibsen and Wagner, Shaw insisted that a work can contain meanings incompletely perceived by its author: "The existence of a discoverable and perfectly definite thesis in a poet's work by no means depends on the completeness of his own intellectual consciousness of it" (*Major Critical Essays,* 12; compare 246). The same, I hope to show, holds true of *Major Barbara*: its resemblances to the *Bacchae* go well beyond those its author may have consciously and intentionally introduced into his drama. In fact, as we shall see, even in the lines he quotes from the Murray translation, Shaw may have intuitively introduced modifications that brought them nearer to the sense of the Euripidean text. Because the meaningful links between the two works are by no means confined to those exhibited in any special or favored reading of Euripides's play, and because being wedded to all the linguistic decisions of a particular translation leaves one at the mercy of its idiosyncrasies and shortcomings as well as its successes, exclusive reliance on any one English version of the *Bacchae,* whether Murray's or another, is more likely to hamper than facilitate analysis.

Accordingly, in order to get as close to Euripides's play as possible for one minimally schooled in Greek, I have adopted instead the more involved but flexible procedure of selecting from among the numerous renderings of individual passages those that bespeak faithful adherence to the intent of the original—so far as that can be ascertained—while eschewing deviations in language or meaning from other translations, and (having met these criteria) that help bring to light latent affinities with *Major Barbara.* Fortunately, assistance in making these choices is available from a wide range of excellent Euripidean scholarship and commentary.[12]

The Way from Athens

When Shaw published the screen version of *Major Barbara* in 1941, among numerous revisions he made were those to the prefatory N.B. crediting and praising the Murray translation of Euripides's *Bacchae,* a passage of which is used in the play. Instead of ending the note with the original "in more ways than one" (which I appropriated as the title of an article of mine), he substituted "in more ways than the way from Athens" (*"Major Barbara": A Screen Version,* v). It is unlikely that this choice of language was accidental, for indeed there was a "sacred way" (*hiera hodos*) leading from Athens to the village of Eleusis, of which Murray was certainly cognizant and which he might well have mentioned to Shaw. This is of course pure speculation given the apparent absence of evidence one way or the other.

Some twelve miles along the sacred way from Athens lay Eleusis, a major religious center, home of the cult of the chthonian fertility deities Demeter and Persephone (Kore), in which Dionysos plays a significant role.[13] Here the secret rites of the Greater Mysteries were celebrated every year in late summer, giving initiates the hope of immortality. The mystery rites, which lasted ten days, included a procession from Athens to Eleusis: "The Sacred Way, along which the procession went from Athens to Eleusis during the celebration of the Mysteries, was lined with tombs of famous men, shrines of local heroes, and temples of the gods" (*Athenian Culture and Society,* 37). It was along this sacred way, moreover, that Plato had a residence and established his Academy:

Some twenty minutes' walk outside the walls [of Athens] on the road to Eleusis, in the retirement of the suburbs, [Plato] had a house and garden. The property was a pleasant one, giving, as it did, on the whispering elms and plane trees and the olive groves of "Academe," a large park and playground laid out and bequeathed to the city by the statesman Cimon, but called after a local hero, or possibly an original owner of the land, named Hecademus. The running waters of the Cephisus babbled near by, and of a still evening "the feathered choir of nightingales" could be heard making their music in the laurel thickets of Colonus. Here, where he had not only his own garden but the shady and quiet walks of the park conveniently at hand for strolling and discoursing, he established himself and set about gathering in his scholars. (*History of Greek Philosophy*, 2:162–63)

Without his realizing it, Shaw's evocation of "the way from Athens" conjoins the Dionysian and Platonic themes in *Major Barbara* to be explored here.

I

Shaw's *Republic*

Convinced that the aesthetic element, creative joy, is the most effective instrument of enlightened teaching, he tirelessly wielded the shining sword
of his word and wit against the most appalling power threatening the triumph of the experiment—stupidity. He did his best in redressing the fateful unbalance between truth and reality, in lifting mankind to a higher rung
of social maturity. He often pointed a scornful finger at human frailty, but
his jests were never at the expense of humanity. He was mankind's friend,
and it is in this role that he will live in the hearts and memories of men.

Thomas Mann, *George Bernard Shaw: A Critical Survey*

The furniture of Heaven has altered little with the centuries; it remains an
idealised replica of the only world we know.

E. R. Dodds, *The Greeks and the Irrational*

Major Barbara clearly invites consideration from a Greek standpoint. It
is Shaw's most "Greek" play. Brimming with Hellenic motifs and allu-
sions, it also bears the author's N.B. that it "stands indebted" to Professor
Gilbert Murray, the classical scholar and admitted model for the character Adolphus Cusins "in more ways than one" (13).[1] More pertinently,
there are two explicit references to Plato's *Republic* in the drama (178,
182). Shaw's own original description of *Major Barbara* as "simply an
ethical discussion in three long acts" ("Terror of a Play," 3:186)[2] suggests
a Platonic type of dramatic dialogue, designed to carry in suspension
and develop conflicts between opposing viewpoints, as well as encour-
age reflection aimed at their resolution.[3]

Platonic Parallels

Before turning to a detailed examination of *Major Barbara* as a Shavian *Republic*, some general parallels between the two works are worth

noting. Though more restricted in philosophic scope than the *Republic*, *Major Barbara*, like Plato's work, is profoundly preoccupied with questions about the best way to order human life in society. The *Republic* is a book in quest of the way to know and attain the good life by the good man in the good state. Viewing as "the most important of all questions, the choice between a good and evil life" (578c), it undertakes "to determine the whole course of conduct which everyone of us must follow to get the best out of life" (344e). Bent on revolutionary reform, it is "written in the imperative mood" (*Greek Political Theory*, 170). The radical spirit in which Plato criticized contemporary beliefs, practices, and institutions "prejudices the calmness and impartiality of his philosophy," in R. L. Nettleship's words. "He is always writing with crying evils in his eye" (*Lectures on the "Republic" of Plato*, 6).

That there were also crying evils in Shaw's eye is evident in both his play and its preface, particularly in the Undershaftian attacks, neither calm nor impartial, on poverty as "the vilest sin of man and society" (Pref. *Major Barbara*, 31). "It is exceedingly difficult to make people realize that an evil is an evil," Shaw writes early in the Preface (23). Near the end of its "Sane Conclusions" he makes his own reforming object clear: "If a man cannot look evil in the face without illusion, he will never know what it really is, or combat it effectually" (61–62). The ills of society—economic, political, moral, and religious—come into sharp focus in the malignant image of poverty. But though "the first need" in curing the disease is money, what is really required as remedy is "a reconstitution of society" (31, 51). It is the existing social order that arouses Shaw's ire and moves him to espouse revolutionary reform:

> Here am I, for instance, by class a respectable man, by common sense a hater of waste and disorder, by intellectual constitution legally minded to the verge of pedantry, and by temperament apprehensive and economically disposed to the limit of old-maidishness; yet I am, and have always been, and shall now always be, a revolutionary writer, because our laws make law impossible; our liberties destroy all freedom; our property is organized robbery; our morality is an impudent hypocrisy; our wisdom is administered by inexperienced or malexperienced dupes, our power wielded by cowards and weaklings, and our honor false in all its points. I am an enemy of the existing order for good reasons. (59)

How reminiscent is this of Plato in the Seventh Letter explaining the basis for his own revolutionary outlook on society:

> When I considered these things and the men who were directing public affairs, and made a closer study, as I grew older, of law and custom, the harder it seemed to me to govern a state rightly. . . . At the same time the whole fabric of law and custom was going from bad to worse at an alarming rate. The result was that I, . . . when I saw all this happening and everything going to pieces, fell at last into bewilderment. I did not cease to think in what way this situation might be amended and in particular the whole organization of the state. . . . At last I perceived that the constitution of all existing states is bad and their institutions all but past remedy without a combination of radical measures and fortunate circumstance.[4]

Major Barbara mounts a comparable attack on the institutions of existing states, and its third act envisages the "fortunate circumstance" of granting power to those best qualified to effect the "combination of radical measures" needed.

Again, like Plato, Shaw is a dramatist who brings opinions and principles to life in the vivid characters who are their exponents. In *Major Barbara* the principal personae not only discuss but represent distinct ideas, principles, and points of view. Clashes of personality are simultaneously doctrinal conflicts. The resolution of the conflicts both terminates an argument and signals that grounds for the meeting and commitment of minds and wills have been reached. Here, as elsewhere, Shaw is the thoroughly dialectical dramatist.[5] Dialectic originated as a form of logic in ancient Greece and came to full fruition in the practice of Socrates and the dialogues of Plato. Shaw's dialectic, despite being filtered through the later Hegelian and Marxian versions of the process, nevertheless retains close kinship to the Platonic dramatic model.[6] In Plato, dialectic is essentially the art of conversation or discourse, in question and answer form, aiming toward a true account of things through critical, cooperative inquiry. It became for Plato both the genuine method of inquiry and the knowledge that method provides. In the *Republic* the term "dialectic" comes to bear a very complex meaning, developed in the context of Plato's metaphysics.

Shaw's use of dialectic, however less complicated, operates correspondingly in the service of his own creative evolutionist metaphysics.

The Shavian dialectic shares with Plato's its basic function as an art of reasoned discussion, presenting in dialogue form the developing opposition and interplay of conflicting persons and points of view. But even more specific features of the Platonic dialectic found in the *Republic* are evident in Shaw's method, especially in *Major Barbara*. For Plato presents dialectic as an instrument of education, interpreted as a process of conversion. Trying to put knowledge into a soul devoid of it, Plato insists, is like trying to put sight into blind eyes. Education must be an art whose aim is to convert the soul's eye from "looking in the wrong direction" by turning it "the way it ought to be" (*Republic* 518d). Dialectic is able to convert because it is "reasoning which is in conformity with facts" (*Lectures on the "Republic" of Plato,* 281), and throughout Plato the objective of the dialectician is to "attain a clear vision of realities as they are in themselves" (*An Examination of Plato's Doctrines,* 2:563).

The Platonic Socrates starts his interlocutor on the way to conversion by showing him the hopeless impasse to which his uncritically held opinions logically lead. This induces a state of *aporia*, or perplexity, a condition of not knowing which way to turn. Then Socrates gently prods him toward the right way out of his predicament. Recipients of such instruction frequently feel that they have been outmaneuvered by superior rhetorical skill more than proved wrong (*Republic* 487bc). This *aporia* is clearly recognizable in Cusins and Barbara (as well as in some of the play's critics). Nonetheless, the learners are disabused of error. "You have learnt something," Undershaft tells Barbara in the third act. "That always feels at first as if you had lost something" (156). But the dialectical process expresses more than learning and conversion: it directly enacts an evolving struggle more important even than the eventual victory over opposition and falsehood. Thus "this intellectual form becomes a dramatic form," in Paul Friedländer's view, "for to be a dramatist means to experience the world directly as a struggle of authentic forces, personalized forces" (*Plato,* 167; compare 367 n. 18). In Shaw's play the experience of Barbara and Cusins conforms to this dialectical pattern of development. And the dialogue that serves as vehicle for the dialectical struggle in which they engage reflects still another Platonic trait: "He was delighted by resounding speeches. . . . He enjoyed the tricks and wily cunning of verbal fencing" (ibid., 167).

Prideful Aristocracy

Plato's classic begins with a critical examination of conceptions of morality prevailing in the Athenian marketplace. The setting is the home of a retired, successful businessman, Cephalus, who, seconded by his son Polemarchus, gives voice to the conventional morality of the day. As innocently as the questions of Socrates initiate an inquiry into the foundations of morality and political life in the *Republic*, the first act of *Major Barbara* introduces us to questions of morality and politics in the contemporary world. Shaw's play also begins in the home of a well-to-do family. Instead of Cephalus and Polemarchus, we meet Lady Britomart Undershaft and her son Stephen, who comparably reflect the respectable morality dominating the British marketplace. In both dramas the parents, coincidentally seated in cushioned comfort, begin discussing inheritance, money, and morality.

The Shavian portraits are more lighthearted, and the moral milieu is etched in the course of a seeming comedy of manners, sitting deceptively on a deep-rooted moral, political, and religious allegory. Lady Britomart launches the play by undertaking to establish her son's hereditary claim to his father's munitions factory and millions, as well as to assure the financial security of her two daughters and their prospective husbands. In the process she sets the stage for posing the play's fundamental question. The basic question of the *Republic,* raised in book 1 and the beginning of book 2, is: What is justice, or rightness in conduct, and how can human society achieve it? Similarly, the first act of *Major Barbara* introduces us to the cognate question of how people in society are to be "saved." The religious question is, as elsewhere in Shaw, identified with the ethical question: "My morality—my religion—" says Undershaft in one breath (90). The salvation question is raised more explicitly in Bill Walker's "What price salvation now?" at the end of the second act (138). And Lady Britomart's haughty "nothing can bridge over moral disagreement," scarcely noticeable in the first act, deftly anticipates Cusins's "abyss of moral horror" and the crucial ethical conflicts of the third act (76, 165).

Lady Britomart and her family represent the ruling class of Great Britain. Confidently *conceiving the universe exactly as if it were a large house in Wilton Crescent*" (67), this daughter of the Earl of Stevenage governs her family for their welfare—as she construes it. "I have always made you my companions and friends," she tells her children, "and allowed you perfect freedom to do and say whatever you liked, so long as you liked what I could approve of" (74).[7] This is precisely her approach to their marriages: "Barbara shall marry, not the man they [snobbish people] like, but the man *I* like"; Charles Lomax, inclined to marry her daughter Sarah, "*has not attempted to resist Lady Britomart's arrangements to that end*" (80); and Stephen learns that, although he is to be consulted, she is "trying to arrange something" for him as well (71).

Her motives are transparently self-interested, but her justifications are clothed in the garments of class privilege and righteous respectability. "In our class," she tells Stephen, "we have to decide what is to be done with wicked people" (73). The principle implicit in this judgment can be understood as a Britomartian version of the Athenian maxim that it is right to render "every man his due," which Polemarchus cites early in the *Republic* (331e), interpreting it to enjoin help to the honest but injury to wrongdoers (334d). Her estranged husband, Andrew Undershaft, in "preaching immorality" while practicing morality (76), has earned Lady Britomart's reprobation by inverting the customarily condoned discrepancy between word and deed. She is, as Undershaft later describes her, "the incarnation of morality," by which he, and Shaw, mean respectable or conventional morality, particularly that of the aristocracy.

Plato viewed with suspicion and mistrust the pursuit of personal profit and family advantage by the governing class, as instituting pressures inimical to the welfare of the community. This led him to propose both communism and the abolition of the private family for the guardian class of his ideal state. Shaw, socialist and proponent of equality of income, underscores in Lady Britomart and Stephen the same demoralizing forces in governmental circles, exposing them to repeated ridicule. He portrays the governing class leadership as otiose and ineffectual. Such ineffectuality finds comic vent in the inanities of Lomax as well as in the moral sententiousness of Stephen, the one an inept heir to wealth, the other to unearned social and political distinction. Even the redoubtable Lady Britomart, for all her imperiousness and hegemonic manipulations, is inevitably bested. At the end of the first act, in a test of her authority, she is virtually deserted by the whole family except Stephen. By Act III even he has asserted his independence of her, although it is evident that he has merely succeeded to her patronizing manner. Unequipped for his father's inheritance, the younger Undershaft has fallen undisputed heir to his mother's self-righteousness. Much as Polemarchus had never seen fit to doubt the accepted precept that it is right to help friends and harm enemies (332d), the *bien pensant* Stephen is at a loss to understand how people can differ about right and wrong. "Right is right; and wrong is wrong; and if a man cannot distinguish them properly, he is either a fool or a rascal: thats all" (76).

If the reigning morality of British aristocratic society thus receives satirical treatment in the first act, so does its religious garniture. The most telling thrusts against the routine role of religion are made at the end of the act. Lady Britomart chides Barbara for lacking a sense of propriety in acting "as if religion were a pleasant subject" (91). If the others are determined to engage in this unpleasant activity, she insists on doing it "in a proper and respectable way." Her attitude is fully exhibited in her peremptory order: "Charles: ring for prayers" (92). All except Stephen rise in dismay at the prospect of such a ceremony and instead withdraw for a cheerful musical service in the drawing room. Cusins, circumventing his future mother-in-law's attempt to detain him, adroitly recoils from "the things in the family prayer book that I couldnt bear to hear you say." She "would have to say before all the servants that we have done things we ought not to have done, and left undone things we ought to have done, and that there is no health in us. I cannot bear to hear you doing yourself such an injustice, and Barbara such an injustice. As for myself, I flatly deny it: I have done my best" (92–93).

The Shavian assessment of established religious practice as sheer hypocrisy is manifest. At the same time, it resembles the complaints in the *Republic* by Plato's brothers, Glaucon and Adeimantus, that according to current Athenian notions morality and religion are externally imposed conventions, accepted because socially necessary, though unpleasant and contrary to natural human desires. What seems to count is the reputation for probity and virtue, not the genuine article. Moral and religious instruction within and outside the family inculcate the same teachings: how difficult is the path of virtue, and how pleasant and easy that of vice. "When children are told by their fathers and all their pastors and masters that it is a good thing to be just, what is commended is not justice in-itself but the respectability it brings. They are to let men see how just they are, in order to gain high positions and marry well and win all the other advantages" (363a). What is more, the rewards of heaven are not confined to the good; for the gods can be won over by prayers, votive offerings, and sacrifices. People learn that "both in this life and after

death, wrongdoing may be absolved and purged away by means of sacrifices and agreeable performances" (364e). This questioning of rituals
of propitiation and absolution parallels the treatment of atonement and
expiation of sin in *Major Barbara*'s second act and Preface (compare also
Pref. *Androcles and the Lion*, esp. 4:469–72).

Glaucon and Adeimantus submit these opinions as challenging re-
statements of the conventional Sophist morality unsuccessfully defended
by Thrasymachus in book 1 of the *Republic*. Thrasymachus's view is that
might makes right: what passes for morality serves the interest of those
in positions of power and superiority. In a manner very different from
that of the haranguing Thrasymachus, Undershaft projects into the play
a similar ethic of power. Unabashedly proclaiming himself "a profiteer
in mutilation and murder," and refusing to take refuge in the customary lame excuse for his trade (that increasing war's destructiveness will
hasten its abolition), he embraces a morality entirely consistent with his
occupation:

> I am not one of those men who keep their morals and their busi-
> ness in water-tight compartments. All the spare money my trade
> rivals spend on hospitals, cathedrals, and other receptacles for
> conscience money, I devote to experiments and researches in im-
> proved methods of destroying life and property. I have always done
> so; and I always shall. Therefore your Christmas card moralities
> of peace on earth and goodwill among men are of no use to me.
> Your Christianity, which enjoins you to resist not evil and to turn
> the other cheek, would make me a bankrupt. My morality—my
> religion—must have a place for cannons and torpedoes in it. (90)

But if Undershaft talks like a Thrasymachus, he operates more like a
Socrates, "as the skillful surgeon of the mind, at his practice of dialectic," in Robert E. Cushman's words: Socrates "can be known only as he
works—now cutting with surgical skill the cancerous presumption of
men by means of *elenchos*, or cross-examination, and then healing with
his protreptic or hortatory art of exhortation" (*Therapeia*, 8).[8] Undershaft performs his major surgery in the second act, reserving his thera-
peutic exhortations for the last act. But propaedeutic to these are his
opening-act pronouncements: "For me there is only one true morality. . . . There is only one true morality for every man; but every man has
not the same true morality" (90). Since his morality is that which fits his
business, this may be taken to be another expression of Thrasymachian

ethical relativism. Yet his generalization about morality is at the same time compatible with the instructional method of Plato as Friedländer describes it: "Plato also inherited the insight from Socrates that there is no ready-made knowledge simply transferable from one person to another. . . . Every philosophical conversation conducted by Socrates is new and different according to the partner—this is the Socratic principle of education. . . . Plato gives wisdom and doctrine; but the Socratic principle is still so commanding within him that for him, too, knowledge would be 'deceit' if it purported to be the same for everybody and everywhere" (*Plato*, 166). A deflating realist, Undershaft first pricks the bubble of moral and religious respectability, but his alternative is hardly a more genuine altruism. Instead, he lays the groundwork for an assault on the underlying religious and moral altruism of Christianity itself, of which Barbara is the play's chief exponent.

The discussion of Undershaftian morality dialectically shifts the issue of the play to a new level with new antagonists. It provokes Stephen's division of people into honest men and scoundrels, and Barbara's Christian rejoinder: "There are neither good men nor scoundrels: there are just children of one Father." All sorts of men—criminals, infidels, philanthropists, and missionaries—are "just the same sort of sinner; and theres the same salvation ready for them all" (90). At this point Undershaft slyly insinuates himself as a tempting minor premise to Barbara's major:[9]

UNDERSHAFT. May I ask have you ever saved a maker of cannons?
BARBARA. No. Will you let me try? (91)

This enthymeme—all sinners may be saved; Undershaft is a qualified sinner—with the lure of the implicit conclusion that he is ripe for salvation, sets the second-act trap for Barbara. Undershaft is primed to undermine her major premise by a demonstration that he is just the "sort of sinner" the Salvation Army, her agency of salvation, is depending on for its very survival; hence he is a sinner beyond their reach. This establishes the pattern of the central agon, the contest between father and daughter. In sharp antithetical strokes, Shaw skillfully sketches in the settings for the contested action of the play's remaining acts in the course of a brisk exchange of challenges, initiated by the businessman's bargain.

UNDERSHAFT. Well, I will make a bargain with you. If I go to see you tomorrow in your Salvation Shelter, will you come the day after to see me in my cannon works?

BARBARA. Take care. It may end in your giving up the cannons for the sake of the Salvation Army.

UNDERSHAFT. Are you sure it will not end in your giving up the Salvation Army for the sake of the cannons?

BARBARA. I will take my chance of that.

UNDERSHAFT. And I will take my chance of the other. [*They shake hands on it*]. Where is your shelter?

BARBARA. In West Ham. At the sign of the cross. Ask anybody in Canning Town. Where are your works?

UNDERSHAFT. In Perivale St. Andrews. At the sign of the sword. Ask anybody in Europe. (91)

The battle of ideas is engaged. Each militant Undershaft stands committed under an opposing shaft and emblem as it were, the cross and the sword: the one symbolizing Christian faith, the other naked power. At issue is the problem of the *Republic:* Which way lies the solution of human social and political problems? What is the way to the good life?

Moral Economics

Most of Plato's *Republic* is devoted to developing a reply to the Sophists' challenge to traditional morality. In its own fashion, *Major Barbara* pits a well-armed, wily, modern archsophist—doubling as Socratic gadfly— against a true defender of the principles of Christian altruism. But the play leads us to consider how to cope with something more than an assault on conventional morality; it confronts us with the threat that war and unrestrained economic might can level against the basic moral foundations of modern life. The operation of religion and morality in our society, brought to the surface in the first act, becomes the dominant concern of the second.

The West Ham Salvation Army shelter in the second act of *Major Barbara* may seem a far cry from the *Republic*, but there are some important points of contact between them. Plato looked upon the extremes of wealth and poverty as socially divisive and disruptive. Every city, he observed, is at least two cities, a city of the rich and a city of the poor, each at war with the other (422a–423a). The oligarchic state, ruled by the wealthy few, is peculiarly prone to such internal economic class warfare (551d). *Major Barbara,* after a first-act visit with the propertied aristocracy, turns to an inspection of the abode of the poor, where a religious ethics of sin, confession, atonement, and redemption operates in a world of poverty and charity.

Adeimantus, in his challenge to Socrates, presents the common belief that the way to fulfill our desires is to "conceal our ill-doing under a veneer of decent behaviour" (366b). Such an outlook receives an ironic Shavian twist among the poor in the Salvation Army shelter. Instead of feigning goodness, they resort to the subterfuge of inventing sins, for which they can then pretend penitence. They court a reputation for wickedness in order to become eligible to participate in the atoning ritual of confession, which helps guarantee their daily bread: "And where would they get the money to rescue us if we was to let on we're no worse than other people?" asks Rummy Mitchens. So they observe the rules of this game of hypocrisy. "I'll play the game as good as any of em," promises Snobby Price (97–98).

Plato undertook an analysis of political society as a guide to the nature and effects of morality in the individual soul. It is easier, he suggests, to understand human nature and ethics when read in the larger letters of social and political life. In other words, social and political knowledge is essential to self-knowledge. Because of the interdependence of ethics and politics, of private and public life, individual development cannot be fully realized in a corrupt political society. This viewpoint is very much in keeping with Shaw's own account of Barbara's second-act lesson, "that there is no salvation . . . through personal righteousness, but only through the redemption of the whole nation from its vicious, lazy, competitive anarchy" (Pref., 36). Plato asks, "is not the public itself the greatest of all sophists, training up young and old, men and women alike, into the most accomplished specimens of the character it desires to produce?" With a human being, as with a plant, if "sown and reared in the wrong soil, it will develop every contrary defect unless saved by some miracle" (492ab).

These considerations make it necessary to dispute Paul Shorey's too facile judgment that Shaw's "dictum that we must reform society before we need try to reform ourselves is the diametrical opposite of the Platonic principle that you have no business to try to reform society until you first have reformed yourself" (*Platonism, Ancient and Modern*, 235).[10] Plato examined the state first not only because of its symmetry with the individual soul but on a larger scale. He was also concerned with the question of priorities, as Ernst Cassirer explains: "We cannot hope to reform philosophy if we do not begin by reforming the state. That is the only way if we wish to change the ethical life of men. To find the right political order is the first and most urgent problem" (*The Myth of the State*, 74).[11] Plato's portrait of society develops from an analysis of human association into elemental and reciprocal needs, which require specialization of function and a division of labor for their fulfillment. Like Shaw's, his inspection of the social order has an economic basis. For Plato the division of labor develops into a moral principle as social justice comes to mean the proper performance of one's peculiar duty and function in the community. Economic relations thus come to be seen in a moral light.[12]

Shaw, too, connects economic and moral conceptions throughout his play, but especially in the second act. The whole act develops a series of moral and religious transactions expressed in economic terms.[13] The characters engage in a kind of moral business with one another as they bid, bargain, exchange and trade money, services, and indebtedness. They are busy trying to pay back what they have received, "rendering to everyone what is appropriate to him" (331e, 332c). They act and react to balance their moral accounts and to find the minimum price for personal salvation. In this way the whole act elaborates Shaw's indictment of conventional moral and religious practice along the lines introduced by Cephalus and developed by Glaucon and Adeimantus in the *Republic*.

As in the first act, Shaw is still presenting unsatisfactory moral, religious, and economic arrangements in Act II. For the poor, life has not even reached the level of Plato's "pig community," with its provision for the physical necessities of life, for bare subsistence is their chief concern. At the same time the society Shaw portrays suffers from luxurious excess not unlike that of the "inflamed" civilized community Plato proceeds to describe (372e–373d). Shaw, like Plato, is proceeding to the ideal community by way of a reformation of existing society.[14] In that reformation he continues to ally himself with Plato in believing that the satisfaction of basic human needs is necessary before virtue and the higher values of civilization can be achieved.[15]

War accompanies the evolution of the luxurious state in the *Republic*. Plato discovers "its origin in desires which are the most fruitful source of evils both to individuals and to states" (373e).[16] Undershaft himself, in his triumphant moment of "saving" the Army by his contribution of five thousand pounds, relentlessly drives home the same lesson: "Think of my business! think of the widows and orphans! . . . the oceans of blood, not one drop of which is shed in a really just cause! . . . All this makes money for me: I am never richer, never busier than when the papers are full of it" (133). As the *Republic* says of the despotic man, "Money he must have, no matter how" (574a). The evils of private property disturbed Shaw as much as they did Plato, and these evils are fully stressed in this play. Plato's opposition to war is more limited than Shaw's, applying only to that between Greeks. Hence if he makes the Undershaftian point that "in no form of work is efficiency so important as in war" (374c), he also would legislate that guardians "are not to ravage lands or burn houses" of Greek enemies (471a).

Will, Reason, Moral Passion

The functional analysis of political society and of human nature into three divisions in the *Republic* has its Shavian counterpart in the central trio of characters in *Major Barbara*. The millionaire Undershaft corresponds to the productive class of craftsmen, merchants, and traders. Barbara and Cusins similarly have roles analogous to those of the guardian soldiers and rulers, and meet the qualifications Plato prescribes for them: "They must have the right sort of intelligence and ability; and also they must look upon the commonwealth as their special concern—the sort of concern that is felt for something so closely bound up with oneself that its interests and fortunes, for good or ill, are held to be identical with one's own" (412cd). Both moreover, have the requisite combination of spiritual high temper and gentleness (375c).

Cusins is portrayed from the outset as combining "an appalling temper" with considerate gentleness, and Barbara as both strong-willed and jolly. In addition, each is appropriately divested of property. Barbara lives on one pound a week, and in the third act Lady Britomart reminds us that "Adolphus hasnt any property" (145). Each also undergoes trials comparable to those proposed for Plato's guardians (413de), involving ordeals of temptation, moral pain, even great toil—"we're worked off our feet," says Barbara of the Salvationists (111). Barbara invites more direct identification with the auxiliary military class. That she belongs to a salvation army has an intriguing aptness in view of the vigilant moral function that Plato assigns to soldiers. It is also dramatically fitting that this

Shavian moral warrior be female, since Plato provided in the *Republic* for women to participate fully and equally in public positions and duties, including ruling (449–57, 540c). Barbara, as a major, is also capable of performing the executive functions expected of the Platonic auxiliaries. Cusins, as we shall see, is properly associated with the class of rulers and counselors. Like those trained for governing the Republic, he has the preparation of long study, but his experience in "warfare" (537a), like Barbara's, is solely of the Salvation Army variety. In the language of the allegory of the metals, then, Cusins would be a golden person, Barbara silver, and Undershaft iron and brass (with foundry and trombone to match). It may be argued that Shaw, too, is prophesying "that ruin will come upon the state when it passes into the keeping of a man of iron or brass" (415c).

Plato's corresponding psychology of the tripartite soul is equally applicable to these characters. Undershaft is associated with the dominating drives of appetite and will (*Republic* 437c); the scholar Cusins is representative of reason; and Barbara symbolizes the passionate, "spirited," or feeling element, whose impulses of righteous and honorable indignation, anger, and ambition side with reason against appetite (*Republic* 440e, 581a–583a). From the Shavian standpoint she is an exemplar of "moral passion," the dawning of which John Tanner so vividly describes in the first act of *Man and Superman,* that passion which dignifies and gives meaning to all the other passions, transforming them from "a mob of appetites" into "an army of purposes and principles" (2:572).[17]

The central role passion plays in Shaw's psychology and ethics strengthens his ties with Plato. "Passion is the steam in the engine of all religious and moral systems," Shaw argues in "The Sanity of Art." "Abstract principles of conduct break down in practice because kindness and truth and justice are not duties founded on abstract principles external to man, but human passions, which have, in their time, conflicted with higher passions as well as with lower ones" (303–4). His definition of passion encompasses both intellect and appetite: "The appalling fact that nobody in this country seems to know that intellect is a passion for solving problems, and that its exercise produces happiness, satisfaction, and a desirable quality of life, shews that we do not yet know even our crude bodily appetites in their higher aspects as passions: a passion being, I take it, an overwhelming impulse towards a more abundant life" (*Sham Education,* 308). In the *Major Barbara* Preface, Shaw appeals to such phrases as "impassioned poetry" and "passionate love of truth" in explaining the sense in which passion is "the life of drama" (34).

These views are very much like those we find in the sixth book of the *Republic,* where the philosophic nature is described as having "a constant passion" for knowledge of reality. "It is not merely natural," Plato adds, "but entirely necessary that an instinctive passion for any object should extend to all that is akin to it. . . . Now we surely know that when a man's desires set strongly in one direction, in every other channel they flow more feebly, like a stream diverted into another bed" (485d).[18] Since this single stream of passionate energy may be directed into each part of the soul, the chief difference in Shaw's doctrine is the priority he gives to moral feelings and will over reason. Thus it is Barbara, the personification of moral passion and volition, who "sounds the highest" note in the drama that bears her name.[19]

In the ninth book of the *Republic* the tripartite distinction is carried over to the three types of people: the philosophic, or lovers of wisdom; the ambitious, or lovers of honor; and the men of business, or lovers of gain. Cusins and Undershaft fit neatly into this pattern as a lover of knowledge and one of profit, respectively. But Barbara is an ambitious seeker of honor, victory, and glory only in a metaphorical sense. She seeks a moral and religious victory culminating in a "Glory Hallelujah!" If, like the *Republic*'s glory-seeker, she is nearer in temperament to the philosopher than to the businessman, her importance is by no means secondary.

The cardinal virtues of wisdom, courage, temperance, and justice or righteousness, which Plato derives from his functional divisions of the state and the individual, are correspondingly operative in *Major Barbara.* They fit the central trio of characters, each of whom, like the virtues, has a public as well as private dimension. Cusins, with his "access to the subtlest thought," symbolizes wisdom that comes from reason and the deliberative function in society. Barbara, as spirited auxiliary guardian, exemplifies the correlative virtue of courage, especially in its fullest Platonic meaning as moral courage.[20] Shaw describes her as "sunny and fearless" in facing the threatening Bill in the second act, and in the last act she is twice linked with courage. Undershaft, proclaiming that whatever can blow men up can blow society up, continues: "The history of the world is the history of those who had courage enough to embrace this truth. Have you the courage to embrace it, Barbara?" (175). In Platonic fashion the challenge to her is personal yet is given a public, historical function. At the end of the play Barbara herself asks Cusins, "Oh, did you think my courage would never come back?" (184).

Undershaft, in his turn, must relate to temperance (*sophrosyne*), which in the *Republic* means self-control or self-mastery.[21] Belonging no more to one of the three divisions than to the others, it involves instead a general agreement that the appetitive desires of the individual and the productive classes (economic forces) of society, respectively, be subordinated to the rule of reason. The complex Undershaft, described as a person with *"formidable reserves of power"* (84), is comparably unattached, but is hardly under the social and political control of reason, let alone moderation, in his public role. Failing thus to fulfill his proper social function—or at least to fulfill it properly—he is an intemperate influence in the state. The result is injustice from Shaw's point of view as well as Plato's.

Justice or righteousness, for Plato, is the principle of each individual or functioning group performing its "own proper work" (433b) for which it is best fitted by nature and nurture, in internal cooperative harmony with the others. It is a peaceful order, "bringing into tune those three parts, like the terms in the proportion of a musical scale, the highest and lowest notes and the mean between them, with all the intermediate intervals" (443d). There is reason to believe that *Major Barbara* is pointing toward a comparable social order. The overweening aspect of Undershaft, displayed in his brutal disregard for human life and in his ruthless arrogation of power, is symptomatic of an unhealthy and disordered condition of society, requiring correction. At the same time Barbara and Adolphus learn through him where the work of saving society must be directed.

It is also well to remember that by the end of *Major Barbara*, the central trio, including Undershaft, acquiesces in Cusins's assumption of authority. In doing so, like Plato's three elements, they "are agreed that reason should be ruler" (442cd). Barbara will join this personification of reason, for "he has found me my place and my work" (184), as she says at the end. In the words of the *Republic*, "at the same time those two together will be the best of guardians for the entire soul and for the body against all enemies from without: the one will take counsel, while the other will do battle, following its ruler's commands and by its own bravery giving effect to the ruler's designs" (442b). But before this can happen, they have to complete the discipline of the educative process.

"Virtue and wealth are balanced against one another in the scales; as the rich rise in social esteem, the virtuous sink" (550e). This moral disequilibrium receives dramatic demonstration in the second-act contention between father and daughter. Undershaft comes as a stranger into the sphere of the Salvation Army, but proceeds to make it his own. That sphere itself reflects some of the features of life under the plutocratic rule of the oligarchic man in the *Republic*. Here, because "a man is allowed to sell all he has to another," is a society with "some men excessively wealthy and others destitute. . . . And you will certainly see beggars in any state governed by an oligarchy" (552b, d). To these Plato adds thieves, but Shaw presents only one instance of stealing, unless with Plato we "call it theft when one is persuaded out of one's belief" (413b), or pursue Shaw's linkage of millionaire and brigand, financier and burglar, in the play's Preface (45–46).

Undershaft, although not fully identifiable with Plato's oligarchic man, does resemble him in a number of respects. There is "his lack of education" ("I was never educated," says Undershaft in the first act [87]) and "his way of always expecting to make a profit and add to his hoard—the sort of person who is much admired by the vulgar" (554a). In addition, he too despises the poor and may also be said to undertake the subjection of reason and of the spirited element, represented by Cusins and Barbara, respectively, in keeping with Plato's description (551a, 553cd).

Irony and Sophistry

This brings us to another important quality in Plato's work, which has its counterpart in the Shavian *Republic* as well: its remarkable irony. Much that Friedländer says of Socratic and Platonic irony is strikingly pertinent to Shavian irony in *Major Barbara*. "Genuine irony," he writes, "contains an element of tension: on the one hand deceptively concealing, on the other uncompromisingly revealing, the truth." Its gentle and hidden dialectical tension makes it seductive: "Irony is the net of the great educator." It causes suffering but also bewitches. "Irony means attraction and repulsion at the same time." Sometimes, as in the *Republic*, the ironic tension is conveyed "through the device of putting a coarse jest side by side with the most solemn expression." The complex irony in Plato veils the highest truth he seeks to show, much as the garment in a Greek statue simultaneously veils and reveals what it veils (Friedländer, *Plato*, 144, 141, 142, 148, 153).

Major Barbara abounds in comparable irony. A few examples will suffice. Much of the play exhibits Undershaft in an ever-expanding process of acquisition. In the second act it is the Salvation Army that he acquires for his purposes. But he begins this operation in Act I by two simple acts of appropriation. First, he takes over the motto of the Army. "Its motto might be my own: Blood and Fire," he informs Lomax. To the latter's protest that it is not the munitions merchant's sort of blood and fire, Undershaft rejoins, "My sort of blood cleanses: my sort of fire purifies" (88). Already the blood and fire have taken on dual and ironic aspects. Near the end of the act when Undershaft counters Barbara's "sign of the cross" with the "sign of the sword" (91), he may well be making subtle use of the fact that both emblems, cross and sword, are emblazoned on the heraldic crest of the Salvation Army itself, where the cross appears between a pair of crossed swords. If so, here is an intimation that Undershaft already has a hand on a weapon in his adversary's arsenal. Early in the play, then, there are these covertly ironic instances of the easy access to proprietary control that the military framework of the Army affords to the dealer in armaments.

In the second act there is Undershaft's inconspicuous but pregnant pun in offering his daughter the "millionaire's mite," within which lurks the millionaire's *might* (123). Cusins and Barbara are alternately attracted and "revolted" by Undershaft. As Cusins puts it in the second act, "Mr Undershaft: you are, as far as I am able to gather, a most infernal old rascal; but you appeal very strongly to my sense of ironic humor" (119). In the first scene of the third act Barbara, after telling her father that she will never forgive him, immediately thereafter is kissing his hands and saying, "You may be a devil; but God speaks through you sometimes." She is eager to learn more: "There must be some truth or other behind all this frightful irony" (156). Undershaft's pedagogic irony inflicts suffering upon both young people and is able temporarily to bewitch each. There is Cusins's "convulsion of irony" at the climax of the second act when, "possessed" by "Dionysos Undershaft," he callously disparages the heartbreak of the woman to whom he is so deeply devoted. She, in turn, after being briefly "*hypnotized*" by Undershaft in the last scene, is able to resume her self-possession "*with a power equal to his own*" (170).

Undershaft himself is a thoroughly ironic character: the incarnation of forces in society that must be overcome, he is at the same time confidently training the adversaries who will replace him. Small wonder that he has been so misunderstood, and with him this play. Bill Walker's pun about the "Snobby Price" of salvation epitomizes a solemn lesson in a coarse jest. Finally, the irony that pervades the second scene of the third act culminates, as we shall see, in an ending in which Shaw masks his teachings in allusive and elusive metaphor. It is in the third act that *Major Barbara*'s strongest marks of kinship to the *Republic* manifest themselves. Here the opposing forces of the first two acts—wealth and poverty, aristocracy and the common people, capitalism and Christianity, morality and power—meet in a comprehending synthesis. In the second scene there is a parallel synthesis in locale, for having already visited the precincts of the arrogant rich and the obsequious poor, respectively, we are introduced to the community in which both could possibly come to live effectively and harmoniously.

A return visit to Wilton Crescent in the first scene prepares the way for the journey to Undershaft's domain. In this scene we witness the *aporia* of Barbara and Cusins and the final elimination of Stephen as a candidate to succeed his father. A perplexed and brooding Barbara has left the Salvation Army after her father's vivid demonstration of its impotence before the might of the millionaire. Adolphus fills us in on the aftermath of the second act. Following the hysterical mass meeting he became drunk on "Dionysos" Undershaft's temperance burgundy. Undershaft himself, who had "*overwhelmed*" Cusins in their first dialectical encounter, and later "*possessed*" him, now according to Cusins, "sat there and completed the wreck of my moral basis, the rout of my convictions, the purchase of my soul" (142). The ironic plutocrat who, according to his wife, "never does a proper thing without giving an improper reason for it," has convinced Adolphus that "I have all my life been doing improper things for proper reasons" (143). So Cusins, too, is perplexed. Shaw's guardians are ready for the next stage in their education, conducted, paradoxically enough, by the demonic Undershaft in the course of a tour of his industrial town, Perivale St. Andrews.

Before that can take place it is necessary to dispose of Stephen's familial claim to the Undershaft succession. His test comes, interestingly enough, in the form of a Socratic cross-examination by his father, in which his moral and political incompetence are satirically exposed.[22] A product of the "public school and university where I formed my habits of mind," and defending "the best elements in the English national character," Stephen, in his father's words, really "knows nothing and he thinks he knows everything. That points clearly to a political career" (152, 151). He therefore invites comparison with the politician questioned by Socrates in the *Apology*, who "thinks that he knows something which he does not know" (*Apology* 21d, trans. Tredennick, *Plato: The Collected Dialogues*, 8).[23] This conversation with his father also resembles the one spoken of in the *Republic* with the aristocratic young man of a great country who is "puffed up with senseless self-conceit": "Now suppose that . . . someone should come and quietly tell him the truth, that there is no sense in him and that the only way to get the understanding he needs is to work for it like a slave: will he find it easy to listen, surrounded by all these evil influences?" (494d). No more is expected from the instruction in the one case than in the other.

Stephen suffers from what Plato calls a "falsehood in the soul concerning reality" (382b); he embodies an incomprehension as abysmal as it is widespread. Indeed, Undershaft goes on to generalize to humanity at large the Shavian indictment of Stephen's claim to know the difference between right and wrong as a matter of gentlemanly birthright:

> Oh, thats everybody's birthright. Look at poor little Jenny Hill, the Salvation lassie! she would think you were laughing at her if you asked her to stand up in the street and teach grammar or geography or mathematics or even drawing room dancing; but it never occurs to her to doubt that she can teach morals and religion. You are all alike, you respectable people. . . . You darent handle high explosives; but youre all ready to handle honesty and truth and justice and the whole duty of man, and kill one another at that game. What a country! What a world! (150–51)

In his famous political parable of the ship of state, Plato complained similarly about the members of the crew, for "each thinks he ought to be steering the vessel, though he has never learnt navigation and cannot point to any teacher under whom he has served his apprenticeship. . . . They do not understand that the genuine navigator can only make himself fit to command a ship by studying the seasons of the year, sky, stars, and winds, and all that belongs to his craft" (488b, d).[24] The implication of Stephen's schooling in the general Shavian censure brings to mind Plato's contention that every Sophist "is teaching nothing else than the opinions and beliefs expressed by the public itself when it meets on any occasion; and that is what he calls wisdom." He will adapt his instruction "to the fancies of the great beast and call what it enjoys good and what vexes it bad. He has no other account to give of their meaning; for him any action will be 'just' and 'right' that is done under necessity . . . to give them [his masters, the public] whatever they like and do whatever they approve" (493ac). Since "the multitude can never be philosophical" (494a), Plato concludes that, excepting the superhuman, "in the present state of society, any character that escapes and comes to good can only have been saved by some miraculous interposition" (492e). "And, by the same token, what sort of ideas and opinions will be begotten of the misalliance of Philosophy with men incapable of culture? Not any true-born child of wisdom; the only right name for them will be sophistry" (496a).

Stephen is a comparable product of his society. He may be taken to exemplify in morality what Plato calls *eikasia* in the simile of the line—"the wholly unenlightened state of mind which takes sensible appearances and current moral notions at their face value," as Cornford describes it (222). It is clear that Stephen lacks the qualifications for guardianship; he fails his test. Unlike his sister Barbara and her suitor, who exhibit the exceptional qualities called for, he never evinces an aporetic condition, even in the face of the most stinging satire. In contrast to the mental outlook just displayed by Stephen are the unstable states of mind of Cusins and Barbara. They contemplate their cannon foundry destination with mixed feelings.

> CUSINS [*moodily* . . .] Why are we two coming to this Works Department of Hell? that is what I ask myself.
> BARBARA. I have always thought of it as a sort of pit where lost creatures with blackened faces stirred up smoky fires and were driven and tormented by my father. Is it like that, dad?
> UNDERSHAFT [*scandalized*] My dear! It is a spotlessly clean and beautiful hillside town. (154)

We are given strong intimations here that the trip ahead is really a spiritual journey. The ambiguous prospect that their destination promises is heightened by Undershaft's account (in a companion speech to the one about the horrors of his trade directed at Mrs. Baines) of the manner in which he exploits the snobbery of his workers to maintain order in his factory and to ensure a colossal profit for himself. Cusins is *"revolted"* by this depiction of a satanic scheme of subjection. When Undershaft rekindles Barbara's faith with the suggestion that she must have left some mark on Bill Walker, although her "spirit is troubled," she is prepared to go with Cusins to "the factory of death" to "learn something more" of the truth behind the irony (156).

Like the beneficiaries of Plato's dialectic, each of the two has reached the stage that Socrates describes in the *Meno*: "So in perplexing him and numbing him like the sting ray . . . we have helped him to some extent toward finding out the right answer, for now not only is he ignorant of it but he will be quite glad to look for it. Up to now, he thought he could speak well and fluently, on many occasions and before large audiences, on the subject" (*Meno* 84b, trans. Guthrie, *Collected Dialogues*, 368). They feel misgivings comparable to those of Adeimantus: "Just as in draughts the less skillful player is finally hemmed into a corner where he cannot make a move, so in this game where words take the place of counters they feel they are being cornered and reduced to silence, but that does not really prove them in the wrong" (487bc).

Stephen's *eikasia*, the aporetic condition of Barbara and Cusins, and the linking of Undershaft's cannon works with hell, suggest that Plato's allegory of the cave (*Republic* 514–21) may contain some helpful clues to the allegorical aspects of the visit to Perivale St. Andrews.[25] The Wilton Crescent home of Lady Britomart and the Salvation Army shelter might seem better analogues of the cave, since Shaw depicts the general run of inhabitants of both places as being, like the cave's captives, imprisoned in a deceptive world of appearance, seeing only shadows of justice and hearing only echoes of truth, their view of reality distorted by prevailing misconceptions and prejudices. But there is more to the cave in Plato's account: there is the fire that casts the shadows of objects on the cave wall, and there is an upward path leading out and beyond. Perivale St. Andrews, perched halfway up a hill, with its foundry fires "*hidden in the depths*" below it (157), thus has both physical and figurative features more closely resembling those of the cave.

The central images in Plato's parable contrast darkness and light, bondage and liberation, and painful upward and downward movements of body and vision. The difficult journey upward represents a dialectical process of education, requiring conversion, or reversal of direction and outlook. Is not the visit to Perivale St. Andrews a comparable journey, in some measure reflecting and refracting the cave imagery? It is at the beginning of the third act that Cusins first calls Undershaft "the Prince of Darkness" (142). Barbara's hellish image of her father's realm as a pit in which blackened victims stir up smoky fires also introduces the image of darkness. Darkness is paradoxically paired with light in Barbara's challenge to her father in the second scene of the third act: "Justify yourself: shew me some light through the darkness of this dreadful place, with its beautifully clean workshops, and respectable workmen, and model homes" (171). She seeks light from the darkness that shines forth as light to others. Clearly she is being prepared for "a conversion and turning about of the soul from a day whose light is darkness to the veritable day" (*Republic* 521c, trans. Shorey, *Collected Dialogues*, 753).[26] As for the others, excepting Cusins, we may well expect that they will perceive only light where she recognizes darkness.

Indeed, at their first encounter with Perivale St. Andrews, the whole entourage is dazzled by its splendor. But all this brightness has its umbrageous side, and in developing irony, this dual aspect of the city is kept before the eyes of its more discerning guests. Its Janus-like image emerges in the alternating and equivocal portrait of the city as hellish and heavenly. Anticipating a hell, Cusins finds that it needs only a cathedral to be a heavenly instead of a hellish city, and the William Morris Labor Church fulfills that need for him. "Not a ray of hope" does he descry in the fact that "it's all horribly, frightfully, immorally, unanswerably perfect" (158). Soon we are concentrating on the remarkable qualities of this community. Barbara alone is silent on its merits until the very end, hers being more "the verdict of one who is not dazzled, like a child, by the outward pomp and parade of absolute power, but whose understanding can enter into a man's heart and see all that goes on within" (577a); but Lady Britomart, Sarah, and Stephen join in a chorus of praise for the town. What attracts Stephen are its substantial fiscal and administrative endowments, although he worries about the demoralizing possibilities of too great provision for the wants of the workmen. Lady Britomart likes the homes and gardens, the linen and china.

These cave-blinded minds, still controlled by the false assumptions with which they grew up, are fascinated by the glittering surface of this shining city. Like Plato's "lovers of belief" or opinion (*doxa*), their affections are set on appearances (480a). Lady Britomart has no interest

in the "ridiculous cannons and that noisy banging foundry" (162)—
she turns her back on that peculiarity of the city. Lomax is the very
paradigm of cave blindness in his comic presumption to knowledge of
explosives, as foolhardy as it is foolish. The shortsightedness of these
views is driven home forcefully by a brief but brutal episode affecting
Cusins, and through him, Barbara. Much as Mrs. Baines's announcement of "good news" in the second act brought in its wake calamitous
consequences for Barbara, Undershaft's "good news from Manchuria"
now precipitates the discomfiture of Cusins. Word has come to the
armament manufacturer that his aerial battleship was a "tremendous
success" at its first war trial, having wiped out a fort with three hundred soldiers. Undershaft's response to Cusins's ingenuous question,
"Dummy soldiers?" and Shaw's stage directions convey the impact of
the scene:

> UNDERSHAFT [striding across to Stephen and kicking the pros-
> trate dummy brutally out of his way] No: the real thing.
> Cusins and Barbara exchange glances. Then Cusins sits on the step
> and buries his face in his hands. Barbara gravely lays her hand on
> his shoulder. He looks up at her in whimsical desperation. (159)

This incident remarkably duplicates for Cusins Barbara's nadir of despair
near the end of Act II. On that occasion, immediately after her ejaculation—"My God: why hast thou forsaken me?"—the stage direction
reads: "*She sinks on the form with her face buried in her hands*" (136–37).
Cusins's virtual repetition of Barbara's earlier despondent gesture clearly
emphasizes the depth of his moral revulsion. Occurring right after he
has proclaimed the unanswerable perfection of the place, it has biting
irony. Occurring, as well, immediately before Stephen's laudatory sentiments about the firm, it dramatically underscores the contrasting moral
obtuseness of the latter, soon shared in by his mother and Lomax. Only
Cusins and Barbara react to the underlying immorality in Undershaft's
model community; the others are lost in admiration, "dazzled by excess of light" (518a). Despite Undershaft's repeated reminders of how
precarious life in his explosive realm must be, they remain oblivious
to the meaning of the place. They illustrate Plato's belief "that the many
conventional notions of the mass of mankind about what is beautiful or
honourable or just and so on are adrift in a sort of twilight between pure
reality and pure unreality" (479d). Their souls are unturned; only those

of Barbara and Cusins become converted to genuine daylight and begin "that journey up to the real world which we shall call the true pursuit of wisdom" (521c).

The Way to Power

What Cushman says of Plato's conception of education is true of Shaw's as well: that "no man is educated, nor has he even begun his education, who has not undertaken critically to examine the reigning dogmas and assumptions of his age and place" (141). But the process of "release from the chains and the healing of their unwisdom" involves anguish, pain, perplexity, and resistance, as well as forceful guidance (*Republic* 515c; compare Friedländer, *Plato*, 67). In Shaw's allegory, Cusins and Barbara undergo the moral equivalent of this kind of experience. There is Cusins's encounter with the devastation of the "accursed" aerial battleships. Barbara graphically depicts her emotional state as resembling her childhood response to an earthquake at Cannes, during which "the surprise of the first shock" mattered little compared to "the dread and horror of waiting for the second." "That is how I feel in this place today," she explains. "I stood on the rock I thought eternal: and without a word of warning it reeled and crumbled under me . . . and in a moment, at the stroke of your pen in a cheque book, I stood alone; and the heavens were empty. That was the first shock of the earthquake: I am waiting for the second" (170). Cusins's replies to Undershaft reflect perturbation as well as resistance, as in his grudging acknowledgment of the political effectiveness of bullets: "I loath having to admit it. I repudiate your sentiments. I abhor your nature. I defy you in every possible way. Still, it is true" (174–75). Barbara is "*bewildered*" by Undershaft's "seven deadly sins," and Cusins is "*desperately perplexed*" when pressed to make his decision (171, 178). Their uncertainty, like that of the cave's prisoner (515c–e), results from a process of compelling guidance directed by a subtle instructor.

It is necessary to consider Perivale St. Andrews, as depicted in the second scene of the third act, in the broader terms of the kind of Shavian "republic" it presents. What does it really represent and signify in this drama? Is it Shaw's ideal community? If so, in what sense? Answers to these questions are crucial for understanding the play. The industrial community of Perivale St. Andrews, operating under Andrew

Undershaft's paternalistic ownership and management, is at the same time the political order he controls. We have already remarked the intimations that the "death and devastation factory" is an underworld or hell, juxtaposed with hints that the model town is a heavenly city. A realm blessed with all the virtues of efficiency, order, and productivity, its products are put to the uses of selfishness, death, and destruction.

How can this city of clean streets and dirty bombs be Shaw's republic? Is the socialist Shaw urging a form of paternalistic welfare capitalism as the solution of our social ills? Is he seriously proposing a materialistic Utopia as the ideal or perfect society, or as a city of heaven? Or is he suggesting the prospect of a hellish and revolutionary Marxian explosion to blow up a capitalist paradise? Before considering possible answers to these questions, we must look at the context of plot development and related circumstances in which this polis is introduced. This means, more specifically, the search for a successor to head the Undershaft firm.

The candidate for the Undershaft throne must be of illegitimate birth. Being a bastard is a necessary but insufficient qualification for munitions making. The incumbent explains the other essentials to his wife: "I want a man with no relations and no schooling: that is, a man who would be out of the running altogether if he were not a strong man. And I cant find him" (146). The only way to keep the foundry in the family, he adds, is to find Barbara a husband with these credentials. This directs attention to Barbara's suitor. Cusins "confesses" that his birth meets the test of technical illegitimacy, the shadow over his parentage arising from the fact that he is the offspring of a widower's remarriage with his deceased wife's sister. Such a marriage, legal in Australia where he was born, is illegal in England at this time. But even "being his own cousin" does not eliminate all the obstacles between Cusins and the succession.[27] "You are an educated man. That is against the tradition," Undershaft reminds him. Cusins meets this challenge with equal ingenuity. He is that *rara avis*, he explains, the schoolboy unspoiled by the educational process. Greek has not destroyed his mind but nurtured it, especially since he did not learn it at an English "public" school (165). Hardly disposed to quibble further, Undershaft declares him fully eligible, and Cusins is on his way to winning the kingdom and marrying the princess.

The succession to Undershaftian authority resembles in important respects the process by which Plato's philosopher-king is selected. In the *Republic* the ruler emerges from a background of anonymity and his ascension to power from a propertyless position is based on competence rather than heredity or kinship to his predecessors. The Undershaft regime similarly is to be directed by a capable "golden" man without hereditary claim to the position. As a "foundling" he is as divorced from family ties as Plato desired his guardian to be. His classless bride-to-be also comes "straight out of the heart of the whole people," to use her own words (183). That the choice of an educated man violates the Undershaft tradition may appear to distinguish this polity sharply from the Platonic one, to which education is indispensable. But Cusins's reply to that objection makes it abundantly clear that it is not education that is being rejected, but rather the failures of conventional schooling. Since Plato, too, found current education inadequate there is no real divergence in outlook on this point. Both writers were seeking an education that would strengthen, instead of weaken, intellect and morality.

With the disposition of the question of Cusins's eligibility to succeed Undershaft, and the settling of the "bargain" over the "price" of his soul in salary, a contest over "the moral question" ensues between the two men. For Cusins now has to decide whether he can conscientiously accept the reins of the factory of death. In making this decision he exhibits much the same reluctance that Plato claimed would characterize the philosopher called upon to govern (520a–521b), an idea that Shaw frequently repeated with favor, and here gives dramatic employment. Both men believe that "access to power must be confined to men who are not in love with it" (521b).

Cusins's reluctance arises from the moral dilemma he faces. His imagination has been kindled by Perivale St. Andrews, as that community provides the opportunity for great accomplishments. But an "abyss of moral horror" stretches out between him and the factory that is the raison d'être of the community. He is faced not only with the prospect of the naked assumption of awesome power, but also with the task of reconciling the Undershaftian creed that accompanies it with the morality and civilization that Cusins himself personifies in the play. Undershaft boldly and uncompromisingly thrusts at him the articles of that creed, "the true faith of an Armorer," daring him to subscribe (168). These articles are given in a series of oracular pronouncements, the substance of which may be summarized as follows: Power, even destructive power, may be used for good or evil. The factory owner who supplies it is only its custodian, merely the earthly agent of cosmic forces. At the same time, he must maintain a strict neutrality. His role is to make the power available; how it is employed is the user's moral responsibility, not his. The point is that no one can be absolved from complicity in the social and political abuse of human resources, natural or civilized.

The Undershaftian assault on Cusins's moral defenses reaches its climax in a surprising reference to Plato: "Plato says, my friend, that society cannot be saved until either the Professors of Greek take to making gunpowder, or else the makers of gunpowder become Professors of Greek" (178). The Undershaftian reading of the famous "until philosophers are kings" passage (*Republic* 473de) is the most palpable and explicit clue to the interpretation of *Major Barbara* as Shaw's *Republic*. Cusins, the professor of Greek, is here unequivocally identified with the Platonic philosopher, and Undershaft, the maker of gunpowder, with Plato's king. Undershaft's identification with political power is implied throughout the play. It is made explicit early in the third act, in a blunt retort to his son:

> *I* am the government of your country: I, and Lazarus. . . . you will do what pays us. You will make war when it suits us, and keep peace when it doesnt. . . . When I want anything to keep my dividends up, you will discover that my want is a national need. When other people want something to keep my dividends down, you will call out the police and military. And in return you shall have the support and applause of my newspapers, and the delight of imagining that you are a great statesman. (151–52)

The doctrine is clear. Economic power, symbolized by Undershaft and his partner, controls political power. Its control over religion has already been demonstrated in the second act. Undershaft, then, represents economic power, and since this translates into political power, he becomes despot as well. But does this exhaust the Shavian symbolism? Is he not also called "Machiavelli," the realistic user of political power, defending its necessity and importance; "Dionysos," embodying the frenzied driving dynamic forces threatening destruction to human life and civilization; "The Prince of Darkness," with the power to produce evil;

"Mephistopheles," bargaining for the soul of the Faustian Cusins? What lifeblood runs through all these incarnations? Is it not the common denominator of power itself?

If so, in his fullest meaning in this Shavian allegory, Undershaft symbolizes power in any guise, including sheer efficacy, the power to act and bring about results. This efficacy requires the mastery of existing forces, however terrible or hideous. But before they can be mastered, these forces must be recognized and reckoned with. Therefore Undershaft also represents the realistic facing of evil, which Shaw regards as an essential prerequisite to all effective change and reform. This is in keeping with Plato's observation that "possessing truth means thinking of things as they really are" (413a).

Triunity

The crux of the problem of interpreting this play lies in the way Undershaft and his teachings are to be construed. Is Undershaft merely the spokesman of the dramatist? Does his creed of power formulate the central message or moral of the play? Is this Shaw's complete or final word on the drama? If *Major Barbara* merely exhibits the process by which Undershaft converts first Barbara, then Cusins to his philosophy, then his model city, Perivale St. Andrews, must be, as it stands, the Shavian republic. If so, the meanings of the play are to be gleaned from Undershaft's philosophy and the way it is illustrated in the streets of his factory city. But surely such a reading of the play distorts its meanings, since it ignores the workings of the Shavian dialectic.

The Platonic parallel and the tripartite soul of the *Republic* can help us here. Three outlooks, three points of view, three facets of human concern, are represented in the three principal characters in the play. And Shaw's perspective, philosophically as well as dramatically, encompasses all three. His viewpoint is trinitarian, with the three aspects of the Platonic soul and society dialectically developed and harmonized. At the conclusion of *John Bull's Other Island*—*Major Barbara*'s dramatic predecessor—Father Keegan presents his dream of heaven: "in my dreams it is a country where the State is the Church and the Church is the people: three in one and one in three. . . . It is a godhead in which all life is human and all humanity divine: three in one and one in three" (2:1021).[28]

This passage has significance for *Major Barbara* also since Undershaft, Barbara, and Cusins comprise a Shavian trinity in which surrogates for state, church, and people meet. They are related to each other in a manner indicated in a letter from a Catholic priest to Shaw anent *Saint Joan*, which Shaw quotes approvingly in the preface to that play: "I see the dramatic presentation of the conflict of the Regal, sacerdotal, and Prophetical powers. . . . To me it is not the victory of any one of them over the others that will bring peace and the Reign of the Saints in the Kingdom of God, but *their fruitful interaction in a costly but noble state of tension*" (Pref. *Saint Joan*, 6:55; italics added). Shaw then comments: "The Pope himself could not put it better, nor can I." The interacting forces that Undershaft, Barbara, and Cusins represent likewise operate in a "noble state of tension." Barbara and Cusins in their encounters with Undershaft display morality and intellect wrestling with the problems of power and efficacy; religion and culture struggling with economic and political realities; Christianity and the Greco-European heritage contending with capitalistic dominion.

The dialectical pressures of the tension serve to break down the barriers separating the three, as each takes on some of the coloration of the other two. The intellectual Cusins is also the "collector of religions" who "can believe them all," as he claims in the second act (115). Captivated by Barbara, he joins the Salvation Army to "worship" her. In the third act he becomes the principal exponent of morality, and is on his way to acquire economic and political power. The religious and moral passion of Barbara is painfully compelled to turn and face the dark might of economic and political authority. Undershaft, the proponent of economic appetite and profit, paradoxically employs his intellect in redirecting the attention and thinking of the other two. At the same time his millionaire's creed of money and gunpowder turns out to be a mystic religion, one in which he serves a "will of which I am a part" (169). The interplay of these three initially related yet opposed forces of intellect, religious morality, and political economy ultimately brings them into a functional harmony in which Cusins is to marry Barbara and become partner, adopted son, son-in-law, successor, and alter ego to Undershaft. The triumphant irony of the drama lies in the fact that when Andrew Undershaft finally prevails he will be Adolphus Cusins, *mutato nomine*, the husband and stepbrother of Barbara. At that point his intrafamilial relations will be almost as complex as those of the Platonic guardian: "He must regard everyone whom he meets as brother or sister, father or mother, son or daughter" (463c).

In the interchanges that establish the relations and continuity between Shaw's trinity of characters, Undershaft is the mentor. But the education of the other two is something more than a simple process of conversion to his doctrines. The hope of the future lies not with him but with them, for they are being trained to replace and supersede him. Is he not the most fitting target of Shaw's comment in the Preface that "the Salvationists divine that they must fight the devil instead of merely praying at him. At present, it is true, they have not quite ascertained his correct address" (37). Undershaft has the ironic task in the play of redirecting the true Salvationists' fire to himself at his proper address.

There is ample evidence for this interpretation in the play. When Undershaft says that society cannot be saved until Cusins becomes Undershaft or Undershaft becomes Cusins (178), he is clearly indicating that neither alone is enough. Since Undershaft represents power, political and economic, and Cusins, knowledge, Shaw is joining Plato in saying that the problems of mankind cannot be solved until knowledge and power meet. But there is a difference. In one respect it is a difference in emphasis. Plato wants knowledge to rule. Shaw is contending that knowledge—and likewise art and altruism—are futile without the power to face realities and to change them. Hence the stress on brutal reality, poverty, death, and destruction in his play. It is not that Shaw is less interested in the lights of civilization: he wants to make sure they are beamed at the darkness.

Power of Life and Death

The cave analogy can be applied to *Major Barbara* only upon close scrutiny of the final dialogue between Barbara and Cusins. The higher Shavian themes emerge when Cusins and Barbara are left alone to decide how to meet the challenge Undershaft has flung at them and to reevaluate their positions. Cusins has decided to accept the offer, and Barbara tells him that had he refused she would have given him up for the man who accepted (180). Each, in turn, explains why. Cusins declares that he wants to "make power for the world." When Barbara then asserts that she would restrict such power to spiritual power, he counters that "all power is spiritual": even cannons will not fire by themselves. To the objection that the power produced in the factory kills and destroys, he responds, "You cannot have power for good without having power for evil too" (181). Mothers' milk may nourish both murderers and heroes. Because higher powers are at the mercy of the power to destroy, that power must be mastered first. That is why he gave his best pupil, going off to fight in a war for Greece, not a copy of Plato's *Republic* but a revolver and a hundred Undershaft cartridges. That act implicated him along with the munitions maker in the killing of every Turk shot by his pupil (182). It also committed him "for ever" to Perivale St. Andrews.

Cusins has learned several Shavian lessons: the indivisibility of human guilt, the irrevocability of moral responsibility, and the need for a useful life of action to supplant literary ineffectuality.[29] Like the Platonic philosopher he realizes "that a state can never be properly governed . . . by men who are allowed to spend all their days in the pursuit of culture" (519bc). Barbara, too, rejects a useless life in an "artistic drawing room" (183). Cusins's conclusion about power is one that Plato reaches about wisdom: "Its use for good or harm depends on the direction towards which it is turned." As for those who misuse it, "there is nothing wrong with their power of vision, but it has been forced into the service of evil, so that the keener its sight, the more harm it works" (518e–519a). Because power may be turned to good or evil, and because all values are at its mercy, Cusins considers it vital that human beings give priority to its effective control and responsible exercise. Undershaft has dared him to "make war on war" (178). That dare he accepts.

He has actually learned more than Undershaft taught. Even his conclusions about power are not strictly Undershaftian. He wants to give power to the people—power against all forces inimical to them:

This power which only tears men's bodies to pieces has never been so horribly abused as the intellectual power, the imaginative power, the poetic, religious power that can enslave men's souls. As a teacher of Greek I gave the intellectual man weapons against the common man. I now want to give the common man weapons against the intellectual man. I love the common people. I want to arm them against the lawyers, the doctors, the priests, the literary men, the professors, the artists, and the politicians, who, once in authority, are more disastrous and tyrannical than all the fools, rascals, and impostors. I want a power simple enough for common men to use, yet strong enough to force the intellectual oligarchy to use its genius for the general good. (181)

That this is not Undershaft's doctrine is evident when it is compared with a passage in the second act:

CUSINS . . . Barbara is in love with the common people. So am I . . . Have you never felt the romance of that love?
UNDERSHAFT [*cold and sardonic*] . . . This love of the common people may please an earl's granddaughter and a university professor; but I have been a common man and a poor man; and it has no romance for me. . . . We three must stand together above the common people: how else can we help their children to climb up beside us? (121)

The romance may be gone for Cusins at the end, but certainly the love for the common people remains. Undershaft has not altered that. If the weapons to be given to the common man are taken to be the literal weapons in the Undershaft arsenal, it could be concluded that Cusins is converted to armed revolution. But surely he does not want to overthrow, remove, or destroy the intellectual professions singled out as antagonistic to the interests of the common people. He wants rather to assure the redirection of their efforts. For this purpose physical weapons can hardly provide the kind of permanent corrective force needed. Only a narrow literalism could construe Cusins's speech as a simple appeal to force and violence, especially when it is noted that his weapon references include those he gave as a teacher of Greek. He now contemplates a much more thoroughgoing revolution.

The power simple enough to compel the intellectual elite to serve the general good must be lasting economic and political power. Undershaft himself expressly identifies gunpowder with such hegemonic power not only in paraphrasing Plato, but even in the precise defining equations that formulate his "gospel" in the second act: "Yes, money and gunpowder. Freedom and power. Command of life and command of death" (120). This is the power that must first be mastered before human beings can effectively develop their higher powers. And if all power is spiritual—that is, moral—then even the power in physical weapons is amenable to the proper social employment of such moral power. What else can be meant by making "war on war"?[30] Nuclear power has only heightened and sharpened the Shavian point: the same power can now be used to wipe out mankind or confer upon it undreamed of energy resources for constructive purposes. What is crucial for effective exercise of moral power is its access to economic and political power; without that it is helpless.

Cusins's conclusions about power express a mistrust for unharnessed intellectual authority and call for having it politically channeled to the common good. This may seem at odds with the unlimited authority Plato was ready to confer upon his philosophers. But Plato, too, was concerned lest selfish interests divert his guardians from public service. He believed "you can have a well-governed society only if you can discover for your future rulers a better way of life than being in office; then only will power be in the hands of men who are rich, not in gold, but in the wealth that brings happiness, a good and wise life" (520e–521a). One way of achieving this goal is to deprive his prospective intellectual and moral leaders of family and wealth. Shaw, in ironic contrast, grants the guardians in his play wealth (and family position) as the very means for accomplishing their social purposes. This brings out another fundamental difference in outlook between Shaw and Plato. For Plato the love of money is a source of evil; for Shaw only the lack of it is evil. "Money," we read in the *Major Barbara* Preface, "is the most important thing in the world. It represents health, strength, honor, generosity and beauty as conspicuously and undeniably as the want of it represents illness, weakness, disgrace, meanness and ugliness" (30). Nevertheless, what counts in the thought of both men is the communal control of this commodity, even though Plato's communism, unlike Shaw's socialism, is limited to the guardian class. Still closer are they with respect to the eventual prospect Plato envisions: "it is better for everyone, we believe, to be subject to a power of godlike wisdom residing within himself, or, failing that, imposed from without, in order that all of us, being under one guidance, may be so far as possible equal and united" (590d).

The play culminates in Barbara's response to her father's challenge, reserved until after that of Cusins. Both her situation and Cusins's may be clarified by returning to the perspective of the cave allegory. As already suggested, the bright material blessings of Perivale St. Andrews blind the eyes of the other visitors. As they concentrate on the model city and the administration of its business, the distastefulness of the community's principal products recede from view. By contrast, it is the moral horror of the hellish death factory that fills the eyes of Cusins and Barbara. Yet in the end they are converted to acceptance of it, even to active participation in its management. But what is the nature of this conversion?

The cave figure traces the progress of "the power of vision in the released prisoner," who, "set free from his chains," eventually climbs up "out of the cavern into the sunshine" (532b). The eye of his soul has been turned and led upward; he has been "made to climb the ascent to the vision of Goodness" (519c). Barbara, too, has come to her pinnacle of vision and freedom. Her lofty speeches in the coda of the play reflect a spirit of liberation, or better still the liberation of a spirit. In a drama so filled with talk about conversion, here is the decisive moment when the soul of the converter is converted, reoriented. What does the eye of her soul now see?

Part of the answer is fairly clear, part is shrouded in mystic language. For Plato the climatic vision is of the sun as a symbol of the good; whereupon those noblest natures who attain to it "must not be allowed . . . to remain on the heights, refusing to come down again to the prisoners or to take any part in their labours and rewards, however much or little these may be worth" (519d). Similarly, although Barbara would prefer to fly heavenward and leave all the "naughty mischievous children of men" (182), she realizes that she cannot. So she turns her thought downward to the meaning of Perivale St. Andrews. A place where good and evil meet, its glowing virtues are conjoined with its macabre and vicious destructiveness. But its sinister side is inescapable; it is necessary to recognize the inextricably guilty involvement of every member of society in its deadly business. The light that Barbara finally discovers shining through the darkness of the dreadful model community is in part the realization of the true locus of the moral challenge for human salvation. Hers is the insight that we must work *through*, not away from, the darkness toward the light.

It is evil—moral and social—that Shaw is undertaking to locate, detonate, and destroy, and "the most sensationally anti-moral department of commerce" is excellently suited to be the shocking, ironic instrument and symbol of his purpose.[31] But if the way to the good life is through the confrontation, control, even devastation if necessary, of the forces conducive to evil, then, as in Plato, the prime pressing need is to turn the soul's eye in the right direction. Also required is perceiving, as Plato did, "that everything has its peculiar evil as well as its good" (608e), and not allowing the good to blind us to the evil.

Barbara has come to know that "life is all one," with its evil not to be shirked but shared. The discovery that life has no isolable wicked side she presents as an admonition to Cusins, who had thought she was "determined to turn [her] back on the wicked side of life" (183). This back-turning phrase recurs in her final speeches, reflecting the cave images in which bodily movements symbolize those of the soul. Because the hands of Bodger and Undershaft "stretch everywhere," she realizes that "if we turn from the churches they build, we must kneel on the stones of the streets they pave. . . . Turning our backs on Bodger and Undershaft is turning our backs on life" (182–83). Were she middle class, she avers, "I should turn my back on my father's business"; so presumably would Cusins, with the consequence that both of them would prove utterly useless as citizens. Her reiterated refusal to turn her back on the problems of society emphasizes a bond of kinship, shared by Cusins, with the Platonic rulers, all of them committed not to turn their backs on the world of the cave.

In the *Republic* knowledge and morality coalesce; in Shaw's play the embodiments of these values, Cusins and Barbara, are soon to wed. Thus the conclusions of Barbara are joined to those of her husband-to-be. Through her father she has learned not to shun realities. But her salvationist goals, like Cusins's, transcend those of her millionaire capitalist father. The important thing in life, she knows, is to be of use and devoted to human purposes. Her work is still to save human souls, but no longer poor, weak, and starving ones; rather those that need saving—the "fullfed, quarrelsome, snobbish, uppish creatures, all standing on their little rights and dignities," who are to be found in Perivale St. Andrews, and presumably right in her own family. That is why she must have this place. Her reasoning is allied to Cusins's: with the mastering of the basic economic powers, people can develop their higher powers. She has learned that salvation cannot be merely private or personal. Where there is moral evil everyone is guilty; accountability for it can neither be absolved nor religiously expiated. She has climbed the path from moral earnestness to social and political responsibility.

In answer to her father's version of Adeimantus's challenge to religious morality—that it is "cheap work" to convert starving people with a Bible and bread—she proclaims her liberation from such bribes. Supplanting her confident declaration to Peter Shirley in the Salvation shelter that "if you did your part God will do his," is a new credo: "Let God's work be done for its own sake: the work he had to create us to do because it cannot be done except by living men and women" (184). Such distinctively human work is here held to be of intrinsic worth and invested with religious dignity verging on the divine.

Raising Hell to Heaven

Friedländer, while denying that Plato was a mystic, has detected mystical elements in the upward path from the cave:

> A path from darkness to light; a path in stages not without numerous labors and not accessible to everybody; a path at the end of which the eye beholds, in dazzling light, something divine; the highest goal shrouded in mystery not arbitrarily posited, and not exposed to profanation by words, because words cannot express it—if we look at these characteristics of Plato's speculation . . . their revelations are seen as allusions . . . to a process of spiritual purification. The contrast between the uninitiated who dwell in the mud of Hades and the purified and enlightened who dwell with the gods represents a contrast between those who seek the truth in the right manner and those who do not. (71)[32]

In her final speeches Barbara's words and thoughts also turn heavenward, toward the divine. She wishes for "the wings of a dove" to "fly away to heaven" (182).[33] In transcending the bribes of bread and heaven, she is "*transfigured*" (184). When Undershaft returns, Cusins reports that Barbara "has gone right up into the skies" (185). But while they are still alone Cusins joins Barbara in celebrating their dazzling revelation very much as if on the sunlit heights. Cusins's question follows Barbara's paean to the divine nature of human work:

> CUSINS. Then the way of life lies through the factory of death?
> BARBARA. Yes, through the raising of hell to heaven and of man to God, through the unveiling of an eternal light in the Valley of The Shadow. (184)

One may discern in this mystical language a meaning related to the cave analogy. The way to the good life is through transforming the actual, with all its evil, into a better world in which humankind may be elevated to godhead. This is the light to be unveiled in the darkness and shadows. Both the Platonic and Shavian works attest to this converse with the universe beyond and with the divine (*Republic* 611). In *Major Barbara* there are hints that the prospective rulers of Perivale St. Andrews are on their way to superhuman or divine status. In the *Republic* Plato writes of the philosophic nature: "if it can ever find the ideal form of society, as perfect as itself, then we shall see that it is in reality something divine, while all other natures and ways of life are merely human" (497bc).

Again: "So the philosopher, in constant companionship with the divine order of the world, will reproduce that order in his soul, and, so far as man may, become godlike" (500cd). Barbara, in particular, speaks of God as from a plane of equality: "When I die, let him be in my debt, not I in his; and let me forgive him as becomes a woman of my rank" (184). She has chosen the ethical goal of making herself "as like a god as man may" (613b), which Plato tells us in the *Theaetetus* means "to become righteous with the help of wisdom" (*Theaetetus* 176b, trans. Cornford, *Collected Dialogues*, 881). Her transfiguration is an apotheosis, succeeding upon her passion.

It is worthy of note that Shaw is undertaking to reform religion in a way comparable to Plato. Plato saw the same principles of order in the state as in the individual; he also viewed these as reflecting an order in the universe. Shaw likewise considers humanity from both a political and a cosmic perspective. Both writers, as a consequence, were led to a criticism of traditional religion. What Cassirer discerns in Plato has its counterpart in Shaw: "He insists that without having found a true and more adequate—conception of his gods man cannot hope to order and rule his own human world. . . . For what man sees in the gods is only a projection of his own life—and vice versa. We read the nature of the human soul in the nature of the state—we form our political ideals according to our conceptions of the gods" (*The Myth of the State*, 78).[34] Barbara's cryptic peroration incorporates a proposed Shavian reformation of established religion—a reformation in keeping with the dramatist's conceptions of economic, political, and moral reform. Shaw would raise "man to God" by evolutionary improvement, working toward the divinity of humankind. Like Plato, he ferments his new religious wine in the old casks, using orthodox phraseology to propound advanced and heterodox religious conceptions. His salvationist is preaching a new religion, not a return to the old.

So, like the Platonic philosopher-kings, these coming leaders of society are preparing to return to the cave to guide others. "They must lift up the eye of the soul to gaze on that which sheds light on all things; and when they have seen the Good itself, take it as a pattern for the right ordering of the state and of the individual, themselves included" (540ab). The eyes of Barbara and Cusins's souls are similarly uplifted toward a Shavian conception of goodness. They too are ready to "take their turn at the troublesome duties of public life and act as Rulers for their country's sake, not regarding it as a distinction, but as an unavoidable task" (540b). Barbara's inclusion in this mission is fully in accord with the reminder Socrates appends to this passage: "All I have been saying applies just as much to any women who are found to have the necessary gifts."

Cusins and Barbara have come to their respective decisions independently yet jointly. Each has chosen a way of life for the future. Like the souls in the Myth of Er at the end of the *Republic* they behold and choose their destiny (617e). In this "supreme choice for a man" (618e) each chooses freely "a life to which he will be bound of necessity" (617e). There is the same interplay of freedom and necessity in their decisions as in Plato's myth. Though freely electing a new life, their commitment is irrevocable; they have "passed under the throne of Necessity" (620e). Barbara would have found it necessary to marry whoever accepted Undershaft's offer; Cusins felt compelled to respond to the challenge. As each soul faces the fates and takes up its lot, it is "a sight worth seeing . . . a sight to move pity and laughter and astonishment" (619e–620a). In their conclusions about moral responsibility each also offers a version of Plato's warning: "The blame is his who chooses; Heaven is blameless" (617e).

The Myth of Er applies to their situation in still another respect. In this myth Plato modifies the traditional Greek mythological belief that every person's soul is possessed by a daimon, personifying his destiny; and depending on whether it is a good or an evil daimon, his life will be happy (*eudaimon*) or miserable (*kakodaimon*). In Plato's view one freely chooses, rather than is allotted, his daimon, and with it his destiny. In

Major Barbara it is Undershaft whom Cusins calls "you old demon" and from whose "possession" he is freed when he makes his conscious decision in the last act. As in the *Republic* this demon is a "guardian spirit" (617d) chosen "to escort him through life and fulfil his choice" (620de). Such a fulfillment, for Cusins and Barbara, will necessitate their free repossession of this demonic Undershaftian force in behalf of the general well-being (*eudaimonia*) of humankind.

Cusins, in his joy at learning that Barbara's decision complements his own, protests that he cannot stand as much happiness as she can. But the happiness of each, given his love of the common people and her classless rise "out of the heart of the whole people," is tied to that of the entire society. For Shaw, with Plato, is seeking to construct "the state which will be happy as a whole, not trying to secure the well-being of a select few." Nor would he "endow our Guardians with a happiness that will make them anything rather than guardians" (420c, d). Having found, with Adolphus, her place and her work, "Major Barbara will die with the colors" (184). She is "Major Barbara" again. Though this signals a return to the Salvation Army, it will be a return with a difference. If there is any merit in the salvation syllogism suggested in Barbara's challenge to her father at the end of the first act, it has additional applicability here. For salvation constituted the major term—the predicate of the conclusion— in that syllogism. Thus the major term describes Barbara's lifework: the saving of souls. At the end of the play she is returning to this major role. The commitment to salvation is the crying imperative facing a leader of the commonwealth whose lot must be cast "in a society congenial to [the guardian's] nature, where he could grow to his full height and save his country as well as himself" (497a).

Return to the Cave

Then, from her apogee of divinity in this penultimate scene with Cusins, Barbara's behavior turns strangely and anticlimactically childish in the final comic moments of the play. Clutching *"like a baby"* at her mother's skirt, she appeals to that lady to decide for her which house in the village to take for her and her "Dolly." If we heed Plato's counsel in responding to this sudden and unexpected infantile behavior on the part of a Shavian guardian, we shall not be surprised to discover "that one who comes from the contemplation of divine things to the miseries of human life should appear awkward and ridiculous" (517d). For the eyes of one who goes back into the cave suddenly from out of the sunlight will be dazed and filled with darkness. If required with such blurred vision to deliver opinions on the shadows in competition with those still imprisoned in the cave, the judgments would appear ludicrous. But when a sensible man sees a soul thus confused by the change from light to darkness, "instead of laughing thoughtlessly, he will ask whether, coming from a brighter existence, its unaccustomed vision is obscured by the darkness, in which case he will think its condition enviable and its life a happy one" (518ab).

In the passage that inspired subsequent heavenly cities, Plato said of his ideal commonwealth, founded "in the realm of discourse": "I think it nowhere exists on earth . . . but perhaps there is a pattern set up in the heavens for one who desires to see it and, seeing it, to found one in himself" (592ab). Plato was a mythmaker, undertaking, as he tells us, to incorporate truths in the fiction of his myths (*Republic* 377a). These Platonic myths are of course not to be interpreted literally. We should likewise avoid taking Shaw's myth literally, heeding his caveat at the end of the Preface: "This play of mine, *Major Barbara*, is, I hope, both true and inspired; but whoever says that it all happened, and that faith in it and understanding of it consist in believing that it is a record of an actual occurrence, is, to speak according to Scripture, a fool and a liar, and is hereby solemnly denounced and cursed as such by me, the author, to all posterity" (63).

In the myth of Perivale St. Andrews we reach the upper dialectical levels of Shaw's drama. The antithesis between Undershaft and Cusins is to issue in the union of wisdom and power, while that between Undershaft and Barbara is to bring a new sense of direction to the glory of fervent salvationism. As Cusins prepares to assume the name and power of Andrew Undershaft and to be joined in matrimony with Barbara, wisdom, power, and glory meet in a symbolic unity prefiguring the kingdom come: Shaw's republic. As in Plato there is the inclination and aspiration to the divine, to the heavenly city, coupled with the commitment to reforming duty in the earthly city.

The marriage of Barbara and Cusins is in the offing. The mating of these exceptional persons has eugenic possibilities along Platonic lines for Shaw: they could breed his supermen. There is even a faint hint in the play that a child of theirs might not have to be disinherited: Undershaft tells his wife early in the third act, "if the tradition be ever broken, it will be for an abler man than Stephen" (146). Plato, too, realizes that "kings and hereditary rulers might have sons with a philosophic nature, and these might conceivably escape corruption" (502a). But whether or not this exception will ever occur, the joint accession to power of Cusins and Barbara will give them their work of transforming Perivale St. Andrews. It is evident that they will not leave it unaltered. Out of their efforts will issue the ideal commonwealth envisaged by the playwright. Shaw's republic, then, is not Perivale St. Andrews, but has its foundation in the potentialities of such a city, with its material wants met, its spiritual life guided by the wisdom and purpose of Cusins and Barbara. Or better still, Shaw's *Republic* is *Major Barbara*, the dialectical drama that considers how to evolve out of existing materials and conditions—so pregnant with potentiality for good and ill—a better life for better human beings in a better society.

II

Shaw's *Bacchae*

1

The Drama of Nutrition

Shaw must either be taken whole or left alone. He must be disassembled and put together again with nothing left out, under pain of incomprehension; for his politics, his art, and his religion—to say nothing of the shape of his sentences—are unique expressions of an enormously enlarged and yet concentrated consciousness.

Jacques Barzun, *The Energies of Art*

However striking the dissimilarities between Euripides's ecstatic tragedy and Shaw's tragicomedy—in content and form, in plot and character, and conceivably in direct meaning and intent—the unmistakable resemblances between them are as illuminating as they are varied. Even the apparent dissimilarity in treatment ought not to blind us to the formal aesthetic features they share. Thus, although the *Bacchae* is written in verse and *Major Barbara* in prose, both utilize a rich undercurrent of musical reinforcement, and both bring music on stage with potent emotional and operatic effect. Euripides does not hesitate to intermingle ludicrous and comic elements in his tragedy, nor does Shaw to infuse the gaiety of his serious comedy with a tragic harrowing of the spirit.[1]

Trenchant irony abounds in both dramas, contributing to the effective interweaving of contrasts in mood and tone. The dramatic agon figures as prominently in the structure of the modern as of the ancient work, and in each case the dialogue makes sparing yet effective use of *stichomythia* (line by line alternation of speakers) and *antilabe* (a line divided between two speakers). What is more, each of these plays evinces a dramaturgical complexity that has earned it a history of wide interpretive controversy.[2] Even the valiant attempts to designate the plays' principal characters have generated sharp critical disagreements.[3] Above all, like the Euripidean classic, Shaw's *Major Barbara* operates on more than one layer of meaning, with each plane of significance interpenetrating and imbruing the others. Hence what Gilbert Murray has said of the *Bacchae* is no less true of *Major Barbara:* "Like a live thing it seems to move and show new faces every time that, with imagination fully working, one reads the play" (*Euripides and His Age,* 128).[4]

Bacchic Parallels

With respect to content, both plays delineate the fate of an expanded single family—a family whose lives and actions profoundly affect the course and destiny of the whole social and political order surrounding them. The characters and action in each work symbolize impelling forces that shape life in nature and society, manifesting conflicting psychological, political, moral, and religious currents circulating in the world. Some of the underlying forces and trends are fundamental and universal; others belong to the specific era of the playwright. In both plays human events acquire a cosmic dimension, with the relation between the human and the divine a central concern.

They also possess a number of motifs and themes in common, exemplified by their distinctive probing into the respective roles of wisdom and power in human civilization, and their vivid reminders of the ironic tension between nature and convention, or from another perspective, between reality and appearance. Initially the most arresting parallels align Undershaft with Dionysos and *Major Barbara's* Salvationists with the *Bacchae's* maenads. But beyond these are others, along with innumerable minor correspondences that, however insignificant they may strike us singly, cumulatively are too impressive to be ignored.

Even where plot is concerned the two plays reveal a marked pattern of congruence beneath the obvious surface differences. The *Bacchae* dramatizes the return of a stranger god, in human guise, to his native city of Thebes, where his relatives, all of whom belong to the ruling family, deny his claims to divine ascendancy and greatness and vainly resist the spread of his cult and its ritual practice. Drawing upon his vast reserves of power, the god Dionysos effortlessly but relentlessly imposes his will—which in the end he declares serves a more basic order in the universe—on a variety of recalcitrants in his family, converting some of them to frenzied worship, others to conforming adaptation, and all eventually to an indefeasible recognition of his overwhelming, indomitable might. The most stubborn resister of all, Pentheus, the young king and cousin of the god, is led by his own Dionysian impulses to unwitting death at the hands of his maddened mother, Agave, and her sister bacchants. At the end of the play Agave, returned to sanity by the ministrations of her father, Cadmus, contemplates with him the tragic aftermath of Bacchic enthusiasm. Her awakening marks the attainment of a state beyond conversion and Dionysianism, which her father, bereft of his sole male heir, fully shares.

In *Major Barbara* we encounter another Dionysian personage in Andrew Undershaft, custodian and dispenser of the awesome power that munitions and wealth confer. His return after a long absence to the home of his estranged wife and family—members of Britain's reigning aristocracy—evokes varied moral resistance, including challenges to his impious religion, and to the heterodox mythical tradition he embodies and defends. All the members of the family, plus a prospective member, fail in some measure to understand and acknowledge his decisive position and influence in the world, but soon receive convincing demonstrations of his latent strength and his ability to overcome with ease even the most stubborn resistance to his will. That will he too interprets as part of a universal cosmic force.

Gradually, but inexorably, the members of the family undergo some degree of conversion to his creed and practice. Their conversions range from expedient accommodation to discerning appreciation of Undershaftian power as a pervasive and inescapable reality in modern civilization, and the consequent need to take it into account socially, politically, and religiously. The sternest resister, his daughter Barbara, ensnared through her own religious zeal, suffers a spiritual laceration to which her "possessed" fiancé, Adolphus Cusins, ironically contributes. But by the end of the play, after decisively supplanting the Undershaft son Stephen as heir, both Barbara and Cusins attain a new level of awareness from which to assess Undershaftianism. Having withstood the trials of conversion, they are jointly prepared to supersede Undershaft himself.

As is evident in both dramas, a warily regarded homecoming stranger with enormous power at his command subtly presides over a complex process of conversion. That Shaw himself conceived of *Major Barbara* along such lines he disclosed in 1905 in a private characterization of his new creation as "Also a Conversion play" (like *Captain Brassbound's Conversion* before it). Later he applied this designation to his entire dramatic output: "All my plays present revolutions in the convictions, in the souls, of my characters. G. K. Chesterton rightly says that every play of mine is the story of a conversion."[5] Each of the two dramas deals subtly with the complexities of conversion. To those complexities we shall return.

Humanity and Divinity

"Many shapes are there of divinity," sings the chorus at the close of the *Bacchae* (1388, trans. Winnington-Ingram).[6] One of the shapes "divinity" assumes in *Major Barbara* is the ample frame of Andrew Undershaft. A mere mortal, he takes on in diverse ways the aspect of a deity—or of a *daimon*, a divinity or divine power, to enlist a word the Greeks at times used interchangeably with *theos* (god).[7] In fact, the word translated as "divinity" in the chorus line just quoted, *daimonion,* is a derivative of this term. It is principally in this divine or daimonic aspect that Undershaft's role is analogous to that of the god Dionysos in the *Bacchae*.

It may seem arbitrary in the extreme to attribute divinity to a patently human character, but for Shaw as for an ancient Greek the boundary between the human and the divine is neither absolute nor inviolable. G.M.A. Grube has summed up the Greek viewpoint succinctly: "There was no impassable gulf fixed between gods and men: as the gods came down to fight men on the plain of Troy, so human heroes became objects of religious worship, and the great Olympians themselves are but glorified humans" (*The Drama of Euripides,* 43). One Greek philosopher, Empedocles, actually proclaimed his own divinity: "I go about among you all an immortal god, mortal no more, honoured as is my due and crowned with garlands and verdant wreaths" (frag. 112, *The Presocratic Philosophers,* 354). Gilbert Murray has described how, in the early and late Greek periods, public benefactors and rulers were similarly deified, as in the case of Alexander the Great, whose extraordinary power, personality, and achievements lent credibility—and discouraged challenges—to his qualifications as a god-man. Indeed, it was impossible to ignore the close approximation of his career to that of Dionysos—each gaining recognition as a god and son of Zeus after a journey of conquest.[8] Yet divine status need not imply moral virtue. Godness does not imply goodness.

Gods may be good, or evil, or ethically neutral and still remain gods. Indeed, as Grube points out, *theos,* the Greek word for god, can also mean "devil," making it as applicable to an evil as to a good power. According to Norwood's definition, *theos* "means a power, usually but not necessarily personal, often outside ourselves and influencing our life," so that "Dionysus, like the other 'gods,' is a permanent fact of life personified."[9]

For Shaw, too, the gap between the human and the divine is traversable. One of his "Maxims for Revolutionists" in *The Revolutionist's Handbook* equates the divine with greatness: "Greatness is the secular name for Divinity: both mean simply what lies beyond us" (*Man and Superman*, 2:789). But even that "beyond" would have to be within human reach. Shaw frequently put his stamp of approval on the pronouncement, "Ye are gods," in Psalms 82:6, subsequently quoted by Jesus in John 10:34.[10] Also like a number of prominent Greek philosophers, including Plato and Aristotle, Shaw considered divinity an end toward which mankind should strive. The more modern idea that "God, as it were, is in the making" recurs in his speeches and nondramatic writings, along with the contention that "we are gods though we die like men."[11] This belief in the realizable divinity of humanity receives subtler treatment in his dramas, and in this respect *Major Barbara* is no exception. Hence we can assert of Shaw what Grube concludes about Euripides: "it was upon humanity that his eyes were fixed, it was humanity that he tried to understand" (62).[12]

In his theology Shaw took keen notice of the special claim to divinity made by and in behalf of rulers. "The consummation of praise for a king," he writes in the Preface to *Androcles and the Lion*, "is to declare that he is the son of no earthly father, but of a god. . . . The Roman emperors, following the example of Augustus, claimed the title of God" (4:476). Yet, he adds, they illogically laid equal stress on their regal human ancestry. In the Greek world before them Alexander did the same, as we have noted. But though this theomorphic tradition was particularly prominent in Roman imperial times, when "the legend of divine birth was sure to be attached sooner or later to very eminent persons" (4:477), even modern theologians have not hesitated to accept it in crediting the miraculous conception (as well as human descent) of Jesus and his mother. Shaw returned to this theme in *The Apple Cart,* where the ruminations of King Magnus on the ancient Roman emperor-god assimilate that legendary notion into the Shavian doctrine of potential human divinity: "The old divine theory worked," he says, "because there is a divine spark in us all; and the stupidest or worst monarch or minister, if not wholly god, is a bit of a god—an attempt at a god—however little the bit and unsuccessful the attempt" (6:291–92). In *Major Barbara* it is the Roman Empire under the Antonines that serves as prototype for the Undershaft weapons firm. At the very outset Lady Britomart tells her son Stephen that in her husband's estimation his company is one of but two successful institutions in history—a distinction realized by emulating its Roman predecessor, whose Antonine emperors invariably adopted their successors (75). The Undershaft lineage is plainly set on imperial lines, and the claim to divine power is merely a step beyond.

But before coming to grips with Undershaft as a Dionysian figure it is necessary to comprehend in some measure the nature, scope, and significance of the Hellenic deity whom Euripides dramatized. An immortal of extraordinary compass, Dionysos was only derivatively and secondarily a god of wine during the Greek classical era. Something of his range and multiformity is evident from his cult titles, in Dodds's listing: *Dendrites* or *Endendros,* "the power in the tree"; *Anthios,* "the blossom bringer"; *Karpios,* "the fruit-bringer," *Phleus* or *Phleos,* "the abundance of life." But his sovereignty extends even further: "His domain is, in Plutarch's words, the whole of the *hygra physis* (wet nature)—not only the liquid fire in the grape, but the sap thrusting in a young tree, the blood pounding in the veins of a young animal, all the mysterious and uncontrollable tides that ebb and flow in the life of nature."[13]

To Dionysos, then, belong all of nature's life-sustaining fluids: wine and water, milk and honey, blood, sap, and semen. Yet the powers of this truly protean divinity defy descriptive containment, as Guthrie cautions: "It is useless to try to account for his nature by an origin in one single functional type, such as that of a vegetation-god, however many characteristics of that type he may display. Always there is something more" (*Greeks and Their Gods,* 145). Rosenmeyer draws virtually the same conclusion about the indefinable and inexhaustible features of the god as described in the *Bacchae* (130). Not only is Dionysos the principle of all animate life and wild, surging potency in nature, but the informing spirit of a human cult as well.

As the daimon of a *thiasos,* a company of worshippers, this mystery deity is both daimonic and human—bearing in mind Dodds's admonition that the *orgia* "are not orgies but acts of devotion" (*Bacchae,* xii–xiii)—Dionysos's orgiastic ritual is a revitalizing religious experience, culminating in ecstatic, mystical union with the divine. Ordinary inhibitory barriers are swept aside in this initiation into the mysterious undercurrents of life, permitting the divine being to enter into and possess his devotee—an identification and transformation that bestows on the possessed individual the god's own name of *Bacchos* or *Bacche* (in the plural, *Bacchoi or Bacchae*). Hence Winnington-Ingram's assertion that "the religion of Dionysus blurred the distinction between god and man" (*Euripides and Dionysus*, 1).

This god "is great in many other ways as well," to quote the first messenger in the *Bacchae* (770, trans. Arrowsmith). For also related to Dionysos are nature's patterns of change: birth and death, generation and decay. His dying and rebirth reflect the annual death and revival of vegetation, kindling hope of a comparable survival of death by humans. A deity of fertility and germination embracing the whole creative and passionate life of nature, he acquired mystic ties with the netherworld and with the souls of the dead. But between the extremes of life and death much more falls under his divine sway: he provides sustenance and drink, bestows riches, brings release from grief and care, inspires and dispels madness. To his involvement with the watery element of nature must be added his close association with the sea and ships. A wandering mystery divinity, the universal power he represents is consequently confined to no one age or locale. The enthusiasm and possession he inspired found expression in music and song, in dance and drama. His ability to enter into the personality of another being and to transmute human life made him a natural choice for the roles he played: god of dramatic art, patron of the Hellenic dramatic festivals, and divine sponsor of both tragedy and comedy. From him comes classical drama's religious framework, a context conducive to the pursuit of its deep-seated interest in the determinative forces, destiny, and meaning of human life. The theater therefore was a peculiarly apposite place to explore his mysteries, as did the *Bacchae* in the god's own Theater of Dionysos in Athens.

The Life Force and Nutrition

In the *Bacchae* Dionysos symbolizes insistent elemental forces, both in nature and human nature, whose demands we can ill afford to ignore or misassess.[14] Accordingly he is the male counterpart of Aphrodite—in particular the Aphrodite of Euripides's earlier play, *Hippolytus*—a goddess with whom Dionysos is directly linked in the *Bacchae* itself (402–5, 773) and elsewhere.[15] For each of these deities is a dramatic personification of the Hellenic life force, expressing fundamental cosmic energies. Of Aphrodite, or Kypris, Dodds writes: "The Kypris of the *Hippolytus* is none other than the Venus Genetrix of Lucretius, the Life Force of Schopenhauer, the *élan vital* of Bergson: a force unthinking, unpitying, but divine" ("Euripides the Irrationalist," 102). William Arrowsmith perceives the metaphysical status of the god of the *Bacchae* to be the same: "What the divinity of Dionysus represents . . . should be clear enough from the play: the incarnate life-force itself, the uncontrollable chaotic eruption of nature in individuals and cities" (Intro. to *Bacchae*, 149).[16]

This conception of a necessitous life force functioning in nature is likewise concordant with the kindred Shavian Life Force doctrine. But to all outward appearances that evolutionary doctrine is strangely muted in *Major Barbara*. There is, of course, express confirmation of its incorporation in the play in Shaw's Preface attestation to Undershaft's "constant sense that he is only the instrument of a Will or Life Force which uses him for purposes wider than his own" (31). But beyond that authoritative affirmation the surface indications of its dramaturgic presence are minimal. Yet this profoundly philosophical drama was written barely three years after *Man and Superman,* which resonates with Shaw's vitalist metaphysics. Since he continued to support and dramatically deploy its teachings throughout his life, it would be truly extraordinary if this weltanschauung left no distinctive mark on *Major Barbara*. How then does the Life Force bear on the intelligibility of this particular drama? Aside from that sole connection avouched by the author, and the possible implications of connecting Undershaft with a life-force deity, is there not, we may ask, a more fundamental way in which *Major Barbara* as a whole fits into the philosophical scheme advanced in *Man and Superman?*

An inconspicuous clue to its place and function may be derived from a suggestive passage in the prefatory Epistle Dedicatory to that earlier play:

Money means nourishment and marriage means children; and that men should put nourishment first and women children first is, broadly speaking, the law of Nature and not the dictate of personal ambition. The secret of the prosaic man's success, such as it is, is the simplicity with which he pursues these ends: the secret of the artistic man's failure, such as that is, is the versatility with which he strays in all directions after secondary ideals. . . . What is wrong with the prosaic Englishman is what is wrong with the prosaic men of all countries: stupidity. The vitality which places nourishment and children first, heaven and hell a somewhat remote second, and the health of society as an organic whole nowhere, may muddle successfully through the comparatively tribal stages of gregariousness; but in nineteenth century nations and twentieth century commonwealths the resolve of every man to be rich at all costs, and of every woman to be married at all costs, must, without a highly scientific social organization, produce a ruinous development of poverty, celibacy, prostitution, infant mortality, adult degeneracy, and everything that wise men most dread. In short, there is no future for men, however brimming with crude vitality, who are neither intelligent nor politically educated enough to be Socialists. So . . . if I appreciate the vital qualities of the Englishman as I appreciate the vital qualities of the bee, I do not guarantee the Englishman against being, like the bee (or the Canaanite) smoked out and unloaded of his honey by beings inferior to himself in simple acquisitiveness, combativeness, and fecundity, but superior to him in imagination and cunning. (Ep. Ded. *Man and Superman*, 2:504–5)[17]

This lengthy paragraph, to be identified hereafter as the "nutrition passage," presents a theme for much of *Major Barbara*. The paragraph immediately following this passage is instructive. It begins with this sentence: "The Don Juan play, however, is to deal with sexual attraction, and not with nutrition, and to deal with it in a society in which the serious business of nutrition is left by women to men" (2:505). In other words, *Man and Superman*, the Don Juan play, like Euripides's *Hippolytus*, is devoted to sex and marital relations, with Aphrodite its patron goddess. *Major Barbara*, on the other hand, is the play of nutrition, Shaw's *Bacchae*, unfolding under the aegis of Dionysos, the divine nourisher, to whom, in the words of Teiresias (in the Greek play), "men owe all their blessings" (284–85, trans. Dodds, Winnington-Ingram).

While Undershaft may not fit this portrait of the "prosaic man" in all respects, does he not fit it in his resolve "to be rich at all costs," following with unswerving drive "the law of Nature" toward nutritional sufficiency? Does the play not concern itself besides with the failings of a versatile "artistic man" (Cusins) distracted by secondary ideals? Is there not, in addition, subsidiary interest in a vital woman (Lady Britomart) who puts her children first, also in keeping with the workings of nature, helping to dramatize the distinct difference in her priorities from those of her estranged husband who places money and nourishment first? What Shaw is saying is that Life-Force motivation gives inevitable precedence to the satisfaction of nutritional, sexual, and reproductive needs, but in a complex civilization the ruthless, undeviating pursuit of such limited ends can only bring poverty and social ruin in its wake. Uninhibited and uncontrolled self-interest is inevitably self-destructive, as in the Hobbesian state of nature (in which life is "solitary, poor, nasty, brutish and short"). Natural power and vitality need to be tempered with political wisdom if human civilization is to survive. Without that wisdom the race will go to the cunningly clever, who will readily overpower those governed solely by their natural instincts for survival. The secondary ideals of the artist, the values of morality and religion, and salutary social growth will all be lost unless the scramble for the more elemental necessities of life acquires rational direction and control.

If this passage is truly anticipatory of *Major Barbara*, then we should not be surprised to encounter in that drama a cunning and imaginative incarnation of natural vitality, single-mindedly dedicated to the pursuit of the money that "means nourishment," hence fully resolved "to be rich at all costs." Nor should we be surprised to find him at the same time posing intellectual and political challenges to the versatility of an artistic man, and moral challenges to an exemplar of Salvationist preoccupation with prospects of heaven and hell. An underlying theme to expect would certainly be the question of how best to use intelligence and political education in pursuit of "a highly scientific social organization" conducive to "the health of society as an organic whole," as Shaw put it in the Epistle Dedicatory just quoted.

Understood in these terms, Undershaft, the resolute champion of wealth and nutrition, may be seen to be the male correlate or complement of Ann Whitefield, the Aphroditean exponent of matrimonial resolve in *Man and Superman* (who has her own reincarnation of sorts in the more mature figure of Lady Britomart). Just as Ann is "Everywoman," he is correspondingly "Everymillionaire," to adopt William Irvine's apt appellation (*Universe of G.B.S.*, 261). Shaw says that "everywoman is not Ann; but Ann is Everywoman" (Ep. Ded. *Man and Superman*, 2:519).[18] Correspondingly, every millionaire is not Andrew, but Andrew is every millionaire. Both characters have deep roots in nature, with Undershaft displaying striking affinities with the nature-god Dionysos. Reflecting potent natural forces, each of these characters raises fundamental and knotty issues for societal resolution. Thus there emerges in Shaw the consequential ancient antithesis, which found its way from Greek philosophy into Greek drama, especially that of Euripides: *physis* versus *nomos*, nature versus convention, custom, law.[19] The conflicting claims and demands of nature and human nature on the one hand, and of society on the other, are weighed and discussed in terms of this contrast—a contrast equivalently germane to Shaw's classical drama, *Major Barbara*. Consequently, this thematic issue is bound to occupy us further.

Myth and Identity

The Dionysian character of Undershaft comes to the fore in the second act of *Major Barbara*, though it pervades the whole play. In contrast to Dionysos, who reveals himself in a soliloquy in the Prologue of the *Bacchae*, announcing in the opening lines, "I am Dionysus, the son of Zeus, come back to Thebes, this land where I was born" (1–2, trans. Arrowsmith), the initial materialization of Undershaft in the first act of Shaw's drama occurs only after elaborate preparation and buildup. One function of the soliloquy in Greek drama, as Dodds points out, is "to stimulate the action in its context of legendary tradition by giving its time and place, a summary of the events leading up to it, and the relationship of the principal characters" (*Bacchae*, 61–62). In *Major Barbara* this expository task is assigned to Undershaft's wife. Whereas Dionysos declares in his soliloquy that it is his mission to teach a lesson (*Bacchae* 39–40), Undershaft is given no opportunity to make such an assertion, but as the play progresses it becomes increasingly evident that this is precisely his objective.

While explaining the family's financial condition to her son, Lady Britomart Undershaft sketches a portrait of her husband in strokes that suggest positive elements of kinship with the Greek god. We learn that he "must be fabulously wealthy," that he and his partner Lazarus "positively have Europe under their thumbs." Furthermore, he is "above the law," able to flout with impunity "every social and moral obligation," as no great political leader could. In vain has she made appeals to Gladstone, to *The Times*, and to the Lord Chamberlain: "They said they couldn't touch him. I believe they were afraid" (72). Clearly conveyed is a status beyond the reach of even the most powerful mortals, carrying with it immunity to human law. "He is always breaking the law," his wife complains; even his birth was extra-legal (73). If in the *Bacchae* a god manifests himself in the guise of a mortal, in *Major Barbara* we encounter an extraordinary mortal storming the precincts of the gods.

Undershaft's motto is "Unashamed." In Greek terminology he is *anaides,* being beyond (*aidos*) a sense of shame or honor. Less narrowly translated, *aidos* is respect for others or for public opinion. According to Bruno Snell, this "spirit of reverence which held men back from rash transgressions," had its origins in religion, man's reactions to the holy. Signifying both deference to the interests of others and respect for honor, it sustains the structure of human civilization and contributes to the preservation and perpetuation of existing institutions. As such it is a conservative virtue: "The *aidos* of religion is the most powerful agency known in the early age for imposing inhibitions upon an agent" (*Discovery of the Mind,* 168). By rejecting *aidos,* Undershaft frees himself from regard for respectability, from accepted religion, and from the established social order. In the *Bacchae* the soldier who has taken Dionysos captive on the orders of Pentheus feels *aidos* (*Bacchae* 441), as does Pentheus himself, briefly, at the thought of donning female garb (828), but no such feeling is ascribed to Dionysos.

Lady Britomart traces the odd genealogy of the Undershafts back to a foundling from the parish of St. Andrew Undershaft in the "city" (London's financial district), who was adopted by an armorer during the reign of James the First. In casually divulging the source of her husband's name (and incidentally, why there is a "Gospel of St Andrew Undershaft" in the Preface [23]), she exposes a rich vein of legend, the ultimate origins of which take us back to pagan antiquity.

In his *Survey of London,* first published in 1598, the antiquary John Stow reported that in the ward of Aldgate there "standeth the fair and beautiful parish church of St. Andrew the Apostle; with an addition, to be known from other churches of that name, of the knape or *undershaft*; and so called St. Andrew Undershaft, because that of old time, every year on May-day in the morning, it was used, that an high or long shaft or May-pole, was set up there, in the midst of the street, before the south side of the said church; which shaft when it was set on end and fixed in the ground, was higher than the church steeple" (*Survey of London,* 1603; reprint 1956, 130).[20]

The custom of erecting a maypole in the middle of the street before the south door of the church every May Day began in the fifteenth century and continued until 1517. An "Evil May Day," so-called because of the insurrection by the London apprentices, ended the practice. Thereafter the shaft was not raised for thirty-two years, but was left recumbent in Shaft Alley beneath the eaves of a row of thatched cottages. There it remained until a Sir Stephen, the curate of St. Katherine Cree Church, a clergyman given to delivering sermons out of a high elm tree in the churchyard, preached against the shaft one day at St. Paul's Cross. According to Stow, Sir Stephen "said there that this shaft was made an idol by naming the church of St. Andrew with the addition of 'under the shaft.'" His sermon so aroused the parishioners that in the afternoon of that same Sunday they took the pole off its hooks and sawed it in pieces. "Thus was the idol (as he termed it) mangled, and after burned."[21]

It is from the maypole, then—"the great shaft of Cornehill," as it is called in some lines of verse Stow attributes to Chaucer—that the name Undershaft derives. Bacchic undercurrents course through the story. The curate preaching from the high tree brings to mind Pentheus in his lofty tree perch; as in the myth, the immediate consequence is an impassioned and climactic *sparagmos* (tearing asunder), though in this instance the sundered victim was not the occupant of the tree but the maypole itself, a scapegoat for the Bacchic rites it symbolized. Indeed, Stow tells us that this shaft was in an earlier period the scene of "great Mayings and May-games, made by the governors and masters of this city" (*Survey of London*, 130). In the reign of Henry VI, a monk celebrated such an occasion in verse, in which the following lines appear:

> Making the vertue, that dared in the roote,
> Called of clarkes the vertue vegitable,
> For to transcend, most holsome and most soote,
> Into the crop, this season so agreeable,
> The bawmy liquor is so commendable,
> That it rejoyceth with his fresh moysture,
> Man, beast, and fowle, and every creature.

(ibid., 90–91)

Truly Dionysian is this paean to "the vertue vegitable" (vegetative power) and the liquid that gladdens all creatures.

In ancient Greece the maypole, or May-tree, as a tree-spirit, was regarded as an embodiment of the spirit of vegetation, very much as Dionysos was. Connected with corn and crops, and even with death, it was at times represented in human form.[22] It is not at all remarkable, therefore, to find it directly associated with the god, especially in connection with the Anthesteria, the Dionysian spring festival. The Bacchic deity is indeed frequently represented in Greek art by a mask nailed to a robe-draped pole, in some instances a maypole. May boughs and maypoles were also carried about in various Greek festivals, while in the Mysteries, as Martin P. Nilsson reports, the May bough was called *bacchos*, indicative of its relationship to Dionysos as a god of vegetation (*Greek Folk Religion*, 39).[23] A. G. Bather, and others after him, have gone on to argue that the myth dramatized in the *Bacchae* itself reflects in some detail an underlying Dionysiac ritual, in which the maypole, bringing in the summer, symbolizes the god in his annual revivification of life out of death.[24]

Even apart from his provenance Undershaft bears a name with strong Dionysian undertones. The *thyrsos*, originally referred to any light straight shaft, and indeed the word is at times translated as shaft, as in "shafts of ivy," "shafts with ivy entwined" (*Bacchae* 25, trans. Arrowsmith). The *thyrsos* actually serves as a missile or weapon (733) hurled at enemies (762, 1099) and is variously described as an "ivied javelin" (25, trans. Murray) or "spear" (25, trans. Kirk), a "violent wand" (114, trans. Arrowsmith, Winnington-Ingram), flung "Lance-wise" (1099, trans. Murray). Dionysos himself brandishes a *thyrsos*—golden, like the scepter of a king—possessing magical powers (553). This material vehicle of the latent energies of nature is equally capable of working alimentary miracles (*Bacchae* 704–11) or of inflicting painful wounds (762–63).

The shaft under which Undershaft operates is a collateral emblem of regal authority, "the sign of the sword" (91). And long before we discover what wonders of sustenance flow from him, we are informed that, Dionysos-like, he supplies miraculous missiles that can maim and kill. Stephen reels off their names early in the play: "The Undershaft torpedo! The Undershaft quick firers! The Undershaft ten inch! the Undershaft disappearing rampart gun! the Undershaft submarine! and now the Undershaft aerial battleship! At Harrow they called me the Woolwich Infant. At Cambridge it was the same" (72). If anything, the power advantage—in deploying the destructive forces of nature on land and sea and in the air—lies by a safe margin with the modern miracle worker and creator of weapons of mass destruction. His *thyrsoi* then, like those of the bacchants, are *hubristic*—prone to cruelty and wanton violence.[25] "I find myself in a specially amiable humor just now," the arms merchant confides to Lomax and the others, "because, this morning, down at the foundry, we blew twenty-seven dummy soldiers into fragments with a gun which formerly destroyed only thirteen" (89).

The foundling of the Undershaft tradition—whatever his modern precursors—has a dramatic lineage traceable to a familiar Greek story pattern, one Euripides used repeatedly and Shaw undoubtedly knew well.[26] "Greek myths," Gilbert Murray has written, "and perhaps particularly the myths of the Greek drama, make great use of foundlings who turn out to be princes. . . . They all start as unknown foundlings with the world against them, and eventually are recognized as of princely birth. The motif has been extraordinarily persistent through the whole history of romantic literature." Andrew Undershaft qualifies without difficulty as a modern equivalent of this "foundling of unknown parentage who grows up, is recognized, and inherits," regularly inhabiting the plays of Menander and later writers, and "clearly descended from the foundling of Euripidean tragedy who turns out to be the son of a god and inherits a kingdom."[27] A version of the foundling story is inherent in the mysterious myth of the double birth of the god Dionysos, born of both his mother Semele and his father Zeus (*Bacchae* 88–98, 242–45, 523–25). The play's chorus relates in song how "while his mother was carrying him, the lightning of Zeus took wing, and in forced pangs of labour she bore him struck out untimely from her womb, and died from the stroke of the thunderbolt. But straightway there received him, in secret recesses of birth, Zeus, son of Cronus, and covered him up in his thigh and fastened him in with golden clasps, safe hid from Hera [Zeus's wife]" (88–98, trans. Winnington-Ingram).

Richard Lattimore has pointed out one way in which Euripides here varies the familiar story pattern: "The foundling story which is plainly discernible in the myth is that modification in which the child is divine, where recognition amounts to acknowledgment of divinity and homecoming is establishment of cult in its proper place."[28] Undershaft has a comparable homecoming, which results in recognition and acknowledgment of his power and authority by the members of his family, who in one way or another eventually accept participation in the "cult" of the armorer, established in his proper "place." In addition, if we pursue the suggestion that the travail of Zeus in the second birth can be explained in natural terms "as a primitive form of adoption, wherein the father pretends to actually give birth to the adopted son" (*Cults of the Greek States*, 5:110), Dionysos and Undershaft have even more in common, each raised by adoption into a new sphere of life and power.

Dionysos feels affronted by disbelief in the legitimacy of his birth, entailing as it does the denial of his status as a son of Zeus. The illegitimacy of Undershaft's birth, on the other hand, is undisputed; indeed, it is used inter alia to flaunt and challenge conventional respectability. Hence, while the legitimacy of Dionysos is mooted, Undershaft is a veritable symbol of illegitimacy, like a force of nature (*physis*) confronting the conventional social order (*nomos*) and its beliefs.[29] Yet in this very respect he resembles Dionysos all the more. "To reveal himself is the natural desire, even the function, of a god: all turns on what he reveals himself to be and how he brings about the revelation." It is in these terms that Winnington-Ingram analyzes the *Bacchae*: "Throughout the play Dionysus is manifesting himself to the eyes and to the understanding: the theme is fundamental." In the process the greater and lesser characters alike "have their partial and incomplete vision of Dionysus" (18, 165–66).

A comparable epiphany occurs in the progressive revelation of the millionaire industrialist in *Major Barbara*. The motif of mistaken identity, expanded to incorporate misidentification of true character and significance, contributes to the unfolding manifestation. There is misunderstanding and gradual recognition (*anagnorisis*) of the terrible reality and power of Undershaft. Stephen, setting out with a dim, distasteful apprehension of his father as the wealthy owner of a munitions firm, is swiftly stunned by the intelligence that this sordid business is the sole source of the family income. Barbara's simple belief that her father "has a soul to be saved like anybody else" (81) affords inadequate preparation for his baffling singularity. Literal mistakes in identity are committed by Undershaft himself who, after having been reassured that he has but one son, first takes Charles Lomax, then Adolphus Cusins to be that offspring, and goes on confusedly to greet his daughter Sarah as Barbara. (Unlike the cognate failure of the *Bacchae*'s Agave to recognize her son, the effect here is comic rather than tragic.)[30]

When Lomax comments, "Takes you some time to find out exactly where you are, dont it?" (86), Undershaft explains the problem he faces in establishing his identity in the immediate situation: "My difficulty is that if I play the part of a father, I shall produce the effect of an intrusive stranger; and if I play the part of a discreet stranger, I may appear a callous father" (86). As in the case of Dionysos, his is the ambiguous role of both intruding stranger and celebrated member of the family. Indeed, his wife has already counseled her children that he would be a stranger to them all (82). He belongs and does not belong in their midst. Hence the "*painfully conscious pause*" following Lady Britomart's reply to his inquiry about what he can do for them: "You need not do anything, Andrew. You are one of the family. You can sit with us and enjoy yourself" (86).

Blood and Fire

Attention now shifts from the millionaire to his outlook on the world. Again the uninitiated learn that they are mistaken about him, matching Pentheus's failure to take the true measure of Dionysos. The irrepressible Charles Lomax registers and blurts out the conventional expressions of dismay. He is "*scandalized*" by Undershaft's suggestion of an affinity with the Salvation Army and its motto, "Blood and Fire," and his confession to a musical past that included earning pennies step-dancing in pubs. "You hardly appreciate my position, Mr Lomax," the industrialist has to demur when the younger aristocrat argues the incompatibility of the cannon business with religion (89). While declaring himself "a profiteer in mutilation and murder," and gratified by the latest improvement in the destructive capability of his guns, Undershaft thwarts Lomax's attempt to justify such preoccupation with devastation as a step toward the abolition of war: the accelerating destructiveness of war makes it all the more fascinating. Undershaft's morality and religion, unlike Christianity, "must have a place for cannons and torpedoes in it" (90). A religion making full provision for destruction and death, it is authentically Dionysian.

For her part, Barbara ingenuously entertains the prospect of her father playing his way into heaven on the trombone as one more sinner being redeemed by the Army. She can even envisage him "giving up the cannons for the sake of the Salvation Army." His openly expressed interest in religion as "the only [subject] that capable people really care for" (91) misleads and tempts her, as does his willingness to join her in an unconventional drawing room religious service. The final misconceptions about Undershaft in the first act are those held by Lady Britomart, who characterizes him as a doting father engaged in stealing her children's affections by petting and spoiling them, and those held by Stephen, who would dismiss the fascination with Undershaft on the part of the others as merely a matter of curiosity. To the extent that audiences are being introduced to the munitions maker through these characters' "partial and incomplete vision" (in Winnington-Ingram's phrase), they too are cultivating illusions about him.

But equally to be taken into account is the direct personal impression he himself creates. A prophetic intimation of the exceptional is latent in the prattling utterance with which Lomax heralds the absent father's entrance: "But this is something out of the ordinary, really" (83). When Andrew Undershaft then appears on the scene for the first time the stage directions picture him as *"on the surface, a stoutish easy-going elderly man, with kindly patient manners, and an engaging simplicity of character. But he has a watchful, deliberate, waiting, listening face, and formidable reserves of power, both bodily and mental, in his capacious chest and long head. His gentleness is partly that of a strong man who has learnt by experience that his natural grip hurts ordinary people unless he handles them very carefully, and partly the mellowness of age and success."* He has and incarnates both power and *sophrosyne,* restraint, self-control.

Although on the one hand the *Bacchae* treats *sophrosyne* as energetic resistance to irrational forces in nature, on the other it has Dionysos, the god who symbolizes such forces, strikingly presenting himself as a possessor of this cardinal virtue. "Throughout the play," as Helen North observes, "he calls himself *sophron* [restrained] and *sophos* [wise, clever] and, in the face of Pentheus's emotional outbursts, displays an unearthly, if ultimately a sinister, calm."[31] One such instance is his account to the chorus of his deportment after the destruction of the king's palace stables: "I walked quietly out of the palace, and here I am. Pentheus does not disturb me. . . . What will he say after this? For all his rage, he shall not ruffle me. The wise man preserves a smooth-tempered self-control" (636–41, trans. Vellacott). Dionysos, like Undershaft, operates in an easygoing, *"watchful, deliberate, waiting"* manner. Earlier in Euripides's play, when Pentheus orders him bound as a prisoner, the Greek god retorts, "I say 'bind me not'—I who am master of my senses [*sophronon*] say it to you who have lost yours" (*Bacchae* 504, trans. Winnington-Ingram).

In commenting on the god's claim to self-control or sanity (*sophrosyne*) in this passage, and to wisdom or cleverness (*sophia*) previously, Winnington-Ingram notes that "Dionysus is *sophos* and *sophron* in normal connotations of those terms. He is *sophos* as a master of tactics. . . . He is because . . . he is calm, collected, and in control of the situation; because he knows what he is doing, as Pentheus does not. What claims Dionysus . . . may have to wisdom and sanity is a fundamental issue of the play. But in this scene the mythological Dionysus is clever and calm with a psychology which is more Olympian than Dionysiac, but Olympian with a characteristic Euripidean twist" (20).

Undershaft is similarly *sophos* and *sophron*: clever and calm; he knows what he is doing. His initial shyness is deceptive: with great equanimity he arranges gradually but surely to extend his control over all around him. Furthermore, concerning *sophia* and *sophrosyne*, North asks: "is not Euripides attacking Dionysus and his *sophrosyne*, just as surely as he is exposing Pentheus and his?" (83). May we not in passing ask the same basic question about Shaw in relation to Undershaft, whose *sophrosyne* in its own way makes ample provision for savagery and carnage on a scale well beyond the reach of frenzied bacchants acting in behalf of the Greek god? By the same token should we not heed Greene's warning that even posing the question of whether Euripides is defending or attacking Dionysos will bring with it the risk of misunderstanding the play? "The poet," he writes, "is not so much concerned either to approve or disapprove of the god as he is to present him as the symbol of something that undeniably exists" (*Moira*, 216).[32] Certainly in the case of each of these dramas recognition of the disturbing reality is made pivotal, but the matter of its assessment by no means ends there.

Dionysos entered Greece as a stranger, *xenos*, representing qualities and views foreign, *barbara*, and disturbing to the Hellenes. Comparably intrusive and "barbarian" is the status of the nongentlemanly, "never educated" Undershaft (87) amid the aristocratic British ruling class into which he married. (The sympathy he quickly feels toward his daughter may accordingly rest on a kinship that goes beyond the blood relationship—a kinship suggested by the Greek connotation of her name, Barbara; for she too is a stranger with traits and beliefs that make her an alien figure in her present environment, a point her mother emphasizes at the very first mention of this errant daughter.) Undershaft's first incursions, in keeping with those of Dionysos, are in the sphere of religious belief and practice. There is a difference, however. When the religion of Dionysos invaded Greece, the established Olympian religion had to make rational and emotional adjustments to the new rival cult. Such adjustments are represented in the *Bacchae* by the rationalized concessions of Teiresias and Cadmus.

But although Undershaft lays claim to a religion and morality of his own in the first act of *Major Barbara*, his most conspicuous "religious" actions in the first two acts are directed to the appropriation of the most vital religious body crossing his path: the Salvation Army, and its principal exponent in the play, his daughter Barbara. At the earliest opportunity he takes special pains to relate himself and his work to the Army and its operations. In short order Barbara's earthly father conveys to her his cognizance of having a role on earth comparable to God's role in heaven. Lady Britomart, taking note of the rapport swiftly developing between father and daughter, attempts the immediate interposition of a

Figure 1. The "Woolwich Infant," mentioned by Stephen Undershaft in Act I of *Major Barbara* (72), dominates the stage as described by the set direction of Act III, scene 2 (157), leaving one to wonder where the actors would find room to perform. The largest gun in the world at the time, the 111-ton cannon was nearly 44 feet long with a 30-caliber bore and a firing range of about 8 miles; intended for sea service, it was produced at Elswick Works by Sir W. Armstrong, Mitchell, and Co. Double-page engraving by W. H. Overend, *Illustrated London News*, June 11, 1887.

concertina solo by Lomax. But before the obedient musician can comply with her order, Undershaft pointedly interrupts:

> UNDERSHAFT. One moment, Mr. Lomax. I am rather interested in the Salvation Army. Its motto might be my own: Blood and Fire.
> LOMAX [*shocked*] But not your sort of blood and fire, you know.
> UNDERSHAFT. My sort of blood cleanses: my sort of fire purifies.
> BARBARA. So do ours. (88)

To the Salvation Army the blood of Christ and the fire of the Holy Ghost represent its two central teachings: salvation and sanctification. On the Army's crimson, blue-bordered flag the "Blood and Fire" motto is blazoned across a yellow star in the center. The blue border symbolizes purity or holiness; the crimson color, the blood of Christ; and the yellow star, the fiery baptism of the Holy Ghost.[33]

Figure 2. The Salvation Army insignia, seal, and flag, bearing the motto "Blood and Fire." The motto is mentioned by Andrew Undershaft in Act I (88). Images provided by and reproduced courtesy of Communications Section, Salvation Army International Headquarters, London.

In focusing on blood and fire as cleansing and purifying agents, Undershaft and Barbara find a direct point of contact (and contention) between his work and that of the Army. But blood and fire have Dionysian import as well. Fire and flaming torches were closely identified with the god and his mystic powers in Dionysian rites. Blood flowed at the climax of ecstasy of the maenads, who seized and tore their animal victim apart (*sparagmos*) and partook of the raw, bleeding flesh (*omophagia*), as a form of communion with the deity. Both blood and fire figure prominently in the *Bacchae*. Within the very first verses we learn about the fire that consumed Semele, the god's mother. Still miraculously burning around her tomb, these flames flare up during the palace miracle (596–99). There is also the chorus's early portrait of the incarnate god carrying aloft a blazing torch as he runs and dances (144–50). Fire again is an element in the miracles on the mountain, described by the first messenger, which have their good side as well. The maenads carry fire on their heads without being burned (757–58). They spill blood in the *sparagmos* of the cattle (734–47) and in wounding the men with *thyrsi* (764); afterward snakes lick away the blood left on their cheeks (768). Blood, shed in the ritual death of Pentheus, who had himself threatened the slaughter of maenads as his sacrificial offering to Dionysos (796), indelibly incarnadines the end of the play.

In representing the whole wet element of nature, Dionysos also stands for the life-blood of animals, the common blood we all share. As a god of the life force, he is a source of vitality, of rejuvenation. *Sparagmos* and *omophagia* were conceived as ways of acquiring the god's miraculous vital powers and strength by the imbibing of fresh blood from the animal (or human) vehicle in which he was thought to be immanent. In this manner, life issues forth from the dying victim; warm, sacred, living blood brings revitalization and renewal. But if "the blood *is* the life" (Deut. 12:23), it flows just as freely in bloodshed and death. Strikingly apt in both senses therefore is blood as a symbol for Dionysos Undershaft.

As did other Greeks, Euripides treats fire as cathartic or purifying both in his *Helen* (865–70) and *Iphigenia in Aulis* (1112). In particular, being struck by lightning fire, as was Semele, made the victim holy, even immortal. In Dionysian fashion Undershaft manifests himself in fire-lit haunts, his Bacchic fires likewise flaming in the area between two peaks (*Bacchae* 307), in a Middlesex hill's analogue to Parnassus. In his case they blaze in a foundry forging weapons of destruction, which the factory owner intimates have cathartic value for life. The same binary powers of life and death appear to reside in the fire as in the blood he takes to be emblematic of his creed.

Maenads and Music

The parallel between Undershaft and the Greek god has its complement in the resemblance between the Salvation Army—which becomes increasingly bound to the millionaire as the play progresses—and the worshippers of Dionysos in the *Bacchae*. Whether Barbara, the key religious challenger of her father, is in any way a counterpart to Dionysos's antagonist Pentheus is another question, but one that may be postponed for the present. When Thomas H. Huxley launched his famous attack on the Salvation Army in letters to the London *Times* in 1890, he described that organization as a form of "corybantic Christianity" whose model could be found among the successful "antique Salvation armies" of Greek and Syrian cults. These, he noted, "also had their processions and banners, their fifes and cymbals and holy chants," along with an official hierarchy; and they too promised "an Elysian future to contributing converts" (*Evolution and Ethics and Other Essays*, 239, 250).[34] A

Greek antecedent definitely was known by Gilbert Murray as well, for in the lines of dialogue he suggested for Shaw's use in revising the first version of *Major Barbara*, he has Cusins say that there was a Salvation Army in Plato's time. In the absence of any further elucidation we cannot know for certain, but in all likelihood he was alluding to the Bacchic followers of Dionysos or to the Orphism that grew out of the worship of Dionysos.[35]

Maenads, *thyiades*, or *bakkhai* (Lat. *bacchae*) were the inspired, frenzied, ecstatic, female followers of Dionysos, joined together in a *thiasos*, a band or company of worshippers. As devotees of a wandering deity, they were free of ties to any officially sanctioned state religion. Instead, they formed a religious body "idealistic in tendency, in the sense that it was other-worldly," with an orgiastic sacramental rite, already mentioned, that was an act of union and communion with their god (*From Religion to Philosophy*, 112). This union occurred in two complementary ways: 1) as *ekstasis* (literally, standing outside oneself) a state transcending the limits of ordinary consciousness and individuality, bringing the feeling of being at one with the divine; and 2) as *enthousiasmos* (being possessed by the god), a state in which persons are having god within them, or are "full of god."[36] Such is the Bacchic orgy. No wonder then that the votaries of Dionysos share even in his name, Bakkhos, in being called *Bakkhai* or *Bakkhoi*.

Women were particularly prominent in this religion, as its most common and characteristic celebrants. Indeed, "the woman-ministrant was more essential generally to this cult than to that of any other male divinity, and was never excluded as she frequently was in the others," reports Lewis R. Farnell. "Even the god himself in his own nature shows a bias towards the feminine." The early conversion of women to this cult was all the more natural because it offered freedom and release from the narrow and constrained existence that was the usual lot of Greek women. Organized into bands, or *thiasoi*, each with a single male celebrant leader, or *exarkhos*—the women were further bound together as maenads "by outward symbols, by a common dress, consisting of fawnskins, headdress and wand, and by a common rallying-cry of *Evoe*—by a uniform and a slogan."[37] "*Evoe*," or "*Euoi*" in Greek, is the ecstatic cry with which they invoked the god Dionysos.

Already discernible are a number of ways in which these zealous attendants of Dionysos parallel the votaries of the Salvation Army, particularly as the latter are represented in *Major Barbara*. In each case they form a distinctive nonconformist religious society, differing markedly from the established state religion, with members who revel in enthusiasm and ecstasy and are united by a unique orgiastic relation to the divine. Both bodies were especially effective in attracting female adherents. "The best men in my Army are the women," proclaimed General William Booth, and indeed the lasses, always outnumbering the male officers, have had free and equal access to every position in the organization he founded (*General Next to God*, 110). In *Major Barbara* the Salvation Army is represented almost exclusively by women—a point not generally noticed; Adolphus Cusins, the sole male member appearing onstage, is "converted" by Barbara—even *to* Barbara, more truly than to the Army.

Todger Fairmile, the other male Salvationist in the play, serves at the barracks in Canning Town, a different community. Barbara, like a Greek woman, has broken from the confines of a home being run under the heavy-handed domination of the head of the family—in this instance a *materfamilias*—to freer life and expression in the Army. There, under the rallying-cry of "Blood and Fire," she too dons a uniform with headdress (though the object nearest to a *thyrsos*, or wand, in her hand is a pen or pencil).

The two organizations resemble each other in still another respect. Early in the *Bacchae* prologue Dionysos refers to his maenads as an army: "I will join that army of women" (52, trans. Vellacott); "then I lead the army of my Maenads into war" (trans. Williams).[38] Neither these *thiasoi* nor the Salvation Army members constitute a military force in the strict sense, but both are comprised of ardent warriors in the cause of religion. Such a warrior is Barbara. Even Cusins's odd attachment to the Salvation Army has its Hellenic precedent. According to a Greek proverb, quoted by Plato, "Many . . . carry the wand, but Bacchants few are amongst them" (*Phaedo* 69d, trans. R. Hackforth).[39] Or, as Undershaft puts it to Cusins, "that drum of yours is hollow" (116).

In dealing with the maenad as a figure transcending differences of name, time, and place, Dodds elaborates one of the grounds for associating the Salvation Army with Dionysiac religion. It "concerns the flutes and tympana, or kettledrums, which accompany the maenad dance in the *Bacchae* and on Greek vases. To the Greeks these were the orgiastic instruments par excellence: they were used in all the great dancing cults, those of the Asiatic Cybele and the Cretan Rhea as well as that of Dionysus. They could cause madness, and in homeopathic doses they could also cure it." Pointing to the similar use of the music of pipe and drum by the frenzied dancers of Saint Vitus two thousand years later, Dodds concludes: "That is certainly not tradition, probably not coincidence: It looks like the rediscovery of a real causal connection, of which to-day only the War Office and the Salvation Army retain some faint awareness" (*Greeks and the Irrational*, 273).

Attention is focused on these musical instruments early in Euripides's play. Tympanum and "reed" (or "pipe") are paired as the orgiastic instruments of the Bacchae, accompanying their song and dance. Before his departure at the end of the prologue, Dionysos bids the maenad chorus play their tympana loudly at the palace of Pentheus (*Bacchae* 55–61). During the *parodos*, their opening ode, the chorus responds with an account of the mythical origin of the instrument itself: "O chamber of the Curetes, and holy secret places of Crete that saw the birth of Zeus, when the Corybants with triple helm devised for me in the cave this circle of stretched hide; and in tense worship [*Bakkheia*] mingled it with the sweet-voiced breath of Phrygian pipes and gave it into the hand of mother Rhea—to beat time for the cries of Bacchanals; and from the goddess mother the mad satyrs won it and wedded it to the dances of the second-year festivals, wherein Dionysus rejoices" (120–34, trans. Winnington-Ingram). The *tympanon*, as these lines indicate, "consisted of a wooden hoop covered on one side with hide," but at times "it had pairs of small cymbals fastened round the rim, like the 'jingles' on a modern tambourine" (*Bacchae*, ed. Dodds, 70), hence its varying designation as tambourine, timbrel, drum, and kettledrum.[40]

The musical instrument translated "reed," "pipe," and frequently mistranslated "flute," is the *aulos*, the name for any wind instrument, but more specifically referring to one akin to the oboe or clarinet in its full deep tone. The Greek word literally means a pipe or tube, and according to the fragmentary knowledge we have of the *aulos* it was a cylindrical pipe, made of cane, wood, bone, ivory, or metal, with a vibrating double reed fitted into its mouthpiece and open at its lower end. Usually played in pairs, it provided exciting musical accompaniment to the choral dances of the dithyramb and to the songs and dancing in productions of Greek tragedy, comedy, and satyr plays.[41]

Just before the end of the hymn the Bacchic leader pairs again the same two orgiastic instruments:

O on ye Bacchae, on ye Bacchae!
In the wealth of Tmolos running with gold

Sing Dionysus
To the tympanum's heavy roar,
Greeting the god of '*Euoi Euoi*'
With answering '*Euoi!*'
Let the shouting of Phrygian voices be heard
Whene'er the sweet-sounding and god-given reed
Adds its strong note to our god-given play.
At one with his bands to the hills, to the hills!"

(152–65, trans. Guthrie)

In *Major Barbara*, as in the *Bacchae*, music is introduced early—both as a thematic strain and as an accompaniment to the action. From the time that the characters of the first act are gathered together, a musical motif, vocal and instrumental, runs through the scene, with an undercurrent of reference to dance and marching. In almost every instance the music emanates from Salvationist Barbara. Immediately after their first entrance we learn that Barbara had been trying to teach Adolphus the West Ham Salvation March, a composition he plays on the drum in the second act. Here, at the beginning, the instruction presumably was vocal, for there is no evidence that Cusins has his drum with him. Upon learning of her father's imminent arrival, Barbara sits on a table, softly whistling "Onward, Christian Soldiers." Hardly is Undershaft guided through the maze of introductions to his unfamiliar family before Barbara once more brings the conversation back to music:

BARBARA . . . Cholly: fetch your concertina and play something for us.
LOMAX [*jumps up eagerly, but checks himself to remark doubtfully to Undershaft*] Perhaps that sort of thing isnt in your line, eh?
UNDERSHAFT. I am particularly fond of music.
LOMAX [*delighted*] Are you? Then I'll get it. [*He goes upstairs for the instrument.*]
UNDERSHAFT. Do you play, Barbara?
BARBARA. Only the tambourine. But Cholly's teaching me the concertina. (87)

As befits a maenad, Barbara plays the tambourine, or *tympanon*, and is also learning to play the concertina. Though the concertina is certainly no *aulos*, nor even a direct modern counterpart of that Dionysian cult instrument in the way a clarinet or oboe would be, it does have some points of kinship with the ancient instrument. A member of the reed-organ family, the concertina is played by forcing wind upon free metallic reeds. The *aulos*, for all its differences, was likewise a wind and reed instrument, bearing resemblance in certain features to the bagpipe and organ; capable of producing a wide range of exciting and sonorous sounds, it could even imitate a trumpet (*European Musical Instruments*, 7).[42] Shaw's own comment on the concertina, written during his music criticism days, suggests a further bridge to the *aulos*: "You can play any instrument's part on a concertina of suitable compass, the B flat being most exactly matched by it in point of tone." Not only is the concertina a versatile alternative to other instruments, but it approximates the *aulos* in timbre, and can therefore serve handily as a modern equivalent of the orgiastic Greek instrument. Hence "the frantic clamour and music of the wind instruments and tambourine" (Shaw's phrase), so characteristic of the Bacchic enthusiast, are equally well suited to the heroine of *Major Barbara* (*London Music in 1888–89*, 78; *Cults of the Greek States*, 5:161).

Barbara's invitation to her father to visit her West Ham shelter again turns the discussion back to musical instruments and dancing:

> BARBARA . . . We're going to march to a great meeting in the Assembly Hall at Mile End. Come and see the shelter and then march with us: it will do you a lot of good. Can you play anything?
> UNDERSHAFT. In my youth I earned pennies, and even shillings occasionally, in the streets and in public house parlors by my natural talent for stepdancing. Later on, I became a member of the Undershaft orchestral society, and performed passably on the tenor trombone.
> LOMAX [*scandalized—putting down the concertina*] Oh I say!
> BARBARA. Many a sinner has played himself into heaven on the trombone, thanks to the Army. (88)

In the *parodos* of the *Bacchae* the chorus also sings the praises of the religiously consecrated life: "O blessed he who in happiness knowing the rituals of the gods makes holy his way of life and mingles his spirit with the sacred band" (72–75, trans. Kirk). Since the Bacchic deity is so closely associated with music, song, and dance, it is more than fitting to find the distinctively Dionysian figure of *Major Barbara* reporting a musical past as a naturally talented dancer and wind instrument performer. In this case the instrument was one in which Shaw shared a long family interest, and whose employment for supernatural effects he called attention to in his music criticism.[43]

Music comes to the fore once more near the end of the first act of *Major Barbara*. After Barbara and her father have each agreed to visit the scene of the other's occupational endeavors, it is proposed that the bargain be consummated in song:

> LOMAX. Hadnt I better play something?
> BARBARA. Yes, Give us Onward, Christian Soldiers.
> LOMAX. Well, thats a rather strong order to begin with, dont you know. Suppose I sing Thourt passing hence, my brother. It's much the same tune.
> BARBARA. It's too melancholy. You get saved, Cholly; and youll pass hence, my brother, without making such a fuss about it. (91)

Barbara's rejection of Sir Arthur Sullivan's song in favor of his hymn prompts Lady Britomart to complain that she is acting "as if religion were a pleasant subject."[44] The imputation typifies what Shaw had previously called an "insular conception of a church as a place where we must on no account enjoy ourselves, and where ladies are trained in the English art of sitting in rows for hours, dumb, expressionless, and with the elbows uncomfortably turned in." Instead he would have people enjoy themselves in their churches, even to the point of adding dancing to their singing: "We sing there: why should we not dance?" (*London Music in 1888–89*, 34–35). In the same vein is his lively sketch in the Preface of the Salvationist as a religious enthusiast who is "always in the wildest spirits, laughing, joking, singing, rejoicing, drumming, and tambourining: his life flying by in a flash of excitement, and his death arriving as a climax of triumph" (Pref. *Major Barbara*, 33). The spirit is authentically Hellenic: "As everyone knows, the Greeks took most of their fun under the sanction of religion," writes Linforth ("Corybantic Rites," 159).

In the *parodos* of the *Bacchae* the chorus sings:

> Onward, O Bacchae, onward, O Bacchae, conducting the Thundering god,
> born of a god, Dionysus,
> down from the mountains of Phrygia home to the broad streets of the broad cities of Greece,
> Dionysus. (83–87, trans. Sutherland)[45]

For all their dissimilarities, is this Bacchic hymn not akin, at least in its fervor and spirit of militant zeal, to the one Lomax found to be such a "strong order"?

Onward, Christian soldiers,
Marching as to war,
With the cross of Jesus
Going on before.
Christ, the royal Master,
Leads against the foe.
Forward into battle,
See, His banners go!

And could not devotees of Dionysus unreservedly join in singing this later verse of the Christian hymn?

Onward, then, ye faithful,
Join the happy throng,
Blend with ours your voices
In the triumph song.[46]

The opening choral ode of the *Bacchae* is cast in the form of a Dionysian cult hymn. In it Dodds has distinguished three elements essential to all religions: dogma, myth, and ritual.[47] In its own way *Major Barbara* exhibits these same components in its first act. The dogma of established religion and morality is there, expounded by Lady Britomart and summarized in the *General Confession* prayer book that Cusins abjures as he takes his leave of that lady: "Well, you would have to say before all the servants that we have done things we ought not to have done, and that there is no health in us" (92–93). Introduced, too, is the myth of the Undershaft tradition. Finally, the act ends in the unusual ritual service Undershaft proposes: "If Barbara will conduct a little service in the drawing room, with Mr. Lomax as organist, I will attend it willingly. I will even take part, if a trombone can be procured" (92). Off they go to the Shavian equivalent of a Bacchic dance, as "Onward, Christian Soldiers" is played on the concertina with tambourine accompaniment. No sound of the trombone intrudes here: it is not as Bromius, the roaring god, that Dionysos Undershaft participates. In joining this innocent celebration of Bacchic joy he displays, characteristically, the more engaging side of the "god most dangerous to man, yet most gentle to him" (*Bacchae* 860–61, trans. Dodds).

The Drama of Resistance

Major Barbara is a play of midwinter. This is entirely in keeping with the ancient belief that Dionysos was on earth for the three months of winter, a period held sacred to the god.[1] One prominent feature of Dionysian worship was the *trieteris* (*Bacchae* 133), a midwinter rite celebrated in alternate years. Unlike spring wine festivals, this biennial orgiastic ritual was marked by libations of milk, honey, and water, as well as by the ecstatic *oreibasia*, or mountain dancing. It probably had as its object some form of revivification of life or crops.

The bleak wintry aspect of Shaw's play is most marked in the Salvation Army setting of Act II. Here, and again in the last scene of the play, Shaw takes religion out of doors, as in Dionysian practice.[2] At the very beginning of the act we encounter two hapless characters, Snobby Price and Rummy Mitchens, drawn by circumstances beyond their control into the Salvation Army milieu. On this *"grindingly cold raw January day,"* they are *"not depressed by the cold: rather are they stung into vivacity, to which their meal has just now given an almost jolly turn"* (95–96). But the vivacity is neither Bacchic nor Salvationist, for these miserable creatures are not true believers; they are dissembling as converts. Their bacchant qualities are enervate, when they are not simply spurious. Accordingly the occasional stepdance Snobby breaks into as he moves about the shelter issues from no ecstatic joy, nor does the dancing take place on a mountain. Ecstasy and ascent to higher ground are reserved for others, and for later.

In the *Bacchae*, liquefactive miracles yield a "land flowing with milk and wine and honey" (*Bacchae* 142–43, trans. Conacher), nourishing the god's followers (*Bacchae* 704–11).[3] In the Salvation shelter Snobby and Rummy, soon joined by secularist Peter Shirley, are fed diluted milk and bread *"with margarine and golden syrup"* (95). It is understandable that an attenuated brand of Dionysian religion, dependent upon appeals to charity rather than on miracles for the sustenance it provides to impoverished hangers-on, would have to settle for diluted milk and ersatz honey. According to Teiresias bread is the divine gift of Demeter, or Earth, the provider of dry foods (*Bacchae* 274–85). The old seer allies her with Dionysos, the giver of liquid nourishment, represented by wine.[4] Bread and drink, and meeting basic nutritional needs, become the subject of serious religious concern and discussion in *Major Barbara* too, as the nutrition passage would lead us to expect.

Snobby, Rummy, and Peter face the necessity of adapting their behavior to unfamiliar cult conditions that, at the moment, are their sole source of food and drink. Snobby offers sophistical socialist reasons for his lot and is ready to play to the hilt the ritual game of confession. Rummy complains because confessions of invented misdeeds by women have to be made in private, and do not receive the same kind of favorable attention as those made in public by men. But since the confessions help the Army raise the funds that keep her from starving, she acquiesces in the ceremonial rite. When the starving Peter Shirley is reluctant to take food offered him, Jenny Hill the Salvation lass bids him, "Come, come! the Lord sends it to you: he wasnt above taking bread from his friends; and why should you be?" (99–100). By mentioning a meal shared with the gods, the *Bacchae* chorus invest a human repast with religious significance (383);[5] Jenny is doing much the same, which only adds to the moral burden it imposes on Peter. His reconciliation to the situation is characteristically secular: he accepts the meal as a debt to be repaid.

This opening scene of the second act, in which these newcomers make their uncomfortable adjustments to the Salvation Army shelter, corresponds functionally with the serio-comic episode in the *Bacchae* in which Teiresias and Cadmus give their reasons for converting to the new Dionysian religion. But the process of Dionysian accommodation in *Major Barbara* is a more gradual and progressive one, developing throughout the play. It begins in the first act, when Stephen discovers his and his family's inescapable dependence on an income provided by his father, "a profiteer in mutilation and murder" (89). Lady Britomart, like Cadmus, gives priority to family considerations. She is concerned that the family should acquire full benefit from its kinship with its notoriously powerful relative. And she silences her son's objections, much more effectively than does Cadmus his grandson Pentheus, concerning such prudential compromise of principle. Teiresias-like arguments in defense of Undershaft and his power are yet to come.

"Hard are the labors of god: hard, but his service is sweet," sings the chorus in the *parodos* (*Bacchae* 66, trans. Arrowsmith). This "labor that is no labor" (trans. Kirk) suggests the effortless Dionysian power that the god transmits to his worshippers. It is simulated in the youthful feelings of Cadmus and Teiresias (*Bacchae* 187–90), mentioned again by Teiresias (194), felt by a deluded Pentheus (945–50), and egregiously manifested by Agave late in the drama (1128). Something like this joyful ease and renewed vigor comes to the work-exhausted Jenny Hill when, as she relates, "Major Barbara just sent me to pray for five minutes; and I was able to go on as if I had only just begun" (100).

Hybris, Aidos, and *Nemesis* in West Ham

Although *Major Barbara* has counterparts to Dionysos and the bacchants in Undershaft and the Salvation Army members, respectively, and to Cadmus in some measure in Lady Britomart, such correspondence as there is between the other characters in the two plays is more limited and indirect. Yet certain traits of the other characters in Euripides's drama, and some facets of their thought and action, are reflected in Shaw's play. This is the case with Pentheus in particular. It could be said that the rending of body and scattering of remains that he undergoes in the *Bacchae* has a dispositional parallel in *Major Barbara,* where may be found something akin to a distribution of fragmentary features of his personality and behavior among a number of characters at different points in the plot.[6]

Dodds characterizes Pentheus as the historical adversary of the god and at the same time his ritual victim. As adversary he is a conservative aristocrat opposing the new religion because it threatens the social order and public morality.[7] Considered as such he invites comparison with Stephen, likewise a young aristocrat rooted in conservative tradition. At the same time Stephen is the victim of a foundling myth that places him in a historical antagonistic relationship with his Dionysian father. The young Undershaft similarly belongs to the ruling class and its political arena, and he betrays incomprehension and intolerance comparable to those of Pentheus. Although more a ridiculous than a tragic figure, he is treated with an irony that wholly escapes him, as is the case with the young Greek king. The tyrannical side of Pentheus is more applicable to

Stephen's imperious mother, Lady Britomart. Something of this domi-nating temper has also been imparted to Stephen's sister, Barbara, who from yet another standpoint better fits the role of challenger to Dionysos undertaken by Pentheus. As in the Euripides drama, each of these char-acters holds a family relationship to the play's Dionysos. The omission of anything like the prurience of Pentheus from a Shaw play should oc-casion no great surprise, but additional Penthean traits are very much in evidence, though in yet another character: the inclination to seek ven-geance, reliance on force and violence, and aggressive religious skepti-cism are all unmistakably demonstrated in the conduct of Bill Walker.

In his first speech Bill voices sentiments similar to those of Pentheus in his initial *Bacchae* monologue. The returning ruler has heard of the misbehavior of the Theban women and is determined to track down and punish those who have evaded capture. Angered by the turn of events, he hurls threats of physical violence at the apparently charlatan stranger whom he has been told is the instigator of the aberrant conduct of the women. In similar fashion Bill threatens Jenny Hill as the interloper who turned his girl Mog Habbijam against him and caused her to leave him. He wants Mog brought out so that he can teach her a lesson in the form of a beating. His concerns are more directly personal and selfish than moralistic, but his mode of dealing with the opposition is Penthean. Bill resents Jenny's religious interference, and subsequently that of Barbara, much as Pentheus resents that of Teiresias. When Bill tells Barbara "Aw don't blieve in your Gawd, no more than you do yourself" (106), he too evinces doubts about the genuineness of a religious leader's beliefs, al-though he stops short of Pentheus's charge of venality against Teiresias: "Yes, you want still another god revealed to men so you can pocket the profits" (*Bacchae* 255, trans. Arrowsmith). Pentheus resorts to force against Teiresias's seat of augury (*Bacchae* 343–51); Bill invades the pre-cincts of the Salvation shelter and strikes both Jenny Hill and Rummy.

It is Pentheus who introduces the theme of revenge, punishment, and retribution in the *Bacchae*, a theme soon to be taken up by Dionysos and the chorus. The king seeks to punish those responsible for the spread of the Bacchic cult in Thebes. First he will punish Teiresias: "By god, I'll make him pay" (345, trans. Arrowsmith), he vows as he orders the destruction of the seer's augural throne. Then he commands that the Bacchic stranger be found and brought to him in chains for execution by stoning (*Bacchae* 352–57). Later he repeats the threats of punishment (*Bacchae* 675–76, 796–97). The captured stranger, Dionysos, concluding his dialogue with Pentheus, leaves the stage promising that the god "will call you to account" (516, trans. Arrowsmith). After his escape he tells the chorus how he had mocked Pentheus, returning "outrage for outrage" (617, trans. Arrowsmith; compare "I out-outraged him," trans. Sutherland). Once he has elicited from Pentheus the admission of his fervid desire to visit Cithaeron, the god again foretells that with death the king will "pay the price" (847, trans. Arrowsmith, Sutherland, and Curry; "pays for all his sin!" is Murray's rendering). "From now onward," comments Winnington-Ingram, "the play is dominated by the note of vengeance. Struck by Dionysus, it echoes in the following chorus" (*Euripides and Dionysus*, 22; *Bacchae* 877ff.). The fourth stasimon, or choral ode (*Bacchae* 977–1032), is also a song of vengeance, and the messenger reports that the attack of the maenads on Pentheus was launched by the voice of Dionysos calling from heaven for revenge (*Bacchae* 1081). Though both a reproachful Cadmus and a somewhat shaken chorus acknowledge at the end that the vengeance wreaked on Pentheus was an act of justice (1249, 1327–28), the drama hardly leaves such morality unquestioned.

Shaw approaches the immorality of revenge and punishment from a different angle. Instead of presenting incidents culminating in vindictive punishment administered by an adversary, he shows a character seeking punishment as a way of balancing out his own violent act and the sense of guilt it has brought him. As Shaw puts it in the Preface:

> Bill Walker, in my play, having assaulted the Salvation Lass, presently finds himself overwhelmed with an intolerable conviction of sin under the skilled treatment of Barbara. Straightway he begins to unassault the lass and deruffianize his deed, first by getting punished for it in kind, and, when that relief is denied him, by fining himself a pound to compensate the girl. He is foiled both ways. He finds the Salvation Army as inexorable as fact itself. It will not punish him: it will not take his money. It will not tolerate a redeemed ruffian: it leaves him no means of salvation except ceasing to be a ruffian. In doing this, the Salvation Army instinctively grasps the central truth of Christianity and discards its central superstition: that central truth being the vanity of revenge and punishment, and that central superstition the salvation of the world by the gibbet. (43)

Unlike the bacchants of Euripides, the Salvationists of *Major Barbara* are arrayed against punishment and vengeance; but both dramas embody a lesson about revenge and justice, and expose the moral bankruptcy proceeding from attempts to pay and repay in order to balance accounts.[8]

Bill proposes going to Canning Town to provoke Sergeant Todger Fairmile into smashing him in the face, harder than he had struck Jenny Hill, as a way of squaring matters with her. He then appeals to Cusins as a gentleman to confirm the fairness of the punishment. The professor of Greek "reflectively" concurs: "Yes: I think youre right, Mr. Walker. Yes: I should do it. It's curious: it's exactly what an ancient Greek would have done" (114). One of several instances in which Cusins relates the conversation to Greek precedents—the Homer citation in Act I being the first (81)—perhaps this response is meant to imply no more than that the standard of justice Bill is invoking is a longstanding one. Cusins does not allude to a particular ancient incident, but to a general moral predisposition on the part of the Greeks. His claim is a defensible one. A passage in Snell's discussion of the early development of Greek ethics seems directly applicable to a situation like Bill's, including the attempt to fine himself after his unsatisfactory encounter with Todger:

> The belief that the good is profitable, and more particularly that the evil is disadvantageous, also affected the concept of punishment. In the early period this is especially striking: no matter whether the punishment is imposed through self-help or through the agency of the State, or even that of the gods, it is always regulated by the categories of profit and damage. The institution of the fine is the most obvious case in point, and it is significant that this business-like arrangement becomes the model for many other types of legal transaction. Whether we are dealing with an "an eye for an eye" or with the custom of blood feud, the "just" penalty is reckoned in figures, and the amount of damage dealt out to the delinquent— the damages—must be commensurate with the amount of damage perpetrated by him. As profit was amenable to prediction and calculation, so also the measures and degrees of justice. (*Discovery of the Mind*, 160–61)

Appropriate too is the thought expressed in the surviving fragment of the philosopher Anaximander, that things in nature (or their elements) "make just recompense to one another for their injustice according to the ordinance of time" (*A History of Greek Philosophy*, 1:76). "The underlying principle," writes Gregory Vlastos, "is that of an *exchange:* equal value rendered for value taken. The same words apply to the closure of a commercial transaction, like barter, sale, or loan, and to the satisfaction of justice" ("Equality and Justice in the Early Greek Cosmologies," 173–74 n. 158). Werner Jaeger visualizes for the same passage the image of a courtroom scene: "When there are two parties to a dispute, the one who has taken more than his share, whether by force or by trickery, must pay damages for his pleonexy to the party he has wronged. To the Greeks for whom the just is the equal, this pleonexy, or taking-too-much, is the essence of injustice" (*Theology of the Early Greek Philosophers,* 35).[9]

It is his conscience that makes Bill want to make reparation. In the case of the Greeks, as Snell points out, "the guilty conscience was not known prior to Euripides," although they experienced feelings of shame, "a sensation of discomfort in the presence of others" (163).[10] *Aidos,* the sense of shame, as explained earlier, and its companion principle, *nemesis,* or righteous indignation, did in fact approximate the idea of conscience in certain contexts. It may be helpful to consider the pertinence of these concepts to Gilbert Murray's commentary on these specific terms in a book originally published in 1907, the year of *Major Barbara*'s first publication. According to Murray, lawless behavior on the part of a strong and apparently fearless Greek who has broken with the old sanctions might produce a "possible action which somehow makes him feel uncomfortable. If he has done it, he 'rues' the deed and is haunted by it. If he has not done it, he 'shrinks' from doing it. And this, not because any one forces him, nor yet because any particular result will accrue to him afterwards. But simply because he feels *aidôs.*" *Aidos* is closely related to *nemesis*: "*Aidôs* is what you feel about an act of your own: nemesis is what you feel for the act of another. Or, most often, it is what you imagine that others will feel about you. . . . (Observe, of course, that Nemesis does not mean Retribution.)" (*Rise of the Greek Epic,* 83–84).[11]

As she goes about "wooing his soul" for salvation, Barbara tells Bill that he feels miserable because of his new friend, the devil. To his agonized complaints that she will not leave him alone, she gently replies, "It's not me thats getting at you, Bill," adding, when he asks who else it can be, "Somebody that doesnt intend you to smash women's faces, I suppose. Somebody or something that wants to make a man of you" (112). Her reproof is in remarkable concord with the spirit of Nemesis, the Greek goddess who personified this moral reaction, especially as Murray explains it: "There are people who have seen your act, and know. But suppose no one sees. The act, as you know well, remains *nemeseton*—a thing to feel nemesis about: only there is no one there to feel it. Yet, if you yourself dislike what you have done and feel *aidôs* for it, you inevitably are conscious that somebody or something dislikes or disapproves of you" (*Rise of the Greek Epic*, 84).[12]

Murray identifies four general kinds of actions that cause the feeling of *aidos* (about one's own actions) and *nemesis* (about the actions of others). These are acts implying cowardice, lying, impudence (or lack of reverence), and—most widespread and significant—cruelty or treachery directed against the helpless, especially strangers, suppliants, and old people (ibid., 85–86; compare Greene, *Moira*, 18).[13] Bill's cruelty toward strangers—some old, and all relatively helpless—is an act of *hybris*, a more familiar but less easily translatable Greek word. Murray calls it "the insolence of irreverence: the brutality of strength." Although generally "a sin of the strong and proud, it has one form in which "it is a sin of the low and weak, irreverence; the absence of *Aidôs* in the presence of something higher" (ibid., 327).[14] There is ground therefore for saying that Bill is guilty of *hybris*, of excess, of going too far, as was Pentheus (for example, *Bacchae* 375).

Bill is like Pentheus in still other respects. Each of these young men is *amathes*, ignorant of his own nature—a "silly young lump of conceit and ignorance," to quote Peter's contemptuous estimate of Bill—a trait that Stephen shares. Each has problems with his identity: "You know not what your life is, nor what you are doing, nor who you are," Dionysos tells Pentheus (*Bacchae* 506, trans. Winnington-Ingram). The puzzled Pentheus answers, "I am Pentheus, the son of Echion and Agave" (trans. Arrowsmith). The god retorts, "You bear a name apt for calamity" (508, trans. Dodds), or in Vellacott's translation, "*Pentheus* means 'sorrow.' The name fits you well," echoing an earlier pun on Pentheus's name: "O Pentheus, named of sorrow!" (367, trans. Murray), or "the name *Pentheus* means grief" (trans. Vellacott). The play is on the Greek word *penthos*, meaning grief, sadness, sorrow, mourning, or misfortune.

More directly, Barbara asks Bill, "Whats y o u r name?"

BILL [*insolently*] Wots thet to you?
BARBARA [*calmly making a note*] Afraid to give his name. Any trade?
BILL. Oo's afride to give is nime? . . . Moy nime's Bill Walker. (106)

When Bill, identified as Jenny's attacker, responds by scouting the Salvation Army and its religious doctrines, Barbara returns with Dionysian assurance and inexorability to the question of his name and identity:

> BARBARA [*sunnily apologetic and ladylike, as on a new footing with him*] Oh, I beg your pardon for putting your name down Mr Walker. I didnt understand. I'll strike it out.
> BILL [*taking this as a slight, and deeply wounded by it*] Eah! you let maw nime alown. Aint it good enaff to be in your book?
> BARBARA [*considering*] Well, you see, theres no use putting down your name unless I can do something for you, is there? Whats your trade?
> BILL [*still smarting*] Thets nao concern o yours.
> BARBARA. Just so. [*Very businesslike*] I'll put you down as [*writing*] the man who—struck—poor little Jenny Hill—in the mouth.
> BILL [*rising threateningly*] See eah. Awve ed enaff o this.
> BARBARA [*quite sunny and fearless*] What did you come to us for?
> BILL. Aw cam for maw gel, see? Aw cam to tike her aht o this and to brike er jawr for er.
> BARBARA [*complacently*] You see I was right about your trade.
> (106–7)

The point is made about Bill, as about Pentheus, that he does not really know himself, his deeds, or his vocation in life. In each case the name of the character comes in for special attention, although the contextual stress does not involve a pun in this passage from *Major Barbara*. This does not mean that Bill's name is necessarily free of paronomastic intent, for plainly he becomes a person who *walks* from place to place concerned about the payment of a *bill*, or debt.[15]

Aeschylus and Euripides frequently resorted to punning character names of this sort, reflecting a Greek presumption that a significant relationship obtained between a person's character or destiny and his name, and even between a name and its object. "To us a pun is trivial and comic because it calls attention to the irrelevant," Dodds remarks, "but the Greek felt that it pointed to something deeply relevant" (*Bacchae*, 116–17).[16] The special attention Shaw paid to the meaning of character names in his plays is accordingly very much in the Greek tradition, as is his conjugate concern with the personal identity theme.[17]

That Barbara treats Bill the way Dionysos does Pentheus may seem incompatible at first with her own Penthean relationship to her father;

but it is actually in line with good *Bacchae* precedent. For in that work too the shifting and reversal of roles exposes identical traits in opposed characters. In the words of Winnington-Ingram, "It is no novelty in this play to find the same items on both sides of the balance sheet" (*Euripides and Dionysus*, 123).[18] Moreover, Barbara has two direct avenues of access to Dionysian identification and power: as a Salvation Army maenad and as natural heiress to "the Undershaft inheritance" (120). All the while the Dionysos of *Major Barbara* is, like his *Bacchae* prototype, "close by . . . peacefully sitting and watching" (221–22, trans. Kirk) as Barbara works on the soul of the young man (111). As for Bill, he feels endangered by his own surprising susceptibility to the practices of the cult he opposes, as does Pentheus.[19]

Bill's close resemblance to Pentheus, especially in his moral failings, makes it possible to affirm of him precisely what Lattimore says of the Theban king: "Pentheus is anti-religious, suspicious, opinionated, jealous, and full of horrid threats, though . . . he is far more given to threatening than to carrying his threats out" (*Poetry of Greek Tragedy*, 130). But there remains another noteworthy parallel between the two young men. In their respective treatment of these characters both Euripides and Shaw make vivid use of wrestling imagery. At his very first meeting with Dionysos, Pentheus greets the captured stranger with taunts about his good looks, adding, "Those long curls of yours show that you're no wrestler" (455, trans. Vellacott). After the departure of the messenger during their long second meeting, the king blurts out in exasperation, "It is hopeless to wrestle with this man. Nothing on earth will make him hold his tongue" (800–801, trans. Arrowsmith).[20]

In *Major Barbara* wrestling, both literally and figuratively, entangles Bill with Todger Fairmile, an offstage bacchant (whom Shaw subsequently made visible in the screen version of the drama). Todger, a type later elaborated in the similarly behaving Ferrovius of *Androcles and the Lion*, is a man of considerable physical strength imperfectly converted to reliance on moral suasion. Almost from the beginning Todger looms over Bill as a figure of prospective nemesis, in the physical terms the latter understands so well. Todger is first proposed for this role by Peter Shirley, and thereafter serves as a model of religious conversion by Barbara. As a defense against Bill's minacity and violence, Peter challenges the young man to match himself against Todger, whose wrestling and boxing prowess he impresses upon Bill. Soon Barbara discloses to Bill that he has been supplanted in Mog's affection by a new "bloke," now a

Salvation Army sergeant. In exhorting Bill to salvation, Barbara sets before him the example of Todger, who "wrestled for three nights against his salvation harder than he ever wrestled with the Jap at the music hall," a public event at which he had earned £20 by holding out for over seventeen minutes (113). Although he complains and threatens, Pentheus-like, at Barbara's relentless rejoinders—"Cawnt you never keep your mahth shat? . . . If you was maw gel and took the word aht o me mahth lawk thet, Aw'd give you sathink youd feel urtin, Aw would" (114–15)—as a result of wrestling with Barbara and his own conscience Bill is driven to a confrontation with his dread antagonist and instrument of nemesis. Todger, as Bill relates afterward, turned the occasion into a combined wrestling entertainment and prayer meeting by downing his hapless challenger, kneeling on his head, all the while leading his audience in prayer for the victim. Thus Bill suffers a humiliation comparable to that experienced by Pentheus, who vainly wrestled with a bull incarnation of the god during the "palace miracle" episode (*Bacchae* 618–41). Each is bewildered by what happens and in the aftermath is regarded with calm amusement, Pentheus by Dionysos and Bill by Barbara.

Viewing Bill Walker in this manner (from the perspective of the *Bacchae*) serves to bring out features of his function in *Major Barbara* that the revenge and punishment motif, stressed by Shaw, partially obscures. A character whose thought and conduct are dominated by considerations of force and power, he is a reflection of Undershaft on a smaller scale, operating within the narrower compass of personal relations, and of course far less effectively. Bill gains sway briefly in an arena where those around him are physically weaker than he. He hurls Jenny across the yard toward the shelter much in the way Undershaft strides on stage and brutally kicks a prostrate dummy soldier out of his path in the second scene of the final act (159). Before striking Jenny again, Bill intimidates the cowardly Price and slaps Rummy Mitchens across the face. His forceful control of the situation is halted first by the resistance and taunts of Peter Shirley, and then by the challenge to strike Shirley's kinsman, Todger—a man unquestionably more than his match in strength and combativeness. Peter adds to the growing array of retaliatory force against Walker the prospect of "goin to the station on a stretcher" because of an offense against the Salvation Army major whose grandfather is an earl. The thought of "wot them people can do" subdues Bill's almost fully expended power (104). But then he encounters a different kind of authority in the moral force that Barbara brings to bear upon him. It

sends him reeling back to invite a beating from Todger as a more familiar and acceptable form of expiation. Frustrated again in this attempt,
he retreats to a quasi-legal act of penance. Through the entire Shavian
apologue Bill's show of violence only serves to actuate superior deterrent
powers, physical and moral. In the end he is rescued by the most formidable power around, Andrew Undershaft. Teiresias's counsel to Pentheus
is, "Be not over-sure that force is what dominates human affairs, nor, if
you have a thought and your thought is sick, mistake that thought for
wisdom" (*Bacchae* 310–12, trans. Dodds). This could equally well be directed to Bill Walker. In a drama that explores the dynamics of power,
Bill's story illustrates the relative impotence in ordinary human affairs of
the impulsive and indiscriminate exercise of force. Bill thus turns out to
be one more foil to the puissance of Undershaft, as the inefficacy of his
impromptu outbursts of violence contrasts sharply with decisive display
of might produced with a minimum of effort by the Dionysian armament king.

Drumming Dithyrambs

The first appearance of Adolphus Cusins in the second act is heralded
by the sound of his drum intruding and breaking the spell at the climax
of Barbara's "wooing" of Bill. The drumming overture brings him on the
scene as a one-person Greek chorus (in this case male, in contrast to the
female chorus of the *Bacchae*). His brief conversation with Barbara and
Bill soon sends the latter off on his penitential mission to Canning Town
and culminates in the two lovers kissing over the drum—an act neatly
epitomizing a relationship sustained by an ability to clear barriers with
Dionysian ease. When Barbara then returns to her offstage duties, she
leaves her fiancé behind for his first solo encounter with Undershaft. In
some ways this confrontation is reminiscent of those between Dionysos
and Pentheus, while at the same time it represents a continuation of the
Cusins choral role. For, in the manner of the chorus of the *Bacchae,* he
is a full sharer in the contest, being personally affected by the action and
affecting it in turn.[21]

If *Major Barbara* bears the direct impress of the *Bacchae* anywhere,
we should assuredly expect to descry it in the ensuing dialogue, for in
this long passage Cusins assumes in earnest the role of translator of Euripides, turning to the *Bacchae* itself for some fairly complex apologetical
support. It is obviously a segment of the play that merits especially close

scrutiny. Before their talk begins Undershaft is "still keenly attentive," retaining the godlike posture of alert and watchful waiting. The two men look hard at one another before speaking. When Undershaft begins the conversation it is evident that in gazing intently at Adolphus he has communicated a judgment that he had reached about his daughter's suitor. It is the same judgment his wife had expressed at the end of Act I:

> LADY BRITOMART . . . I have a very strong suspicion that you went to the Salvation Army to worship Barbara and nothing else. And I quite appreciate the very clever way in which you systematically humbug me. I have found you out. Take care Barbara doesnt. Thats all.
> CUSINS [*with unruffled sweetness*] Dont tell on me. [*He steals out.*] (93)

Without having discussed the matter with Lady Britomart, Undershaft in effect picks up and pursues her charge against Adolphus.

> UNDERSHAFT. I fancy you guess something of what is in my mind, Mr Cusins. [*Cusins flourishes his drumsticks as if in the act of beating a lively rataplan, but makes no sound*]. Exactly so. But suppose Barbara finds you out! (115)

Both parents call into question the sincerity of his religious commitment, accusing him of worshipping the worshipper Barbara while pretending to worship with her. The mimed rataplan signifies empty gesticulation, fury without sound, and imputes imposture. Underscoring the accusation is the appended Undershaft warning, to be reiterated subsequently, that Barbara "will find out that that drum of yours is hollow" (116).

The worship of Barbara remains in the background, where we too may leave it for the present. But a burden is laid on Adolphus to answer the rest of the indictment he dodged when Lady Britomart first thrust it at him in the previous act. In the process, we may notice, the question of his true character and identity is raised. There is, accordingly, a gradual revelation of the nature of Adolphus Cusins in the play, paralleling that of Andrew Undershaft, before the two identities interweave in their final intricate pattern of kinship. Cusins launches his defense against Undershaft's charge gingerly:

> CUSINS. You know, I do not admit that I am imposing on Barbara. I am quite genuinely interested in the views of the Salvation Army. The fact is, I am a sort of collector of religions; and the curious

thing is that I find I can believe them all. By the way, have you any religion? (115)

After a brief reaffirmation of his own "religion" of money and gunpowder in response to this diversion, Undershaft, by his "hollow drum" admonition, puts Adolphus back on the defensive.

> CUSINS. Father Undershaft: you are mistaken: I am a sincere Salvationist. You do not understand the Salvation Army. It is the army of joy, of love, of courage: it has banished the fear and remorse and despair of the old hell-ridden evangelical sects: it marches to fight the devil with trumpet and drum, with music and dancing, with banner and palm, as becomes a sally from heaven by its happy garrison. It picks the waster out of the public house and makes a man of him: it finds a worm wriggling in a back kitchen, and lo! a woman! Men and women of rank too, sons and daughters of the Highest. It takes the poor professor of Greek, the most artificial and self-suppressed of human creatures, from his meal of roots, and lets loose the rhapsodist in him; reveals the true worship of Dionysos to him; sends him down the public street drumming dithyrambs [*he plays a thundering flourish on the drum*].
> UNDERSHAFT. You will alarm the shelter.
> CUSINS. Oh, they are accustomed to these sudden ecstasies. (116–17)

In the *Bacchae* the god, rather than his cult, is extolled, and the praise comes primarily from the bacchants in their dual role as followers of Dionysos and dramatic chorus. Although newly joined to the Dionysian cause, Cusins offers here a paean to the Army that is closer in spirit to the hymning of the chorus. Through the words of the chorus, Arrowsmith notes, we come "to feel what Dionysus means for suffering mortality, the direct eruption of deity in blessing and miracle" (*Bacchae*, trans. Arrowsmith, 151).[22] For them, as for Cusins, joy, love, and courage are gifts of Dionysos. They "sing praise of Dionysus to the beat of the rumbling drums, in joy glorifying the Lord of Joy . . . when the sweet and holy music of the pipe peals its holy gaiety" (*Bacchae* 155–64, trans. Dodds). As for love, "if there is no god of wine, there is no love, no Aphrodite either" (*Bacchae* 773, trans. Arrowsmith), the herdsman-messenger avers, reinforcing the chorus's association of Dionysos with Aphrodite (*Bacchae* 402–5). But in this association, the goddess, like the life force she symbolizes, represents something more than sheer sexuality: the liberation, harmony, and well-being that stem from joyful assent to vital natural impulse.[23]

The courage to be gained from Dionysos is also abundantly attested in the messenger's account of the way in which the maenads on the mountain turned on the men who tried to ambush them. Just as Cusins credits the Army with reviving the lowly and the high, the chorus votaries in the *Bacchae* glorify a democratic divinity whose beneficence is available to all: "The god, the son of Zeus, rejoices in feasts, and loves Peace, the giver of prosperity, the goddess who nurtures the young. And in equal measure to the prosperous and to the lowly has he given to have the griefless delight of wine. But he hates him who cares not for these things—to live the life of blessedness by day and through nights of joy" (*Bacchae* 416–26, trans. Winnington-Ingram). Theirs is "a mysticism which includes democracy as it includes love of your neighbor," was the way Murray, the model of Cusins, put it.[24] We have already called attention to the parallelism between the music and musical instruments of the *Bacchae* and those of the Salvation Army. To the corybantic music of the Army Adolphus adds dancing, equally characteristic of bacchant behavior. He himself drums "dithyrambs"—originally songs sung to Dionysos—down the public streets, thereby emulating the chorus in the *parodos* of the *Bacchae* (83–87, previously quoted). And he playfully describes his drum flourish as a particular instance of sudden "ecstasies" familiar to the Army. Most significant of all, the Salvation Army reveals to him "the true worship of Dionysos" (117).

Cusins's panegyric reflects features of Shaw's own appreciation of the renewed vitality the Army brought to Christianity: "Joyousness, a sacred gift long dethroned by the hellish laughter of derision and obscenity, rises like a flood miraculously out of the fetid dust and mud of the slums; rousing marches and impetuous dithyrambs rise to the heavens from people among whom the depressing noise called 'sacred music' is a standing joke; a flag with Blood and Fire on it is unfurled . . . Fear, which we flatter by calling Self, vanishes; and transfigured men and women carry their gospel through a transfigured world" (Pref., 39–40). Adolphus puts his stress on the aesthetic and inspirational qualities in such religious activity, along with its powers of moral conversion. In the process, he himself is set before us as an artistic man, religiously catholic—a believer in all religions—commending a life devoted to the joyful pursuit of what Shaw designated as secondary ideals in the *Man and Superman* "nutrition" passage, discussed earlier.

It is the religion of Barbara, in which he is a partial participant, that her suitor celebrates. Juxtaposed is the prosaic religion of Undershaft, given its first thematic statement at the start of their conversation. In the millionaire's religion, money and gunpowder are the "two things necessary to Salvation." Without these one cannot afford honor, justice, truth, love, and mercy, judged to be "the graces and luxuries of a rich, strong, and safe life" (116). Stated otherwise, in the value scheme of the industrialist these too are secondary ideals, with priority accorded to money and power as vital necessities. But although the Dionysian Undershaft allows these graces and luxuries only subsidiary status, he by no means rejects them. In like manner the chorus in the *Bacchae* counts as auxiliary to Dionysos not only Aphrodite, but Pieria, the haunt of the muses, where reside the Graces and Desire (*Bacchae* 402–15).

Eudaimonia, Sophia, and Indeterminate Divinity

The religions of Undershaft and the Salvation Army are developed contrapuntally. After putting down his drum, Adolphus asks the millionaire if he remembers "what Euripides says about your money and gunpowder" (117). He then proceeds to quote from Murray's translation of the *Bacchae* (905–11). This passage comes from the epode, the closing stanza, of the third stasimon, or choral ode. The generally ignored and minor alterations that Shaw made in the lines he borrowed may best be discerned by setting Cusins's version alongside the Murray translation from which it was derived.[25]

Murray's translation	Cusins's version
For strangely graven	
s the orb of life, that one and another	One and another
n gold and power may outpass his brother.	In money and guns may outpass his brother;
And men in their millions float and flow	And men in their millions float and flow
And seethe with a million hopes as leaven;	And seethe with a million hopes as leaven;
And they win their Will, or they miss their Will,	And they win their will; or they miss their will;
And the hopes are dead or are pined for still;	And their hopes are dead or are pined for still;
But whoe'er can know,	But who'er can know
As the long days go,	As the long days go
That To Live is happy, hath found his Heaven!	That to live is happy, has found his heaven. (117)

Besides skipping Murray's first three and a half lines, Shaw also passes over the opening words (unique to Murray) of the sentence with which

Cusins begins—"For strangely graven / Is the orb of life, that . . ."; he alters the "gold and power" phrase to "money and guns"; "the hopes" becomes "their hopes," and "hath" becomes "has." There are also a number of punctuation and capitalization changes: substitution of a semicolon for the period after "brother" and removal of the comma after "know" and "go"; a period replaces the final exclamation point; and in the last line the capitalizations of "To Live" and "Heaven" are reduced to lowercase.[26] (In reducing "Will" to lowercase both times Shaw may simply have been following this modification in the separate 1904 edition of Murray's *Bacchae*.)

It may be helpful to consider a different translation of the same lines from the *Bacchae*, in this case Arrowsmith's:

> In various ways one man outraces another in the race for wealth
>   and power.
> Ten thousand men possess ten thousand hopes.
> A few bear fruit in happiness; the others go awry.
> But he who garners day by day the good of life, he is happiest.
>   Blessed is he.[27]

Dodds's excellent analysis of the "thought-structure of these deceptively simple lines" develops the view of E. Fraenkel that they compose a priamel, that is, "a series of detached statements illustrating either by analogy or by contrast a rule of wisdom in which the passage culminates; the reader is left to make the connexion" (*Bacchae*, 190). These particular statements Dodds connects in this fashion: "'There is the happiness of peril escaped, the happiness of hardship overcome, the pride of victory in the race for material success; there is besides the pleasure of hope, which may or may not be fulfilled: but it is the happiness of the *here* and *now* that I call truly blessed.' All other *eudaimonia* (happiness) rests on the fading memory of yesterday's achievement or the insecure prospect of to-morrow's; what the Chorus long for is the *immediate eudaimonia* of present experience which Dion. [Dionysos] gives." A better designation for this so-called hedonism of the *Bacchae*, Dodds suggests, is "religious eudaemonism," conferred by the god who is "the dispenser of natural joys."[28]

The lines Shaw chose for Cusins to declaim come from what Kirk has called "one of the densest of Euripides' odes" (94–95 n. 911). But the problems involved in interpreting the passages chosen probably did not figure importantly in their selection by Shaw. Where questions of

Euripidean interpretation were concerned the most obvious authority he would turn to would be Murray. But since this part of the second act of *Major Barbara* was written in Ireland, when Shaw was not in direct communication with his Greek scholar friend, it is worth examining what he would have found in Murray's writings at that time. Most certainly he had read the commentary of the introductory essay to the volume in which Murray's translation of the *Bacchae* first appeared. In that introduction the translator concludes that the *Bacchae* contains a "real and heartfelt glorification of Dionysus," notwithstanding its implicit criticism of the god. In addition, he infers that some of the sentiments uttered by the chorus reflect the personal thoughts and feelings of Euripides himself. More specifically, he believes that in the very epode we are presently considering the Greek poet clearly "expresses his own positive doctrine." After quoting his own translation of the opening lines of the stanza, Murray comments:

> Men strive with many ambitions, seethe with divers hopes, mostly conflicting, mostly of inherent worthlessness; even if they are achieved, no one is a whit the better.
> But whoe'er can know, As the long days go,
> That *to live is happy*, hath found his Heaven!
> Could not the wise men of Athens understand what a child feels, what a wild beast feels, what a poet feels, that to live—to live in the presence of nature, of Dawn and Sunset, of eternal mysteries and discoveries and wonders—is in itself a joyous thing? (*Euripides*, lvii, lxii–lxiii)[29]

As Murray would have it, the Euripidean doctrine expressed in this and other choral odes in the *Bacchae* has as its essence: "That the end of life is not in the future, not in external objects, not a thing to be won by success or good fortune, nor to be deprived of by the actions of others. Live according to Nature, and Life itself is happiness. The kingdom of Heaven is within you—here and now. You have but to accept it and live with it—not obscure it by striving and hating and looking in the wrong place" (*Euripides*, lxvi).

Such a reading of the *Bacchae* obviously makes Euripides out to be a precursor of the Stoics, but Murray discerns here much more; a moral line leading to the Platonists, the Epicureans, and early Christian thought, in quest of the "city of Man's Soul," or the City of God. At the same time he detects in the *Bacchae* a strong aesthetic strain, "an appeal to the almost mystical faith of the poet or artist who dwells in all of us." This experience, which most people have had momentarily, even on the top of an omnibus or in the crowded streets of London, is one "of being, as it seems, surrounded by an incomprehensible and almost intolerable vastness of beauty and delight and interest—if only one could grasp it or enter into it!" (*Euripides*, lxviii, lxvi). In Shaw's play Cusins identifies himself as the translator of the verses he quotes; to the extent that he can be presumed to subscribe to the opinions of the actual translator, it may be that something along the lines of Murray's gloss—modified to fit the Salvation Army—is what he is trying to communicate to Undershaft. And Murray's ascription of attitudes and opinions of the chorus to the tragedy's author could have served as stimulus and warrant for having Undershaft address Cusins as "Euripides."

But quite apart from such speculation about the extrinsic influence of Murray's views, analysis of the first *Bacchae* quotation itself can supply clues enough to its function in Cusins's argument. It is only natural that he should ally himself with the chorus of the *Bacchae* in undertaking to present a case for "the true worship of Dionysos" that he has found in the Salvation Army. In the manner of the chorus he is celebrating the immediate Dionysian joy and release from care that the Army can inspire. The Euripidean choral ode he invokes presents grounds for challenging Undershaft's money and gunpowder religion. That is because it contrasts the struggle for wealth and power, and the insecurity of relying on uncertain hopes (which confer no *eudaimonia*), with the direct benefits and everyday blessings that come from achieving the right personal relation to the divine power (the root meaning of *eudaimonia* is to have a good *daimon*; Winnington-Ingram, *Euripides and Dionysus*, 114 n. 1, 156). The inner happiness this relation brings is inaccessible to those who pursue material prosperity (*olbos*).

But Undershaft converts the last lines of the stanza into an admonitory restatement of his own doctrine: "I think, my friend, if you wish to know, as the long days go, that to live is happy, you must first acquire money enough for a decent life, and power enough to be your own master" (117–18). (His retort, be it noted, could easily be supported by any translation of these *Bacchae* lines.) Despite this "damnably discouraging" rejoinder the young "translator" goes on to another quotation from the same stasimon—actually a passage from the stanzas immediately preceding the one he had just finished (*Bacchae* 892–901).

Murray's translation	Cusins's version
Is it so hard a thing to see,	Is it so hard a thing to see
That the Spirit of God, whate'er it be,	That the spirit of God—whate'er it be—
The Law that abides and changes not, ages long,	The law that abides and changes not, ages long,
The Eternal and Nature-born—these things be strong?	The Eternal and Nature-born: t h e s e things be strong?
What else is Wisdom? What of man's endeavour	What else is Wisdom? What of Man's endeavor,
Or God's high grace so lovely and so great?	Or God's high grace so lovely and so great?
To stand from fear set free, to breathe and wait;	To stand from fear set free? to breathe and wait?
To hold a hand uplifted over Hate:	To hold a hand uplifted over Fate?
And shall not Loveliness be loved for ever:	And shall not Barbara be loved for ever? (118)

Once more Shaw makes some word changes—"Hate" to "Fate," and "Loveliness" to "Barbara" (the latter jauntily advanced by Cusins as a defensible equivalent)—along with a number of alterations in capitalization and punctuation: dropping the initial capital letters of "Spirit" and "Law" (although not until the Standard Edition in the case of the latter word), and adding the initial capital letter in "man's"; removal of a comma after "see" and the addition of one after "endeavour," characteristically modified in spelling to "endeavor"); spacing of "these" for emphasis; and substitutions of dashes for commas around "whate'er it be," of a colon for a dash after "Nature-born," and of question marks both for the comma after "free" and for the semicolons after "wait" and "Hate" ("Fate"). In Cusins's version Shaw combined the last four lines of one stanza (*Bacchae* 892–96) and the refrain that follows it (897–901, a repetition of 877–81). (The stanza division that Shaw removed has been restored here to enable line-by-line comparison of the two versions.) Since these two components of the passage are distinct in the original, they will be better understood if we analyze them separately, assessing for each the implications of Murray's phraseology and of Shaw's further modifications.

The first part of the quoted passage is the end of the antistrophe of the third stasimon, and, as Dodds points out, the antistrophe in several of the *Bacchae*'s stasima turns away from the immediate situation and universalize it by stating the underlying conflict in more general terms. What is universalized in this instance, in Kirk's formulation, is "the inescapable power of the gods and the inviolability of established law" couched "in the language of philosophy as much as of pure poetry." The last part of the antistrophe (890–96), our particular concern, Dodds interprets as "drawing a highly generalized moral—not that man must worship the personal god Dionysus, but that he must respect 'the rules' and 'the unknown daemonic.'"[30] It is reverence of this sort that brings the *eudaimonia* that is lauded in the first of the *Bacchae* passages quoted by Cusins.

To Murray the choral song conveys an appeal by Euripides against the essential irreligion of proud men who "worship the Ruthless Will" (his translation of the preceding lines, 885–86)—that is, realists such as Cleon who reject the ideals of "Pity and Eloquent Sentiments and the Generosity of Strength."[31] But if we are to decipher what Winnington-Ingram calls "the obscure generalities of this passage," it is again necessary to go beyond the confines of both Murray's translation and the biographical interpretation he attaches to it. Here is Winnington-Ingram's rendering: "It costs but little to believe that it is with the divine—whatsoever the divine may be—that power lies, and that what has been accepted through long ages is eternal and grounded in nature" (*Euripides and Dionysus*, 110). The central ideas expressed in these lines are the need to recognize that there is power in divinity, and to accept longstanding *nomos* (convention, tradition, custom, law) as rooted in nature (*physis*). The immediate object of the chorus in invoking such tenets—to sanction a call to vengeance—need not concern us since it plays no part in the lines that Cusins declaims in *Major Barbara*, leaving us free to concentrate on the general principles, which do.

The attribution of power to the divine—the "indeterminate formulation is an expression of religious humility in face of the unknowable," Dodds explains[32]—is inherent, even if not as apparent in the Murray translation Shaw employs: "That the spirit of God—whate'er it be—. . . be strong." His espousal of this belief shows Cusins still addressing himself to the theme of power introduced by Undershaft. As in his first *Bacchae* quotation, he is affirming the superiority of religious power over the economic power that Undershaft persistently prescribes. The "indeterminate formulation," the "whate'er it be" of the divine, is particularly appropriate to the stance of a believer in all religions. At the same time this indefiniteness is entirely consonant with the workings of the Shavian Life Force.[33] Viewed in this light the two quotations from the *Bacchae* may be seen to function as lyrical elaborations and extensions of the previous arguments by Adolphus in behalf of the Salvation Army. In the process he remains a close ally of Barbara, his personal link to the Army.

The implicit appeal to *nomos*, to tradition, is also especially suited to Cusins, who is not only a classical scholar and poet, but is at the moment engaged in establishing the kinship of the Army with Dionysian religion. Dodds observes that in this passage the *Bacchae*'s chorus anticipates in principle Plato's solution of the problem of the antinomy between *physis* and *nomos,* namely, that when both terms are correctly understood, *nomos* is found to be based on *physis,* nature.[34] Aristotle reconciled *nomos* with *physis* similarly, and Cusins, in quoting these lines, is drawing on a reinforced post-Socratic philosophic tradition in responding to the challenges of a formidable modern sophist. The emphasis Shaw adds by spacing "these" in "t h e s e things be strong" helps bind together all three concepts: *nomos* (law, traditional belief) and *physis* ("the Eternal and Nature-born") with divinity ("the spirit of God—whate'er it be"). The result is another Shavian trinity. Lattimore's translation of these lines makes the triadic conjunction succinctly:

> It costs so little to believe
> in the strength of divine
> power, whatever divine power is,
> which has been established by long belief
> and has been established by nature. (892–96)[35]

Divine power has deep roots in both traditional belief and nature. By glorifying the divinity in nature that ever triumphs over its irreverent challengers, Cusins is carrying his defense of the Salvation Army one step further: the Army draws its strength from a tradition that goes back to antiquity, and more fundamentally from springs in the nature of things (especially human nature) linked to cosmic sources of power and inspiration.

The "What else is wisdom?" refrain (*Bacchae* 877–81, 897–901) introduces knotty terminological difficulties that seriously complicate the problem of interpretation. Grube uses these very lines to give an object lesson in the vagaries of Euripidean translation, with Murray cited as the worst offender in straying from the original. The words of the chorus, reflecting the increasing cruelty of the god, have the meaning of "to hold down one's enemy," Grube maintains, whereas Murray's "'uplifted over Hate'" implies the opposite of the Greek."[36] In his own note on the refrain Murray admits, "I have practically interpolated the third line ('To stand from fear set free, to breathe and wait')." He has done so, he says, "in order (1) to show the connection of ideas; (2) to make clearer the meaning (as I understand it) of the two Orphic formulae, 'What is beautiful is beloved for ever,' and 'A hand uplifted over the head of Hate.'" Believing that the chorus exhibits two antagonistic spirits as "furious Bacchanals" and as

"exponents of the idealized Bacchic religion of Euripides," he opted here
for the idealization. "If I am wrong," he acknowledges, "the refrain is probably a mere cry for revenge."[37] That it does indeed sound such a cry has
long since become the generally accepted view of Euripidean scholars.

By way of contrast to Murray's more lively treatment of the refrain,
Grube offers his own more literal and prosaic rendering: "What is wisdom? Or what a finer prize from the gods among men, than to press
down one's mightier hand upon the head of one's enemies? And what
is fine is ever loved." With this we may compare (as does Grube) the
prosaic translation of Hadas and McLean: "What is wisdom: What boon
from the gods is fairer among men than to hold a victorious hand over
the head of one's enemies? What is fair is ever dear." To these it is possible
to add a few more specimens. First, Rosenmeyer's attempt to translate
the refrain "as literally as the sense allows":

> What is wisdom? Or what is more beautiful,
> a finer gift from the gods among men,
> than to extend a hand victorious
> over the enemy's crown? But beauty
> is every man's personal claim.[38]

Then there is Dodds's: "What is wisdom? Or what god-given right is
more honourable in the sight of men than to keep the hand of mastery over the head of a foe? 'Honour is precious': that is always true."
Conacher's translation runs: "What, then, is 'cleverness' . . . ? Or, mid
mortals, what prize from the gods is nobler than to hold a triumphant
hand over the heads of one's enemies. And what is noble is forever dear."
And Kirk's metaphrase is: "What is wisdom? or what fairer gift from the
gods in men's eyes than to hold the hand of power over the head of one's
enemies? And 'what is fair is always followed'" (99).

Rhymed versions tend to bring wider variations, which ought to be
kept in mind in judging Murray's version. Here are two such examples,
the first by Vellacott, the second by Sutherland:

> What prayer should we call wise?
> What gift of heaven should man
> Count a more noble prize,
> A prayer more prudent, than
> To stretch a conquering arm
> Over the fallen crest

Of those who wished us harm?
And what is noble every heart loves best.

What can our wits contrive, or what more glorious
gift can come from the gods to men than a high hand
over the foe, heavily held, fully victorious?
Glory's the thing men cherish, ever and in every land!

As is evident the greatest discrepancies appear in the last line. In fact, the range is even greater:

Glory is crown and sum of human bliss. (Way)
Glory is sweet and that I know. (Birkhead)
Fair is fame, and dear its prize. (Lucas)
What is fairest still is dearest. (Milman)
Honor is precious forever. (Arrowsmith)
And what is good is dear, always. (Lattimore)
Good has many faces, I know.
Yet, let it always be on my side. (Volanakis)
What is lovely is always welcome. (Ferguson)
Whatever beautiful, always personal. (Rosenmeyer)
The fair, the noble, how we cherish,
how we welcome them. (Williams)[39]

Grube's comment on a smaller sampling of these lines in translation merits reiteration here: "*All* the words in the original are words commonly used in prose. Yet how differently we all translate them: *sophon* is uniformly 'wisdom,' but this is not really satisfactory; *kalon* becomes 'lovely,' 'fair,' 'glorious,' 'fine,' the difference being due to the meaning 'beautiful' and the association with 'triumphant.'"[40]

Understandably, there is critical disagreement about the precise meaning of this "sententious and cryptic" refrain, as Kirk describes it. To this its heady mixture of Dionysian extremes undoubtedly contributes. Certainly the lines cut deeper than the conclusion Kirk extracts from them, namely, that "revenge is sweet and is sanctioned by the gods" (*Bacchae*, 94). For Rosenmeyer the refrain, through its last line in particular, affords a glimpse, swiftly obscured, of "a vision which comprehends man in the sum total of his powers and feebleness." To which he adds: "The refrain may well be the closest approach to poetry shedding its disguise and showing itself as metaphysics pure and simple" (*Masks of Tragedy,*

137). Its remarkable melding of poetry and philosophy is germane to *Major Barbara* too, but we need only delve into as much of it as survives in Shaw's play.

Dodds notes that in this refrain the chorus somewhat uneasily quotes two traditional maxims in support of Dionysos's wisdom in avenging himself on Pentheus: "To punish an enemy is by general consent a *kalon geras*, a privilege to which one is honourably entitled; but men and gods are rightly jealous of their honor (*hoti kalon philon*)." The first maxim expresses the long accepted opinion, hardly questioned before Euripides's day, that justice requires doing good to friends and harm to enemies.[41] Since Murray eliminated the revenge motif from his translation of this passage, and Shaw further modified Murray's language in another direction, there is no point in pursuing further that popular standard of Greek morality (to which neither Euripides nor Plato subscribed). The other maxim, which appears in the last line of the refrain, is an old Greek proverb according to Plato (*Lysis* 216c). It is given an egoistic interpretation by the chorus, apparently with Greek precedent, accounting it "fine" (*kalon*) to pursue one's own advantage. But the proverb itself is enigmatic and elusive, composed as it is of two highly ambiguous key terms: *to kalon* and *philos*.[42] As for *philos*, it can mean "friend," "dear to," "loved by," and "fond of." As Plato says (in the same place), its soft, smooth, and slippery character allows it to slither easily through our fingers, hence the bewilderingly diverse translations of the last line of the refrain. But it would be a mistake, I believe, to deem such teasing and entangling ambiguity foreign to Euripides's purposes.

The ambiguity is of value to Shaw as well. But in dealing with the version of the stanza in *Major Barbara* it is essential to keep in mind that more is involved than Murray's variations on the Euripidean source: there are also Shaw's own modifications of Murray. For just as Cusins himself is a Shavianized Murray, so is what he quotes. First of all, by eliminating the break between the refrain and the preceding lines Shaw emphasizes their continuity of thought. "What else is Wisdom?" is in this way made to refer to the previous glorification of divine power. Consequently a basic thematic question of the drama, the relation between wisdom and power, into which the *Bacchae* also inquires, receives poetic statement by way of the ancient drama. Second, by doubling the number of question marks in the remaining lines, Shaw imparts an aura of philosophic questioning to the passage. Beyond this, the references to godly grace and loveliness add intimations of beauty to the power already attributed to the divine, and relate human effort to both. The freedom from fear in the interpolated Murray line reflects the fearlessness engendered by the Salvation Army, which won praise from Cusins earlier. Latent perhaps in "breathe and wait" is a hint about inspiration. More remarkably, by changing "Hate" to "Fate," Shaw intuitively escaped Murray's unwarranted reversal of the justification of revenge; what supplants it is the more characteristically Shavian notion of *mastering* one's destiny (indeed, "mastering" is another sense of the verb *katechein*, which Murray renders as "to hold . . . uplifted").[43]

The ambiguous final line of the stanza carries its own unique implications for *Major Barbara*. We have already remarked the wide range of meanings of *kalon*. It can mean the beautiful, lovely, fair, glorious, graceful, delightful; it can also refer to the morally beautiful, virtuous, excellent, fine, noble, honorable. It is a term that expresses a human ideal of intrinsic value (*Paideia*, 1:416 n. 4). There is accordingly a good deal more to it than the "loveliness" Cusins identifies with Barbara. Yet are not the ethical dimensions of *kalon* equally applicable to her? Does she not represent moral virtue, excellence, goodness, honor, nobility—even glory—in this drama? Virtually any translation of the Greek line *hoti kalon philon aei* can be applied to Barbara, as Adolphus has done with "Loveliness" in "And shall not Loveliness be loved for ever?" As for *philon*, she—and the values she represents—are befriended, loved, held dear, and prized as precious by her young lover. Furthermore, this evaluation is no isolated afterthought: it ties in with all that precedes it in the quotation, incorporating a commitment to aesthetic and moral values in Cusin's religious credo. The poet-translator thus equates and syncretizes wisdom, beauty, and goodness with power, tradition, and nature. His philosophy, his religion, is comprehensive and sweeping. Purged of the *Bacchae*'s vengeance theme, it embodies the substance and spirit of the classical intellectual, ethical, and cultural tradition. And all this is invoked as an answer to the Undershaft religion of money and gunpowder.

The apologia of Cusins began with a defense of the Salvation Army. It culminates in a glorification of Barbara. Her name is brought in as a light and comic touch crowning his lyrical Euripidean philosophizing. But in this case there is a great deal more beneath the surface, for the feeling he evinces toward her harks back to Lady Britomart's accusation that it is Barbara he really worships. This thought recurs in the play, with Adolphus eventually confessing its truth openly in the last scene of the drama. The recurrence can hardly be accidental, or trivial in significance.

It will be worth recalling this second-act tribute when we come to the later scenes between Adolphus and Barbara, especially their final one.

Meanwhile, we should take special cognizance of the indefiniteness in Cusins's eschatology. The divine, "the spirit of God—whate'er it be," matched by the ambiguity of the worshipped *kalon* in Barbara (and in the Salvation Army) resembles what the chorus of the *Bacchae* celebrates as the "Other Things" that "are great and shining" (1006–7), and what the Nurse in Euripides's *Hippolytus* speaks of as "that Other—whatever it be—that is more precious than life" (*Hippolytus* 191).[44] In a similar vein is Eve's musing in Shaw's *Back to Methuselah:* "But is [life] long enough for the other things, the great things?" (5:377). "I grudge not the wise their wisdom," sings the *Bacchae* chorus, "My joy is in hunting after those other things which are great and manifest, and they lead man's life toward honour" (1005–7, trans. Winnington-Ingram), "towards the good" (trans. Dodds), or "to what is fair" (trans. Kirk), variant readings of *kalon* again. But this metaphysical suggestiveness is not all that the mystical ambiguity drawn from the *Bacchae* passages contributes to the drama. It has an ancillary use as well: it assists Cusins in negotiating during the second act a nimble tactical shift from tenuous affiliation with the Army to an alliance of convenience with the redoubtable Andrew Undershaft.

Divine Mania

The insertion of Barbara's name into the last line of Murray's translation allows the dialogue to glide smoothly into a consideration of her prospects as the wife of Adolphus. To Undershaft's questions about how well Barbara will fare from the match, Cusins answers "with polite obstinacy" that despite his own weakness in character and health, and his dislike and fear of marriage, he is determined to wed her; so any discussion of this inevitability would consequently be a waste of time (118–19). In the *Bacchae* too, although Aphrodite is allied with Dionysos, as already indicated, her role is subordinate and secondary. This response of Cusins also reflects the workings of the Life Force as played out in *Man and Superman*, but in the drama of nutrition the love interest cannot be expected to hold the foreground for long. Accordingly the conversation immediately returns to the Salvation Army and to Dionysos:

> UNDERSHAFT. You mean that you will stick at nothing: not even the conversion of the Salvation Army to the worship of Dionysos.

CUSINS. The business of the Salvation Army is to save, not to wrangle about the name of the pathfinder. Dionysos or another: what does it matter?

UNDERSHAFT [*rising and approaching him*] Professor Cusins: you are a young man after my own heart.

CUSINS. Mr Undershaft: you are, as far as I am able to gather, a most infernal old rascal; but you appeal very strongly to my sense of ironic humor.

Undershaft mutely offers his hand. They shake. (119)

In this exchange the two come to a rapprochement solemnized by the handshake. It is instructive to trace the steps by which they arrive at this point in their agreement. Undershaft's immediate reply to Cusins's insistence on the incontestability of his decision to marry Barbara seems oddly unresponsive. Adolphus has been talking about Barbara; Undershaft answers by accusing him of being unscrupulous, to the extent of converting the Salvation Army to Dionysos worship. This answer would appear more opportune if given directly in response to Cusins's earlier speech championing the Army, in which he praised that organization for revealing to him the true worship of Dionysos. No doubt Undershaft had that speech, among other things, in mind. But what more?

A clue to his intent may be found, first of all, in another part of their earlier dialogue. After hearing and thoughtfully digesting Undershaft's initial affirmation of a religion of money and gunpowder, Cusins told the millionaire, "Barbara wont stand that. You will have to choose between your religion and Barbara." "So will you, my friend," was Undershaft's rejoinder (a comment subtly prophetic of the young man's third-act dilemma), backed up by the "drum is hollow" charge. To meet that charge Adolphus argued that he was a sincere Salvationist, worshipping Dionysos. But what Undershaft was calling to the young lover's attention was the impossibility of embracing both his Dionysian religion and Barbara—that the two enticements would inevitably collide. An alternative course, however, lay open to him: to convert the Army to his own religious purview. That would involve converting Barbara as well, or rather, in particular. Thus Undershaft perceives in Cusins's stubborn determination to let nothing prevent him from marrying Barbara a willingness to go so far as to try to bring the Army, and with it Barbara, around to his pagan belief. (Like Shaw, Cusins is adept at translating Christian concepts into a heretical creed.)

Through all of this runs an ironic undercurrent, for there is no more than a simple short step from the indeterminate divine "whate'er it be" of Cusins's Dionysos to the discovery of its direct incarnation in the imposing figure of the mighty munitions maker. Such a discovery would render pertinent the advice of the *Bacchae*'s herdsman-messenger: "This god, then, master, whoever he may be, receive into this city; for he is great" (769–71, trans. Winnington-Ingram). Therefore when Cusins explains that the name, and presumably the identity, of the "pathfinder" matters not—that it could be "Dionysos or another"—it is apparent to Undershaft that his daughter's suitor is firm and intransient about *her*, but quite flexible and adaptable in his religious affiliation.[45] Stated otherwise, Undershaft sees that the young man is committed to his daughter, not to her specific faith, hence his willingness to make him his confederate.

But an even deeper vein of irony is exposed, for Undershaft has accused Cusins of being willing to do exactly what he himself contemplates doing; he too "will stick at nothing: not even the conversion of the Salvation Army to the worship of Dionysos." Hence Cusins's answer signals their *identity of purpose*. No wonder that the wily father can say that the professor is a "young man after my own heart"! And no wonder they can join forces so readily. That Cusins is far from oblivious to this ironic twist in their relationship is evident from his final words before the handshake. From here on the Dionysian energy of the millionaire progressively asserts itself. As Shaw explained to Louis Calvert, the first actor to play the part, up until the handshake Undershaft had been studying Cusins and allowing him to talk. The shaking of hands shows that he has decided that Cusins is the one to understand him. He proceeds to lead the conversation and dominate the younger man in a display of steadily mounting force.[46] Yet Cusins makes important contributions to the scene along the way.

Attention now focuses on Barbara. Undershaft tells her fiancé that "it is through religion alone that we can win Barbara" (119), confirming that they are joined in a common effort. Cusins even relegates his own love for Barbara to a lower footing than "the most dangerous of all infatuations"—that exhibited in a father's love for a grown daughter. Thus the religious wooer is to be wooed, the converter to be converted. This affords a Shavian counterpart to the theme of the hunter hunted, so predominant in the *Bacchae*. As Undershaft steers his companion back to the problem of how to win her, sectarian and heterodox approaches are dismissed as equally irrelevant. What is crucial, Cusins brings out, is a matter of *power*, in this instance the wellspring of power that moves Barbara and by which she moves others. That is what they must gain access to if they are to convert her.

> CUSINS. . . . The power Barbara wields here—the power that wields Barbara herself—is not Calvinism, not Presbyterianism, not Methodism—
> UNDERSHAFT. Not Greek Paganism either, eh?
> CUSINS. I admit that. Barbara is quite original in her religion.
> UNDERSHAFT [*triumphantly*] Aha! Barbara Undershaft would be. Her inspiration comes from within herself.
> CUSINS. How do you suppose it got there?
> UNDERSHAFT [*in towering excitement*] It is the Undershaft inheritance. I shall hand on my torch to my daughter. She shall make my converts and preach my gospel—
> CUSINS. What! Money and gunpowder!
> UNDERSHAFT. Yes, money and gunpowder. Freedom and power. Command of life and command of death. (119–20)

Power is manifested in and through Barbara. Uniquely inspired, she is the fountainhead of her own inspiration. In Greek terms she is *entheos:* divinity resides within her. Yet the inspiration has been acquired hereditarily—she is her father's daughter. Like him, she is possessed of the gift for wielding great natural power and influence. Interestingly, it is his "torch" that Undershaft proposes to pass on to his daughter. This metaphor is particularly well suited to a Dionysian character, as torches were an important feature of the Dionysian winter rites, especially the *trieteris*, in which the god himself was represented as carrying a torch during his epiphany. As noted earlier, Dionysos (or the celebrant in whom he is temporarily incarnate) is so depicted in the *Bacchae* (144–50, 306–8) and elsewhere. The torch of the god, like the *thyrsos*, bore his mystic power.[47]

What excites Undershaft is the realization that it is *physis,* nature, inborn disposition, that is strong in his daughter, not the *nomoi,* the prescriptions of any particular religious dogma or tradition. Both affinity and spiritual filiation are established between the father, himself an embodiment of Dionysian natural forces, and his Salvationist daughter. Already he has watched her cast a spell over Bill, exercising an influence akin to that at his command. Now he perceives clearly the groundwork from which his conversion can proceed. Since her religious powers, like his own, are rooted in nature, not convention, he sees in her a potential disciple of his creed. At the same time he knows that it is in the realm of *nomos* that she is vulnerable: there he can attack. The "money and gunpowder" gospel, explicated as a way to freedom and power, to command of life and death, constitutes a call to *physis,* an appeal beyond the boundaries and constraints of *nomos.*

In the attempt to bring his ecstatically towering companion "down to earth," Cusins accuses him of being mad, an indictment promptly flung back at him "with redoubled force." For his part, Adolphus admits to the "secret" of being "mad as a hatter." But he is astonished to learn that a madman can make cannons. Dionysos-like, the cannon maker simply turns on more current:

> UNDERSHAFT. Would anyone else than a madman make them? And now [*with surging energy*] question for question. Can a sane man translate Euripides?
> CUSINS. No.
> UNDERSHAFT [*seizing him by the shoulder*] Can a sane woman make a man of a waster or a woman of a worm?
> CUSINS [*reeling before the storm*] Father Colossus—Mammoth Millionaire—
> UNDERSHAFT [*pressing him*] Are there two mad people or three in this Salvation shelter today?
> CUSINS. You mean Barbara is as mad as we are?
> UNDERSHAFT [*pushing him lightly off and resuming his equanimity suddenly and completely*] Pooh, Professor! let us call things by their proper names. I am a millionaire; you are a poet; Barbara is a savior of souls. What have we three to do with the common mob of slaves and idolaters? (120–21)

This catechismal attribution of madness to the three central characters in the drama invites Greek commentary. Madness is an equivocal term, equally capable of implying praise or censure. Teiresias puts it to both uses in the same speech in the *Bacchae,* lauding Dionysos whose "worshippers, like madmen are endowed with mantic powers" while condemning Pentheus for being "mad, grievously mad, beyond the power of any drugs to cure" (299, 326–27, trans. Arrowsmith). Linforth explains: "When a Greek spoke of madness (*mania, mainesthai*) he used a word which had a wide scope of meaning. At one extreme it might be sheer insanity, at the other it might imply no more than a mild unreasonableness or perversity or queerness. Any startling and unexpected proposal might provoke the exclamation, 'You are mad' exactly as in English" ("Corybantic Rites in Plato," 127–28). Shaw himself comments in the Epistle Dedicatory to *Man and Superman* that "the man whose consciousness does not correspond to that of the majority is a madman, and the old habit of worshipping madmen is giving way to the new habit of locking them up" (2:510).[48]

Madness (*mania*), a condition in which a power or influence from external nature is experienced as a form of "possession" (*enthousiasmos*), raising the individual out of his normal level of consciousness and rationality, was viewed as an important religious phenomenon in developed Greek religion.[49] The discussion of such "divine mania" in Plato, especially in the *Phaedrus*, has repeatedly been associated with its dramatic expression in the *Bacchae*. As R. Hackforth puts it in his commentary on the *Phaedrus*, "The idea of 'divine madness' or *enthousiasmos* is no Platonic invention: it belongs in origin to the religion of Dionysus . . . ; in literature its most splendid embodiment is of course the *Bacchae* of Euripides" (58).[50] According to Plato there are "two kinds of madness, one resulting from human ailments, the other from a divine disturbance of our conventions of conduct" (*Phaedrus* 265a, trans. Hackforth). Earlier he denies that madness is invariably bad, for the *mania* may be a divine gift: "in reality, the greatest blessings come by way of madness, indeed of madness that is heaven-sent" (244a). This leads him to defend "the superiority of heaven-sent madness over man-made sanity" (244d). In the *Bacchae* scene in which Pentheus confronts the two old men ridiculously clad in Bacchic costumes (*Bacchae* 248–369), the accusation of being mad is hurled back and forth. First Teiresias, then Cadmus, tells Pentheus that his mind is distracted. After Pentheus in violent reaction calls their actions mad folly, Teiresias concludes that the king's madness has worsened. By means of these imputations the scene raises questions about what conduct is mad, what sane.

Shaw, in his own fashion, uses the device of questioning sanity in play after play to highlight comparable moral and social issues. More specifically he brings to the fore the very issue explored with great interest by both Euripides and Plato: the relative worth of inspiration and what passes for sober judgment. Shaw's fascination with this theme finds expression very early in the *Major Barbara* Preface. The novelty in Charles Lever's *A Day's Ride*, he tells us, is that Lever deals seriously with what was formerly deemed comic: "the contrast between madness and sanity."

Shakespeare, too, displayed originality in taking the lunatic Hamlet, previously a comic figure, "sympathetically and seriously, and thereby making an advance towards the eastern consciousness of the fact that lunacy may be inspiration in disguise, since a man who has more brains than his fellows necessarily appears as mad to them as one who has less" (17).[51]

It is precisely the contrast between "Divine madness" and "manmade sanity" that emerges in the exchange between Cusins and Undershaft. But instead of encountering conflicting claims of sanity or madness, we have thrust at us Undershaft's claim of a common madness shared by the millionaire, the poet, and the savior of souls, set over against the "sanity" of the "common mob of slaves and idolaters." What about this claim? Do the three have the same form of "madness"? In terms of Plato's distinction, is the madness of each "divine," or of the ordinary human kind? In the *Phaedrus* Socrates names four varieties of divine madness, ascribing them to patron gods: "the inspiration of the prophet to Apollo, that of the mystic to Dionysus, that of the poet to the Muses, and . . . the madness of the lover, to Aphrodite and Eros" (265b, trans. Hackforth). The first three of these types figure prominently in the *Bacchae,* as James Adam has shown, but even the fourth, the madness of the lover, comes in for some passing attention as well.[52] The previously cited yearning of the chorus for Aphrodite and for the abode of Desire (402–16) and the herdsman-messenger's point in associating Aphrodite with Dionysos (773–74), testify to its presence in Euripides's play. In *Major Barbara* the "possessed" lover aspect of Adolphus receives considerable minor treatment. Though he is *"obstinately bent on marrying Barbara,"* as Shaw's stage direction informs us, this resolve results from *"the operation of some instinct which is not merciful enough to blind him with the illusions of love"* (80). Yet even in this "instinct" is discernible the working of Eros, producing "a 'given,' something which happens to a man without his choosing it or knowing why," as Dodds characterizes Plato's fourth type of divine madness. Equally well does the Shavian portrait fit Plato's description of the lover as one transported and moved to reverence by the sight of beauty expressed in a godlike face or bodily figure (*Greeks and the Irrational*, 218; *Phaedrus* 255d, 251a).

But Adolphus also happens to be a poet, and as such better exemplifies the third type of madness, which inspires the soul it seizes "to rapt passionate expression, especially in lyric poetry, glorifying the countless mighty deeds of ancient times for the instruction of posterity" (*Phaedrus* 245a, trans. Hackforth). Such madness inspired by the Muses brings us knowledge of past heroic achievements and virtue, which is what Cusins as Greek scholar-poet does. Plato goes on to say: "He who knocks at the doors of poetry untouched by the madness of the Muses, believing that art alone will make him an accomplished poet, will be denied access to the mystery, and his sober compositions will be eclipsed by the creation of inspired madness" (*Phaedrus* 245a, trans. Cornford, in *Principium Sapientiae*, 66). Adam declares that no Greek poem illustrates Plato's conception of poetical frenzy as well as does the *Bacchae,* adding that there is "none in which the writer is himself so truly 'possessed'" (*Religious Teachers of Greece*, 315).[53] Undershaft and Cusins carry this thought one stage further by denying that anyone "sane," that is, uninspired, would be capable of translating the works of Euripides.

Barbara, already represented as inspired (*entheos*), typifies the second type of possession, religious inspiration, which Adam associates with the *Bacchae's* maenads. Plato describes it as a variety of divine mania that reveals the means of deliverance from misery and sin by recourse to prayer, worship, and rites of purification (*Phaedrus* 244e). Sources of salvation of this sort are the Dionysian and corybantic forms of ritual madness, such as is portrayed in the *Bacchae,* effecting catharsis through Bacchic frenzy and orgiastic music and dancing.[54] As a "savior of souls" who can transform a waster into a man and a worm into a woman, Barbara evinces a cathartic divine madness along similar lines.

That leaves Undershaft. The case for taking him as an example of prophetic inspiration, Plato's first type of divine madness, would appear to be unjustified: he has little to do with divination or foretelling the future, nor is he in any sense Apollonian. No Teiresias is he. So if the madness he attributes to himself is to fit the Platonic classification, it would have to be of a radically different sort than those of Barbara and Adolphus. But insofar as his claim to madness has its basis in the making of cannons, it is difficult to think of it as a "divine" or salutary form of mania at all. Perhaps then, it should be assigned to the opposite kind of madness, that stemming from human infirmity. Yet Undershaft does contribute a divinelike disturbance to conventional conduct, or "emancipation from conventional rules" (*Phaedrus* 265a10, trans. Crombie), and an incursion of Dionysian energy and power.[55] This is fully recognized by Cusins, who is overwhelmed by it. Clearly that comparative religionist comes to perceive its kinship with the Bacchic fervor that moves Barbara and himself. Undershaft is moving forcefully to preempt the divine "whate'er it be" that inspires his daughter and her young poet-translator with their particular varieties of madness or "enthusiasm." Thus if the mania he exhibits as a maker of cannons strikes us as something less than a divine gift or blessing, that definitely is not the case with the madness he lays claim to at the end of his speech in his proper name as millionaire.

Cusins's "Father Colossus—Mammoth Millionaire—" attests to the forcefulness of the Undershaftian madness, which is now threatening to engulf those of Barbara and her lover. It is not then as prophet of an Apollonian religious substitute for his own money-and-gunpowder faith, but as a competing Dionysian *source* of "enthusiasm" that the millionaire joins the other two as a "madman." Already he has advertised his cathartic powers—"My sort of blood cleanses: my sort of fire purifies" (88). Soon he will be proposing alternative means to salvation and deliverance.

Power of the People

"But what the common people do, the things that simple men believe, I too believe, and do" (*Bacchae* 430–33, trans. Arrowsmith). This declaration of faith by the chorus at the end of an ode to Dionysos expresses the same spirit as that with which Cusins greets Undershaft's haughty disdain of the lowly mob. He cites Barbara's love for the common people, the romance of which love he shares. In doing so he once more takes on a choral role, offering a Bacchic interpretation of the Salvationist's creed. Like the Salvation Army, Dionysian religion was accessible to all, with membership in the god's *thiasoi* open even to slaves. The strong democratic appeal of Dionysos, remarked earlier, helped install him as a god of the common people. Hence his followers tended to side with the instinctive feelings and intuitive wisdom of the simple and ordinary people against the encroachments of the socially or intellectually pretentious. Embracing wholeheartedly the beliefs and practices of the common people, they shunned the clever subtleties of sophisticated intellectuals (*sophoi*).[56]

The corresponding stance of Cusins is sardonically attacked by Undershaft as a love of poverty, dirt, disease, and suffering. Barbara, an Earl's granddaughter, and Cusins, a university professor, may find satisfaction in loving the common people, presumably from positions of superiority, but such love holds no attraction for one who has been both common and poor as he has. Rejecting both poverty and the religion that disguises cowardice as humility, Undershaft presents himself at this time as no Dionysian democrat, but rather as an aristocratic or Nietzschean moralist. From this standpoint he propounds the paradox that only those who do not come from the people can really love them. In so characterizing Barbara and Adolphus, he implies that Earl's granddaughter and university professor—their social roles—are not their "proper names" (120), and that their love of the common people is patronizing. Their "proper names"—"savior of souls" and "poet"—designate their distinctive achievements; in the same way Undershaft's passage from "common man" and "poor man" to "millionaire" has won him his own "proper name." The revelation of personal identity thus continues as a persistent motif in the drama. Barbara, it should be noted, eventually utters what is tantamount to a categorical rejection of this (unheard) allegation by her father when she announces near the close of the play that she has sprung from the heart of the whole people (183).

If Undershaft's antidemocratic views strike an un-Dionysian note, it must be remembered that his Dionysian role is that of a rival power; he is proffering an alternative worship to the slavery and idolatry he sees in the mob of Salvation Army devotees. It is the Army that offers democracy, and he is undertaking to dislodge his daughter and prospective son-in-law from their attachment to the Army and its *anschauung*. He interprets the situation very much as did Gilbert Murray in his 1902 commentary on the same choral passage in the *Bacchae* (430–33), which he translates:

The simple nameless herd of Humanity
Hath deeds and faith that are truth enough for me!

"It implies," writes Murray, "that trust in the 'simple man' which is so characteristic of most idealists and most reformers. It implies the doctrine of Equality—a doctrine essentially religious and mystical, continually disproved in every fresh sense in which it can be formulated, and yet remaining one of the living faiths of men" (*Euripides*, lxiv). This is precisely the idealism that Undershaft repudiates. But he does not entirely repudiate the common people—only the love of them as they are. "We three," the millionaire insists, "must stand together above the common people: how else can we help their children to climb up beside us?" This Dionysos would have his followers ascend the mountain to where he dances. As such he can still serve as godly patron to the common people, or at least to their progeny.

When Cusins predicts that Undershaft will not succeed in getting Barbara away from the Salvation Army by such talk, their dialogue turns stichomythic, spoken for the most part in alternate lines. The excitement of the stichomythia—"a kind of verbal fencing" to borrow Albin Lesky's description—is intensified by a shift to *antilabe* (dividing a line between speakers), accelerating the pace of the interrupting, and topping, in the agon (*History of Greek Literature*, 402). The use of *antilabe* in the *Bacchae* is equally sparing but pointed.[57] Undershaft's assertion that he never asks for what he can buy arouses the ire of Cusins, who takes it to mean that her father proposes to buy Barbara. But the businessman makes clear that it is her religious base that he is shopping for, and meets every objection the young defender of the Army raises with succinct and incisive answers. Not only does the canny merchant maintain that the Army is for sale, but he points out how valuable to his own commercial interests are its ministrations to the poor. Just as Dionysos does with Pentheus in the *Bacchae*, he cleverly parries every thrust, giving replies that baffle, silence, and frustrate his adversary rather than convince him. The Pentheus-like fury of Cusins is kindled only when he believes Barbara's integrity impugned, not when that of the Army is called into question. Hence his position remains consistent: adamant and unswerving where devotion to Barbara is concerned, yet amenable to entertaining charges of weakness brought against the Army.

Although Cusins sits down "*overwhelmed*" at the end of this segment of dialogue (123)—replicating Stephen's condition after his first-act colloquy with Lady Britomart (94)—Undershaft has not really succeeded in advancing his case materially with the young scholar; in fact, he appears to have lost some ground. Yet he has laid the foundation for a triumph to come. In this respect the conversation with Adolphus is a development in detail of the exchange of challenges between Barbara and her father in Act I. From this point on Cusins recedes into the background of the action, becoming once again a quiet choral observer, not to reemerge as a key figure until the climactic moments at the end of the act (133ff.).

Undershaft's contention that he could buy the Salvation Army is put to the test when he meets its commissioner, Mrs. Baines. But first he prepares the ground for that meeting by successive mischievous bids of financial aid to Barbara, prompted by her complaints about the paucity of funds for the continuance of the Army's work. These bids she rejects summarily because the traffic in armaments that provides his income has stained his hands "with bad blood," which "good blood" alone can cleanse. (His money, like that of Sartorius and Mrs. Warren in Shaw's early plays, is tainted.) Yet she dearly longs to be free to make converts instead of being compelled continually to beg for the Army in a way that would be humiliating if it had to be done for herself. The "*profound irony*" of her father's response—"Genuine unselfishness is capable of anything, my dear"—escapes her but not Cusins, who in an aside calls the crafty plutocrat "Mephistopheles" and "Machiavelli" (124). As Mephistopheles, Undershaft is after the soul of his daughter; as Machiavelli, he is not averse to deception in the exercise of power. The irony resides in the fact that it is his genuine selfishness that is "capable of anything." Compounding the irony is the prospect that it will eventually prove capable of giving Barbara just the opportunity she is pleading for: to devote herself to the work of conversion without having to beg for money to sustain the enterprise.

Mrs. Baines's name enters the conversation as that of a potent champion of the Army and potential agent to effect Undershaft's conversion. Jenny informs Undershaft that the Salvationists expect to get the money they need by praying for it. Their most effective advocate in such campaigns is Mrs. Baines, who "has never prayed for it in vain: never once," and she has just prayed for it the night before (125). From his daughter he learns that Commissioner Baines, who has come to march with them to their big meeting that afternoon, is eager "for some reason or other" to meet him. "Perhaps she'll convert you," adds Barbara. In this way she reminds us of the ongoing contest in proselytizing between father and daughter, and intimates that the commissioner could prove decisive in tipping the scales in her own favor.

The subject is dropped temporarily upon Bill Walker's return from his encounter with Todger Fairmile. Once more the tycoon offers a monetary contribution to his daughter—this time to augment the modest peace offering that Bill makes in seeking to absolve himself of guilt. But Barbara rebuffs the overtures of both men as vain attempts to buy her and the Army, neither of which, she says, is for sale. Now, at last, the stage is set for the entrance of Mrs. Baines. Not only does Commissioner Baines represent high officialdom within the Salvation Army; she is also credited with an efficacious relation to the divine, endowing her with special powers concerning future events. While she bears some resemblance to the Dionysian worshippers whom Teiresias describes as possessing mantic powers conferred by the god (*Bacchae* 298–301), prophetesses or priestesses, she is a much closer counterpart to Teiresias himself, the practical-minded, politically adaptable ecclesiastic. Despite her leadership status in her *thiasos* (band of worshippers), she, like Teiresias, cuts a rather sorry figure as an exponent of her sect. Teiresias appears on the scene costumed and ready to walk to the mountain where he will sway in expedient dance. Mrs. Baines, in her cult costume, is as fully prepared to step out in a march of equivalent expedience. As the Greeks were given to describe a march or procession as a dance, the correspondence is even closer.[58]

Admitting to being hampered by the filial relationship—"He wont listen to me, because he remembers what a fool I was when I was a baby" (128)—Barbara immediately turns over the task of converting Undershaft to her superior, much as Cadmus left the bulk of the argument with his relative to the professional *sophia* of Teiresias. Perhaps Barbara expects Mrs. Baines to woo her father's soul as she has been wooing Bill's—unaware that all the while her father is in paternal pursuit of her own soul. The commissioner loses no time in bringing up the Army's need for money, in effect picking up where Barbara left off. (Soon Undershaft is to be similarly confronted at the familial level by his wife.) Mrs. Baines's tactic—by no means unheard of in other times—is to hold out the threat of riots of the poor against the well-to-do, which the work of the Army serves to prevent. But the millionaire is moved merely to applaud the efficacy of such drastic measures by the needy. The weakness of the commissioner's case is further exhibited by her credulous introduction (and misidentification) of the hypocritical Snobby Price as a sample convert in order to illustrate the Army's effectiveness in drawing the teeth of the poor, as Undershaft had previously characterized the process. "You see how we take the anger and the bitterness against you out of their hearts, Mr Undershaft," is her proud boast to the industrialist (130). Hardly has he ironically but politely acknowledged the convenience to "all large employers of labor" of such tranquilization by the Army, when Mrs. Baines announces to Barbara and Jenny that she has "good news: most wonderful news." In divulging her glad tidings she reinforces her reputation as prophetess: her prayers have been answered, as she had promised Jenny they would. The answer is Lord Saxmundham's munificent promise to donate five thousand pounds if others will contribute an equal sum (130).[59]

Once Lord Saxmundham is identified as Sir Horace Bodger, the philanthropic distiller, Mrs. Baines turns to Undershaft, supplementing her already partially successful prayers by further supplication, now addressed to the mighty presence in their midst. Will he help them gain the remaining five thousand? If only she could announce at the great gathering that afternoon that another benefactor had joined Lord Saxmundham, additional supporters would rally to the cause. Her plea for his intercession grows in fervor as with tearful eyes she implores him to "think of those poor people, Mr Undershaft: think of how much it means to them, and how little to a great man like you" (131). It seems safe to assume this to have been the tenor and style of her preceding prayers. The present entreaty proves equally successful as the "*sardonically gallant*" Undershaft agrees to match Bodger's gift. To her "Thank God!" he responds with the question, "You dont thank me?" Having graciously received her homage to his greatness and unhesitatingly answered the crucial part of her prayer, he daringly challenges—as misdirected—her ceremonial thanksgiving. In doing so he arrogates to himself unabashedly the role of a rival providence, with a legitimate claim to her thanks and devotion, but he does not press the claim, which she dismisses as a cynical pose (131).

Meanwhile, eager to have his signed check in hand for the meeting, she directs Jenny to fetch pen and ink. But Undershaft is armed with his own pen, as potent as the dread weapons it symbolizes, and he is prepared to wield it like a modern *thyrsos* in an effortless and convincing display of his overwhelming power. Appropriately "*all watch him silently*" as he writes the check, for *hesuchia* (stillness, quiet, calmness) not only belongs to a god as such, but is also traditionally the natural response to a divine epiphany: indeed the silence of Bacchae was proverbial.[60] (Additional instances of such Bacchic silence are to be found in Act III of *Major Barbara*.) Here the silence is abruptly broken by Bill's "Wot prawce selvytion nah?" taunt, followed by Barbara's desperate and determined effort to prevent Mrs. Baines from taking the money (132). The interruption straightway diverts attention from Undershaft to Bodger and the intoxicating spirits that the latter purveys.

Undershaft, the Dionysos of *Major Barbara*, unlike his Greek counterpart, is not directly representative of the vine and its fruits. But he is brought into close association with Bodger, who is. This sort of compartmentalization echoes a similar de-emphasis in the *Bacchae*, where Euripides takes pains to circumscribe and minimize the Dionysian connection with wine and drinking.[61] Undershaft and Bodger are united in a common relationship to the Salvation Army acquired by their joint benefaction to it. From this moment to the very end of the play Barbara closely links the two industrialists in her thinking. Much of the indictment she levels against the distiller, whom she condemns as worse a foe to her Salvationist efforts than the devil, is equally applicable to her father. The same holds true of Mrs. Baines's ex parte plea in behalf of the liquor baron: "If heaven has found the way to make a good use of this money, are we to set ourselves up against the answer to our prayers?" In her attempt at extenuation the commissioner even echoes Barbara's very first words about Undershaft in Act I, "My father has a soul to be saved like anybody else" (81); she does so by reminding the young major that "Lord Saxmundham has a soul to be saved like any of us." As for Barbara, she is willing enough to help save Bodger's soul, but protests against allowing him "to send his cheque down to buy us, and go on being as wicked as ever" (132). That is of course exactly what her father intends to do.

No wonder then that Undershaft, with pointed irony, joins Mrs. Baines in her special pleading. It is not the distiller he defends but the "inestimable gift" of alcohol despite his own teetotalism:

> UNDERSHAFT [*with a reasonableness which Cusins alone perceives to be ironical*] My dear Barbara: alcohol is a very necessary article. It heals the sick—
> BARBARA. It does nothing of the sort.
> UNDERSHAFT. Well, it assists the doctor: that is perhaps a less questionable way of putting it. It makes life bearable to millions of people who could not endure their existence if they were quite sober. (133)

This in substance is Teiresias's case for the social utility of Dionysos's gift of wine: "For filled with that good gift, suffering mankind forgets its grief; from it comes sleep; with it oblivion of the troubles of the day. There is no other medicine for misery" (*Bacchae* 280–83, trans. Arrowsmith). The same praise for its power "to give ease from care" comes from the chorus (381, trans. Winnington-Ingram) and from the herdsman-messenger, for whom it is "sorrow's antidote" (772, trans. Coleridge). Undershaft's argument that it is not Bodger's fault that less than one percent of the poor abuse the valuable gift of alcohol is homologous with Teiresias's reply to Pentheus's accusation that the Dionysian cult sponsors sexual license (221–25). *Sophrosyne*, self-control, he tells the king, is the responsibility of the individual not the god: "Dionysus compels no woman to be chaste. Chastity is a matter of character, and she who is naturally chaste will partake of Bacchic rites without corruption" (314–18, trans. Guthrie).

Still, the burden of defending the cause of compromise with the corruptive influence of the Army's moneyed patron falls to the complaisant Mrs. Baines. She justifies her actions as Teiresias does: their occupational survival demands acceptance of the practical realities. Concern for the fate of the city at the hands of a vengeful god is a key factor in the Greek prophet's decision that "dance we must" (324, trans. Winnington-Ingram, Arrowsmith, Kirk, Curry, Hadas and McLean). Mrs. Baines asks Barbara whether drinking would increase or decrease were the souls they are saving to find all the shelters shut down tomorrow. Her decision, too, is that it is necessary to dance attendance on the prevailing powers. According to Teiresias, men owe all their blessings to the intercession of Dionysos (*Bacchae* 284–85). According to the commissioner, "Lord Saxmundham gives us the money to stop drinking—to take his own business away from him" (133).

The sophistry of this remark prompts an impish outburst from the long-silent Cusins: "Pure self-sacrifice on Bodger's part, clearly! Bless dear Bodger!" His last previous utterance was the aside ("Mephistopheles! Machiavelli!") educed by Undershaft's equivocal assertion to Barbara that genuine unselfishness is capable of anything. Adolphus is obviously fascinated by the revelation of what such "unselfishness" is actually capable of doing, especially in light of Undershaft's earlier prediction as to what his money could buy. The keenest and best informed observer on the scene, Cusins is beholding both the corroboration of Undershaft's judgment that all religious organizations, including the Church of the Poor, survive by selling themselves to the rich, and the fruition of the scheming that proceeded from that judgment. This is the turning point for Adolphus, occurring right after he has witnessed Undershaft's signing of the check and Mrs. Baines's attempt to rationalize away Barbara's moral objections. The commitment of the Army, represented by its officer, has been fully compromised. A new power now controls it, and an understandable consequence is for its votaries to be caught up, however undiscerningly, in a subtle shift of allegiance. In full appreciation of the irony of the situation, Cusins is going the way of the Army, which is Undershaft's way. Since Barbara is not, he fails her at this trying moment.

Undershaft, check in hand, now makes painfully explicit whither the Army is going. In doing so he builds upon the swelling and enveloping motive of "unselfishness":

I also, Mrs Baines, may claim a little disinterestedness. Think of my business! think of the widows and orphans! the men and lads torn to pieces with shrapnel and poisoned with lyddite! . . . the oceans of blood, not one drop of which is shed in a really just cause! the ravaged crops! the peaceful peasants forced, women and men, to till their fields under the fire of opposing armies on pain of starvation! the bad blood of the fierce little cowards at home who egg on others to fight for the gratification of their national vanity! All this makes money for me: I am never richer, never busier than when the papers are full of it. Well, it is your work to preach peace on earth and goodwill to men. [*Mrs Baines's face lights up again*] . . . Yet I give you this money to help you to hasten my own commercial ruin. [*He gives her the cheque*]. (133)

Dionysos Undershaft stands revealed, his great destructive power made fully manifest amid blood and fire. From his standpoint, and that of his business, the exercise of this power is detached from human ethical considerations, expressing "a little disinterestedness." The "oceans of blood" shed in unjust causes are sacrifices to a morally indifferent divinity whose wealth and power this blood-flow nourishes.

The words of the munitions maker conjure up visions of the Dionysian ritual acts of *sparagmos*, the tearing to pieces of a living victim, and *omophagia*, the eating of its flesh.[62] In the *Bacchae*, *omophagia* is mentioned only once (138) and once more hinted at (1184), but the play contains two dramatic instances of *sparagmos*, both described in macabre detail. First Theban cattle, then Pentheus, are rent asunder by the frenzied maenads on the mountain, led by his mother Agave. There is obviously less reason to look for *omophagia* amid the vegetarians of *Major Barbara* than in the *Bacchae*, but Undershaft's vivid visualization of men and boys "torn to pieces with shrapnel" thrusts at us an egregious modern manifestation of *sparagmos* attending Bacchic mania. Certainly the ready recourse to destructive warfare and terror in our era, with the prodigious sacrifice of human life and limb it entails, qualifies as an example of irrational possession and surrender to daemonic forces. Shaw himself drew this parallel in one of his speeches during World War I. In it he likened the plight of German and English mothers caught up in the patriotic war delirium of the time to that of the frenzied Agave in Euripides's *Bacchae*, "who discovers that the head which, in her transport, she supposed herself to have torn from a wild beast, is that of her own son."[63]

The final point Undershaft makes to Mrs. Baines is that in giving her money for the Army he is working against his own business interests, since the converts she makes by preaching peace and goodwill will vote against war, from which his wealth and commercial success derive. The ironic coloring with which this imbues the whole speech is heightened when we recall what he said to Lomax in Act I about the relation between his business morality and religion:

> I am not one of those men who keep their morals and their business in water-tight compartments. All the spare money my trade rivals spend on hospitals, cathedrals, and other receptacles for conscience money, I devote to experiments and researches in improved methods of destroying life and property. I have always done so; and I always shall. Therefore your Christmas card moralities of peace on earth and goodwill among men are of no use to me. Your Christianity, which enjoins you to resist not evil, and to turn the other cheek, would make me a bankrupt. My morality—my religion—must have a place for cannons and torpedoes in it. (89–90)

In both speeches Undershaft maintains that Christianity, especially in its advocacy of peace and goodwill, would be ruinous to his business. In the earlier statement he is, of course, setting forth his own beliefs; in the later one he is weighing with Mrs. Baines the consequences of *her* preaching and practice. His own sincere conversion to Christian doctrine, were that to occur, might conceivably drive him into bankruptcy, but he plainly does not expect any such effect from Mrs. Baines's best efforts. Even more interesting is the fact that the "oceans of blood" speech establishes Undershaft's contribution to the Salvation Army as an action contrary to his own convictions about philanthropy. Or rather, it shows that this particular action differs markedly from donating conscience money. Obviously the contribution is an exception to his rule, expressly designed to bring about the conversion of his daughter.

In another letter to Louis Calvert, Shaw advised him about the acting of Undershaft in this scene: "There is that frightful speech where Undershaft deliberately gives a horrible account of his business, sticking detail after detail of the horrors of war into poor bleeding Barbara in order to show her what Mrs. Baines will tolerate for the sake of £5000. Cusins, who sees it all, is driven into an ecstasy of irony by it: it is sort of fantasia played on the nerves both of him and Barbara by Machiavelli-Mephistopheles."[64] These instructions to Calvert should help us trace the devious threads of intent that extend from the words of "Machi-avelli-Mephistopheles" to the responsive nerves of his oblique targets. Although addressed to Mrs. Baines, the savage speech is directed mainly at "bleeding" Barbara as a special victim now on the verge of her own spiritual *sparagmos,* and at her carefully preinstructed lover-observer. To Barbara it imparts a more developed version of the lesson her brother learned in the first act: the Army is now as fully implicated in the bloody operations of the munitions firm as are the members of the Undershaft family, who owe their income to it.

Epiphany: Ecstasy and Resistance

Stirred to mischievous ecstasy, Cusins provocatively amplifies the ironic theme of unselfish interest, proclaiming that the unselfishness of Un-dershaft and Bodger will inaugurate the millennium. The drumsticks he flourishes while exclaiming "Oh be joyful!" (134) are handy equivalents for *thyrsoi,* and as he wields them thus it is tempting to picture him tossing back his head in the characteristic attitude of a bacchanal. His cry itself strikes a Bacchic note, for Dionysos, identified with Iacchus, is "Lord of Cries" (725, trans. Dodds, Winnington-Ingram), or in Guthrie's phrase, "god of the joyful cry."[65] The "unselfish" beneficence of Under-shaft and Bodger has bought for them the independence and integrity of a moral adversary, the Army, and a consequent increase in their power. Hence the words of the tearfully grateful Mrs. Baines as she takes Un-dershaft's check are fraught with the most telling irony: "The longer I live the more proof I see that there is an Infinite Goodness that turns everything to the work of salvation sooner or later. Who would have thought that any good could have come out of war and drink? And yet their profits are brought today to the feet of salvation to do its blessed work" (134). Her reading of the developments exactly inverts the true state of affairs, a fact evident to all but the obtuse maenad, Jenny, now the hopelessly gullible auxiliary of the ecstatic Cusins.

Adolphus proceeds to organize the march to the great orgiastic meet-ing, which Mrs. Baines reports will celebrate the "saving" of the Army. "Straightway the whole land will dance," sing the devotees of Dionysos in the *Bacchae* (114, trans. Winnington-Ingram). Mrs. Baines invites the savior millionaire to an analogous spectacle, predicting that he will be-hold "a thousand people fall on their knees with one impulse and pray" (134). The impressionable Jenny has already taken up her tambourine, and Cusins now brings from the shelter both a flag for Mrs. Baines and a trombone for Undershaft, who, in the guise of a "gifted trombonist" will "intone an Olympian diapason to the West Ham Salvation March" (134).[66] In calling the swelling outburst of sound "Olympian" Cusins connects Dionysos Undershaft with Olympus, just as the chorus does their god in the *Bacchae* (411, 554, 561).

Addressed by Cusins in an aside once again as "Machiavelli," the arms maker agrees to do his musical best, adding that he could vamp a base— a rather weak attempt at an Olympian diapason—if he knew the tune.[67] In taking the trombone he fires an aside of his own at Cusins: "The trumpet in Zion!" The allusion is to either of two passages in Joel, chapter 2—"Blow the trumpet in Zion, sanctify a fast, call a solemn assembly; gather the people. Sanctify the congregation, assemble the elders; gather the children, even nursing infants. Let the bridegroom leave his room, and the bride her chamber" (Joel 2:15–16). Or more ominously, the first verse of chapter 2—"Blow the trumpet in Zion; sound the alarm on my holy mountain: let all the inhabitants of the land tremble, for the day of the Lord is coming, it is near, a day of darkness and gloom" (Joel 2:1–2). Perhaps, with appropriate ambiguity, Undershaft is alluding to both verses.[68]

"Whoso leads our bands is Bromius," sings the chorus of the *Bacchae* (115, trans. Guthrie), and Bromius (or Dionysos), the roaring or thundering god, is what Undershaft with his trombone parallels. The celebrant too assumes the identity of the god: "Bromius is he who leads the cry of Evoe" (141, trans. Winnington-Ingram).[69] Thus in true Dionysian spirit Cusins takes the lead and sings, with drum obbligato, a wedding chorus from Donizetti's *Lucia di Lammermoor,* converted by the Army into the West Ham Salvation March: "For thee immense rejoicing—immenso giubilo—immenso giubilo." "We convert everything to good here, including Bodger," is Cusins's double-edged musical commentary (135). For truly this Bacchic scene is a celebration of conversion and converters. "This is his kingdom: to make men one in the dance; to be gay with the music of pipes [*auloi*]; to set an end to cares" (378–81, trans. Dodds). Over such a kingdom Undershaft now reigns, having appropriated Barbara's realm as easily as he had taken over her mother's in Act I. (There remains his own special kingdom to be visited in Act III.)

The *ecstasis* of Cusins at Undershaft's triumph over his daughter brings to mind that of the chorus leader in the *Bacchae* when apprised of the fate of Pentheus: "Dionysus, god of rapture! Your power is revealed!"

When the messenger bearing the news is shocked at such exultation in disaster, the leader replies, "I am no Greek; I sing for joy in a foreign tune" (1031–34, trans. Vellacott). An Australian, Adolphus too is an exultant foreigner, singing "immenso giubilo" in Italian. His unfeeling response to Barbara's sad plaint that he is breaking her heart—replying "What is a broken heart more or less here? Dionysos Undershaft has descended. I am possessed" (135)—is again essentially that of the chorus leader, who shows the same disregard for Theban sensibilities: "Dionysus, Dionysus, not Thebes, has power over me" (1037–38, trans. Arrowsmith, Kirk). Cusins acts *entheos*, his "enthusiasm" or "possession" coursing through the whole scene in frenzied counterpoint to the deepening despair of the disenchanted Barbara.[70] His impetuous strophic movements rouse his companions to a fever pitch of excitement and action. As organizer of the procession, he even attempts to beguile Barbara into it, mutely offering as lure the tambourine he has snatched from Jenny, only to toss it "recklessly" back to that maenad when all it elicits from Barbara is a decisive shudder of rejection.

It is Cusins who ignites a fire in the band, his drum setting the time and starting the jubilant offstage march. The dithyrambic processional that he animates re-echoes the impassioned strains of the *Bacchae parodos* (already quoted in another rendering) in which the chorus "sing praise of Dionysus to the beat of the rumbling drums, in joy glorifying the Lord of Joy with Phrygian crying and calling, when the sweet and holy pipe peals its holy gaiety" (155–65, trans. Dodds).[71] Cusins's unusual behavior is in complete accord with what Plato says in his *Ion* about such inspired "possession." Corybantes so affected "have a quick ear for only one tune, the tune of the god by whom they are possessed, whoever he may be, and they are ready with words and gestures to suit that tune, while they are heedless of all others" (536c, trans. Linforth).[72] It applies to Barbara as well; for though the enthusiasm in this case swiftly spreads "like a wildfire" (*Bacchae* 778, trans. Milman) to Mrs. Baines and Jenny, it fails to enkindle Barbara, whose ear hearkens to a different ethical tune.

The *Bacchae* dramatizes a resistance myth. *Major Barbara*, correspondingly, unfolds its own drama of resistance. Barbara's unyielding stand brings her experiences that parallel in important ways those of both Pentheus and his mother Agave. Like Pentheus she alone tries to withstand the relentless intrusion of an irresistible daemonic power only to find herself in consequence isolated and desolated. Steadfastly she declines invitations from Mrs. Baines, Jenny, and Adolphus to join in their orgiastic celebration. In the *Bacchae*, Cadmus bids Pentheus "come, let me wreathe your head with ivy. Along with us give honour to the god" (341–42, trans. Winnington-Ingram). Mrs. Baines makes an equivalent request: "Come, Barbara: I must have my dear Major to carry the flag with me" (135). But the self-restraint that marks Barbara's refusal contrasts sharply with the violence of Pentheus's rejection of his grandfather's suggestion. That rejection leads Teiresias to urge, "Let us go, Cadmus, and pray for him, wild though he is" (360–61, trans. Winnington-Ingram). Barbara's *sophrosyne* prompts a befittingly variant response about prayer from Mrs. Baines: "Barbara: if you wont come and pray w i t h us, promise me you will pray f o r us" (136).

But Barbara can no longer pray. This loss of the ability to worship directly follows the surrender of her badge of identification with the Army. Before destroying Pentheus, Dionysos has him dress in the ritual costume of the cult. Barbara already wears the uniform of her cult; her father's effortless usurpation of its devotion calls for diametrically opposite action. She removes the silver brooch from her collar; before long she will remove the entire uniform. To give ritual significance to what has happened, she publicly pins the badge on Undershaft in bitter tribute to his conquest. Much as Pentheus cast away the *mitra*, or headband, at the moment of recognition (*anagnorisis*) of his fate, Barbara at her time of crisis discards the distinctive insignia of dedicatory religious service that she has been wearing. "*Almost delirious*" herself, Barbara sends her tormentors away. The beat of Cusins's drum outside sends forth the band of bacchanals on their *parodos*-like religious procession, playing "I m m e n s o g i u b i l o" in homage to Bromius the Thunderer, who marches with them (136). As Mrs. Baines is caught up in the frenzy, the optimistic nonsense she blurts out to Barbara betrays her growing obliviousness to the realities of the situation: "I must go, dear. You're overworked: you will be all right tomorrow. We'll never lose you." Like the wild mountain maenads of the *Bacchae* she is in the grip of forces that overwhelm her senses, incapable of attending to anyone who is unswayed by the movement of their mesmeric dance. With the cry of "Blood and Fire!" she beckons Jenny and starts a stichomythic chain of feverish exclamations:

MRS BAINES. . . . Blood and Fire! [*She marches out through the gate with her flag*].
JENNY. Glory Hallelujah! [*flourishing her tambourine and marching*].

UNDERSHAFT [*to Cusins, as he marches out past him easing the slide of his trombone*] "My ducats and my daughter"!
CUSINS [*following him out*] Money and gunpowder!
BARBARA. Drunkenness and Murder! (136)[73]

Each of these five successive emotional outbursts explodes on the scene a capsulated expression of the dramatic perspective of the speaker, with Undershaft's utterance strategically set in the middle. They form a series of pithy dualisms—with the less sophisticated Jenny contributing merely a two-word phrase instead of two concepts—taking their cue from the basic duality of the patron daemon and his dyadic creed. So concatenated they afford both a triumphant epiphany in glory and a thematic compendium of the whole act. Let us examine each of these clarion calls in order.

"Blood and Fire!" Mrs. Baines's war cry is ironically syncretic. Undershaft had announced in the first act, with oracular ambiguity, that this motto of the Army "might be my own." Now it is! With the purchase of the Army comes its appurtenances, including its rallying cry and the flag upon which it is inscribed. Barbara has just given him the Army's badge. Mrs. Baines now literally bears the banner for the millionaire. Salvation hereafter is to be through Undershaft's "sort of blood," not Jesus's, and sanctification will be through the baptism of his "sort of fire," rather than through that of the Holy Ghost. Or rather, in terms of Shaw's philosophic perspective, blood and fire acquire new evolutionary meaning. So viewed the Holy Ghost "is the Christian name of the Life Force," which, as in Undershaft's operations, "creates disquieting doubts by acting occasionally in a very unholy manner, as if it had no conscience" (*Everybody's Political What's What?*, 240, 238).[74] The polar opposition between Mammon and religious altruism is moving dialectically—and evolutionarily—to higher ground, although at this point in the drama the eventual goal is by no means clear. Looking ahead, we should expect blood and fire, however inconspicuously, to function dramatically in the final act of the drama.

"Glory Hallelujah!" In the prologue to the *Bacchae*, Dionysos declares that he has established his worship in Thebes, making the city resound with the cries of exultant, ecstatic women. "Thebes is first to ring / With my halooing" (*Bacchae* 24, trans. Birkhead), or in Dodds's translation and clarification, "I stirred to women's cries, roused Thebes to the joy-cry 'ololu.'" The *ololuge* is a women's ritual cry of ecstasy, triumph, or thanksgiving.[75] This characteristic shout is given again at *Bacchae* 689. The corresponding cry of praise to the Lord, "Glory Hallelujah!"—likewise expressing joy and gratitude—is uttered three times in Act II of *Major Barbara*. Rummy shouts it in feigned fervor (100), but the other two exclamations come from "Hallelujah Lasses," as the female members of the Army were popularly called; its final use is reserved for Barbara near the end of the third act (184). Bill Walker relates how Mog Habbijam gave the cry just before Todger downed and kneeled on him in prayer in the snow. Now an ecstatic Jenny utters the same cry as she flourishes her tambourine in another joyous celebration of the triumph of power. Unsuspectingly, she joins the march a converted maenad.

"'My ducats and my daughter'!" Undershaft, readying his trombone as he marches out, hurls these words of Shylock (*Merchant of Venice* 2.7.17) at Cusins.[76] The allusion heaps irony on irony. Shylock was bemoaning the loss of both his ducats and his daughter; Undershaft has similarly given up five thousand pounds and his daughter is alienated from him. But in his case the forfeit of the money is more than willingly accepted: it is the result of his own deliberate action and initiative. For him the loss paradoxically betokens a victory because the ducats that have apparently cost him his daughter have really won her freedom from the Army, according to plan. The Shylock outcry frames a subtle and elliptical message to Cusins, succinctly summarizing the lesson the millionaire has taught this former skeptic: that with Dionysian ease and swiftness he could "buy the Salvation Army" and liberate his daughter from it, as he had predicted.

"Money and gunpowder!" In his own ritual enactment of their new relationship, Cusins follows Undershaft out of the shelter. He does so echoing the creed of the millionaire, in open acknowledgment of its efficacy and power. But his conversion as we have seen, has been largely a matter of identifying another "spirit of God—whate'er it be," the perception of whose strength he had earlier held to be a token of wisdom. Already, like the millionaire, committed to "the conversion of the Salvation Army to the worship of Dionysos" (119), as Undershaft had recognized, Cusins was also disinclined "to wrangle about the name of the pathfinder," whether it be "Dionysos or another." Once again he is sent ecstatically "down the public street drumming dithyrambs" (117), this time to one whose revealed might entitles him to the Dionysian appellation.

Not only does Cusins clearly comprehend Undershaft's kinship to what the orgiastic Salvation Army worships, but he has good reason to rejoice in the success of the millionaire's undertaking, having made common cause with him in the scheme to convert Barbara from her Army commitment. What Adolphus has so expeditiously learned, from the vantage point of his alliance with Undershaft, is that, and how, this could be done. The ironies of the process he alone savors to the full, being privy to the considerations that move each of the parties. These ironies help make him ecstatic, yet, like Hamlet, he is "but mad north-north-west" (Hamlet 2.2.239), knowing full well what is happening. As matters stand, it would only jeopardize his own purposes to help Barbara preserve her allegiance to the Army. Hence his inability to side with her in her hour of crisis and defeat. Instead he avails himself of the opportunity to revert to the role of choral commentator on the machinations of the daemonic power he has been so perspicaciously studying.

"Drunkenness and Murder!" Barbara's anticlimactic cry cuts through the irony and translates "money and gunpowder" into its moral obverse. Her words recall her earlier expostulation with Mrs. Baines about "what my father is," and the concomitant denunciation of Bodger, as she tried in vain to prevent the Army's capitulation to the two capitalists. To her Bodger stands for drunkenness and her father for murder, and both have now prevailed. "My God: why hast thou forsaken me?" The chain of cries culminates in the *pathos,* the suffering and passion of Barbara.[77] For the effects of Dionysos cut both ways. "A famous hymn of victory have you made—but the end is lamentation, the end is tears," sing the chorus in the *Bacchae* (1161–62, trans. Dodds). The deepest despondency follows in the wake of the greatest exultation, the darkest desolation reflects the supremely radiant jubilation. The extremes of exaltation and repulsion, of the holy and the horrible, as Dodds explicates, mark the "violent conflict of emotional attitudes that runs all through the *Bacchae* and lies at the root of all religion of the Dionysiac type" (*Bacchae,* xvii; compare *Greeks and the Irrational,* 277). The same kind of sharply conflicting attitudes finds expression in *Major Barbara.*

As victim of a kind of ritual *sparagmos,* Barbara's plight at this point is akin in spirit to that of Pentheus, as already noted. Her defeat, like his, results from a mistake about identity—a failure to understand the true character and power of a deceptive and resourceful antagonist. In the *Bacchae* it is a mother who unwittingly commits an act of *sparagmos* on her son. In *Major Barbara* it is a father who knowingly and willfully performs the emotional equivalent of a *sparagmos* on his daughter. But because for Pentheus it ends his life, while for Barbara it marks a beginning as well as an end, it is more worthwhile to consider the ways in which Barbara's experience resembles Agave's, both here and subsequently. Like Agave she comes to an agonizingly painful realization of what has happened and its dread significance. Disparate as are the devastating experiences the two women undergo, they are similar in origin and in emotional effect. To each woman the religious life in which she gloried has brought her the "uttermost anguish" she has ever known (*Bacchae* 1282, trans. Way). In the aftermath, each finds herself suddenly alone in a changed world, with only an older man left behind vainly trying to console her.

"Wot prawce selvytion nah?" It is left to Bill to raise the moral issue and, by a crowning pun (in the Greek manner) on the name of Snobby Price, to underline for Barbara his would-be moral instructress, the lesson they have both just learned. She thus becomes the teacher taught. Agave holds her son's body in her hands and mourns because she destroyed it. Barbara, as she herself later puts it (155), had Bill's soul in her hands, and grieves because she failed in her endeavor to save it. Bill's retaliatory ironic comment is superadded to the others. He will not accept the return of his pilfered pound, for now it is his turn to refuse to be bought by Barbara. Unexpectedly he has his moral freedom; it is she who bears the burden of an expensive sellout.[78] "That which was expected has not been accomplished; for that which was unexpected has god found the way" (*Bacchae* 1390–91, trans. Hadas and McLean).[79]

Barbara's experience at the end of this act recapitulates, on a larger scale and with added dimensions of meaning, those of her own mother and brother one act earlier. At that time Lady Britomart arranged for a religious service only to find the nature of the observance quickly transformed when her Dionysian husband suggested a compromise (91–92). Barbara then swept her father out of the room to attend the Bacchic-like rite in the drawing room. Lady Britomart was deserted by Adolphus, whom she sought to keep, and by all the others with the exception of Stephen. Concurrently, Barbara was preparing everyone for the next day's march to the great Salvation Army meeting. But still another compromise with her father—this time by the Army—has wrought a change in the character of the projected religious celebration. This time it is Cusins who sweeps everyone out as she had before, deserting her much as they both had previously deserted her mother. Barbara is left behind with Peter Shirley, as Lady Britomart had been left behind with Stephen.

Yet there is a difference. Notwithstanding her complaints and tears over the injustice of her abandonment, the inconsolable Lady Britomart was unable to hold out and in the end joined the others in the unconventional rite. When she temporized in this manner, allowing herself, like Cadmus, to be caught up in the Bacchic currents that eddied around her, she ceded the role of Penthean resister to her son. Stephen's refusal to be drawn into the religious celebration, which meant following in his father's train, foreshadowed the very same behavior by his sister one act later. Of these cognate acts of resistance the first was petty and comic, the second fateful and tragic; but both were ineffective, bringing discomfiture and ethical isolation to brother and sister alike. As in the *Bacchae* it is the Dionysian relative who triumphs.

Meet it is that Barbara's companion in defeat is Peter, this act's minor figure of moral scruple, as she is its major. Ironically she had earlier bade him "give that conscience of yours a holiday" (111) just before her own was to become so desperately ensnared. Now her conscience too has been relieved of its work and given an enforced holiday. Despite the high hopes with which Barbara set out in her agon with her father, "all the victory she carries home is her own grief" (*Bacchae* 1147, trans. Arrowsmith). But the drama is still far from having run its course, and no more than in the *Bacchae* do these circumstances convey the whole message of the play.

The Drama of Heaven and Hell

The third act begins by focusing attention on Barbara's alienation from the Army, made conspicuous by her assumption of "*ordinary fashionable dress.*" "LOMAX. Youve left off your uniform! *Barbara says nothing; but an expression of pain passes over her face*" (140). When Cusins appears a few minutes later, he "*starts visibly*" at the sight of Barbara out of uniform (141).[1] As suggested earlier, Barbara's predicament reverses that of Pentheus: the dressing of Pentheus in female guise marks his dedication as victim, the Dionysian livery serving as a material link to the god who gains control over his mind and person.[2] "I could not put on woman's dress," says Pentheus (836, trans. Winnington-Ingram), and Dionysos admits that the young king would never do so of his own accord (851–52). Dionysos himself dresses Pentheus in the Bacchic costume the latter must wear for his departure to Hades (857–59).

Like Pentheus, and like the heroine of Shaw's *Saint Joan*, Barbara dons such apparel unwillingly. She puts a rhetorical question to her father a little later in the opening scene of Act III: "Do you think I can be happy in this vulgar silly dress? I! who have worn the uniform" (155). But at the moment this "Warrior Saint" is brooding over the realization, soon to be acknowledged at Perivale St. Andrews, that instead of being in the power of God, as she had supposed, she is "in the power of Bodger and Undershaft."[3] That realization dictated her reluctant abandonment of the Army and its trappings. As in the *Bacchae*, bodily adornment reflects spiritual condition. The change of habit thus symbolizes Barbara's dislocation, and to a marked degree, the loss of her distinctive identity. A serenely self-confident Major Barbara has been reduced to a disquieted, unsettled Barbara Undershaft.[4] Barbara discards the Salvationist garb that linked her materially to the Army once that religious body begins dancing to her father's tune, yet her present attire is itself a visible indication of a new vulnerability to his influence. Before long he will remind her that these garments, like those worn by other members of her family, have been bought with his money (171). Hence she is properly attired as an Undershaft in embarking on a journey to the hidden, low-lying, hellish foundry that is the source of that money.

As for Cusins, we soon discover that he has learned by direct experience that wine, along with music and dance, is a source of Bacchic ecstasy. After the Army meeting, he relates, he spent the night in the company of Undershaft, drinking a "most devilish kind of Spanish burgundy." The wine was supplied by his host-companion but, he theorizes, "I think it was Dionysos who made me drunk," adding to Barbara: "I told you I was possessed" (142). Dionysos, however, is more than the bringer of madness; he is also the liberator "who delivers us from the ill effects of his own gift or from the madness of his revel."[5] As Liberator (Lysios) he "enables you for a short time to *stop being yourself,* and thereby sets you free" (*Greeks and the Irrational,* 76). That is what Undershaft has done to Cusins, and more indirectly to Barbara.

As he comes back to his senses the young professor proceeds to analyze what has happened to him. But first he wonders how Lady Britomart could have married "the Prince of Darkness" (142). Even this satanic epithet does not rule out a Dionysian parallel, since Dionysos too has a chthonian aspect, with cult titles that imply a "god of night" and "of the dark world below," a "dark god" connected with the world of souls, a mysterious "divinity of the underworld."[6] The early Greek philosopher Heraclitus went so far as to identify this god of life with Hades, the god of death, declaring "Hades and Dionysus are the same, in whose honour they go mad and celebrate the bacchic rites." In conferring this and other titles on Undershaft, Cusins is still closer to Bacchic precedent, for Dionysos himself was a god of many names, among them the various titles he bears throughout the *Bacchae.*[7]

Assessing what he has undergone, Cusins concedes that Undershaft has "completed the wreck of my moral basis, the rout of my convictions, the purchase of my soul" (142). Indeed this is what happened to the Army itself; Cusins was caught up in the process, but with heightened awareness of its far-reaching implications. All were "possessed by Bacchus" (*Bacchae* 1124, trans. Arrowsmith). It becomes increasingly clear that, despite outward appearances, the Undershaftian machinations have the same ultimate effect on Adolphus as on Barbara: the uprooting of his philosophical underpinnings. In contemplating the tribulations still to come, he also realizes where he is most vulnerable: "He cares for you Barbara. That is what makes him so dangerous to me." This reminds us that it was only the recognition of the love for Barbara they shared that made it possible for Cusins to arrive at his entente with her father in the Salvation Army shelter.

Barbara, despite her disillusionment, waves aside such preoccupation with merely personal affection:

> BARBARA. That has nothing to do with it Dolly. There are larger loves and diviner dreams than the fireside one. You know that, dont you?
> CUSINS. Yes: that is our understanding. I know it. I hold to it. Unless he can win me on that holier ground he may amuse me for a while; but he can get no deeper hold, strong as he is.
> BARBARA. Keep to that; and the end will be right. (142)

In effect they establish a pact representing a joint rededication to higher ideals, as they gird for the moral struggle they know awaits them. Their bargain harks back to the one in the first act between Barbara and her father, which brought him into the Army quarters and is about to take her to Perivale St. Andrews. Cusins is by now totally absorbed in the conflict: he as well as Barbara is a prize to be won. Armed with knowledge of how difficult it is to elude Undershaft's clutches, he is marshalling his defenses, preparing to pit his own strength against that of the formidable millionaire. That at this point he has even more in mind the sequel will show. The "understanding" the young lovers have reached also foreshadows "the right end" of the play: the kind of life to which they will pledge themselves from the "holier ground" occupied during their final conversation at Perivale St. Andrews. Meanwhile Barbara wants to know what happened at the meeting she had expected to attend.

Aftermath, *Amathia*, and Awakening

In the *Bacchae* two messengers recount the details of the Bacchic *orgia* on the mountains. The herdsman-messenger tells Pentheus: "I have seen the holy Bacchae, who in madness went streaming bare-limbed out of the city gates. I have come with the intention of telling you, my lord, and the city, of their strange and terrible doings—things past all wonder" (664–67, trans. Vellacott). In *Major Barbara* two characters undertake analogous tasks. Bill has already given a vivid account of the rites in Canning Town at which he served as ritual victim. Now Cusins describes what took place at the great Bacchic assembly to which Barbara had watched him march off in the previous act. He, like the herdsman-messenger, has a tale of wonder to relate:

> CUSINS. It was an amazing meeting. Mrs Baines almost died of emotion. Jenny Hill simply gibbered with hysteria. The Prince of Darkness played his trombone like a madman: its brazen roarings were like the laughter of the damned. 117 conversions took place then and there. They prayed with the most touching sincerity and gratitude for Bodger, and for the anonymous donor of the £5000. (142–43)

Clearly Mrs. Baines and Jenny were frenzied modern maenads, and Undershaft with his trombone a roaring Bromius, inspiring prayers from the devout. Like the revels of the wild mountain maenads in the *Bacchae*, this climactic religious celebration occurs outside the action of the play and is recounted by an appreciative witness. The orgiastic gathering bears further resemblance to the proceedings on Mount Cithaeron in incorporating both wild and calm behavior, although the order in which they occur is reversed.

Cusins, recovering from his encounter with ecstatic possession, discloses what he has gleaned from the experience. The wreck of his moral basis involved being convinced that all his life he had "been doing improper things for proper reasons" (143). Like Dionysos, Undershaft forces the reexamination of philosophical foundations. All this has come in the wake of Adolphus's liberation from the Army. He fends off "*disingenuously*" Barbara's query about how serious his previous attachment to the Army would have been without her, taking refuge in the possibility that he could have joined "as a collector of religions," the position he had taken earlier when discussing his motives with her father. That may well have been his "proper reason" for improperly masquerading as a Salvationist.

By the time her husband arrives Lady Britomart has taken over, sending all the others away to prepare for their trip to the Undershaft cannon factory and bidding Lomax to summon Stephen to join her in five minutes. Before considering what ensues it will be worth examining this whole scene in relation to Act I, which shares the same setting. If we survey the first act from Lady Britomart's standpoint we find that, after carefully engineering her husband's visit and divulging her aims in inviting him, she was completely thwarted in her efforts even to communicate her wishes to him. Her objectives were twofold: to persuade him to provide additional financial support for her daughters because of their impending marriages to spouses with limited resources, and to prevail upon him to abandon the negative application of the Undershaft tradition to her son. But when all were gathered together the conversation and events took a different tack, resulting in the contraposition of Undershaft's and Barbara's religious convictions.

The domineering Lady Britomart, so adept at steering the colloquy with her son Stephen to a foregone conclusion, found herself, with her husband on the scene, unequal to the task of maneuvering the family talk into the plotted and charted channels. Instead, the unexpected electricity generated between father and daughter activated powerful new currents, causing the well-laid maternal plans to be sidetracked. As already shown, Lady Britomart's mission much like that of Cadmus in the *Bacchae* is to come to terms with a great power in behalf of family interests. In both plays the powerful relative quickly and easily establishes his ascendancy over most of the members of the family. But in *Major Barbara* the resistance to him, not concentrated in any one person, itself undergoes dramatic development through the play. It shifts from the initial moralistic refractoriness of Stephen in the first act to the deep-seated moral recalcitrance of his sister in the second. In the third Cusins comes to join her in opposition before they both are able to discover the grounds for eventual reconciliation with this overwhelming force.

Early in Act III Lady Britomart returns resolutely to her unfinished business. Having carefully contrived to be alone with her husband for no more than five minutes, she abandons further dilatory tactics, thrusting her case at him with startling directness: "*She comes to the point before he has time to breathe*," as the stage direction puts it (144). He readily though "*resignedly*" accedes to her monetary demands in behalf of the two daughters and their prospective husbands. But when he goes on to ask if anything more is needed, for herself in particular, she immediately introduces the other matter close to her heart: Stephen and the inheritance.

Here the distinctive myth of *Major Barbara* reasserts itself. The singular position and power of Undershaft derives from a breach in the customary hereditary process, not unlike that of Dionysos, who instead of being reared by his mother was "adopted" into the Olympian pantheon by means of a second birth from Zeus. In his conversation with his wife, Undershaft reaffirms and defends the foundling tradition. All that her insistent protestations in behalf of their son are able to extract from him is a declaration of dissatisfaction with the available candidates, all of whom are "exactly like Stephen" (146). What he seeks is an able foundling, unschooled and free of family ties, who would be disqualified were he not "a strong man." The only way to keep the foundry in the family is to arrange for an eligible foundling to marry Barbara. If Act III were a separate play this could be its Dionysian prologue, for in effect it outlines the remaining dramatic action, in which Barbara's fiancé proves to be such a foundling and keeps the factory in the family. As in a Greek drama there is no great mystery about the myth; what counts is its enactment.

Undershaft dismisses his wife's appeal to his sense of duty toward their son as a trick of the governing class, unavailing against another member of that class such as himself. In characteristically Dionysian fashion he strips all moral considerations from the issue, reducing it simply to an issue of power. And in the present circumstances, he reminds his wife, the power resides in him. In words that fittingly prepare us for Stephen's entrance, Lady Britomart takes a moralistic stance in defeat: "Andrew: you can talk my head off; but you cant change wrong into right" (147). In the first-act tête-à-tête with her son she kept that young man nervous and uncomfortable by asking him to stop fiddling with his tie and watch chain. Now, unable to bend her husband to her will at the level of their real differences, she has to settle for disconcerting him at the surface level of outward appearance by shifting attention to his askew tie, asking him to straighten it. Once again articles of clothing and adornment provide protective covering for the psyche as well as the body, and moves to manipulate them represent attempts to work on the minds of their wearers. Such Shavian use of apparel and its arrangement to highlight personal relationships, especially as these reflect contests for ascendancy, comports well with the precedents in Euripides's play (*Bacchae* 341–44, 925–44).

In the *Bacchae* Cadmus abdicates his throne in favor of his grandson Pentheus, and at the end of the drama mourns the loss of this last male heir of the family. The guiding principle of his life is family loyalty, which Dionysos violates (*Bacchae*, ed. Dodds, 229). As the aristocratic custodian of the interests of her family, Lady Britomart is likewise devoted to family solidarity while advancing the hereditary claims of her single male offspring. That young scion now joins them, according to her prearranged plan, all in furtherance of her determined effort to salvage her rapidly waning case. Although from different motives, Stephen too repudiates his champion within the family, asserting full independence from his mother before coming to a face-to-face confrontation with his Dionysian father. In that confrontation he makes explicit a claim inherent in Pentheus's attacks on Dionysian religion: the claim to "know the difference between right and wrong" (150). His contention that this precise ethical knowledge is the birthright of "any honorable English gentleman" makes it possible for Undershaft to generalize his rejoinder into an indictment of all respectable people, who, like Stephen, make sophistic pretensions to wisdom, ethical and religious.

The question of genuine and spurious wisdom (*sophia*) is again posed in Shaw's drama, much as we find it recurring in the *Bacchae*.[8] The Undershaftian denunciation of "those mortals who hold in honour obstinate folly" (*Bacchae* 884, trans. Winnington-Ingram) contrasts their admitted ignorance and incompetence in technical matters (including the handling of armaments) with their rash pretensions to knowledge and proficiency in conduct and faith. Here too Shaw is operating within the framework of the Greek tradition, in which *sophia* referred to practical skill and craftsmanship as well as to high-level understanding and insight. In proclaiming, as he soon does, that "*I am the government of your country*" (151), Undershaft returns to the correlative theme of power that looms so large in both plays. This speech, in which he arrogates to himself the supreme political authority in the land, makes manifest his decisive Dionysian might, capable of exercising far greater control over the forces of war and peace than was attributed to the Hellenic god (*Bacchae* 302–4, 419–20). Throughout the political sphere it is the moneyed industrialist who pays the aulete and calls the tune.[9]

As for Stephen, this "normally well-meaning man" (Kitto's characterization of Pentheus) suffers from a "complete lack of imagination" (*Greek Tragedy*, 373). The narrowness of his vision makes him, like Pentheus, an exemplar of false wisdom (*Bacchae* 311, 332, 394). Each of these young men is convinced of the natural superiority of his own countrymen over others (*Bacchae* 483, 779); each fails to recognize when he is bested in argument; each is *amathes*, self-ignorant, blind to his own weaknesses. "He is a fool and talks like a fool," is the final judgment of Teiresias about Pentheus (*Bacchae* 369, trans. Ferguson). "He knows nothing and he thinks he knows everything," says Undershaft of his son. "That points clearly to a political career" (151)—one in the very domain in which Pentheus operates. At the same time Stephen is not far removed from the stated beliefs of Teiresias. Upholding "the best elements in the English national character" (152), he is a defender of *nomos* in complacent agreement with the sentiments of the sophistic Greek ecclesiastic: "The traditions which we have received from our fathers, old as time itself, no argument shall overthrow them, whatever subtleties have been invented by deep wits" (*Bacchae* 201–3, ed. Dodds). As Helen North has noted, both Euripides and Plato (in the *Laws*) hold to the view "that under the influence of Dionysus, character is revealed" (*Sophrosyne*, 84 n.; *Bacchae* 314–18, 918–70). The same is true of encounters with Dionysos Undershaft in Shaw's drama.

From the very beginning of the *Bacchae,* in the prologue delivered by Dionysos, we learn of Cithaeron, the mountain where most of the vital offstage action of the drama takes place (*Bacchae* 33, 62). Thereafter—during the *parodos*, the speeches of Pentheus, and the reports of the messengers—Cithaeron and the maenads who wander there are kept constantly before our mind's eye. In *Major Barbara* Undershaft initially mentions Perivale St. Andrews as the location of his works near the end of the first act, and it is not until the close of the first scene of Act III that we discover it too is situated in hill country. There is only one visit to Undershaft's *oros* (mountain, hill) but the entire long final scene of the drama is devoted to it. The members of Undershaft's family go there together, rather than in separate trips as Cadmus's family does. In Euripides's play Cadmus considers taking a chariot to the mountain until Teiresias talks him into walking instead. In *Major Barbara,* too, the mode of transportation comes in for brief consideration, with Lomax and Sarah rejecting Undershaft's bulletproof motorcar in favor of the family carriage.

In the *Bacchae* prologue Dionysos announces that he has maddened the Theban women who denied his legitimacy and driven them to dance wildly on Cithaeron. "I have stung them with frenzy, hounded them from home up to the mountains, where they wander, crazed of mind, and compelled to wear my orgies' livery" (*Bacchae* 32–34, trans. Arrowsmith). At the conclusion of the prologue he himself departs to join them in their dancing. Pentheus is convinced that these mountain maenads are drunken and engaged in sexual excesses, but from the herdsman-messenger comes a decidedly different account of their conduct. He describes their waking as "a lovely sight to see" (*Bacchae* 693), and impressively recounts their miracle-working in making water, wine, and milk flow from the earth, and honey pour from their *thyrsoi*. "If you had been there and seen these wonders for yourself," he assures Pentheus, "you would have gone down on your knees and prayed to the god you now deny" (*Bacchae* 712–13, trans. Arrowsmith). In Shaw's play, when Barbara envisions the Undershaft factory as a chthonic domain peopled by "lost creatures with blackened faces . . . driven and tormented by my father," that scandalized parent's reply is that it is actually "a spotlessly clean and beautiful hillside town" (154). Both Dionysos and Undershaft have surprises in store for their skeptical and misconceiving relatives. But the millionaire's milk and honey miracles are reserved for later revelation.

Disarming as is Undershaft's disposition of his daughter's dark forebodings about his realm, it should not mislead us into believing that his "creatures" are any the less "lost" for living in lovely surroundings. Although his men "are all strongly religious," their faith is essentially precautionary: they dare not risk the presence of agnostics among the high explosives (154). Their religious persuasion is therefore no more free and voluntary than that of the maenads on the Grecian hills. Moreover, as the munitions king's added explanation makes plain, they are equally at the mercy of his ulterior interests, their thralldom rendered all the more insidious by the Dionysian facility of the process that effects it: a hierarchical snubbing order relying on each man's insistence that he retain a status of social superiority and uncontestable managerial authority over his immediate subordinate. Undershaft thus achieves his ends through the agency of his followers very much in the manner of Dionysos, who employs Agave and her sisters to wreak vengeance on Pentheus, a deed which in turn ruins Cadmus and his city.

With equally deceptive ease Undershaft brings his great power to bear upon his daughter. Cusins, "revolted" at the bald admission of how the munitions maker exploits the snobbishness of his workers to augment his profit and power, once again terms him an "infernal old rascal" (155), this time merely by alluding to that epithet he had employed the day before.[10] Deflecting the criticism, Undershaft asks his daughter whether he has really made her unhappy, as Cusins believes. Since he can hardly have any doubts about the effect on her of what he has done, obviously he is ready at last to respond to her remonstrations. His query about her happiness has peculiar pertinence since, as already explained, *eudaimonia,* the Greek word for happiness, etymologically means being on good terms with a favorable *daimon.* At the moment Barbara is unmistakably not *eudaimon* (itself a key word in the *Bacchae*)[11] and her father's question is all the stimulus she needs to unloose her hitherto pent-up indictment of his conduct:

> Do you understand what you have done to me? Yesterday I had a man's soul in my hand. I set him in the way of life with his face to salvation. But when we took your money he turned back to drunkenness and derision. [*With intense conviction*] I will never forgive you that. If I had a child, and you destroyed its body with your explosives—if you murdered Dolly with your horrible guns—I could forgive you if my forgiveness would open the gates of heaven to you. But to take a human soul from me, and turn it into the soul of a wolf! that is worse than any murder. (155–56)

Here at last is her delayed response to Undershaft's "oceans of blood" speech of the previous day, picking up its *sparagmos* (tearing apart) motif. In charging that he has committed a moral *sparagmos* exceeding in gravity any of the physical ones he had described—even if the victim were her own beloved or child—Barbara is inviting comparison with a tragic predicament very like Agave's. Her accusation that Undershaft has engaged in conduct more reprehensible and less pardonable than the more customary forms of *sparagmos* for which his arms-making is responsible—because he has returned Bill to a life of drinking and bestiality—expands on her "Drunkenness and Murder!" outcry in the Army shelter. The suggestion that Bill's soul has become that of a wolf is the first appearance in *Major Barbara* of the Dionysian idea of a connection between human and bestial life, another dominant motif in the *Bacchae.*[12]

"Was your courage then so broken . . . ?" Dionysos inquires of his votaries (*Bacchae* 610, trans. Lucas). Undershaft speaks to his daughter in a similar vein. Instead of defending himself, he shifts to the attack: "Does my daughter despair so easily? Can you strike a man to the heart and leave no mark on him?" This surprising answer lights up Barbara's face: "Oh, you are right: he can never be lost now: where was my faith?" (156). Judging by her reaction, her father's questions have an immediate and profound impact. Cusins's comment—"Oh, clever clever devil!—further attests to its effectiveness. (The words, we may note, approximate those of Pentheus to Dionysos: "You are clever, clever" [*Bacchae* 655, trans.

Winnington-Ingram].) Yet it is far from clear on the surface why Undershaft's remarks should so suddenly change Barbara's whole attitude and perspective. It would seem advisable to review for clarifying clues the second-act scene in which she was wooing Bill's soul under the watchful gaze of Undershaft.

In that scene she told Bill that it was the devil who was making him miserable; that it was not she who was "getting at" him, but "somebody or something that wants to make a man of you"; that he should put out his strength against being converted too easily; that perhaps he lacks a heart; and that it is not she but his soul that is hurting him. Finally, as she exhorts him to come with them to "brave manhood on earth and eternal glory in heaven," he is on the verge of breaking down when a stage direction tells us that Cusins's drum breaks the spell, and with a gasp Bill escapes (113). It must be to this near-conversion experience that Undershaft alludes to in speaking of her having struck a man to the heart. For in spite of Cusins's interruption, Bill was launched thereafter on a pilgrimage to Canning Town and on other attempts to escape the burden of his conscience. And what immediately followed that scene between Barbara and Bill was the conversation between Undershaft and Cusins in which the millionaire stated that he would hand on his torch to his daughter, who "shall make my converts and preach my gospel—" (120).

What Undershaft is doing, then, is reminding Barbara of her magnetism, her talent, her ability to influence conduct, as well as of her success in reaching Bill's conscience, all almost obliterated from her memory by her father's subsequent powerful intervention. His two questions pose an inspiriting challenge and an appeal to her deep-rooted but damaged faith, all of which she recognizes. With remarkable succinctness the questions also manage to draw a sharp distinction between her work in the Army shelter and the official Army actions that compromised it. Part of their effectiveness derives from the fact that they are flung at her by the very person who inflicted the damage. With these works her father begins the process of reviving her powers, but for employment in a different milieu. Though a new faith is being kindled, there remains in it an echo of the Salvation Army past. For Barbara's renewed confidence that "he can never be lost now" recalls Mrs. Baines's parting words to her—"We'll never lose you"—correctly prophesying, "you will be all right tomorrow" (136).

Many years later, in 1940, Shaw provided an expansion of Undershaft's lines in his correspondence with Gabriel Pascal about the filming of *Major Barbara:*

What you really miss is a more complete reassurance of Barbara as to the loss of Bill's soul. But the only way to mend that is by enlarging Undershaft's speech to her before they go to the factory when she reproaches him with having turned her convert into a wolf, like this—

"Did he not spit in Todger's eye to save his honor? Did he not give up his hard earned pound to save his soul? Do you not know what a pound means to such a man?: more than ten thousand pounds to me! Will he ever strike a woman again as he struck Jenny Hill? It is your faith that is failing, not his. You have sent him on the road to his salvation: it may not be your road; but he will not turn back. You have finished with Bill: your work is done in the Army. So put on your hat and come and have a look at my work."

You can put that patch into the reel if you like: it will give Barbara a better cue for recovering her joyousness; but that is all that can be done.[13]

Cusins, alert to all the ironies of the situation, knows very well what Undershaft is doing; hence his "clever clever devil!" For her part, Barbara is discovering the other side of the complex duality in her Dionysian parent, making it possible for him to round out her first Undershaftian lesson with a paradoxical moral:

BARBARA. You may be a devil; but god speaks through you sometimes. [*She takes her father's hands and kisses them*]. You have given me back my happiness: I feel it deep down now, though my spirit is troubled.

UNDERSHAFT. You have learnt something. That always feels at first as if you had lost something. (156)

The abrupt psychological change Undershaft inspires in Barbara is reminiscent of the sudden alteration that Dionysos effects in Pentheus at *Bacchae* 810 by suddenly reaching into the recesses of the king's mind. But that change led Pentheus to a diminishing contact with reality until the moment of death, whereas Barbara's experience is an awakening leading toward heightened sensibility. Hence once more her state of mind bears an even closer resemblance to that of Agave, in this case during the initial stages in the clearing of her clouded vision, as Cadmus guides his daughter's thoughts back to the ineluctable realities of her situation. In each case there are the first glimmerings of light, the gradual changing of perspective as things begin to clear up, and the dawning of a new expanding awareness. "I don't understand what you mean," says Agave. "But my head is somehow . . . clearing: something has changed in my mind" (1269–70, trans. Dodds).[14] Barbara too is on her way to an *anagnorisis,* a sudden realization of truth. At last she is ready to go to the "factory of death" to ascertain what "truth or other" lies behind all the "frightful irony," and accompanying her is the equally concerned and wary Cusins.

For the third and last time in the play Undershaft leaves with the others in tow. This time there are no abstainers, as Barbara and Stephen—however uncomfortably—join the procession, setting out for an incalculable experience in the hills. Stephen, who had sided with his mother against his father to the very end of the first act, is by the end of the last act's first scene more at ease with his father than with his mother, who thrusts at him that he has "outgrown" her (157). When Dionysos is finished with Agave, her father Cadmus tells her that he can be of little further help to her (1367). Similarly, when Undershaft has disposed of Stephen as an heir, the latter is beyond the reach of his mother's ministrations.

Dionysos or Another

"You may be a devil; but God speaks through you sometimes" (156). Barbara's characterization of her father provides an introduction and text for what lies ahead in Perivale St. Andrews, Undershaft's model factory community. Like Dionysos, Undershaft bears the aspects of both god and devil, of the divine and satanic, being, according to an already quoted *Bacchae* line, "most terrible, and yet most gentle, to mankind" (861, trans. Arrowsmith). As such he symbolizes a combination of civilized and savage traits at work in the governance of humankind. What Rosenmeyer says of Dionysos and of the *Bacchae* affords an enlightening suggestion about Undershaft and *Major Barbara* as well: "The double nature of man is what the play is really about; the ambivalence of Dionysus is pressed into service largely in order to illumine the ambivalence of human cognition reaching out for its object, for the elusive pageant of truth" (*Masks of Tragedy*, 131). In Shaw's drama the uncertain search for truth takes place amid the apparent contradictions of Undershaft's enigmatic realm, with its own correlates both of his benign and terrible features. Underlying the ambiguities that pervade this provocative community are the ultimate tensions and intimately connected realities of life and death. Perivale St. Andrews is patently a domain and symbol of the Life Force.

In discussing some difficulties of interpreting the *Bacchae*, Gilbert Murray once suggested imagining as a helpful analogue a modern "play in the style of the old Mysteries on some legend of a medieval saint. The saint, let us suppose, is very meek and is cruelly persecuted by a wicked emperor, whom he threatens with hell fire; . . . in such a play one would not be . . . shocked . . . to find the Mouth of Hell situated in the same street as the emperor's lodging" (*Euripides and His Age*, 120–21).[15] Less melodramatically, and with his own distinctive twists, Shaw provides us with a Saint Barbara (the original was the patron saint of armorers) and her "wicked emperor" father. More pertinently, he puts the "Mouth of Hell" in the vicinity of the lodgings both of the "emperor" and his subjects.[16] Barbara and Cusins are immediately caught up in the polarities and antinomies of Perivale St. Andrews. Anticipating a "hellish" city, Cusins finds it wonderful and perfect, more like a "heavenly" one (158). As if in confirmation of this, we learn that Peter Shirley has been employed as a gatekeeper and timekeeper in a "splendid" lodge, but is not yet at ease in his new role of Peter at the heavenly gates. Soon Barbara's brother and sister join in a chorus of praise for what they have beheld. "Heavens! What a place!" is Sarah's opening exclamation.

But all this agreement about what Cusins calls its horrible, immoral, unanswerable perfection culminates in a rude reversal as Undershaft appears and announces the "tremendous success" of his aerial battleship in destroying a fort manned by three hundred soldiers. This *peripateia*, or reversal of fortune, is punctuated by the brutal kick he administers to the dummy soldier lying across his path, and by the emotional deflation of Barbara and Cusins—especially the latter—that it brings in its wake.[17] Suddenly and unceremoniously their soaring spirits are sent plummeting by a depressingly dismal glimpse at the substructure of Perivale St. Andrews. The brutality of Undershaft's business, set vividly before the eyes of the young couple, is immediately conjoined with its Dionysian moral neutrality, introduced by the industrialist's declaration that "which side wins does not concern us here" (159). Barbarity and amorality are in this fashion sharply etched in as background for the agon to come.

Guided by the perspicacity of Cusins, now beginning to be shared by Barbara, we confront the hellish side of the city. In sharp contrast is the reaction of Stephen. Lost in admiration of the financial and industrial organization of the firm, he is moved to quote Milton (*To the Lord General Cromwell*): "Peace hath her victories no less renowned than War," a testimonial from still another quarter to the Dionysian duality of his father (160). But the young aristocrat, Pentheus-like, has misgivings about what "luxury" and "pampering" by Undershaft's generous provisions will do to the workmen's characters. His father's response has a Hobbesian tone: underlying any effort to organize civilization is a prior decision about the value of trouble and anxiety; if a premium is placed on these as character-building experiences, they can be found in abundance in uncivilized existence. But he hastens to assure Stephen that the Damoclean peril of being blown up at any time affords sufficient anxiety to protect everybody's character (160).

The ultimate thrust of his words is ambivalent: one more reminder of the dark and hellish side of Perivale St. Andrews to counterbalance the heavenly side emphasized initially. Undershaft's city sits on explosives, its foundations vulnerable and insecure. Life in this community is precarious, ever poised on the brink of death and destruction. The monuments that peace builds, war and its arsenals can quickly demolish. Implicit is a lesson about the necessity for civilization to master and harness the dread power it generates. For in this city, as elsewhere, life depends on the wisdom with which the instruments of death are handled. This is all the more true in the twenty-first century.

Illustrating this need for wisdom in dealing with power, Lomax enacts a comic parable. With the foolhardiness bred of cocksure ignorance, he has lit a cigarette in the high-explosives shed and tossed away the uncooled match. Saved by the watchfulness of the factory foreman Bilton, he is singularly unappreciative, lecturing that worker on his want of nerve. Undershaft, who had already explained that the explosives were confined to isolated, cheap, expendable sheds, and equally expendable people in their vicinity, suggests that Lomax put his knowledge of gun cotton to the test at home. Assuring Sarah that there is no danger, Lomax caps the incident by sitting beside her on a loaded bombshell (162)—the one that Undershaft later indicates as the means for making war on war.

The behavior of this prospective millionaire and potentially influential member of government in such a simple encounter with explosive power provides a graphic Shavian commentary on some of the hazards we face from foolish societal leadership. For Lomax is a fool, and as Shaw wrote in 1922, "there is a great deal to be said for a sharp reminder to us that good intentions are no excuse for stupidity, and that if people are to be damned at all, it had better be the fools than the rascals" (*Shaw on Religion*, ed. Smith, 161). Those who wield the *thyrsos* in the modern world need to know what they are doing. As for Undershaft, he is on the side of

"Necessity, ever ironical towards Folly," to quote Shaw again (Pref. *Three Plays for Puritans*, 5:17). That becomes even clearer in the ensuing dialogue between Undershaft and his wife. The entrance of Lady Britomart reintroduces the succession plot, since she immediately reproaches her husband for having kept the town to himself all through the years. His reply—that the town, like the Undershaft inheritance, does not belong to him but he to it—renews his insistence on the framework of necessity within which he operates, in this case the stipulations of an inheritance tethered to a tradition of adoption. This thematic emphasis on necessity, *ananke* in Greek, is soon reiterated.

As Dodds observes, citing Teiresias (314–18), for us Dionysos is "what we make of him" (*Bacchae*, xlv). The same holds true of Undershaft—and of his community. Each of the visitors perceives Perivale St. Andrews in a different light and from a different angle. What impresses Stephen is the business enterprise and financial management it represents. Cusins, persisting in his collector of religions role, concentrates on the places of worship provided for inhabitants. Back at Wilton Crescent, before coming to the factory town, he wanted to know if the place had a Methodist chapel. Once on the scene, he concluded that it would take only a cathedral to transmute the hellish city into a heavenly one. Upon learning that Lady Britomart was presented with flowers at the William Morris Labor Church, he exclaims, "It needed only that. A labor Church!" Then "*distractedly*" mounting the firestep, he turns his back on the others (162). It is unclear how much heed he pays to Undershaft's cynical comment that the workers take no more notice of Morris's words, "No man is good enough to be another man's master" (162), inscribed in ten foot high letters round the church's dome than they do of the Ten Commandments in church. Probably very little, else he might have responded again to the irony of the situation—one in which the occupant of a position of overwhelming mastery over other men thinks nothing of setting so conspicuously before them a patent condemnation of their subservience.[18] Once more Undershaft shows himself to be beyond the reach of moral assaults by "paper apostles and artist-magicians," as Shaw refers to reforming writers and artists in the Preface (39).

Ironically counterpoising Stephen's belated attraction to the business is his mother's antipodal abandonment of interest in the "noisy banging foundry" (162). Attempting to relegate the elusive Undershaft inheritance to that bothersome facet of the firm, she now proposes to take over and manage the domestic side of Perivale St. Andrews—its houses, gardens, and orchards, its furniture, linen, and plates—laying claim to them as strictly female property, of no proper interest to a male. *Physis*, "the law of Nature" in the nutrition passage of *Man and Superman*, continues to exercise its control over her, guiding her again to womanly concerns of home and family, which she carefully carves out of Undershaft's domin- ion. Indeed, in a reiteration of the madness motif, she thinks her hus- band "out of his senses" to consider giving up these possessions. Barbara alone, be it noted, is noncommittal about the place. She remains aloof, a skeptical inquirer and observer. Cusins, in marked contrast, gravitates from heaven to hell and back, alternately fascinated and disheartened as he encounters one after another the constructive and destructive forces within this ambiguous realm. Like the artist in the nutrition passage, "he strays in all directions after secondary ideals," his ambivalent and mer- curial condition reflecting the developing moral struggle within him, soon to surface.

Perivale St. Andrews having revived Lady Britomart's familial in- terest in the inheritance, her managerial instincts reassert themselves, prompting her to a new proposal. Building upon her functional division of the place into male and female spheres of authority, her plan provides momentum for a resolution of the inheritance problem and plot. "Why should not Adolphus succeed to the inheritance?" she asks. "I could manage the town for him; and he can look after the cannons, if they are really necessary" (163). Presumably having reflected on Undershaft's suggestion back at Wilton Crescent—"If you want to keep the foundry in the family, you had better find an eligible foundling and marry him to Barbara" (147)—she characteristically deprecates the weighty demands connoted both by foundry and foundling. But if she would shunt aside the necessities of the situation, her husband cannot. Appealing as her idea is, he will have nothing to do with it since Adolphus cannot qualify as a foundling.

We now learn why Perivale St. Andrews has so perturbed and dis- tracted Cusins: he has been nursing thoughts about his odd eligibility, tenuously acquired by the circumstances of his foreign birth. For, ironi- cally again, it is possible for him to establish the legitimacy of a claim to succession in the Undershaft inheritance. "Customs differ," as Dio- nysos says (484, trans. Arrowsmith, Curry). The professor's qualifica- tions, those of native endowment and character, still have to be assessed, as do the ethical challenges the succession raises; however, Undershaft already recognizes in Cusins "the sort of new blood wanted in English business" (163). Adolphus sets forth his foundling claim in the guise of a confession. In this parody of what Shaw refers to in the Preface as "the nasty lying habit called confession" (41), Adolphus essays a more sophisticated version of the game Snobby and Rummy played in the Salvation shelter: he casts himself in the role of an adventurer who misrepresents himself in order to wed a rich wife. What Lady Britomart and Undershaft surmised long before he now divulges to all: his overriding desire to win Barbara—a desire transcending his craving for "the approval of my conscience" (163). Openly he admits the truth of Lady Britomart's accusation that he had joined the Army "to worship Barbara." Barbara had bought his soul "like a flower at a street corner," but she alone became its possessor: "she bought it for herself." "What! Not for Dionysos or another?" asks Undershaft. "Dionysos and all the others are in herself," is Cusins reply. "I adored what was divine in her, and was therefore a true worshipper" (164).

These lines take us back to Cusins's second-act contention that the Salvation Army's business was to save rather than to wrangle about the pathfinder's name: "Dionysos or another: what does it matter!" (119). The pointed repetition of "Dionysos or another" at this juncture suggests a connection between the present "confession" of Cusins and the earlier dialogue in which the phrase first appeared. During that conversation, it may be recalled, Undershaft found the scholar-poet equivocal and pliant in his underlying religious commitment—his worship of "Dionysos or another," a divine "whate'er it be"—while steadfast and unwavering in his devotion to Barbara. But at the same time it had appeared to Undershaft that Cusins, like himself, would go to any lengths, even to converting Barbara and the Army to his own uncertain Dionysian purposes. Now the young scholar confesses that Barbara herself was the real object of his worship. It was she in whom he found "Dionysos and all the others." Of particular interest here is his view of himself as a "true worshipper" because he "adored what was divine in her."

Evidently to him Barbara is a divinity too, a "Dionysos" and much more, to be adored and worshipped. This, Adolphus perceives, gives her something in common with her father. The indeterminate nature of the divine object of his worship had rendered him peculiarly susceptible to Undershaft's Dionysian powers, but his possession by those powers was as temporary and transitory as his attachment to the Salvation Army. For all his flirtation with Undershaftian irony, his fundamental religious convictions did not really alter. For if Undershaft allied himself with Cusins as a way of winning his daughter away from the Army, it is equally true that Cusins did the same with Undershaft, and for the same purpose. And in the third act the goal of that alliance having been realized, Cusins has no more reason to follow Undershaft's lead. Consequently he can reaffirm his allegiance to Barbara, now detached from the Salvation Army milieu. Thus the transparent cozenage of Cusins's "confession" becomes the vehicle for his genuine confession of faith—the first of a series of such testaments in this act. And his faith, it may be noted, has something in common with that of Father Keegan in *John Bull's Other Island,* whose "madman" dream of heaven included "a temple in which . . . the worshipper [is] worshipped" (2:1021).

As Cusins presents the case for his legal illegitimacy, Barbara climbs to the cannon that dominates the scene, from which lofty vantage point she quietly watches and listens (165), much as her father had looked on in Dionysian silence and detachment in the Salvation Army shelter. Barbara's elevated position also parallels that of Rummy Mitchens during the latter part of Act II. Perched in the loft, Rummy was a silent observer of the action below, including Snobby's appropriation of Bill's pound. Although in the *Bacchae* Pentheus meets his death after being hurled from his treetop perch, in *Major Barbara* no ill effects result from assuming a high vantage ground. A distinctive feature of Shaw's dramaturgy is the inclusion of situations in which a character silently observes what is being said or taking place for a period of time, and *Major Barbara* is replete with instances of this. All of the central characters—Rummy, Cusins, Undershaft, Barbara—become observers, during which time they remain prominent but unobtrusive.

Importantly, Barbara moves through this long scene toward a symbolic divinity much like that of her father. Once more, as in the second act, it is Cusins who makes the attribution of divinity. A pivotal character, he supplies the vital ties that bind these three central characters into a complex triadic unity. In the process he has to undergo a subtle metamorphosis, involving a radical change of identity. In one sense this transformation could be viewed as a kind of mystical union with the drama's chief Dionysian figure, a more fundamental case of becoming *entheos* than that which he experienced in the Salvation shelter. Equally Dionysian is Undershaft's contribution to the process as a "great transformer" (*History of Greek Literature,* 227).[19] To the Greeks, as we have noted, one form of union with the divine was adoption as the son of a deity. As already indicated, adoption itself was interpreted as a rebirth, and Undershaft's adoption as heir to a munitions-maker made him in this respect twice-born, like Dionysos. The same kind of experience awaits Cusins. But indispensable to a second birth are the qualifying conditions of the first, and a good deal of preliminary attention is devoted to these implications in the play.

The discovery that Barbara, instead of being a "woman of the people" as he had thought, actually overshadows him in wealth and social position, caused him to stoop, Adolphus says, "to deceive her about my birth" (164). He had kept secret from her the outcast status imposed on his parents by the English illegality of their marriage. Once these very circumstances render him eligible before Undershaft as a foundling, we learn that the potential consequences of his eligibility have already been weighing heavily on the mind of the professor.

> BARBARA. Dolly: yesterday morning, when Stephen told us all about the tradition, you became very silent; and you have been strange and excited ever since. Were you thinking about your birth then?
> CUSINS. When the finger of Destiny suddenly points at a man in the middle of his breakfast, it makes him thoughtful. (165)

A number of characteristically Greek ideas turn up in these comic lines. The change Barbara has noticed in the behavior of Adolphus is remarkably Bacchic. Not only was it imbued with the Dionysian excitement exhibited in the second act, but in addition with a silence befitting a bacchant, of which we were previously unaware. Destiny (capitalized by Shaw) is the Greek *aisa* or its synonym, *moira*, personified in the Moirai, or Fates, who among other things are birth-goddesses, giving an infant his luck or lot or destined portion, and are so alluded to in *Bacchae* 99.[20]

Of more immediate significance in *Major Barbara* is Cusins's admission that he has been thinking about his eligibility for the Undershaft succession for some time, a point duly seized on by the incumbent owner of the firm: "Aha! You have had your eye on the business, my young friend, have you?" (165). What is more, Barbara's query tells us just how long Adolphus has been contemplating this prospect: ever since breakfast the morning before. This means that he began to think about it prior to his second-act appearance in the Army shelter later that same morning.[21] It follows then that an important motive for Cusins's conduct in the second act, hidden from the others at the time, was the realization that he could possibly become the next Andrew Undershaft. Evidently no one, not even Undershaft, was as aware as he of the wider ramifications of the proceedings in the shelter. Beyond this, his susceptibility to Undershaft's Dionysian influence may also be traceable to an affinity by nature of an heir with his benefactor; for a relationship in *physis* clearly existed between them before any attempt was made to establish it in *nomos*. Still, a disturbing uncertainty attends Cusins's *anagnorisis* (realization by a character of the true situation). Ruefully aware as he is of the dark uses of Dionysian power now within his reach, "an abyss of moral horror" stretches between him and the products of the Undershaft factory (165). His confrontation with the owner of that factory confers on him advantages Pentheus lacked in his engagement with Dionysos: having been initiated into the ways of his adversary, he enters the lists stripped of illusion, his eyes fully opened. Yet his very identity is now also at stake, beginning with the requisite sacrifice of his name. Since he has no intrinsic objection to relinquishing that name, the issue turns on the modification in moral identity and character that the change in cognomen entails.

Some of the nuances of Cusins's agon with Undershaft over the succession can best be appreciated by comparing it with the earlier discussion between Stephen and his father. For Stephen's shortcomings do more than pave the way for his prospective brother-in-law: they help clarify the crucial differences between the two men as possible Undershaft heirs. Each case contains an appraisal of the aptitude of the candidate for business, for independent action, and above all for handling the complex ethical challenges that the inheritance poses. In addition, the tone of the conversation *inter familia* is more strained, that with the outsider more familiar and free. So far as the cannon firm is concerned, Stephen haughtily renounces all "intention of becoming a man of business in any sense," owing to a complete lack of capacity and taste for it (148). But this incapacity turns out to be chronic, as his father exposes his want of knowledge about, sympathy for, and interest in various other fields of endeavor. In sharp contrast is the ingenuity of Adolphus, who arrays as "capital" that he would bring to the business: his "mastery of Greek," his "access to the subtlest thought" as well as to humanity's "loftiest poetry," along with his character, intellect, life, career, and soul. His consequent success in negotiating a higher salary for himself earns Undershaft's compliment: "You are a shark of the first order, Euripides. So much the better for the firm" (167).

Stephen declared his independence from his mother before undertaking to do the same with his father. Yet in point of fact he remains dependent on each: on his mother for his status and ethical perspective, on his father for his income. In his turn Adolphus, early in his bargaining with the industrialist, asserts something more than independence: that he is operating from a position of strength. Taking the offensive, he has no hesitation in using to full effect this most powerful argument—"You cannot do without me; and I can do without you" (166)—especially in the salary negotiations. Toward his father Stephen takes a stand as moralist, presuming to absolute knowledge of the distinction between right and wrong. His son's fatuity provokes Undershaft to derisive flattery: "Why, man, youre a genius, a master of masters, a god!" (150). Behind this irony may be recognized the substance of Teiresias's criticism of Pentheus as one who speaks foolish words in the glib manner of a wise man (*Bacchae* 268–69). "The ready speaker who owes his influence (solely) to his self assurance," he adds, "proves a bad citizen; for he lacks good sense" (270–71, trans. Dodds). When the bargaining over Adolphus's salary is concluded and the figure settled, he too turns to a discussion of morality—specifically the barrier that separates him, along with all the others, from the munitions manufacturer. "The real tug of war is still to come," he says. "What about the moral question?" (168). For him there remains a question to be resolved, its outcome uncertain. Indeed it is a "real tug of *war*" he introduces, for war has to be the ultimate proving ground of his candidacy. It will test how closely he approximates to the desiderated character of an ideal successor, one who can be epitomized in Undershaft's own words, stripped of their irony: "a genius, a master of masters, a god!"

Both Stephen and Adolphus stand their ground against Undershaft, the former denying his father's claim that his money rules England, the latter that the millionaire has true power of his own. According to Stephen, his father's judgment is adversely affected by his having associated only with those who defer to him because of his wealth. According to Adolphus, Undershaft is controlled by "the most rascally part of society" (169). Each of the young men is, in addition, forced to defend his intellect and its cultivation. Stephen is convinced of the superiority of his own habits of mind, formed in public (that is, private) school and university. The case that Adolphus makes for his mental acumen, conversely, is that his learning has come from a native intelligence uncorrupted by formal schooling. His knowledge of Greek, untainted by instruction in an English public school, far from being a handicap, has "nourished" his mind

(165). Looking back, we can see that Cusins had struck a strong blow for Greek almost as soon as he had met Undershaft in the first act. At the time he had advised Undershaft himself to study Greek, because "Greek scholars are privileged men" enjoying an unchallengeable social position, Greek being "to a man of position what the hallmark is to silver" (87). Hence in this play Greek itself serves as an important touchstone of ability in establishing the credentials of a candidate for the succession.

As in the *Bacchae* (196, 268, 312, 332), we are presented with a contrast between real and merely apparent intelligence or good sense (*phronein*).[22] That of Cusins is the genuine article, a gift of *physis;* Stephen's is the specious product of a misguided *nomos*. Whereas Undershaft laughed off the views of his own son, to Cusins he offers an elaborate doctrine in justification of his beliefs. It begins with an affirmation of "the true faith of an Armorer." Understanding this and succeeding speeches by Undershaft is crucial to the interpretation of *Major Barbara*. Too many interpreters have tended to take Shaw's apparent espousal of Undershaft's position at face value, reading the meaning of the play in greater or lesser degree from the creed pronounced by the millionaire in these passages. It is all the more essential that we become clear on what Undershaft's doctrine is, and then consider to what extent and in what manner it is interwoven into the drama's fabric.

The Armorer's Creed

The speech comprising the Undershaftian profession of faith is analyzable in two parts: first the creedal canon, and second a series of aphoristic mottos proposed by successive Undershafts as derivative articles of faith. The creed enjoins the armorer to "give arms to all men who offer an honest price for them, without respect of persons or principles: to aristocrat and republican, to Nihilist and Tsar, to Capitalist and Socialist, to Protestant and Catholic, to burglar and policeman, to black man, white man and yellow man, to all sorts and conditions, all nationalities, all faiths, all follies, all causes and all crimes" (168). This formulation expands on Undershaft's previous announcement of his indifference to the question of which side proves victorious. It sets forth a doctrine of absolute commercial impartiality as well as of moral, political, religious, and racial neutrality in the distribution of arms, and consequently of the power they provide.

Once more Undershaft reveals himself to be an exponent of Dionysian amorality, beyond good and evil. Like Dionysos he represents raw power, a *physis* presumably accessible to all. Particularly to be noted is the religious idiom of his declaration. Not only does the gospel of St. Andrew Undershaft incorporate a clear-cut dogma, complete with foundational creed and determinate articles; it has evolved a myth and a tradition as well. The Undershaftian business enterprise, in fine, operates like a religion. And as in the case of the Dionysian cult it "rises above mere morality," in keeping with the fact that "Dionysus in his public functions left morality alone" (*Cults of the Greek States*, 5:238–39). Undershaft continues:

> The first Undershaft wrote up in his shop if God gave the hand, let not Man withhold the sword. The second wrote up all have the right to fight: none have the right to judge. The third wrote up to Man the weapon: to Heaven the victory. The fourth had no literary turn; so he did not write up anything; but he sold cannons to Napoleon under the nose of George the Third. The fifth wrote up peace shall not prevail save with a sword in her hand. The sixth, my master, was the best of all. He wrote up nothing is ever done in this world until men are prepared to kill one another if it is not done. After that there was nothing left for the seventh to say. So he wrote up, simply, unashamed. (168–69)

The creed harks back to what the armament maker avowed in Act I: "My morality—my religion—must have a place for cannons and torpedoes in it" (90). If the form is inspirational and the language prophetic, the content is an unabashed justification of recourse to armed might in political affairs. Like Dionysos he "also has a hand in Ares' work of war" (*Bacchae* 302, trans. Curry). What he is propounding is an apologia for "the faith that sees God in the sword," as Ferrovious in *Androcles and the Lion* puts it (4:621), reminding us that it is under "the sign of the sword" (91) that Undershaft operates.[23]

The truth is that, prefiguring his appropriation of the Salvation Army, he and his predecessors had long before taken unto themselves its evangelical mode of expression and its consecrated zeal. Abundant irony lurks here, as elsewhere, in the promulgation of the Undershaft doctrine. In the *parodos* of the *Bacchae* (113), the chorus utters what Dodds calls "a strange phrase," which he translates as, "Be reverent in your handling of the violent wands." Conjoining reverence and *hybris,* Dodds explains, the phrase "expresses the dual aspect of Dionysiac ritual as an act of *controlled violence* in which dangerous natural forces are subdued to a religious purpose. The *thyrsus* is the vehicle of these forces."[24] The sword is an Undershaftian hubristic *thyrsos*. Like the Bacchanals, the arms manufacturer harmonizes *hybris* with holiness. But Shaw has reversed Euripides's approach. Instead of subduing natural forces to a religious purpose, Undershaft is attributing religious purpose to natural forces. It is the power of *physis* that the religious sententiousness upholds.

The mottos fall into two groups, divided by reference to the fourth, nonliterary Undershaft. The initial trio is fairly abstract, the first and third claiming divine support and value for man's use of sword or weapon, the second sanctioning combat while repudiating moral judgment. All three advocate a gladiatorial view of the *physis* of man and a natural "right" to warfare, such as may be found in the teachings of some of the Greek Sophists and in Thomas Hobbes's state of nature. As for the final trio, the mottos of the fifth and sixth Undershafts argue the ultimate necessity of coercive force in achieving human ends, including peace. They continue the Hobbesian argument in behalf of the exercise of power, or alternatively the earlier Sophist contention that ultimate political decisions rest on superior might—doctrines to be returned to presently. Finally, "UNASHAMED" proclaims the moral stance of the incumbent Undershaft—a motto known to everyone, as we learn from Lady Britomart very early in the play (73).

In Greek terminology, such a person is *anaides*, above *aidos*, that sense of shame touched on before in connection with Bill Walker's conduct in the second act.[25] *Aidos* is respect for others or for public opinion. Religious in origin, "this spirit of reverence which held men back from rash transgressions," is a bulwark of civilized society, contributing materially to the preservation and perpetuation of existing institutions. As such it is an inhibitory, conservative virtue (*Discovery of the Mind*, 167–68).[26] "The more things a man is ashamed of, the more respectable he is," observes John Tanner in *Man and Superman* (2:547) as he details the constraints of shame. Tanner rues his inability to "wholly conquer shame." Presumably Undershaft is more successful. By abjuring *aidos* he flouts public disapproval, loosing himself from the fetters of respectability, accepted religion, and the established social order. In the *Bacchae* the soldier who has taken Dionysos captive on the orders of Pentheus feels *aidos* (441), as does Pentheus himself, fleetingly, at the idea of dressing in female apparel (828). On the other hand it is understandable that Dionysos—like Undershaft, impervious to the strictures of conventional morality—nowhere surrenders to such a feeling.

Of the seven Andrew Undershafts, the fourth is conspicuous for being motto-less. Special attention is thereby directed to his *actions*, which clearly convey the practical import of the others' words. No national or political considerations withheld his hand from selling cannons to an enemy conqueror. That is what the Undershaft creed amounts to in practice. Put simply, the stress is on armaments, not faith, in the "true faith of an Armorer." The armor of faith is converted into faith in armor.[27] This is a faith in the use of force, indifferent to the character of the user. It is quite understandable then that in responding to the Armorer's faith Cusins addresses his adversary as "Machiavelli," for like Machiavelli the cannon king is committed to power and its uses, which are to be sustained at all costs. As the prospective eighth Undershaft, Cusins announces that he will furnish a seventh motto for the wall, but will write it in Greek, rendering it unintelligible to his predecessor. This is but one of a number of instances in which the putative successor serves notice that the course he intends to follow will diverge from the one charted for him by his precursors. As to the sort of motto Cusins might compose, it is reasonable to expect some clue in his private conversation with Barbara later on. There are several motto possibilities in what he then affirms, one of which, as we shall see, seems a more likely prospect than the others.

As the third-act conflict of *Major Barbara* evolves in the course of their ethical discussion, the metaphors of noose, snare, and hunt are introduced by Cusins's disavowal of the Undershaft creed: "But as to your Armorer's faith, if I take my neck out of the noose of my own morality I am not going to put it into the noose of yours" (169). This echoes one of the most prominent metaphors in the *Bacchae:* that of the hunt. Involved in the hunt motif is the frequent and ironical reference to noose, nets, snares, and traps as devices for use in capture.[28] Dionysos, in particular, is alternately hunted and hunter. First he is the quarry of Pentheus, then later he emerges in the dominating role of hunter. "For our lord is a hunter" is the eventual proud cry of the chorus (1192, trans. Winnington-Ingram). Herdsmen and Bacchae similarly exchange positions as prey and hunters, and Agave comes on the scene in the equivocal role of hunter whose very triumph is a hideous defeat. The noose image that Cusins attaches to his own and to Undershaft's antithetical moral perspectives suggests that he finds them both unduly restrictive, intimidating, if not deadening.

Once again we find Cusins maneuvering to maintain flexibility of position. Since it is precisely a moral issue that separates them, simple acceptance of the "Armorer's faith" would mean the abandonment of his own moral convictions for those of the millionaire. At the same time he is trying to keep free of the Undershaftian toils, with whose subtlety and effectiveness he, more than anyone, has become conversant. Characteristically he maintains that he will decide as he pleases to whom to sell or refuse to sell cannons. But the munitions maker warns him that in becoming Andrew Undershaft he will never again do as he pleases, appending an admonition against coming to the firm "lusting for power." Thus the drama returns yet again to the theme of power and revives the challenge to the might of Undershaft. In this instance the power motif is intertwined with the conception of an underlying and controlling force, as in the second *Bacchae* quotation of Act II, while continuing with the hunt metaphor:

> CUSINS. If power were my aim I should not come here for it. You have no power.
> UNDERSHAFT. None of my own, certainly.
> CUSINS. I have more power than you, more will. You do not drive this place: it drives you.
> UNDERSHAFT [*enigmatically*] A will of which I am a part.
> BARBARA [*startled*] Father! Do you know what you are saying; or are you laying a snare for my soul?
> CUSINS. Dont listen to his metaphysics, Barbara. The place is driven by the most rascally part of society, the money hunters, the pleasure hunters, the military promotion hunters; and he is their slave. (169)

Undershaft's avowal that he is part of a will that drives the place elicits Barbara's first words to her father since their arrival at Perivale St. Andrews, and they reflect the same spirit that animated her words to him just before their departure from Wilton Crescent. At that time, she concluded that though Undershaft might be a devil, God spoke through him sometimes. Now the suggestion that he is an instrument of a mystic will startlingly renews and reinforces her earlier thought. Yet in her troubled state of mind she cannot overlook the possibility that her father is merely resorting to subterfuge, relying on religious intimations to entrap her in his enterprise. So her attitude toward him remains ambivalent—her judgment suspended.

Adolphus is much more skeptical, insisting that Undershaft belongs to "the most rascally part of society." The figures of noose and snare portray Undershaft as a canny hunter. But pari passu he is depicted as being himself at the mercy of "hunters"—hence a hunted hunter. Thus an ambiguity comparable to that of the enigmatic Dionysos clings to the munitions maker. Cusins thinks him a hunter, but equally the slave, if not the prey, of the predatory groups in society in their hunt for pleasure, money, and military advancement. As such he is the quarry of luxury-seekers who hunt appearance and unreality in the world.[29] In much the same vein as Cusins, the chorus of the *Bacchae* (in a Murray rendering cited earlier) sings of "them that worship the Ruthless Will" (885–86), meaning those who are proud, pitiless, and lacking in moral sensitivity. The chorus members have Pentheus in mind, but as Dodds indicates, the general description could fit others just as well, especially those committed to a philosophy of "realism" and violence (*Bacchae*, 188, 122).

The key issue in this *Major Barbara* passage, however, is the reality and locus of power. Cusins's contention that Undershaft is without power sounds strange indeed, especially coming from one who has witnessed its efficacy and proclaimed its greatness. Strikingly enough, the very words he uses are precisely those of Pentheus's hubristic boast to Dionysos: "I have more power than you" (*Bacchae* 505, trans. Grube, Sutherland).[30] But Cusins is no Pentheus, nor has he taken leave of his senses. He knows well the power Undershaft wields. What he is maintaining is that the owner of the firm draws on a source of power not his own. Yet not long before he had vehemently declared himself to Stephen to be the true government of their country, the decisive force behind its institutional façade. The assertions appear contradictory. Which are we to believe? Is Undershaft a powerless power, a pseudo-Dionysos? If not, what is the nature and extent of his power? He does not deny Cusins's contention that "the place" drives him. What drives the place, then, must drive him too. Attention is thus clearly focused on the enigmatic answer, on the will of which he is a part.

As noted near the beginning of this essay, the Preface to *Major Barbara* contains a brief passage in which Shaw mentions this will, and identifies it with the Life Force. Arguing that the nation's crying need is for money, and that poverty is the evil to be attacked, he adds that if you fix your eyes on this truth "Andrew Undershaft's views will not perplex you in the least. Unless indeed his constant sense that he is only the instrument of a Will or Life Force which uses him for purposes wider than his own, may puzzle you. . . . All genuinely religious people have that consciousness. To them Undershaft the Mystic will be quite intelligible, and his perfect comprehension of his daughter the Salvationist and her lover the Euripidean republican natural and inevitable" (31). Evidently Undershaft's power is not illusory, but he is exercising it not simply on his own but as an agent of the Life Force.[31] In some measure the faith of the Armorer likewise represents the standpoint of a custodian of natural power, and its religious cast is to that extent fitting and appropriate. Shaw's attribution to him of "perfect comprehension" of Barbara and Cusins is an additional suggestion of superhuman capabilities. Yet this explanation hardly suffices, for Undershaft operates in terms of narrow selfish purposes as well as of wider, more inclusive ones. Witness his "oceans of blood" speech to Mrs. Baines and the related one about the snubbing order among his workmen yielding him a "colossal profit."

The summum bonum of the *Man and Superman* Epistle Dedicatory would seem to afford a better standard of judgment for Undershaft. There Shaw expounds the view that "the true joy in life [is] the being used for a purpose recognized by yourself as a mighty one . . . the being a force of Nature instead of a selfish little clod of ailments and grievances complaining that the world will not devote itself to making you happy." To this he adds that "the only real tragedy in life is the being used by personally minded men for purposes which you recognize to be base. . . . This alone is misery, slavery, hell on earth" (2:523). Undershaft may be an agent of purposes wider and mightier than his own and may perform as a "force of Nature," but he also uses others for base purposes, giving his realm its slavish, hellish aspect, all in keeping with his double-edged Dionysian character.[32]

In reply to Cadmus's reproach in the *Bacchae* that gods should not be subject to human passions, Dionysos says, "My father Zeus willed all this long ago" (1349, trans. W. C. Greene). Commenting on this, Dodds quotes Wasserman: "Because Dion[ysus] as god represents a universal law, the operation of this law is not to be measured with the measure of human good and evil" (*Bacchae*, 238). Winnington-Ingram similarly explains: "The appeal to Zeus is an appeal to ultimate mystery, to a world structure in which the forces Dionysos represents are an inescapable element. With that there is no quarrelling" (146). The lines that follow in Euripides's play further stress the operation of necessity. Undershaft, attributing his power to a will that works through him, is elaborating his earlier assertion to his wife that the town, as part of the inheritance, does not belong to him but he to it. In both instances he appeals, as Dionysos did, to a necessitous power underlying his actions and beyond moral judgment. As with the Greeks, in *Major Barbara ananke,* necessity, is a force stronger than the gods. At the same time Undershaft continues to bear the same kind of relation to the Armorer tradition as Dionysos does to Zeus.

"The Life Force," Shaw wrote many years later, "when it gives some needed extraordinary quality to some individual, does not bother about his or her morals. . . . Apparently its aim is always the attainment of power over circumstances and matter through science, and is to this extent benevolent; but outside this bias it is quite unscrupulous, and lets its agents be equally so" (Pref. *Farfetched Fables,* 66–67). Undershaft, an embodiment of *physis,* is a beneficiary of such natural power, and is equivalently without scruple. A further indication of how to understand him may well be contained in an independent passage written by Shaw at the time he was composing *Major Barbara.* At the conclusion of the Preface to *The Irrational Knot* he refers to the Life Force as "a stupid instinctive force that has to work and become conscious of itself by means of human brains." He continues: "If we could only realize that though the Life Force supplies us with its own purpose, it has no other brains to work with than those it has painfully and imperfectly evolved in our heads, the peoples of the earth would learn some pity for their gods; and we should have a religion that would not be contradicted at every turn by the Thing-That-Is giving the lie to the Thing-That-Ought-To-Be" (Pref. *Irrational Knot,* xix).[33] The Dionysian Undershaft is a god of the Thing-That-Is, a powerful reality needing to be recognized and somehow dealt with in the world. His religion accordingly is ontologically rather than ethically oriented.

Of this he reminds Cusins in dismissing the charge that the rascals of society drive him and his place. The Armorer's faith establishes a neutrality that makes it equally possible to take orders from good or bad men. Hence his challenge to Cusins and the "good people" to buy his weapons and fight the rascals, instead of "preaching and shirking" (169). A maker of cannons, he cannot make "courage and conviction" any more than Dionysos can make men moral, for as Teiresias explains (*Bacchae* 314–18), that depends on human nature and character (*physis*). The Undershaftian point is additional evidence for his amorality, and for the fact that his sphere is *physis,* nature, not *nomos,* convention. Small wonder then that he turns impatiently from the "morality mongering" of Cusins to deal with his daughter as a prototype of the kind of courage and conviction, grounded in nature and temperament, that he has in view. "Ask Barbara: s h e understands" (169). In this manner the dialogue shifts subtly and smoothly from Undershaft's agon with Cusins to one with his daughter; as the young couple exchange positions, the male adversary assumes for a while the attentive silent observer role that Barbara has so long maintained.

Power Struggle

The first opportunity Undershaft has to converse with his daughter is on the next day. He proceeds from Barbara's startled response at his mention of a "will" behind his work. His disdainful abandonment of Adolphus at this point is patently motivated by his desire to get at Barbara and implement the "snare" for her soul. It is his turn to work at her conversion, to make good on the prophetic prospect that seemed so unlikely when first broached, along with the invitation to visit his cannon works: "Are you sure it will not end in your giving up the Salvation Army for the sake of the cannons?" (91).

The relation between Undershaft and Barbara at this juncture strikingly parallels that between Dionysos and Pentheus in the *Bacchae*'s "temptation" scene (*Bacchae* 810ff.), during which the god begins to prevail over the resistant will of the young king. That marks the *peripeteia* of the *Bacchae*, the critical turning point in the action. It is reasonable to ask whether the encounter between father and daughter at this moment in *Major Barbara* is not of comparable significance. In Shaw's drama of conversion, is not this the beginning of the obligatory and decisive confrontation between the principals? After remaining for so long unobtrusively outside and above the agon between her father and suitor, Barbara is about to descend.[34] Before the end of the play she will rise again.

There has been wide-ranging disagreement among critics about the nature of the psychic influence Dionysos exerts over Pentheus. It is the precipitating cause of an abrupt volte-face and a gradual but irreversible loss in the king's control over his mind and will, despite brief gestures of resistance. Pentheus's yielding has been variously interpreted as a case of infatuation, intoxication, mesmerization, enchantment, imposition of will, possession, madness, loss of identity, alteration of personality, and symbolic death. Murray, among others, suggests that Dionysos exercises something like hypnotism on Pentheus. Dodds, rejecting the hypnosis hypothesis, explains the process as a "psychic invasion" of his victim by the deity, in which the "poet shows us the supernatural attacking the victim's personality at its weakest point—working upon and through nature, not against it. The god wins because he has an ally in the enemy's camp . . .—the Dionysiac longing in himself. From the first that longing has been skilfully excited by the Stranger [Dionysos]."[35]

Undershaft, who had announced in the second act of *Major Barbara* that he would hand his torch on to his daughter, has been adroitly redirecting the Dionysiac inspiration he had at that time recognized as coming "from within herself" (120). He too is "working upon and through nature," drawing on their blood affinity. The stage direction—"*He suddenly reaches up and takes Barbara's hands, looking powerfully into her eyes*" (169–70)—remarkably duplicates Winnington-Ingram's visualization of the corresponding scene in the *Bacchae*: "'Ah!' says Dionysus, perhaps with an intense stare, and a grasping of Pentheus's hands, as he begins to exert some kind of psychic power over his victim" (*Euripides and Dionysus*, 102). The stage direction in Shaw's play tells us that Barbara is "*hypnotized*" as she responds to her father's request, "Tell him, my love, what power really means" (170).

But her resistance proves stronger than that of Pentheus, for by the time she has delivered the first sentence of her second speech, she is once more a free agent: "*She resumes her self-possession, withdrawing her hands from his with a power equal to his own.*" No longer "possessed" by her father, she has regained full self-control (*sophrosyne*) as she brings to bear, in Shaw's decisive phrase, a power equal to Undershaft's own. The power theme dominates the action on more than one level. Not only is power under discussion but there is a power contest under way among the three central personalities, for Cusins's engagement in the struggle is only temporarily relegated to the background. Undershaft's gripping and then surrendering his hold on Barbara's hands enacts a kind of "tug of war" between them, visibly and symbolically, reflecting the underlying moral tug of war that both the young people are waging with him.[36]

The "*hypnotized*" Barbara's explanation of the meaning of power manifests the same religious consciousness Shaw claims for Undershaft in the Preface passage about the Life Force. Before joining the Army, she had power over herself without knowing what to do with it. After joining, she had more to do than time permitted. Asked by her approving father why that was so, she tells him that yesterday her answer would have been "because I was in the power of God" (170). Presumably that is why she was startled when he claimed to be part of a more pervasive will. As Undershaft has keenly discerned, she too thinks of true power as proceeding from *physis*, from the underlying nature of things. Such a source gives meaning, point, and joy to their labors. Both are Stoics in this respect, seeking to live in concord with a providence and purpose immanent in Nature.

But Barbara has been disillusioned in her faith. With her hands freed from her father's, she explains the alteration her beliefs have undergone as a result of his instruction. What he demonstrated was that she was in the power not of God but of Bodger and Undershaft. In this revealing juxtaposition the two merchants are ranked as powerful rivals to divinity. Later on Barbara will interpret to Cusins the full import of this discovery. But now, in an attempt to depict her emotional state, she finds a dramatic analogue in the unnerving repercussions from a cataclysm in nature:

> Sarah: do you remember the earthquake at Cannes, when we were little children?—how little the surprise of the first shock mattered compared to the dread and horror of waiting for the second? That is how I feel in this place today. I stood on the rock I thought eternal; and without a word of warning it reeled and crumbled under me. I was safe with an infinite wisdom watching me, an army marching to Salvation with me; and in a moment, at a stroke of your pen in a cheque book, I stood alone: and the heavens were empty. That was the first shock of the earthquake: I am waiting for the second. (170)

In the *Bacchae* an earthquake occurs during the "palace miracle" scene (576–641).[37] The voice of the god calls upon *Ennosis*, the spirit of Earthquake ("the destructive potency in Nature," in Dodds's phrase), to shake the ground. Dodds gives this account of what ensues: "Thereupon a chorister predicts that the palace will be shaken, and in a moment another points to the physical results of the shock. The voice speaks again, calling now upon the lightning: the Chorus claim to see the flames leap up 'about the holy tomb of Semele' [Dionysos's mother], and in fear and awe they fling themselves upon their faces. Their god has manifested himself—but as the master of dangerous magic, the Son of the Lightning."[38] As they fall to the ground they announce that Dionysos is turning the place *ano kato*, upside down or topsy-turvy—a phrase equally descriptive of the upheaval caused by Undershaft at the end of the second act, the episode Barbara is recalling. At the end of the scene, exactly like Barbara, they "await what further catastrophe may come," in Winnington-Ingram's recounting. What counts most, he points out, is the symbolism—the use of earthquake, lightning, and fire as symbols of nature in its moods of violence, ruthlessness, and destructiveness.[39]

Shaw's selection of the earthquake metaphor was far from accidental, for he resorted to it a number of times, at least twice making its moral connotation explicit. In the Author's Apology (1902) for *Mrs. Warren's Profession,* he exulted as author in "that sense of the sudden earthquake shock to the foundations of morality" that produces consternation in critics (1:233). And even more germane to *Major Barbara* is this 1909 observation in the Preface to *Three Plays by Brieux:* "Those who have felt earthquakes assure us that there is no terror like the terror of the earth swaying under the feet that have always depended on it as the one immovable thing in the world. That is just how the ordinary respectable man feels when some man of genius rocks the moral ground beneath him by denying the validity of a convention" (xxxv). Such moral innovators and critics, he adds, are always described as wishing "to turn the world upside down" or as "standing on their heads" (xxxvi).[40]

Barbara of course is no ordinary respectable person, but that only makes her experience of shock all the more catastrophic. She depended not merely on an "immovable" earth but on a rock she thought "eternal." The moral ground beneath her did not just rock, it "reeled and crumbled." The stroke of her father's pen removed a watchful "infinite wisdom" shielding her and a whole army with whom she was marching to salvation. The pen whose stroke can wipe out an army is certainly mightier than the sword; to empty the heavens as well it would have to carry the impact of a stroke of lightning. Nor is it at all odd or inappropriate to think of this manufacturer of modern thunderbolts as a "Lord of Thunder" (*Bacchae* 592, trans. Dodds) or master of lightning (594). Although direct references to lightning and fire are missing from Barbara's earthquake speech, it must be remembered that she is harking back to a transaction in the second act during which the imagery of bursting shrapnel and "the fire of opposing armies" emerged prominently (in Undershaft's "oceans of blood" speech), as did "Blood and Fire" and "letters of fire against the sky" with accompanying flourishes of thunder from Cusins's drum.[41] And before long Undershaft will be discussing the way to overturn a whole social system, which would be turning or heaving it "upside down."

Even apart from such intimations of thunder, lightning, and fire, however, the basic parallel with the *Bacchae*'s earthquake symbolism stands.

What Winnington-Ingram says about the miraculous events in Pentheus's palace is equally true of the circumstances that brought Barbara her earthquake shock: "the keynote of the episode is the calm and easy exercise of power on the one side, the flurry and futility on the other" (*Euripides and Dionysus,* 21). The outcome of Barbara's earthquake experience is the wreck of her moral basis—a condition she now shares with Cusins. And yet, though the stroke of her father's pen disposed of the Army and the rock of faith that sustained her, it failed to convert her. Even as she awaits in dread the prospect of a second moral shock, she still resists him "with a power equal to his own." His recent comments having paved the way, the time has now come for Undershaft to endeavor to overcome her remaining resistance by an affirmative frontal assault.

From Undershaft's initial response to Barbara's earthquake speech— "Come, come, my daughter! dont make too much of your little tinpot tragedy" (170)—through about twelve speeches thereafter, Shaw explains in a letter to Calvert, Undershaft "must go over everybody and everything" up to and past the point where Lady Britomart temporarily deflects him. His present conduct, like his managing to overwhelm Cusins in the second act, is authentically Dionysian. Full of "conviction and courage," as Shaw insists, this Niagara, this force of nature, sweeps all before him ("Shaw's Advice to the Players of *Major Barbara,*" 10). Here, then, is his climactic epiphany, a torrential display of power, illuminated with thunderbolt tenets that consummate the doctrine of Dionysos Undershaft. In the revelation and its backwash, crucial currents of the drama's meaning swirl.

Initially, Undershaft proposes a new quality standard for morality and religion based on the analogy of quality control in his armament production. No matter how great the funds already expended on it, a defective weapon is immediately scrapped; the same should be done to a morality or religion that "doesnt fit the facts": it should be replaced by one that does (170). The world does well in machinery but is failing in morals, religion, and politics because it scraps its obsolete engines while refusing to scrap its outworn prejudices, conventions, and institutions. In other words, Undershaft is again arguing that *nomos* should be based on *physis,* the true nature of things. Having shaken his daughter's former view of *physis,* he proceeds to urge its supercession: "If your old religion broke down yesterday, get a new and better one for tomorrow" (171).

Barbara, who is more than willing to embrace a better one, protests that what he offers is something worse. Vehemently she challenges him, "shew me some light through the darkness of this dreadful place, with its beautifully clean workshops, and respectable workmen, and model homes" (171). Once more we are greeted with a paradoxical reminder of the Dionysian duality and ambiguity of the Undershaftian "place." Prior to departing from Wilton Crescent, Barbara had introduced the imagery of light and darkness by visualizing Undershaft's cannon factory as a pit where sooty-faced workers stirred up smoky fires. Yet even after careful inspection has apparently vindicated her father's defense of his community, she persists in viewing it as shrouded in darkness, standing in need of light. Eventually she will find the kind of illumination she seeks, but at the moment the answer elicited by her call for light is that cleanliness and respectability justify themselves. Denying her allegation that there is darkness and dreadfulness in Perivale St. Andrews, Undershaft hurls back essentially the same charge at her Salvation shelter: it had darkness and dreadfulness in the form of poverty, misery, cold, and hunger. Dramatically reversing positions, he argues that her former sphere of operations is truly a realm of darkness, while his is a source of light. In doing so he contrasts what he has to offer with the benefits she gave in the shelter. Instead of bread and treacle and dreams of heaven, he pays good wages and looks after the drainage, leaving his men to their own devices so far as their dreams are concerned.

To this discussion the nutrition passage is a relevant and helpful guide. Undershaft exhibits the natural vitality that puts nourishment first, and definitely accords heaven—if not hell, and ideals or "dreams"—a secondary status. Barbara, characteristically, gives priority to heaven and dreams. She asks about the souls of Undershaft's people, only to receive the second earthquake shock she awaited, when Undershaft replies: "I save their souls just as I saved yours" (171). Shaw describes the effect on her of this unexpected answer with the same word used to describe Cusins's reactions twice before: she is "*revolted.*" That was how the young poet reacted in the Army shelter when the millionaire explained why it was worth his while to buy "the Church of the poor," and again at Wilton Crescent in response to Undershaft's account of how the social snobbishness of the workers brought their employer "a colossal profit." On each occasion Cusins called Undershaft "an infernal old rascal," the second time by recalling the first. Barbara casts no such chthonian epithet at her father, but instead incredulously exclaims, "Y o u saved my soul!" and wonders at his meaning.

Salvation through *Physis*

Barbara, "a savior of souls"—so styled by her father—had been successfully tempted by him from the outset to undertake the saving of his soul. Yet not only had he thwarted her every effort in that direction, but now in crowning irony he goes so far as to claim that she is the one saved and *he* the savior. This would make her a "savior saved," ringing still another change on the ironic Euripidean theme of the "hunter hunted." Saotes, "the savior," was one of the minor cult titles of Dionysos, and in the *Bacchae* the god does in fact offer to "save" Pentheus (the Greek reads *sosai*, 806), a proposal the king foolishly spurns.[42]

Undershaft's claim to savior status is fittingly based in part on nutrition: he fed, clothed, housed, and lavished money enough on his daughter to assure her an abundant life, even allowing for the luxuries of waste, carelessness, and generosity. To her bewilderment he adds, "That saved your soul from the seven deadly sins." These "sins"—which he enumerates as "food, clothing, firing [heating], rent, taxes, respectability, and children"—are millstones weighing down the human spirit; money alone can remove them and free that spirit to soar (171–72).[43] Being necessary rather than sufficient conditions of modern communal existence, the seven "sins" impose burdensome demands on all. As a deliverer from these oppressive responsibilities of life, Undershaft carries on in the tradition of Dionysos Lysios, "the Liberator" or deliverer.[44]

Undershaft here manifests himself as the Great Provider. The first act showed the whole family dependent on his provision. In the second act he claimed and demonstrated that religious institutions needed benefactions from men of wealth, such as himself, for their very survival. That he paid the piper and called the tune for government and other social institutions he made abundantly clear earlier in the final act. The current lesson drives home to Barbara her own special inclusion in this network of universal economic dependence. Already made painfully aware of her subjugation by the power of Bodger and Undershaft, Barbara now learns how far more extensive and pervasive than she had imagined is the power these industrialists wield, since it is they who control the indispensable apparatus that sustains the modern civilized world. Access to *physis*, the nature upon which *nomos* rests, must come through them. Undershaft in particular is able to supply the basic needs of nourishment, shelter, and civilized comfort without which secondary ideals are impotent. Truly a primal power, he has, like Dionysos, his bountiful as well as his baneful side.

By freeing Barbara's spirit from the seven millstones, her father continues, he saved her from the crime of poverty, the worst crime of all. Undershaft denounces poverty as the plague of cities, the moral and physical contaminator of society, the destroyer of happiness (*eudaimonia*), and the corruptor of social institutions (*nomoi*).[45] Answering at last his daughter's earlier indictment, he invites her to bring him the "half-saved" Bill, whose soul she had charged him with redirecting to perdition. By providing that errant soul with permanent employment, decent wages, and adequate housing rather than empty words and dreams, he will set the young man back on the path to salvation for her. In a foretaste of Shaw's *Pygmalion* he promises the young ruffian's transformation within a year or two into a political Conservative who "will shake hands with a duchess at a [Tory] Primrose League meeting." Bill's improvement will consist in being "better fed, better housed, better behaved; and his children will be pounds heavier and bigger" (172–73). Her father forcefully contrasts this route to salvation with that taken in Barbara's shelter, where conversion depends on the compulsion of "knee-drill"—exacting thanks to heaven in return for bread and treacle. Rather than engaging in such "cheap work" of converting with bread and Bible, which could as readily "convert West Ham to Mahometanism," he bids her to "try her hand" on his men whose "souls are hungry because their bodies are full" (173; note the use of "hand" again).

Thus Undershaft preaches the gospel of the "full-fed" man, an appropriate goal for an alimentary power. But though the beneficiaries of Undershaftianism have full-fed bodies, their souls remain undernourished. May we not reflect with Hamlet, "What is a man, / If his chief good and market of his time / Be but to sleep and feed? A beast, no more" (*Hamlet* 4.4.33–35)? Just as the emphasis in Perivale St. Andrews is on cultivation of the beast, on supplying animal necessities, so the kinship of Dionysos and his followers with animal nature, as we have learned, is a recurrent motif in the *Bacchae*. The god as a force of nature brings man and beast together, fulfilling the universal demands of animate life. Revealing the divine within elemental being, the god binds the bestial to the celestial. So does Undershaft. From him flow milk and honey miracles that feed the creaturely appetites of his people, exposing a residual spiritual void in the process. To a query such as that of Pentheus about the benefits of Bacchic rites—"What profit do they afford to the votaries?" (*Bacchae* 473, trans. Hadas and McLean)—the answer for Perivale St. Andrews is that its blessings are those extolled by the maenad chorus of the *Bacchae* in the first passage quoted by Cusins: "But who'er can know / As the long days go / That to live is happy, has found his heaven" (*Bacchae* 910–11). And these blessings result from having, as Undershaft holds at the time, "money enough for a decent life" (118). Undershaft's other requisite, "power enough to be your own master" (ibid.), his underlings obviously have not.

When arguing his case, Undershaft sets before his daughter a choice between two imperfect alternatives. On the one hand there is the Army's salvationist way, succoring underfed stomachs and warped souls, or as Barbara puts it later, "weak souls in starved bodies" (183). On the other there is Undershaftian salvationism, producing full bodies with starving souls. These people are equally unsaved, but Undershaft's way has the advantage of affording Barbara a greater opportunity for genuine salvationism, freed from debilitating and distracting preoccupation with urgent survival needs. Undershaft proves himself a savior of bodies; his claim to save souls is patently an exaggeration. What he does is liberate them from vassalage to bodily wants. At that stage they still suffer from spiritual malnutrition, standing in need of an authentic "savior of souls," Barbara's "proper name" and special calling.

Soon she will take up the challenge. Meanwhile there is more Undershaft doctrine to ponder. Her reluctance to leave the East Enders to starve, conjures up in her father bitter memories of his own life in the East End. He "moralized and starved" until the day he swore he would become "a full-fed free man at all costs" (173). Hence Undershaft, like his workers, is fully fed, emancipated from slavery to the body. And if, as he says, filled bodies bring hunger to the soul, then even this "savior" must in some measure share the soul-hunger of his beneficiaries. His vow, that nothing but a bullet would stop him, "neither reason nor morals nor the lives of other men," is strictly Dionysian in its insensibility to rationality, morality, and human life. He found that adopting the precept, "Thou shalt starve ere I starve," made him "free and great."[46]

As in the Armorer's faith, what is being professed is a radical egoism appropriate to the Hobbesian state of nature. In classical times a similar doctrine emerged in the conception of *physis*, with which Sophists such as Antiphon and Callicles interpreted human nature.[47] Amplifying his particular version of this individualistic philosophy, Undershaft relates that he was "a dangerous man" until he had his will, whereupon he became "a useful, beneficent, kindly person" (173). His own testimony thus both confirms his Dionysian polarity and shows how well he typifies Shaw's *naturally* great" man, who "in order to produce an impression of complete disinterestedness and magnanimity, . . . has only to act with entire selfishness."[48] But Shaw made no secret of his own repudiation of the selfish morality embodied in the motto "Thou shalt starve ere I starve," for he vented it on a variety of occasions. Perhaps his most forthright statement is in *Everybody's Political What's What?* where long-range thinkers and planners are said "to find out that the worst species of vermin is the human sort whose motto is 'Thou shalt starve e'er [*sic*] I starve' whilst their own is 'We must stop killing and robbing and eating one another or we shall all starve'" (133).[49]

Undershaft presents his aggressive occupational case history as typical of "most self-made millionaires," neglecting in doing so to take into account the unique adoptive circumstances that landed him at the head of his firm. But then the myth of Dionysos had its problems of credibility, which Teiresias in the *Bacchae* tries to explain away (272–325). Undershaft makes no like effort to clear up this seeming inconsistency in the details of his myth. Perhaps that is because the inconsistency is only apparent: since he undoubtedly had to meet criteria for adoption that went beyond mere unconventional birth and schooling, the ruthless determination he displayed may well have been a decisive factor in his selection and adoption as heir. That would warrant his laying claim to being a "self-made" millionaire and commending his kind of pertinacity to all Englishmen as the way to a good life (173). It was Dionysos's desire to disseminate his religion as widely as possible; Undershaft similarly promotes his own gospel, calling for its universal acceptance. Both hold out to their adherents the promise of salvation.

The Undershaft gospel that is militantly preached in the play and roundly championed (selectively) in the Preface has misled many to equate Shaw's own tenets with those of this character indiscriminately—however antinomic or incredible the result. But no more is Undershaft a mere spokesman for Shaw than is Dionysos for Euripides. Each dramatist had complex ideas to express through and about his *daimon* character. The case for the death merchant as social savior is founded on the dictates of nature, which the nutrition passage tells us must be *transcended*. So likewise, then, must the thinking of Undershaft. Confirmation of this conclusion fortunately survives from Shaw himself. In several letters to Thomas Demetrius O'Bolger, a prospective biographer, he delineates incisively how Undershaft's reasoning fits into the wider Shavian Socialist perspective, and protests against being interpreted exclusively in Undershaftian terms. On April 24, 1919, Shaw wrote:

You will have to balance my views on Money carefully. Samuel Butler was, I think, the first writer to give anything like its proper modern weight to money. In Major Barbara I have carried this further by attacking it from the other end, and demonstrating that poverty is a crime, and should no more be tolerated than highway robbery or bad sanitation. I then develop this to the point which no previous Socialist had really tackled by shewing that the central object of Socialism is the establishment of rigid equality of income and its complete dissociation from its present use as *the reward of industry in pursuing it: in short the reward of sordid rascality.* The reply to the crucial question as to what evil justifies a decent man in cutting his neighbor's throat sooner than endure it is the evil of his having a penny more to spend than any other man. All this stands together quite logically and consecutively. *Undershaft was right in resolving to have enough money at all hazards; but the others were wrong in allowing him to get a farthing ahead of them;* for inequality of purchasing power means disaster economically, politically, and biologically.[50]

The words I have italicized bring out the point that Undershaft's success is "the reward of sordid rascality"—an echo of Cusins's accusation (169)—but the criticism is really directed at those who permit him to pursue his private advantage at their expense.

During the course of a long letter to O'Bolger dated August 7, 1919, Shaw addressed himself again to the limitations of Undershaftianism:

Now that we are on the subject of wifely virtues I must tell you that your remarks on economics, Undershaft, &c, are not criticism. They are, quite simply, *nagging*: that is, you keep contradicting things I never said and complaining of idiotic positions which, if I had ever taken them, would have relegated me to obscurity. If, in dealing with Undershaft, you demonstrate that the social problem will never be solved by the Henry Fords and Leverhulmes, well and good: I shall heartily endorse your conclusion. But if you keep accusing me of trying to impose Undershaft on you as the Saviour of the world, I can only drop my inherited kindness for a moment and tell you to go to hell. In fact I think you *will* go there soon if you do not pull your faculties together.

My plays are no more economic treatises than Shakespear's plays are. Who on earth ever said they were after the first moment when the critics announced that they were not plays as all, but Fabian tracts? Economics played an important part in my education. An educated man, according to the old formula, is one who knows everything of something and something of everything. The everything of something may be Greek or mathematics. In my case it was economics, thoroughly learnt for a vital purpose, *not* for passing an examination in which I should have been plucked for giving up-to-date answers. . . .

But as to the economics and their effect on my plays. It is clear that Widowers' Houses and Major Barbara, being dramas of the cash nexus (in plot), could not have been written by a non-economist. It is also clear that Mrs Warren's Profession is the work of an economist. There is an economic link between Cashel Byron, Sartorius, Mrs. Warren & Undershaft, all of them engaged very capably in infamous activities prosperously and proudly. But would anyone but a buffle headed idiot of a university professor, half crazy with correcting examination papers (another infamous activity pursued under economic pressure) immediately shriek that all my plays were written as economic essays, and that I did not know that they were plays of life, character, and human destiny as much as Shakespear's or Euripides's?"[51]

Two months later he returned to the same topic in another letter to O'Bolger (October 9, 1919), this time without vituperation: "As to Undershaft, read the preface again. It deals with all your points. Undershaft has something to say worth listening to. So has Keegan in John Bull's Other Island. Why do you forget all about Keegan and see nothing but Undershaft-red?"[52] Worth recalling in this connection is Keegan's comparison of businessman Broadbent to an ass: "efficient in the service of Mammon, mighty in mischief, skilful in ruin, heroic in destruction" (2:1016). Socialist Shaw conceived of Undershaft as something less than savior, something less than the embodiment of ultimate answers to our social problems. A vital ingredient in Shavian dramatic and dialectical strategy, the industrialist by no means consummates it.

Just as Pentheus commands Dionysos to "stop talking" (*Bacchae* 809, trans. Grube), so Lady Britomart somewhat belatedly tries to silence her husband, ordering him to stop making speeches. Neither attempt succeeds. Undershaft, only momentarily deflated and distracted, continues in the same vein as before. Far from being put on the defensive by his wife's allegation that he owes his success solely to selfishness and un-scrupulousness, he argues in rebuttal that his opposition to poverty and starvation is a more principled position than that assumed by moralists, who construe these evils as virtues. If the unwelcome choice were forced on him he would follow the morally preferable and more courageous course of being a thief rather than a pauper, a murderer rather than a slave (173–74). Because poverty and slavery have withstood sermons and editorials for centuries, Undershaft presses his listeners to abandon at-tempts to preach at and reason with these hated crimes. The prescribed alternative is the use of his machine guns to "kill" them. When Bar-bara wants to know whether killing is his remedy for everything, he replies, "It is the final test of conviction, the only lever strong enough to overturn a social system, the only way of saying Must" (174). The same thought of applying a lever in order to turn something "upside down" (*ano kato* again) appears in the *Bacchae* when Pentheus issues orders for the destruction of Teiresias's seat of augury: "lever it up and overturn it" (*Bacchae* 348–49, trans. Winnington-Ingram).[53] Subsequent references to using a lever, *mochlos* (*Bacchae* 949, 1104), and overturning (602, 741, 753) are more immediately connected with Dionysos.

"Killing" poverty and slavery must mean taking action to destroy or eliminate them instead of writing or talking about them. But killing as a test of conviction and as the means of overthrowing a social system suggest a more direct and less figurative sense of the word. Undershaft is proposing the destructive use of force to accomplish change, put-ting special stress on its necessitous character, as saying "Must." Force is being invoked as a corrective to human misuse of the generous vital powers of nature, much as the denial of surging Dionysian life-currents causes them to erupt counteractively in deadly rampage and destruction. "When that has happened," as Dodds observes, "it is too late to reason or to plead: in man's justice there is room for pity, but there is none in the justice of Nature; to our 'Ought' its sufficient reply is the simple 'Must'" (*Bacchae*, xlv). Undershaft's machine guns may not be raw forces of nature, but they mobilize physical forces at their deadliest and propel them at human targets with equivalent irrationality, inexorability, and indiscriminacy.

The political exercise of force is, in Undershaft's view, the natural basis of all government. What differentiates a parliament from a gathering of fools is the ability and readiness to exert death-dealing power. His description of the process by which such fools are transformed into a governing body—"huddle them together in a certain house in Westminster; and let them go through certain ceremonies and call themselves certain names until at last they get the courage to kill" (174)—sounds a good deal like the ritual behavior of possessed Bacchants. Dionysos asks Pentheus about the maenads, "Would you like to see them as they sit / Huddled together on the mountain side?" (*Bacchae* 811, trans. Curry). The word *synkathemenas,* generally translated as "huddled together" or "seated together," Sutherland notes, "plainly means 'in conclave' or 'in session together'" (*Bacchae of Euripides,* 110). Not long afterward the vindictive choral devotees of Dionysos repeat once more a furious ode in which they piously invoke the retaliatory forces of nature to punish their humbled foe: "Let Justice come, manifest and sword in hand, stabbing through the throat and killing the godless, the lawless, the unjust man" (*Bacchae* 991–95; 1011–16, trans. Winnington-Ingram). They are summoning up the courage to kill, though the deed itself is left to their counterparts on the mountain—not unlike the practice of parliaments that implement their death-dealing decisions vicariously.

Pursuing his theme of force, Undershaft insists that even democratic governance rests on the bullet, not the ballot. Voting only changes the cabinet names. Force, in other words, is an unfailing instrument of historical necessity: "When you shoot, you pull down governments, inaugurate new epochs, abolish old orders and set up new" (174). Cusins, now addressed as "Mr Learned Man," is asked to confirm or deny the truth of this reading of history. The scholar, invited back into the fray after taking vigorous moral exception to the allegation, grudgingly concedes its truth, yet protests that it ought not to be so. Indignantly repeating "ought" five times, Undershaft, true to the cause of nature, calls upon Cusins to quit spending his life vainly saying ought, like all the other moralists. "Turn your oughts into shalls, man. Come and make explosives with me. Whatever can blow men up can blow society up. The history of the world is the history of those who had courage enough to embrace this truth" (175). He concludes by inquiring of Barbara whether she has the courage to embrace it, in this manner involving both his young adversaries in the challenge.

The fulminatory visions his speech evokes represent a further development of the *ano kato,* or violent upheaval motif. They also suggest that Rosenmeyer's aperçu is as apposite to *Major Barbara* as to the *Bacchae*: "it is a portrayal of life exploding beyond its narrow confines, of reality bursting into the artificiality of social conventions and genteel restrictions" (*Masks of Tragedy,* 134). Still, what dominates this passage is the conflict between factual truth and morality, between what is and what ought to be. The apologist of power repudiates oughtness because, as Dodds says of Dionysos, "for such gods as these the human 'ought' has no meaning" (*Bacchae,* 238). The conflict is epitomized in the ensuing brief exchange between Undershaft and his wife. Criticizing Adolphus for "saying that wrong things are true," Lady Britomart asks, "What does it matter whether they are true if they are wrong?" To which Undershaft retorts, "What does it matter if they are wrong if they are true?" (175). As usual, the millionaire brushes aside the moral alternative and cleaves to the ontological one.

The exhortation to courage and the emphasis on its vital role are fitting from one named Andrew—derived from *andreia,* the Greek word for courage.[54] Despite his repudiation of reason, morals, and human life as effective deterrents to his conduct, he does offer a partial moral warrant for his broadside at poverty and slavery, and ends up calling for a morality of courage in support of forceful action. Yet through it all his ethical position remains at bottom an affirmation of natural virtue—a claim of right to the nutritional gifts of nature and an incitement to free, undaunted doing and daring. To preserve these vellums, indeed, it may be necessary to rob, even to murder. Hence in this ultimate appeal to what T. H. Huxley called "tiger rights" and with it his aversion to all moral protestation, Undershaft shows himself a wholehearted exponent of nature.[55] In effect, then, Lady Britomart and her husband stand at opposite extremes, each holding to an exclusive, one-sided position: an unrealistic morality versus an unmoral realism. But if morality without realism is likely to be misguided and vain, realism without morality is bound to be violent and destructive.[56] In the end, the task of reconciling the competing claims of brute power and morality will devolve on Barbara and Cusins; they give voice to what they derive from this discussion later in the third act.

Undershaft's Machiavellian analysis of government in terms of power to kill enlarges on what he had previously said to Stephen on this subject. It is Undershaft who really governs the country because he commands not only the undergirding economic power, as he has already made clear, but also the power of weaponry the country's nominal rulers need in order to reign. As for his advocacy of force and violence, though evangelical in tone, it is empirical in content and intention. His bold declarations on the efficacy of force are advanced as stern lessons from experience and unvarnished inferences from history: killing tests conviction; there is no other method of coercion, no other mechanism capable of overturning a social system; government rests on the courage to use bullets; historically it is true that shooting removes governments, annihilates the old and brings forth the new; explosives that can blow men up can do the same to society.

Were Undershaft himself eager to overturn the social system, launch a revolution, blow up society, inaugurate a new era, he would have the requisite ordnance by his own admission. He could, then, do what he says has to be done. On the other hand, it is consonant with his favored position in the social order, and the privileges it confers on him, that he eschew such action. In fact, it would be suicidal for him to agitate successfully for revolution. Yet his impassioned arguments about the vulnerability of social institutions (*nomoi*) to attack from the weapons he manufactures are flung defiantly at his moral opponents. What he is doing is daring them to make good on *their* moral claims. If *they* wish to change the world, he has the most effective means: theirs are ineffective. But the moral mission is theirs, not his. It can hardly be otherwise since he himself is an obvious target for the kinds of attack he describes.

Yet castigating sinners is not the way for Barbara and Cusins to accomplish their mission. How to deal with wickedness is the burden of the next segment of the play. Lady Britomart forbids Barbara to heed Undershaft's "abominable wickedness" now that she has found him "wickeder than ever" (175), but her remonstrations are to no avail. Barbara is not alone in declining to go along with her mother's moralistic demands: both Sarah and Charles Lomax side with her. Particularly instructive are the respective reasons offered by the two sisters; Sarah's are expanded into a general principle by her young man. Reversing the order in which they are put forth, Sarah refuses to cut her father for making cannons, very wicked though that may be. Lomax's disinclination to support any wrongdoing is mitigated by the recognition of how much dubious conduct goes on in the world. He would have them "look at facts," explaining this to mean "you cant go cutting everybody," thus "there is a certain amount of tosh about this notion of wickedness" (175–76). His counsel, on a different tack, converges with Barbara's. There is "no use" in running away from wicked people, she tells her mother. According to Lomax, "it doesnt work"; according to Barbara, "It does not save them" (175). Lomax is conciliatory toward sinners; Barbara wants to reform them. These simple words of hers could all too easily escape our notice, yet they betoken the revival of her original intention to *save* her father, the focal object of all these reflections about wickedness.

Shaw's comment in a letter to Gilbert Murray that "the moral is drawn by Lomax" in this "tosh" sentence should be taken with a grain of salt ("'In More Ways Than One,'" 128): it bears the earmarks more of a Shavian polemical sally than a revelation of dramatic intent. More helpful guidance is afforded by an observation about Lomax that the same line elicited from Shaw many years later: "The point is that though he is a foolish figure he always says something sensible."[57] (This time the "always" needs to be scanned.) What Lomax is saying here does contain more than a kernel of truth: the handling of wickedness is an important theme in the drama, and "it doesn't work" is certainly a pertinent judgment on the moralistic stance. But Charles freely acknowledges that his own complaisance toward Undershaft is dictated by his and Sarah's selfish interests, when Lady Britomart levels that charge at him. He cites Matthew 24:28—"For wheresoever the carcass is, there will the eagles be gathered together"—a moral that draws once more upon the animal world of nature (176).

Unsurprisingly, Undershaft immediately warms to Lomax, whom he now wants to address by his first name. But when he goes on to call his wife "Biddy," the colloquial name for a chicken or hen (a domestic creature this time), as he had done back at Wilton Crescent, she rebukes him with far greater vehemence than before—but with no more success (176).[58] The motif of name and identity comes into play once more as the morally indignant Lady Britomart, "like Jove hurling thunderbolts," assails with denunciatory epithets each of the company in turn, with Sarah alone escaping the general censure.[59] Not to be overlooked in this display of divine wrath is the identification of Barbara as "lunatic," reviving the madness theme as well. Undershaft rounds out his wife's critical catalogue of characters by returning the compliment: in dutifully clearing her conscience by name-calling she shows herself to be "the incarnation of morality" (176). More accurately, we should say, the incarnation of *conventional* morality and, as such, understandably at odds with a spouse who incarnates amorality.

4

The Drama of Transfiguration

The turning point in the *Bacchae* comes when Pentheus, on the verge of marching against the maenads, calls for his armor (809). Dionysos diverts him from this course of action by proposing instead a surreptitious visit to their mountain haunts. Weakening to the influence of the god, the king nevertheless wants to deliberate on his decision; he retires to his palace with the announcement that "either I will march out under arms or I will take your counsel" (843–45, trans. Winnington-Ingram). The construction of the Greek itself reflects the division in his mind, Winnington-Ingram observes; "the decision is not yet made, his will is still free," helping to sustain the dramatic suspense (104–5).[1] The decision on which *Major Barbara*'s plot pivots, by comparison, is aimed at other issues, and Cusins, who must make that decision, has a freer choice based on a far clearer understanding of the pitfalls before him. "Come Euripides!" Undershaft beckons him—as avatar of the *Bacchae*'s author—to make up his mind and delay no longer (176). To the "old demon" Cusins sets forth his "horrible dilemma" in the form of two ostensibly conflicting desires: first, to gain Barbara, and second, to keep from becoming a rascal (177). His predicament, more implied than stated, merits analysis.

Each of Cusins's desires, be it noted, articulates his basic motives and in itself poses no dilemma. Through the first desire, wanting Barbara, he remains in the grip of *eros* and *pothos,* love and desire (or longing).[2] The second desire takes us back to Cusins's allegation that the Undershaft establishment is "driven by the most rascally part of society." His conviction that armament-making is an unsavory business, inescapably implicating its owner in rascality, obviously has not yielded to Undershaft's expostulations. Still, there is no inherent incompatibility between winning Barbara and avoiding rascality; the complicating factor unquestionably is his attitude toward the succession. We can rule out the bare possibility that he thinks it necessary to become a rascal (by agreeing to succeed her father) in order to win Barbara, because, among other odd consequences, that would make nonsensical his subsequent surprise at Barbara's favorable reaction to that decision. Rather he must think that inheriting the firm would cost him Barbara's favor and love—and turn him into a rascal to boot. Thus, one of the horns of his dilemma must be the prospect of accepting the succession, and in doing so both lose Barbara and become a rascally Undershaft. The other horn would be the necessity of refusing her father's offer in order to win Barbara and preserve his moral integrity.

For this to be a genuine dilemma *both* alternatives have to be undesirable. That can be the case only if Cusins very much *desires* to succeed to the position, something he has hitherto failed to admit openly. Yet there were earlier signs of his being strongly inclined in that direction: in his claim of eligibility, in his bargaining over salary, in the prediction that he would write a motto on the wall, in the avowed feeling of being singled out by destiny, as well as in the Undershaftian warning, "Dont come here lusting for power, young man" (169). Now his susceptibility to the temptation is virtually conceded. Accordingly, the dilemma implies Adolphus's assumption that Barbara is firmly opposed to his acceptance of the Undershaft inheritance.

In fact his quandary is even deeper; for notwithstanding his suspicions, he really has no way of knowing which alternative will gain her favor and which will alienate her. Hence his "horrible dilemma" consists in having to choose between the risks to his conscience in taking over the firm and the exceptional loss of opportunity that turning down the new position would entail. Furthermore, if he makes the wrong decision—whichever one that turns out to be—he will *in addition* lose Barbara. That she is his major objective, taking precedence even over the conscience that now troubles him, he divulged earlier in the act: "Until I met Barbara . . . I wanted the approval of my conscience more than I wanted anything else. But the moment I saw Barbara, I wanted her far more than the approval of my conscience" (163). The stakes are high, his fate and future riding in the balance. Meanwhile the whole issue still hinges on the moral question—on the "abyss of moral horror" yawning between him and the Undershaft works. Early in the play Lady Britomart took the stand that "nothing can bridge over moral disagreement" (76), yet in the end it is incumbent on Cusins to find such a bridge and cross it.

Traversing the Abyss

At the beginning of the third act Cusins had reported to the family that, after the Salvation meeting, Undershaft "only sat there and completed the wreck of my moral basis, the rout of my convictions, the purchase of my soul" (142). His report must have overstated what happened then, for this is exactly what the daemonic industrialist now sets about doing. As the nutrition passage might lead us to expect, he proceeds to deflate Adolphus's commitments to secondary ideals, including the "gospel of love." "The artist . . . as poet," Shaw avers in a portion of the nutrition passage not hitherto quoted, "cannot see, as the prosaic man does, that chivalry is at bottom only romantic suicide" (2:504). The prosaic Undershaft seems to subscribe to that opinion, judging by his derogation of the devotees of Aphrodite. The poet's desire for Barbara he dismisses as a young man's magnification of the difference between one young female and another. Even more contemptuously he interprets the desire to avoid rascality as "lust" for personal righteousness and self-approval; for to his way of thinking what Cusins takes to be "a good conscience" and Barbara "salvation" amount to patronizing those less fortunate than oneself (177). The inclusion of Barbara's "salvation" endeavors in his censure would seem to indicate that Undershaft is not merely slating self-righteous moralizing, but more altruistic moral pursuits as well, deeming moral activity in general to be rooted in condescension and conceit. The denunciation of morality is sweeping.

Cusins denies the validity of the imputation, just as he had denied earlier that he was "lusting" for power. The poetic aspect of his nature, he says, balks at being a good man. If "a good man" is a fair translation of the sort of person Undershaft has just denounced, his earlier assertion that under the terms of the Armorer's faith he would "take an order from a good man as cheerfully as from a bad one" (169) acquires a somewhat altered coloration. Undershaft had been quite caustic at the time about the "preaching and shirking" of "you good people." His present blanket condemnation of the morally good suggests the denial of any appreciable value distinction between "a good man" and "a bad one." So viewed, the armorer's amorality becomes all the more comprehensive and Dionysian.

But loath as Cusins is to be identified as a good man, he has other feelings not so readily dismissed: pity and love. Undershaft pulverizes pity with a phrase: "The scavenger of misery" (177). Shaw offered his own commentary on this line in 1909: "I do not disapprove of scavengers any more than I disapprove of dentists. But scavenging is only a remedy for dirt, just as dentistry is only a remedy for decaying teeth. He who aims at a clean world and sound jaws aims at the extinction of the scavenger and the dentist."[3] Still, such extinction of the remedy must be a consequence or by-product of the eradication of the evil it palliates. Pending the elimination of misery from the world, pity, by Shaw's own argument, has the merit of a remedy, and as such merits something more than unqualified disapproval. The extirpation of misery from the world, moreover, would appear to require the mastery of natural as well as human resources. Contemplating action on such a scale, Undershaft assumes superhuman dimensions yet again, and like the god in the *Bacchae*, places himself well beyond the reach of human pity. But in the spirit of Cadmus's reproach that, though just, Dionysos has been too harsh and merciless (*Bacchae* 1249, 1346), it is permissible to conclude that Undershaft's criticism, while morally unexceptionable, is likewise unduly severe and uncompromising toward human imperfection.

Having disposed of love as *eros* and *pothos*—especially in the moral formulation as lust for self-aggrandizing righteousness—Undershaft goes after the cooler form of love, *philia*, affection or fondness, and the related *philanthropia*, love of humanity, benevolence.[4] Though handled with a lighter touch, it fares no better than pity at his hands. Putting to the test Cusins's love for the downtrodden, needy, and outcast everywhere, Undershaft trips him up on the question of love for the English. The determinant for the young scholar is again ethical: the English are wicked, their success "a moral horror." When he in turn asks whether even love for his "father-in-law" is proscribed, the proffer of affection is repudiated as an impertinence: "I will have your due heed and respect, or I will kill you. But your love!" The alternatives of heed and respect or death are the fateful ones Dionysos exacts, as the Bacchant chorus avouches: "Slow but unmistakable the might of the gods moves on. / It punishes that man, infatuate of soul . . . who disregards the gods"

(882–87, trans. Arrowsmith). The imperative in each case is a respectful attitude toward necessitous power. "The powers which govern human life cannot be denied but they may be hated," Winnington-Ingram reminds us; in any event they need not be loved.[5]

But *philia* is not entirely ruled out by Undershaft. His answer to Barbara's query whether there is anyone he loves is, "I love my best friend" (178) who, it turns out, is his "bravest enemy," the one who keeps him up to the mark. Rigorous as it is, the criterion is still compatible with a quantum of affection for Barbara and Cusins (and even Lady Britomart) as dauntless moral opponents despite their inability to qualify as full-fledged enemies. A possible source for this self-imposed Undershaft standard is an old political precept Shaw quoted with approval in 1917: "Treat your friend as one who may someday be your enemy, and your enemy as one who may someday be your friend."[6] It yields yet another instance in which the perspective of the daemonic industrialist conjoins polarities. Pointing to the failures of pity and love, which like weak swords have broken in the hand of his adversary (whom he has just described as "fencing"), Undershaft suggests forgiveness as a "last weapon" (178), thus advancing the verbal agon with apt support from the hand-and-weapon image of the Armorer's faith. But Cusins rejects forgiveness as the refuge of a beggar, agreeing with his challenger that their debts must be paid. So at last they are met on common ground, securing a footing for the next uncertain steps across the intervening abyss.

The *Bacchae* chorus warns of the craftiness of the divinities: "The gods are cunning: they lie in wait a long march of time to trap the impious" (*Bacchae* 888–90, trans. Hadas and McLean). So Undershaft's subtle paraphrase of Plato—that there is no possibility of saving society until professors of Greek undertake the making of gunpowder, or makers of gunpowder become professors of Greek (178)—lays a philosophical snare for Cusins's soul. The latter's exclamation, "Oh, tempter, cunning tempter!" carries an echo of his earlier retort—"Oh, clever clever devil!" prompted by the ease with which Barbara's father revived her flagging faith at Wilton Crescent. The same cleverness (*to sophon*) is now aimed at himself, enticing him with an inspired Platonic Hellenism. The maneuver could afford sufficient ground for Undershaft to reply, with Dionysos, "Where most I need it, there I am most clever" (*Bacchae* 656, trans. Winnington-Ingram). Yet not to be obscured by all his shrewdness is the tacit admission that the gunpowder maker is unable to save society by himself.

This Platonic paradox in *Major Barbara* builds on the extended Undershaft-Cusins dialogue in the second act, where the question of relating wisdom and power was first raised. It also draws upon the professor of Greek's claim of scholarly "access to the subtlest thought . . . yet attained by humanity" (166). What he lacks is power, symbolized by the gunpowder he is now being tempted to make. His second quotation from the *Bacchae* had identified wisdom with the strength to be found in "the spirit of God—whate'er it be—," the *physis* imparting permanence to *nomos*. Now the armorer, the repository of the forces of *physis*, abetted by "the subtlest thought" of Plato, proposes a union of his power with the *sophia* of the professor of Greek. As Arrowsmith notes, *sophia* is "nearly synonymous with 'civilization,'" or with culture. Understood in this larger sense it includes "that ideal Athenian fusion of moral and artistic skills which, fostered by *eros*, creates the distinctive *arete* [virtue, excellence] of the civilized polis" (*Greek Theater of Ideas*, 27, compare 34). Undershaft holds out no real hope for the social order unless these cultural skills can gain control of the natural energy generated and mobilized in his factory. His thesis is the inverse of the one in the nutrition passage, that "there is no future for men, however brimming with crude vitality, who are neither intelligent nor politically educated enough to be Socialists." According to Undershaft, instead of love, pity, and forgiveness, the values most needed for the improvement of human society are power (*dynamis*) and wisdom (*sophia*).

Our analysis has shown that both *Major Barbara* and the *Bacchae* explore the deep-seated conflict between *nomos* and *physis*, dramatizing the vital need for its resolution. In *Major Barbara*, however, Undershaft represents economic and political power as well as the forces of physical nature symbolized by Dionysos in the Euripidean drama. The two works also challenge claims and claimants to true *sophia*, wisdom. But neither is Cusins self-ignorant (*amathes*) nor Barbara repressively moralistic as Pentheus is. Moreover, Shaw's play works toward reconciliation rather than catastrophic tragedy. Nonetheless each tracks contrapuntally the critical consequences of the undercurrent conflict Arrowsmith finds in Euripides: "a carefully construed clash between myth (or received reality) on the one hand, and fact (or experienced reality) on the other. *Logôi men . . . ergôi de*, as the Greeks put it, contrasting theory (*logos*) and fact (*ergon*), appearance (or pretence) and reality, legend and truth."[7]

Under pressure to come to a decision, yet "desperately perplexed" when Barbara confirms his fear that she may not marry him if he makes the wrong choice, Cusins raises one final objection: he is being driven against his nature, for he hates war. Undershaft has another gnomic utterance ready: "Hatred is the coward's revenge for being intimidated" (178). While failing to recognize that this diagnosis is just as applicable to his own hatred of poverty and slavery, he does prescribe the same remedy for war as for those other social ills. For the "killing" of poverty and slavery he had proposed the use of his machine guns; now he dares Adolphus to "make war on war" (178), suggesting as means the bombshell on which Lomax is sitting.

The bombshell corresponds to a set of images that Rosenmeyer detects in the *Bacchae*: "the container filled to the bursting point," compressing a force that eventually explodes; "Dionysus disrupts the settled life, he cracks the shell of civic contentment and isolation" (*Masks of Tragedy*, 139–40). So does Undershaft. Explosion imagery, with its "overturning" (*ano kato*) correlate, permeates *Major Barbara*. At Perivale St. Andrews the outburst of infinite force from its finite container is an ever-present peril, threatening *sparagmos* to everyone and everything. The bombshell concretizes the threat and, like the machine guns, symbolizes unlimited destructive power. Yet how it can be brought to bear against war itself is left provocatively unexplained. What Shaw may have had in mind is suggested by two lines that are cancelled in the original Derry manuscript: to Cusins's protestation of hatred for war, Undershaft had first replied, "Then come and help to perfect the means by which those who hate war can destroy those who love it." After his dare, and the indication of the means, he then added, "England, America and one European Power could stop war forever with those means if they wanted to."[8] Making war on war would thus entail the exercise of superior destructive force against those who would start or engage in wars.

But, as argued earlier, cancelled lines are imperfect guides to interpretation since they disclose no more than possibilities tentatively entertained by the author. Their evidential value is more than offset by the fact that the writer decided to abandon them, and probably did so because they failed to express his artistic intent satisfactorily. I suspect that in this instance Shaw concluded that, irrespective of his own views on the subject, it was better to leave open and unspecified in the play the mode of waging war on war. The idea is nonetheless one that Shaw reiterated over a span of years. For example, in 1899 he wrote to Arthur Conan Doyle, "what I *do* believe in is a combination of the leading powers to police the world and put down international war just as private war is put down," and in 1907 to Felix Moscheles, "I believe in making war on war—policing the world by a terrific international armament which shall destroy any national armament which attempts to begin fighting." In *What I Really Wrote About the War*, Shaw recollected the pre–World War I disparity between the disarmament and pacifist commitments of his Socialist and Labor confreres, on the one hand, and his own advocacy of "additional armament for threatening war on war," on the other.[9]

Cusins makes no immediate reply to Undershaft's dare, as Lomax and Sarah weigh the consequences of being seated on the live shell. Undershaft attempts to settle matters by attempting to persuade his presumptive successor to agree to arrive for work at six the following morning, but Cusins "firmly" refuses to arise at five, holding out for his own "healthy, rational" hours of eleven to five. Content that the position would make its own inroads on the fledgling executive's time, the confident host arranges to take the others away through the guncotton shed, leaving Adolphus and Barbara to themselves, free to take their bearings and contemplate their altered prospects. On a grander scale they confront the problem neatly epitomized in the stationing of the other young couple on the loaded bombshell. Indeed, the whole *exodos* is marked by successive reminders of the volcanic nature of the place. The unexploded shell does not frighten Sarah, who, if she is to be blown up, prefers it to be done thoroughly. Cusins would have the whole establishment blown to pieces by its own dynamite rather than rise at five o'clock. Bilton bars the entrance, refusing to allow anything explosive in the shed. This turns out to be, not the volatile Lady Brit, as she presumes, but Lomax's matches in Undershaft's pocket. And Sarah is notified that it is necessary to wear list slippers in the shed for protection. The dramatic undercurrent of danger swelling beneath the comic surface of this scene accents the daring inherent in Cusins's decision.

The departure of the family culminates in a brief exchange between the successful and unsuccessful candidates for the Undershaft inheritance. Stephen offers friendly counsel to his prospective brother-in-law (greeted for the first time as "Dolly, old fellow") advising him, before he decides, to consider whether he is practical enough to assume the responsibilities of such a "huge undertaking" (180).[10] Stephen thinks that the business will be Greek to Cusins, but the professor replies it will be "much less difficult than Greek," reminding us that what may be "Greek" to others will not be so to him. (Once more "Greek" represents cultural distinction.) But Stephen's main object is to put his moral imprimatur on the whole succession transaction and its two principals. With a new-found filial pride welling up in him, he bestows a fervid blessing on his father's industrial enterprise, esteeming it "of the highest character and a credit to our country" (180). No qualm of conscience stirs any longer; he stands in awe, sympathetically attuned to the vastness of the business. Well might Undershaft address to him, with equivalent irony, the words of Dionysos to Pentheus after the king has experienced his "change of heart": "Your mind was once unsound, but now you think as sane men do" (*Bacchae* 994, 947–48, trans. Arrowsmith). The most complete convert in the play, Stephen makes his final exit zealously trailing after the joyful *thiasos* of his father, in striking contrast to his behavior at the end of the first act, His enthusiasm typifies the condition of the departing members of the family (including Lomax), now entirely caught up in the orbit of the powerful paterfamilias, as "possessed" as Pentheus when he tells the Greek god," I am in your hands completely" (*Bacchae* 934, trans. Arrowsmith). The only uncertain converts are the two left behind, Barbara and Cusins, who have yet to reveal their ultimate verdicts on Undershaftian Dionysianism. (How ironic that some critics have viewed the two of them as the only converts, ignoring what has happened to the others.)

"Like an irresistible current that overwhelms a swimmer or like the mysterious helplessness that frustrates the dreamer, the magic power emanating from the neighbourhood of the god took complete possession of the worshipper and drove him whither it willed. Everything in the world was transformed for him; he himself was altered. Every character in the play falls under the spell as soon as he enters into the magic circle" (*Psyche*, 286). Rohde's vivid description of the impact of Dionysos in the *Bacchae* is applicable, mutatis mutandis, to Undershaft and his nonworshippers. But Rohde neglects to mention that at the end of the *Bacchae* Agave and Cadmus are thoroughly disenchanted. The terminal balance of forces is different in *Major Barbara;* the outcome is closer to the eventual response of Greece to the coming of Dionysos and his cult, the legend of which the *Bacchae* celebrates. In the Greek world Dionysianism was Hellenized, modified, and reconciled with the more Olympian Greek mentality, a development also presaged in Euripides's tragedy (306–9).[11]

Power and Wisdom

Before proceeding further it will be useful to recapitulate the course of Cusins's agon with Undershaft about the succession. Throughout, we should observe, the young man retained not only his wits but his *sophrosyne*, his self-control. There was no further succumbing to the kind of "possession" that seized him in the second act, nor to the subtler kind that snared Stephen at Perivale St. Andrews. Winning out in the skirmish over salary, Cusins took a firm and unyielding stand in the matter of his working hours. Although he did not fare as well in this moral "tug of war," his losses consisted for the most part in conceding cogent points.

On the other hand, the initiative lay throughout with Undershaft, who overwhelmed the defenses of his young challenger in the moral struggle. Yet the ironic consequence was not defeat or death—the fate of Pentheus in his conflict with the god—but Cusins's triumphant designation to supersede the armorer and reap his Dionysian power and influence. In becoming the new Andrew Undershaft, he is expected to incorporate in that novel identity all that the professor of Greek brings to the making of gunpowder. Hence his convictions at the end of the play are of critical moment, pointing as they do to the kind of amalgam to be expected from the merger of Undershaftianism with the thought and ideals of Adolphus Cusins. Heightening their significance is the fact that it was Undershaft who sought to win him over, rather than the other way around. In the final analysis the decision was his alone to make, as he tells Barbara at the beginning of their final dialogue. Before uttering a word, he and Barbara "look at one another silently" (180). Once more we are greeted with a Bacchic silence, broken at last by Cusins's announcement that he is accepting Undershaft's offer.

All in all Cusins is a much more complex and compelling figure than has generally been recognized. That he was conceived with strengths other than the surface variety is clear from the play's introductory character sketch, which depicts him as uniting and controlling (with *sophrosyne*) radically conflicting impulses. Combining a subtle sense of humor with an "*appalling temper*," a "*high conscience*" with "*fierce impatience*," he is truly "*a most implacable, determined, tenacious, intolerant person who by mere force of character presents himself as—and indeed actually is—considerate, gentle, explanatory, even mild and apologetic, capable possibly of murder, but not of cruelty and coarseness*" (79–80).

Shaw explained to Murray that he wanted Cusins "to go on his quality wholly" rather than on any "show of physical robustness or brute determination," and expected him to puzzle believers in strong, silent melodramatic heroes.[12]

Unfortunately Cusins has puzzled many others as well, and has suffered a long-standing underestimation even on the part of otherwise perceptive critics. To Maurice Valency, for example, he appears to be "a young man deeply concerned with matters that have nothing to do with the play" and "mysteriously aloof from the action," while Charles Berst questions his intellectual and philosophical credentials, turning back to G. K. Chesterton for support. But such conclusions are bound to be superseded through a better purchase on the way the professor's "quality" is realized in the play and a richer understanding of the dynamics and nuances of the role, especially in the second act. Not only does he meet Undershaft's demanding standards for "a strong man" (146), but he establishes himself as a more than worthy successor with a subtle mind and indomitable spirit of his own.[13]

Initially Cusin's decision is open to interpretation as conversion, capitulation, or accommodation; Barbara calls it the sale of his soul (180). In his earlier confession, it will be recalled, he had described his joining the Army (to worship Barbara) as her purchase of his soul "like a flower at a street corner" (164). Not wanting him to sell his soul (again) for her, nor wanting him to sell it for the inheritance, she had disassociated herself from the bargaining process. But Cusins is no longer troubled by the selling of his soul, having done so, he says, many times before: for a professorship, for an income, and in allowing himself to be coerced into paying taxes for executions and unjust wars. Like everyone else, regularly and repeatedly he has compromised his moral integrity for trifles; now he is doing it neither for money (*nota bene*), nor position, nor comfort, but "for reality and for power" (181).[14]

From this speech it is evident that Cusins regards his acceptance of the inheritance as a moral compromise. As such it amounts to something less than conversion to Undershaft's amoral philosophy. Furthermore, his moral concessions are not dictated by motives of personal gain. Of Undershaft's "money and gunpowder" religion he is adopting *only* the gunpowder half. Plainly the moneyed capitalist side of Undershaftianism holds less attraction for him. His new access to reality entails an abandonment of appearance and pretense and a penetration beneath surface societal arrangements to the ineluctable necessities of nature. In *Major Barbara*, as in the *Bacchae*, the underlying forces are Dionysian, and the crying need is to recognize and take them into full and respectful account. Transcending the limitations of the artistic man of the nutrition passage in his random pursuit of secondary ideals, Cusins is prepared at last to devote his attention to primary determinants as well.

Paired with reality is the objective of power, easing us into the play's climactic elaboration of this pervasive and fundamental theme, along with that of its inevitable correlate: wisdom. Barbara's admonition that the power will no more be his own than is her father's (181), brings home to him his own insistent point; his concurrence shows him still convinced of its truth. But then the power is not being courted for private advantage; rather he wants it "for the world." Barbara seconds this desire, provided that the power is spiritual. Refusing to dichotomize it in this manner, he argues that power is always spiritual: cannons do not fire themselves. Indeed, power is a manifestation of will—an idea intimated in his prior boast to Undershaft: "I have more power than you, more will" (169). His professional endeavors to create spiritual power by teaching the dead language and civilization of Greece, Cusins realizes, have made no appreciable impact on the world. It is the people beyond the reach of Greek who need power, and the power generated in Perivale St. Andrews is the kind that every man can wield. In other words, its power is less subtle, more elemental and universal, hence more accessible and efficacious.

Cusins here bridges the ancient Greek world and the modern in his own life, a palpable reminder of how chronic and enduring is the problem of harmonizing power and civilization. In making the transition from cultural power to a force within the democratic reach of all, he is moving in a Dionysian direction. Barbara's response accents this Bacchic strain. It is *sparagmos* that lingers in her mind, planted there by her father's "oceans of blood" speech: "Power to burn women's houses down and kill their sons and tear their husbands to pieces" (181). Her visions are of Undershaft's sort of "blood and fire" in action, making manifold versions of Agave's sort of dire loss.

In his next two speeches Cusins sets forth his final conclusions, indicating the nature of the compromise he has made, how much of Undershaftian doctrine he will make his own, wherein his distinctive brand of Undershaftianism is likely to vary from that of his predecessors, and the new identity he is on his way to acquiring. His immediate rejoinder to Barbara enlarges on his new conception of power. Restating in his own terms Undershaft's Dionysian argument that force may be put to good or bad uses, he carries it a step further: power for evil is an inevitable concomitant of power for good. The lesson is given further Dionysian emphasis: mother's milk—one of the gifts of liquid nature from the god—provides nourishment to murderers and heroes alike. (That Cusins should begin to pay some attention to nourishment is also significant from the standpoint of the nutrition passage.) But mother's milk sustains life, while the power the Undershaft factory produces destroys it, a distinction Barbara has just drawn. To answer this objection her suitor turns to a comparative appraisal of the ways in which power has been abused.

There has been less abuse of the power that wreaks bodily *sparagmos,* he declares, than of "the intellectual power, the imaginative power, the poetic, religious power that can enslave men's souls." That is to say, greater harm has resulted from corrupt spiritual forces than from physical devastation. Perhaps implied besides is the just expressed thought that cannons can do their damage only when activated by an animate being. The fault lies not with *physis*, but with human *sophia,* the artistic and cultural skills we have misdirected. These too are gifts capable of being put to beneficent or harmful use; their misuse wounds our souls, the misuse of natural forces only our bodies. Whereas Undershaft laid great stress on bodily ills and health, his chosen successor continues to concern himself chiefly with the pathology and well-being of the soul.

Cusins interprets his teaching of Greek as a way of arming the intellectual man against the common man. What he seeks is to arm the common man against the tyranny and disaster wrought by intellectuals in positions of authority: lawyers, doctors, priests, literary men, professors, artists, and politicians. His opposition to the arrogance of professional people allies him again with the *Bacchae* chorus, to whom "the world's Wise are not wise" (395, trans. Murray; "cleverness is not wisdom," trans. Dodds), and their distrust of "superior persons" (*perissoi photes*) yields a different perspective on *sophia*: "Wisdom is it to keep the mind and heart aloof from men of excess" (427–29, trans. Winnington-Ingram; "men of power and ambition," trans. Lattimore). The parallel with the chorus extends to his enduring feelings of affinity with the common man—feelings unshaken in spite of all the strictures of Undershaft. "The life that wins the poor man's common voice, / His creed, his practice—this shall be my choice," sing the *Bacchae's* maenads (430–33, trans. Vellacott). "I love the common people," says Cusins in a reprise of the sentiment he had expressed in the Salvation shelter. The constancy of this love registers a dismissal of Undershaft's second-act instruction: "We three must stand together above the common people" (121).

Though Undershaft did desire to help the children of the common people climb to a level higher than their parents, his heir-designate gives no sign of willingness to wait for another generation before bringing power to the people. Cusins wants access to "a power simple enough for common men to use, yet strong enough to force the intellectual oligarchy to use its genius for the general good" (181–82). The intellectual oligarchy cultivates the most highly developed skills in society, and Cusins would have these skills serve the public interest rather than the private or professional special interests of their practitioners. The clearly intended aim is to find a means of exerting socialized control over civilized *sophia*, the cumulative worldly wisdom so selfishly squandered at present. One so bent on societal sanctions may safely be assumed to have taken himself out of the ranks of those men "neither intelligent nor politically educated enough to be Socialists," for whom the nutrition passage predicts an empty future. The scholar successor to capitalist Undershaft is therefore something more than a "Euripidean republican" (Pref. *Major Barbara*, 31): he is a fully committed democratic socialist.[15]

Because the people cannot handle *sophia*—they "cannot have Greek," as Cusins puts it—they must have what they can handle: power. A power simple and strong enough to ensure that skill and wisdom are devoted to the common good has to be political, but according to Undershaft the exercise of political authority rests ultimately on the power to enforce its edicts. It requires military and police power to operate effectively, and such power relies on the force of arms. Cusins has apparently found this part of Undershaft's argument persuasive. Otherwise there would be no reason to go into the armament business. At the same time we should not overlook the fact that in seeking to use the products of the firm for the benefit of the common man he would have to abandon the neutrality and impartiality of the Armorer's creed.[16] In these arguments, moreover, we can pinpoint a number of possible choices for his motto as the next Andrew Undershaft: for example, "Power for the world," "All power is spiritual," or "Weapons for the common man."

Pointing to the bombshell already used to symbolize the destructive power of Perivale St. Andrews, Barbara asks whether there is no higher power than that. Cusins answers, "Yes; but that power can destroy the higher powers just as a tiger can destroy a man: therefore man must master that power first" (182).[17] Again it is an analogue from nature that furnishes the lesson for civilized life (and another possible motto). Just as humankind must gain mastery over the stronger and more primitive Dionysian animal forces of nature if it is to preserve itself, so too do the security and advancement of civilization require tight control over its own threatening elemental forces and mechanisms of devastation. Once more the stress is on making *sophia*, wisdom and culture, face up to the stern necessities of *physis*, lest the undirected energies of rational life proceed without regard to their empirical ground and practical implications. By calling for institutions to be based on the hard realities of existence, Cusins reveals his agreement not only with Undershaft but with the asseverations of Don Juan in *Man and Superman*: "Nature . . . is what you call immoral. . . . Nature is a pandar, Time a Wrecker, and Death a murderer. I have always preferred to stand up to those facts and build institutions on their recognition" (2:677).

If the moral of the *Bacchae* is that we ignore at our peril the Dionysian demands of nature and human nature, the homologous moral of *Major Barbara* is that we ignore at our peril the power basis of morality and civilized society. Both works dramatize the need to fortify wisdom with power and temper power with wisdom. Like Euripides, Shaw is constantly probing the relationships between civilization and nature, between human aspiration and the demands of existence, between variable convention and inexorable necessity, between *nomos* and *physis*, wisdom and power, life and death. In this drama especially has he undertaken a penetrating exploration of the nonmoral natural foundations of society.

Cusins finds corroboration for his latest conclusions about power in one of his own past deeds: to his best pupil, departing to fight for "Hellas" in the war between Greece and Turkey—another bridging of ancient Greece and the modern world—he made a gift of a revolver and a supply of Undershaft cartridges. Consequently his complicity is no less than Undershaft's in whatever Turkish blood his pupil may have shed with that weapon. Undershaft's guilt is not isolable; to blame him alone would be to ignore the inevitable implication in his works of all who resort to force. Having abetted the use of that weapon, Cusins had inextricably committed himself to Perivale St. Andrews. It is Undershaft's challenge, he explains, that has "beaten" him. That challenge was his dare to make war on war. "I dare. I must. I will" (182). Necessity and freedom, obligation and commitment, converge in his decision. To try to annihilate war he must achieve mastery over its means, and that he will now venture to do. Yet nothing in his demeanor or affirmations in taking over the Undershaft firm suggests that he will do so "unashamed."

Torch in Hand

Teiresias's prediction in the *Bacchae* reads, "Hereafter shall you see the god himself even upon the rocks of Delphi, leaping over the twin-peaked plateau, torch in hand, poising and shaking the Bacchic branch—and great throughout Hellas" (306–9, trans. Winnington-Ingram).[18] In *Major Barbara* the elated Cusins, realizing that he has resolved his dilemma without losing Barbara, erupts into one of the rhapsodic "sudden ecstasies" he had indulged in as a Salvationist. Crying "Oh for my drum!" and flourishing imaginary drumsticks, he is once more eager to play the exultant Bacchic worshipper of his beloved. Meanwhile Barbara undergoes equally rapid changes of mood. Touched by his dread of her judgment, she is moved at first to affectionate reassurance, then abruptly flares up in anger at the levity it engenders in him. Probably contributing to her displeasure is the memory of how she felt when he last acted so jubilantly back in West Ham. But no sooner does she warn him to "take care" than a yearning to escape surges over her: "Oh, if only I could get away from you and from father and from it all! if I could have the wings of a dove and fly away to heaven!" (182). This allusion to Psalm 55 is the second passage from the Psalms that she invokes to express her distress; the first was her lamentation at the end of Act II.

So too the Lydian maenads in the *Bacchae* long to take flight "to the land of fairest Pieria, the holy slope of Olympus, where the Muses have their abode" (409–11, trans. Festugière).[19] This theme of escape turns up frequently in the writings of Euripides. Even closer to Barbara's "escape prayer" is Creusa's in Euripides's *Ion*:

Oh, to flee on the wings of a bird
Through the ocean of air, and from Hellas afar to
the stars of the west! (796–98, trans. Way)[20]

But Barbara knows well that escape is impossible—from Adolphus, from her father, and from "all the other naughty mischievous children of men"

(182). The truth she had so recently tried to impress upon Lady Brit-omart—"It's no use running away from wicked people, mamma" (175)—Barbara herself cannot elude. Apparently her escape prayer was in some measure a parting nostalgic cry for a felicity lost. For in taking a retro-spective look at her Salvation Army experience once more—as she had done when her father asked her to explain the meaning of power—she realizes how escapist was that life too. "We aim high, and miss the things within our reach," comment the Bacchants (397–99, trans. Ferguson). Barbara's *eudaimonia* in the Army, she tells us, arose from a flight from the world into "a paradise of enthusiasm and prayer and soul saving" (182), but reality, in the shape of Bodger and Undershaft, intruded when the money ran short. Then the two daemonic capitalists, whose "hands stretch everywhere," were revealed as the ironic saviors of the Army's people. They are the ones who do the saving, providing the vital gifts of bread to the starving and healing to the sick (in their hospitals); they build all the churches and pave the streets (182–83). While such power is firmly in their grip, no escape from them is possible—a conclusion Shaw underscores in the Preface (40, 49). "Turning our backs on Bodger and Undershaft," Barbara sums up, "is turning our backs on life" (183). Thus these industrialists—one of them directly representative of the wine de-ity and his deliverance from care—symbolize Dionysian forces deeply implicated in the provision of human sustenance and the essentials of communal life.

Both Cusins and Barbara have had to come to terms with unregen-erate Undershaftianism. While Cusins focused on assessing the moral import of its destructive power, Barbara was occupied with its ubiqui-tous control of nutritional and economic lifelines. The conclusions she reaches nonetheless come as a surprise to Cusins, who presumed that she had adamantly turned her back on "the wicked side of life"—the side that Bodger and Undershaft embody. The basis for this presump-tion must have been her determined stand against the benefactions of both men in the Salvation shelter. But her perspective is much broader: "There is no wicked side: life is all one" (183).[21] This thought, however, is no fresh discovery on her part: in the first act she had repudiated the di-chotomy of good men and scoundrels, regarding all humans as "children of one Father" (90). That this conviction is congruent with her previous religious commitment Barbara herself spells out: never had she sought to evade her "share" in any evil that had to be endured, whether in the form of sin or suffering. A full participant in humanity, she willingly accepts her allotted portion of its guilt and pain. Like Cusins, she recognizes human guilt to be socially shared, a view Shaw expounds in the play's Preface (52–53). If there is a touch of the saint in her willingness to partake of human suffering, there is a tightening grasp on Bacchic sympathies as well.

As in the *Bacchae*, the philosophical reflections in *Major Barbara* arise out of the experiences of a particular family. The *Bacchae's* mortal family, its sole heir slaughtered, is doomed to extinction. The prospect in *Major Barbara* is just the opposite. The futures of both the Undershaft family and the usurping tradition that repeatedly disinherits its heirs— two ways of succession contrasted in Acts I and III—are being renewed and synthesized in the marriage of a daughter and her adopted-brother spouse. As Barbara formulates her reexamined beliefs, she is defining and refining a revitalized identity—an individuality reflecting facets of kinship with, and divergence from, each of her parents. Her stand on wickedness is thus particularly illuminating when compared with her mother's. Lady Britomart counseled her son in the first act: "It is only in the middle classes, Stephen, that people get into a state of dumb helpless horror when they find that there are wicked people in the world. In our class, we have to decide what is to be done with wicked people; and nothing should disturb our self-possession" (73). Barbara is her mother's daughter in desiring to "cure" Adolphus of "middle-class ideas" about wickedness. But his protest that this amounts to a social snub administered by a foundling's daughter elicits an explanation of her true social status—one that sharply differentiates her from her mother. "That is why I have no class, Dolly: I come straight out of the heart of the whole people" (183).

Her words confirm his original impression of her as "a woman of the people" (164). They also relate her to her foundling father. Through that parent has come an independence from traditions of family and class reminiscent of the Greek god: "These things say I Dionysus, born of no mortal father but of Zeus" (*Bacchae* 1340–41, trans. Hadas and McLean). (Adoption will confer on her fiancé a similar status, and in a very special way he and Barbara will be "children of one father" [90].) Yet in egalitarian persuasion the daughter is much closer than the father to the democratic spirit of the Greek god. For not only does Barbara, like Dionysos, transcend class distinctions (*Bacchae* 421–22), but by her own admission she too is *demotikos*, of the people.[22] Since the lowly have already won a loyal advocate in Cusins, their cause has two staunch champions at the end of the drama. Wholehearted devotion to the well-being of the common people remains as important a motif in *Major Barbara* as it is in the *Bacchae*.

Barbara's ethical position develops along lines indicated for her in the Preface, where Shaw argues the need to establish societal institutions on the basis of social and moral equality. Taking "straightforward perception of the fact that mankind is practically a single species" to be a distinguishing mark of "the master-minds of the world," he singles out for praise leaders who have, like Barbara, held fast to "the scientific fact of human equality" (47–48). Those who believe in a *natural* division of men into lower, middle, and upper classes either socially or morally are alike mistaken. What Barbara is affirming is "the sacred mystery of Equality" (56). What she is renouncing is the specious superiority and uselessness of middle-class life in an artistic drawing room. Along with Cusins and the votaries of Dionysos in the *Bacchae* (427–29), she reprehends the way of the contemptuous, superior (*perissos*) person. Rather than live in such a manner, she would undertake the socially more useful work of sweeping out the guncotton shed or become a Bodger barmaid (183). Nor is it at all likely, we may add, that she will settle for the self-possession, the peculiar *sophrosyne*, in which her mother takes such pride.

The only significant change in Barbara's thinking to emerge thus far is her recognition of the protean and inevasible tentacles of power that Bodger and Undershaft extend to all who would save lives. What she has learned from her father, and the extent to which she has been "converted" by him, must be gleaned from her two remaining long speeches. These proclaim the gospel of Saint Barbara Undershaft—her third, climactic confession of faith in this act.[23] First, however, comes her disclosure to Cusins that she might have forsaken him had he made the wrong choice. Had he refused the proposition, she was prepared to marry the man who accepted it. The implications of this avowal are far-reaching, for Barbara is binding herself unreservedly to the Undershaft inheritance, becoming an integral part of the prize and—more important—a potent influence on its future.

Her decision, in its own way as fateful as that of her husband-to-be, resolves an ambiguity latent in her father's excited utterance to Cusins during their discussion in the shelter: that Barbara's inspiration, issuing from within herself, "is the Undershaft inheritance" (120). It was this revelation that prompted him to declare that he would hand on his torch to his daughter. His exclamations are interpretable as alluding to direct biological heredity: a parent's pride at learning of inherited capability in his or her offspring. But "the Undershaft inheritance" has another— and to all purposes diametrically antithetical—meaning in the play. As a legacy of money and power from the munitions firm, the inheritance is mandated by tradition not to go to any of the owner's progeny. In which of these two senses did Undershaft conceive of the inheritance he would be handing on as a torch to the daughter who would make his converts and preach his gospel? Or did he intend it in both senses? Was he perchance adumbrating something more than he was able to envision at the time? Given a multilayered drama such as *Major Barbara*, "where everything that is said seems to cut two ways" (*Meaning and Truth in the Arts*, 25), ambivalence of this sort should be regarded neither as unusual nor as unintended.

Whatever may have been in Undershaft's mind, the passage initially would appear to convey its surface, genetic meaning. But viewed in light of Barbara's resolve to marry the successful candidate for the firm's own-ership—for all the world like a fairytale princess consenting to wed the daring suitor who surmounts extraordinary obstacles, survives peril-ous trials, or solves baffling riddles in order to win her hand—the per-spective shifts, and the recessive meaning moves to the fore. The idea of inheritance in terms of the Undershaft tradition, seemingly doubly inapplicable to Barbara as filial and female, is suddenly seen to loom large in her thinking, making manifest that she has been a possible in-direct legatee all along. Undershaft may also have had some intimation of things to come. After all, back at Wilton Crescent he told his wife that the only way to keep the factory in the family would be to arrange the marriage of an eligible foundling to Barbara. In any event, Barbara's marital commitment brings to fruition what Lady Britomart (and all her predecessor Undershaft wives) had been vainly striving to accomplish: to keep possession of the business in the family.

Apposite then is Barbara's admission that her feelings about Perivale St. Andrews were akin to those of her mother, whom she credits with an intuitive good sense (*sophia* or *phronein*)[24] that is wanting in the rest of them. Like Lady Britomart, having laid eyes on the place she felt impelled to have, hold, and never relinquish it. In effect the community took possession of her, though until this moment she had betrayed no hint of the kind or intensity of its impact. With her father she could now truthfully say, "It does not belong to me. I belong to it." The family heir, as it turns out, is an heiress who will come into her patrimony by matrimony—by wedding the Undershaft tradition's stipulated extrafamilial adopted heir. So Barbara will indeed take up the torch from her father. But will she go so far as to make his converts and preach his gospel, as he further predicted? A harmonizing force, she is planning to realize the one objective pleasing to both her conflicting parents. And even if she falls a shade short of circumventing or nullifying the tradition, her manner of embracing it will ironically manage to loosen its longstanding, invariant hold on the business. In the process she will bolster materially the languishing cause of heredity in its competition with adoptive selection. The development is dialectical and evolutionary, in line with Shaw's conviction that "the law of God is a law of change" (Pref. *Saint Joan*, 6:57).

Barbara goes on to explain the difference between her mother's enchantment with Perivale St. Andrews and her own. Lady Britomart is charmed by its domestic appurtenances: the houses, kitchen ranges, china, linen. But Barbara's vision goes beyond things to people: the real significance of the place, and its fascination for her, lies in "all the human souls to be saved." In the spiritual state of these souls evidently she has discerned the truth lurking "behind the frightful irony" of her father's domain; they have vouchsafed her a glimpse of the light she wanted to be shown shining "through the darkness of this dreadful place, with its beautifully clean workshops, and respectable workmen, and model homes" (171). Her mother's soul was bought by the "darkness" of the model housing. Barbara has been won over by the moral shortcomings of the human beings who reside in the houses. Unlike the infirm and obsequious souls in starved bodies to whose salvation her life had previously been dedicated, these "fulfilled, quarrelsome, snobbish, uppish creatures, all standing on their little rights and dignities" and rightly believing that Undershaft ought to be indebted to them for his wealth, are the ones truly in need of salvation (184). At last her father has been revealed to her in his true guise as a nutritional power, and her mother as the complementary natural exponent of home and children. But the vitality that concentrates on these ends is ultimately deficient, as the nutrition passage argued. In managing to satisfy the elemental wants of food and shelter, it renders more acute the famine of the spirit.

To a reformer like Barbara who cannot rate "heaven and hell a remote second," Perivale St. Andrews represents an unregenerate, spiritually impoverished territory. Much of this lesson she has learned from her father. He had bade her try her hand on his men, whose "souls are hungry because their bodies are full," after derogating as "cheap work" her reliance on Bible and bread to effect the conversion of the starving. Now she is resolved never again to give him grounds for accusing her of bribing her converts with bread. Rid of the bribe of bread and heaven, a "transfigured" Barbara enunciates her own credo: "Let God's work be done for its own sake: the work he had to create us to do because it cannot be done except by living men and women. When I die, let him be in my debt, not I in his; and let me forgive him as becomes a woman of my rank" (184). Her transfiguration celebrates not a conversion, but an apotheosis.[25] "The worshipper of Bacchos became Bacchos simply enough, because in reality the God Bacchos was originally only the projection of the human Bacchoi," Murray informs us. A development from this conception is the Greek Stoic teaching formulated by Pliny: "God is the helping of man by man; and that is the way to eternal glory."[26]

If Cusins will supplant her father on earth, Barbara will do so in heaven, and her role as a new divinity will be the Shavian (and Greek) one of elevating humankind to divine status. No difficulty arises from her being female. In the *Bacchae* Dionysos transcends sexual distinctions, possessing feminine as well as masculine traits (235–36, 353, 455–59).[27] Shaw himself remarked on the arbitrariness of conceiving of the godhead as male: "Clearly, if you have a personal God, one of the first difficulties is to determine the sex of that god." In a lecture delivered about one year after the original production of *Major Barbara* he suggested that if it was necessary to personify God "why not personify Him as a woman?" In particular he wanted all religions to remind us "of woman's place in Godhead."[28] The gospel Barbara is preaching during her epiphany in glory is patently not Undershaft's, nor is it likely to be *his* converts that she will be making. Her Dionysianism is of a different cast, readily distinguishable in doctrine from the "money and gunpowder" religion of her father.

Her new religious creed—revealed in a sermon preached on a mount overlooking Perivale St. Andrews—esteems "God's work" to be of intrinsic worth (184). That means that it is not to be done for the sake of reward, heavenly or earthly. Such a tenet takes her (with Cusins) to a stage beyond the monetary concerns that loom so large in her father's creed. "God's work" she defines as work achievable only by living human beings created for that purpose. The underlying notion is the keystone proposition in Shaw's metaphysics: our purpose comes from the instinctual operation of the Life Force, which by trial and error and experiment evolves human creatures as its effective instruments. Elsewhere in his writings and speeches Shaw made more explicit the ideas compressed into Barbara's two sentences. A compendious guide to their meaning is an undated brief manuscript entitled "The Life Force," in which he wrote: "The Life Force must not be conceived as a force that has mankind at its mercy. It is not something outside humanity: on the contrary, mankind is its highest organ, agent, and instrument yet created; and the chief evidence of its existence is that certain men and women have dreams of perfection, and will sacrifice their comfort and risk their lives in the pursuit of knowledge as a step towards the achievement of power over their circumstances."[29] The eventual goal he explained in a 1907 speech:

> The object of the whole evolutionary process is to realize God . . . to conceive of the force behind the universe as working up through imperfection and mistake to a perfect, organized being, having the power of fulfilling its highest purposes. In a sense there is no god as yet achieved, but there is that force at work making God, struggling through us to become an actual organized existence, enjoying what to many of us is the greatest conceivable ecstasy, the ecstasy of a brain, an intelligence, actually conscious of the whole, and with executive force capable of guiding it to a perfectly benevolent and harmonious end. . . . When you are asked, "Where is God? Who is God?" stand up and say, "I am god and here is God, not as yet completed, but still advancing towards completion, just in so much as I am working for the purpose of the universe, working for the good of the whole of society and the whole world, instead of merely looking after my personal ends."[30]

Barbara is committing herself to earning divine status as the proper end of human work, so that the Life Force will owe her more than she owes it. Her old religion, her father argued, did not fit the facts; it misconceived *physis*. In keeping with his bidding she has acquired "a newer and a better one for tomorrow." Unsurprisingly it is, in essence, Shaw's Creative

Evolutionism. "The Life Force," says the brief manuscript bearing that title, "is only a hypothesis: but it fits the facts as far as we know them, and thus enables us to think without substituting fairy tales for the facts. It gives you a credible 'frame of reference' without which reasoning is impossible" (1). Hence the emphasis at the end of the *Major Barbara* Preface on the need for creeds to become "intellectually honest" (63). Barbara is prepared to forgive God, or the Life Force—for what? Ostensibly for its omissions and blunders: "for all the starvation and mischief he is responsible for," as Shaw once phrased it. Hence her lofty forbearance really cloaks a Shavian unriddling of the problem of evil.[31]

The intellectual scaffolding for her stance is to be found once again in the argument of "The Life Force":

The Life Force is not new, its old name was Providence. But it was assumed that Providence is omnipotent, omniscient, infallible, and beneficent: and this is contradicted by the existence of evil, vice, poison, disease, and all the other mischiefs. The Devil had to be invented to account for them. . . . The novelty about the Life Force is that though, like the Holy Ghost, it is impersonal and unaccountable, yet it is fallible, and proceeds by trial and error, leaving the world full of its well meant failures as well as its well meant successes, and thereby creating evil as well as good without intending it. It makes the flea and the scorpion, and then has to make mankind to kill them. This solves the problem of evil. (1)

The theory posits a Shavian alternative to traditional theological efforts to resolve the difficulties posed by the conception of an omnipotent and omnibeneficent deity creating a world indisputably filled with all sorts of existential evils.

The forgiveness envisaged by Barbara will be such "as becomes a woman of my rank." Her rank manifestly is that of a divinity in process, rising above the source of her being.[32] In taking up Undershaft's torch his daughter assumes divine attributes. But as becomes an evolutionary goddess she does more than just carry on: she moves to higher ground from which to surpass her father. If he "strikes the deepest note in the play," as the author indicates, "Barbara sounds the highest." Her lofty creed, built on the factuality of his, constitutes an advance to a stage beyond. If in the *Bacchae* "Teiresias tells us, in effect, that man cannot live by bread alone," Barbara in Shaw's play tells us that he cannot live by the bread of Undershaft (and Bodger) alone.[33]

Not to be overlooked in this *confessio fidei* is the fact that, contrary to Cusins and Undershaft, she does find a place for forgiveness in the scheme of things. Perhaps that is because the Life Force cannot use it as "a beggar's refuge." Nor does the mere repayment of debt, with which Cusins rules out forgiveness, suffice for her. Rather, her intention is to put the forgiven Life Force under obligation to her. It may be remembered that in the passage quoted earlier from the Preface to *The Irrational Knot* Shaw suggested that recognition of the limitations of the Life Force would teach people "some pity for their gods" (Pref. *Irrational Knot*, xix). And in his rehearsal notebook for the original production of *Major Barbara* he jotted down alongside Barbara's line, "as becomes a woman of my rank": "not earthly pride, pity for God in it."[34] Pity and forgiveness, it would appear, are reserved for the forces of nature, disdained for the exculpation of human beings. The religion of *Major Barbara* is magnanimous and compassionate toward nature, ethically stringent toward humankind. In this respect it inverts the outlook reflected in the *exodos* of the *Bacchae* (and other Euripidean tragedies), where the humans find moral meaning and worth in compassion and fellow feeling, after learning so painfully how unequal they are to the exigencies the divine powers of nature remorselessly impose (*Bacchae*, trans. Arrowsmith, 152–53). Yet each dramatist points to something indomitable in the human spirit, and locates its singular strength in moral growth.

Resurrection: Life through Death

Interpreting Barbara's thought in gnomic form Cusins asks, "Then the way of life lies through the factory of death?" (184). Affirmatively stated this could well be what the eighth Andrew Undershaft will end up inscribing on the wall, in Greek, as his distinctive motto.[35] For it epitomizes and consummates a theme running through the whole Perivale St. Andrews episode in the drama: the inseparability of life and death. The *Bacchae* reveals the life-giving and death-dealing powers of Dionysos; *Major Barbara* correspondingly shows Undershaft as both builder and destroyer, dispensing the life-sustaining powers of food, clothing, and housing, while trafficking in lethal weapons and explosives. "Command of life and command of death" (120) was the scope of the dominion the armament king claimed for money and gunpowder, and each of these resources he possesses in abundance. Throughout their visit to Perivale

St. Andrews Cusins and Barbara were made acutely aware of both the vital and destructive potency latent in the place. Now, during this penultimate scene, they are intent on gaining the right purchase on this problematical community.

With the emergence of the dark side of Dionysos's nature in the *Bacchae*, "the power of salvation has become the power of destruction," as Ferguson puts it (*A Companion to Greek Tragedy*, 476). The reverse, and more paradoxical, development takes place in *Major Barbara*: the power of destruction becomes the power of salvation. "And is it not the very diagnostic of true salvation that it shall overcome the fear of death?" asks Shaw in the play's Preface (41). Belief in personal immortality is a surrender to that fear; salvation requires overcoming the fear by facing up to one's mortality and seeing that life persists only in the succession of generations. Death, he subsequently argues in the Preface to *Misalliance*, makes room for new births, bringing fresh hope for evolutionary improvement. He would have us "rejoice in death as we rejoice in birth; for without death we cannot be born again," and we should surely wish to be born again, he adds, and born better (Pref. *Misalliance*, 4:17).

The coming of Undershaft in Act I has brought to Barbara a passion and a spiritual death in Act III; at the dénouement she is being reborn.[36] A rebirth is in process for Cusins too—as Andrew Undershaft. In consequence, both become twice-born, and as in the case of Dionysos, the second birth is from a paternal divinity. A double resurrection is added to the other dualisms of the drama, eventuating in a Dionysian trinity.[37] The demigods in this Shavian pantheon are in fact on their way to realizing the crowning aspiration of Father Keegan's trinitarian dream of heaven in *John Bull's Other Island*: "a godhead in which all life is human and all humanity divine: three in one and one in three" (2:1021). The complete unwrapping of the identities issuing from these rebirths is left to the future, but the resultant configurations and interrelations are clearly preindicated. Cusins, already his own cousin, as Lady Britomart tartly observed (165), is undergoing a Platonic metamorphosis from professor of Greek into gunpowder maker, and moving to shared identity with his predecessor Undershaft. Adopted son, he will marry his new sister, and in due course will assume his wife's surname while, in this feminist Shavian inversion, she will retain hers. He will thus become son, son-in-law, and heir to Undershaft: "three in one and one in three."

The original draft of the play's third act contains a cancelled rejoinder by Cusins to Lady Britomart's calling him his own cousin: "It is quite true that the confusion of relationships has given me a sort of manifold nature that makes me several different sorts of people in one."[38] Premature and overstated in that earlier context, the remark fits him neatly in the final version of the play. The same kind of multiple identity belongs complementarily to Barbara, who will become the wife, stepsister, and presumptive partner of one Undershaft, as well as daughter, daughter-in law, and heiress of the other. The one father, father-in-law, and senior partner, meanwhile, will be bequeathing a portion of his identity along with his regime and fortune to them both. Truly they are all "three in one and one in three."

The social consequences of the resurrections of Barbara and Cusins are likely to include those advocated by John Tanner in the first act of *Man and Superman*. Describing himself as an iconoclastic reformer whose moral passion directs his destructive impulses to moral ends, he commends the uses of destructiveness: "Destruction clears it [construction] and gives breathing space and liberty" (*Man and Superman*, 2:573).[39] No doubt death and destruction can open new reformational vistas of this sort for the collaborative zeal of Barbara and the newly chosen heir to the Undershaft firm. But death can do even more. It furnishes an acid test of reality, as Shaw explained in a wartime symposium on ethics some years later: "Everyone who has been face to face with death knows that it has the power, by the intensity of its reality, to reduce many of what we believed to be our gravest concerns and most important convictions to the idlest vanities and the shallowest affectations. It also, by the extraordinary efforts we find ourselves able to make to escape from it, reveals reserves of power in ourselves which we had never before discovered."[40]

It was to "the factory of death" that Barbara asked to be taken just before leaving for Perivale St. Andrews so that she could learn something more. What both initiates have succeeded in discovering in the factory of death is the machinery, the vehicle, for the way of life. Death is an ineluctable condition and concern of life; it is the crucible of power, the touchstone of authenticity. Short of facing it in all its inexorability, these reformers nourish in vain any hope of accomplishing something enduring. An inspired Barbara answers Cusins's question concerning the way of life: "Yes, through the raising of hell to heaven and of man to god, through the unveiling of an eternal light in the Valley of The Shadow" (184). In this mystical sentence the motifs of hell and heaven, light and darkness, return. Much as the philosopher Heraclitus linked Dionysos with Hades, Cusins and Barbara have associated Undershaft and his domain with hell. At the same time they have descried in Perivale St. Andrews a potential heavenly city. Its Dionysian ambiguity leaves it capable of going either way.

What these ways are can be gathered in part from the definitions of hell, earth, and heaven stipulated by Don Juan in *Man and Superman*, according to which "hell is the home of the unreal and of the seekers for happiness," heaven "the home of the masters of reality," and earth "the home of the slaves of reality" (2:650). In these terms Wilton Crescent is representative of hell, its denizens concerned with illusion and the scramble for happiness; and the Salvation Army shelter represents earth, where people's bodies drag them down, as "hunger and cold and thirst, age and decay and disease, death above all makes them slaves of reality," to apply Don Juan's reading (2:650).[41] But Perivale St. Andrews is not, as one might expect, simply symbolic of heaven. Instead it totters twixt heaven and hell through the greater part of the last act. It embodies concurrently the clear-cut alternatives Father Keegan articulates near the close of *John Bull's Other Island*: "For me there are but two countries: heaven and hell; but two conditions of men: salvation and damnation" (2:1020).

Clarifying the heaven-earth-hell triad is Shaw's own gloss, submitted in the form of a program note on the scene of Don Juan in hell in *Man and Superman*. Explaining that localizations such as "the heavens above, the earth beneath, and the waters under the earth" are wholly figurative, he embraces the contemporary "higher" theological interpretation of heaven and hell as "states of the soul"—the soul being defined as "the divine element common to all life." Such a theology maintains "that this world, or any other, may be made a hell by a society so lacking in the higher orders of energy that it is given wholly to the pursuit of immediate individual pleasure, and cannot even conceive the passion of the divine will. Also that any world can be made a heaven by a society of persons in which that passion is the master passion—'a communion of saints' in fact."[42] At the end of *Major Barbara* the saints have begun to commune as Barbara and Cusins embark on the divine mission of raising from hell to heaven the community they will before long be governing.

Raising Man to God

At this point a parallel episode from John Bunyan's *Pilgrim's Progress* affords a crucial interpretative clue to Shaw's thematic design in juxtaposing heaven and hell in *Major Barbara*. At the end of the first part of *Pilgrim's Progress*, as Christian and Hopeful enter the gates of the Celestial City, they are "transfigured" (*Pilgrim's Progress*, 140), which is precisely what happens to Barbara when she offers her Creative Evolution–inspired prayer, quoted earlier: "Let God's work be done . . . by living men and women" (184). Shortly thereafter the two Shining Ones (angels) who had escorted the pilgrims to the city gates proceed to bind Ignorance, take him from those same gates, and put him into the doorway to Hell. "Then I saw," Bunyan pointedly concludes, "that there was a way to Hell even from the Gates of Heaven, as well as from the City of Destruction" (*Pilgrim's Progress*, 142).

Shaw suggestively set forth his own revealing exegesis of this familiar Bunyan passage in two disparate commentaries, penned decades apart. Expounding his Diabolonian ethics in the Preface to *Three Plays for Puritans* (1900), published five years before the composition of *Major Barbara*, he incorporated the following commentary: "Our newest idol, the Superman, celebrating the death of godhead, may be younger than the hills; but he is as old as the shepherds. Two and a half centuries ago our greatest English dramatizer of life, John Bunyan, ended one of his stories with the remark that there is a way to hell even from the gates of heaven, and so led us to the equally true proposition that there is a way to heaven even from the gates of hell" (Pref. *Three Plays for Puritans*, 2:33–34). Writing twenty-eight years later in *The Intelligent Woman's Guide to Socialism and Capitalism*, he is more explicit and expansive:

John Bunyan, with his queer but deep insight, pointed out long ago that there is a way to hell even from the gates of heaven; that the way to heaven is therefore also the way to hell; and that the name of the gentleman who goes to hell by that road is Ignorance. The way to Socialism, ignorantly pursued, may land us in State Capitalism. Both must travel the same road, and this is what Lenin, less inspired than Bunyan, failed to see when he denounced the Fabian methods as State Capitalism. What is more, State Capitalism, plus Capitalist Dictatorship (Fascism), will compete for approval by cleaning up some of the dirtiest of our present conditions: raising wages; reducing death rates; opening the career to the talents; and ruthlessly cashiering inefficiency, before in the long run succumbing to the bane of inequality, against which no civilization can finally stand out. (298)

Not to be overlooked in these two passages are Shaw's subtle corollaries to Bunyan's view of the heaven-hell nexus. In the first of these he adduces the additional inference that there is a way to heaven even from hell's gates. In the second, the inference drawn is that the same pathway leads to heaven and hell. Whether deliberately intended or not, these Shavian variations on the derived Bunyan theme are strikingly applicable to *Major Barbara,* where the dramatic focus is on the way from hell to heaven, and from heaven to hell, and the very close proximity of the two destinations.

Equally apposite to the play is Shaw's extension of the heaven-hell symbolism to socialism and capitalism. Not only state capitalism, but paternalistic capitalism as well may be confused with the genuine socialist article (as he indicates in "Sham Socialism," the next section of *The Intelligent Woman's Guide*). Barbara and Cusins are confronted at the end of the play with the forbidding task of turning the enlightened capitalist "hell" at Perivale St. Andrews—organized to bring its owner "a colossal profit," as Undershaft openly admits (155)—into a socialist "heaven." Shaw's belief that both socialism and capitalism must at this stage of the evolutionary process "travel the same road" is undoubtedly one of the reasons why some critics have mistakenly detected in *Major Barbara* an inclination toward compromise with capitalism on the part of its author.[43]

The alliance of Barbara and Cusins conjoins them with the Superman in "celebrating the death of godhead" (2:33). Barbara expresses this celebration paradoxically in prayer and transfiguration. That is because she is shedding one religion and assuming another, one in which humanity must undertake to establish its own salvation and its own divinity. Her father had challenged her to "get a newer and a better [religion] for tomorrow" (171): straightaway she has done so. In Bunyan's allegory, the peregrinations of Christian represent a process of psychological conversion. The course of the progression is more concise in Shaw's drama, but it comparably unfolds the conversion of Major Barbara. Her progress as pilgrim is evolutionary in both development and doctrine.

Barbara, imbued with "the passion of the divine will," could sing with the choral maenads of the *Bacchae*: "My joy is in pursuing these other aims, being high and plainly set (for they lead man's life toward the good), day-long and through the night to be pure and reverent" (1006-7, trans. Dodds). In this passage Murray detected an appeal to mystic faith, anticipating the longing in later Hellenistic thought for the city of God.[44]

"Would you not be expecting this earth to be fulfilling its real destiny, to be transforming itself into the Kingdom of Heaven?" Shaw once asked in his speech on "The Crime of Poverty."[45] It is to the fulfillment of such an expectation that Barbara is dedicating herself. What is called for is the redirection of the chthonic energies of Perivale St. Andrews from hedonistic self-interest toward the realization of higher evolutionary goals for humankind, thereby raising "man to God" (184).

The torches of Dionysos bring light to darkness (144–50); so do all the fire images in the *Bacchae*. Darkness of night and light of day as influences enter into the exchange between Pentheus and the god about the character of Bacchic worship (*Bacchae* 458–59, 485–88). Again, light and darkness are contrasted in the imprisonment of Dionysos (509–18) and during the "palace miracle," during which he effects his escape (576–607). The chorus greets the returned god as a liberating light whose illumination is immediately juxtaposed with the darkness of the dungeon (608–11). When the voice of Dionysos cries out in his terrible epiphany on the mountain, a miraculous light shines forth between heaven and earth (1082–83). The manifestation of supernatural light, the sign of a divine presence or divine inspiration, was especially associated with the cult of Dionysos.[46] In *Major Barbara* the "eternal light" Barbara sees unveiled likewise intimates a revelation of the divine in human life. Contrasts of light and darkness pervade Perivale St. Andrews, as already indicated, including the light Barbara sought within the darkness of her father's "dreadful place." Now, with the introduction of light into "the Valley of The Shadow" where "the factory of death" is located, her vision is bright and clear. As radically as her *anagnorisis* differs from the awakening of Agave, for Barbara too the sky "is brighter and shines with a holier light" (*Bacchae* 1267, trans. Kirk; "More shining than before, more heavenly bright!," trans. Murray).

Turning from the mystical annunciation of her gospel, Barbara seizes Cusins "with both hands," using them to communicate her fervor in this culminating expression of the hand theme. Transported to new heights of moral passion and enthusiasm, she glories in the return of her courage. *Andreia*, courage, her father's special virtue, is once more hers as well, dovetailed with her conviction. That *andreia* is a manly quality poses no barrier to a liberated savior of men such as Barbara. Courage and conviction were the desiderata Undershaft stressed in his dialogue with Barbara and Cusins, although in his daughter's case the appeal was directed solely to her courage. Having regained both, Barbara is ecstatic:

"Oh, did you think that my courage would never come back? did you believe that I was a deserter? that I, who have stood in the streets, and taken
my people to my heart, and talked of the holiest and greatest things with
them, could ever turn back and chatter foolishly to fashionable people
about nothing in a drawing room? Never, never, never, never: Major
Barbara will die with the colors" (184). Like the Dionysian worshipper at
the peak of ecstasy, she is one with her god, *entheos,* possessed of divinity, and inspired with invigorating new power. Her *enthusiasmos* is thus
Bacchic, celebrating the identification of devotee with deity. The recol-
lection of her evangelical life in the streets in holy and edifying communion with her people brings us back to the excitement and exultation
of the *parodos* of the *Bacchae* and its hymn to Dionysos: "—Ah, blessed
is he whom the gods love, who understands the secret rites of the gods,
whose life is consecrated, whose very soul dances with holy joy. In the
mountains he knows the bacchic thrill, the holy purifications" (*Bacchae*
72–75, trans. Hadas and McLean).[47]

The contrast Barbara draws between the enthusiastic vitality and joy
of religious activity and the foolish vanities of the fashionable drawing
room typifies the difference between her life and the colorless existence
of her sister Sarah. In affirming that she is no deserter and that she will
"die with the colors" Barbara recognizes an essential continuity between
her previous Salvationist activity and the work she will now undertake.
There was a homecoming, a "bringing home" or "bringing back," of Dionysos in the *Bacchae* (85) and of Undershaft in Shaw's play.[48] In her turn,
Barbara too is being brought back to her true home and work. Elated
because "I have my dear little Dolly boy still; and he has found me my
place and my work," she exclaims, "Glory Hallelujah!" and kisses him.
Her affection toward him evinces a touch of the maternal, if not of the
patron goddess. Mingled with it is a feeling of gratitude for the rediscovery of her identity, for having been shown her life's vocation and the
right environment in which to practice it. What deserves special notice
in her attitude, however, is that the individual to whom she feels grateful
for these benefits is not the present but the future Andrew Undershaft. It
is a symptom prognostic of her growing independence from her father.

Her "Glory Hallelujah!" recalls not only the Salvation Army and its
maenads, but also the *ololuge,* the joy-cry "ololu," the triumphant or
thanksgiving ritual shout of the women in the *Bacchae* (23–24). Like
Thebes (*Bacchae* 23–24), Perivale St. Andrews will henceforth stir to
such ecstatic cries of joy from Bacchic women. Barbara's own rapture

is bodied forth in the aptest of gestures in the course of this apocalyptic scene; for in looking heavenward during this speech, she would have to be "in ecstasy flinging back" her head and turning up her throat in the characteristic gesture of a bacchanal (*Bacchae* 864, trans. Dodds).[49] Assuming a Cusins taller than she is, her head would retain this carriage for the consummating kiss. Shaw undoubtedly had this speech (as well as her preceding one) uppermost in mind when he wrote to an actress preparing to play Barbara that she could carry the last act "to the wildest limits of your imagination without the least fear of over-acting or extravagance."[50]

The *eudaimonia* of Barbara resembles that of which the Bacchae sing: "Blest is he who triumphs over trial" (904–5, trans. Vellacott). Responding to the blithe caveat of Cusins that he cannot stand as much happiness as she, Barbara concedes that being in love with her "is not easy work," but she thinks it nevertheless good for him.[51] These lines revive thoughts about their personal life touched upon lightly in the second act. Bill Walker, on being introduced to Cusins, expressed grave fears for the latter's fate as Barbara's future husband, forewarning him of a premature death from exhaustion should he fail to stop her tireless tongue-wagging. To Barbara, affronted that Bill's warning should give him even a momentary pause, Adolphus explained: "Yes, my dear, its very wearing to be in love with you. If it lasts, I quite think, I shall die young" (115). But he would not mind, he then assured her with a kiss. The two conversations intimate that even love and happiness with Barbara Undershaft have a Dionysian double edge: for all their benefits, love is demanding and hazardous, happiness risks death. The delights of Aphrodite, comprehended within the framework of the couple's larger moral mission, acquire a characteristic Bacchic duality. At the same time the way is clear for Cusins to continue dauntlessly to adore what is divine in his saintly Barbara.

Descent from the Heights

"Then indeed the bacchant maid rejoices and gambols, light-footed, like a foal by its mother's side in the pasture" (*Bacchae* 165–69, trans. Hadas and McLean). From her beatific transfiguration and ensuing confident exercise of personal female dominance over her lover, Barbara suddenly turns "childlike," running to the shed and calling for her mother, the parent from whom she derives her propensity to dominate. The move to seek out her mother rather than her father receives special emphasis in the stage action. For it is not Lady Britomart who emerges first from the shed, but Bilton and Undershaft, and it is they who are greeted with the unexpected demand, "I want Mamma" (184). In the initial draft of the third act, prior to its revision, Barbara adds to her father, "I didn't call you," and in his rehearsal notebook for the first production Shaw wrote the instruction, "Hit him," as her line, leaving no doubt about its paternal target.[52] At the personal level the act registers a definite shift away from father toward mother, reversing the trend of her interest throughout the play. But it has additional significance, both negative and positive. Negatively, it presents us with yet another display of independence from Undershaft by his autonomous daughter—further evidence that she is no mere convert to his gospel. Transcended is her father's brand of Dionysianism, very much as Agave at the close of the *Bacchae* has passed beyond belief in the religion of Dionysos. On the positive side, we see Barbara beginning to take action on the basis of her newfound affinity with her mother. Relishing her close sympathy with Lady Britomart's *sophia* about Perivale St. Andrews, she is eager to ally it with her own.

After reporting that his wife is removing her list slippers, Undershaft bypasses his daughter—presumably sensing from her mien that he will learn nothing by direct questioning—to inquire about her decision from Cusins. Dramatic interest continues to be concentrated on Barbara, for it is *her* decision that her father wants to know, not that of Cusins. Through her, as we have seen, the inheritance will remain in the family, even if only by indirection. Remove the god's irony, and what Dionysos prophetically promises to Pentheus is hers: "You shall win a glory towering to heaven" (972, trans. Arrowsmith). "She has gone right up into the skies," Cusins reports to Undershaft.[53] Barbara is triumphant in her ascension; her triumph, unlike the one Pentheus expects (or Agave believes she has won), is neither ironic nor illusory. Retaining her identity as Barbara Undershaft even in marriage to the next Andrew Undershaft, she will acquire her father's daimonic power while preserving a spirit free of his control, as her final actions disclose. But although her life is again consecrated to "larger loves and diviner dreams than the fireside ones" (142), she is not entirely ready to forsake those of the fireside, judging by her oddly filial behavior toward her mother.

Barbara's new relationship to her mother is one of climactic—or rather anticlimactic—irony and dramatic reversal in a number of respects. For in this crowning *peripeteia* she makes a speedy and incongruous descent from the skies, from adoration by her beloved, and from a new position of strength vis-à-vis her father, to cling to her mother in infantine dependence:

> LADY BRITOMART [*coming from the shed and stopping on the steps, obstructing Sarah, who follows with Lomax. Barbara clutches like a baby at her mother's skirt*] Barbara, when will you learn to be independent and to act and think for yourself? I know as well as possible what that cry of "Mamma, Mamma," means. Always running to me! (185)

This dégringolade plunges us precipitously into backwashing emotional currents from the first act. Barbara has swiftly acted to restore her mother in some measure to the matriarchal status she enjoyed when the play began. At the time Lady Britomart expressed her firm intention of having Barbara marry, not the man snobbish people like, but "the man *I* like" (71), and set in motion her plans to assure financial support for both daughters' households. Her manipulation of Stephen eventually led him to insist, as he did before the family's departure for Perivale St. Andrews, that "there must be an end of treating me as a child" (148). He thereby won his latchkey and his independence, as his father duly noted. Sarah's relationship to her mother nowhere comes up for inspection, but it would seem to be encapsulated in the stage action during the concluding moments of the play. On the shed steps stands the returning Lady Britomart "*obstructing Sarah*," who thereupon puts her fingertips to her mother's ribs and in imitation of a bicycle horn calls out, "Pip! Pip!" Her noncompliant behavior, like Stephen's before, runs directly counter to that of Barbara, who is eagerly appealing for maternal guidance. At Wilton Crescent Undershaft had explained to his wife, "it is only the big men who can be treated as children" (149). Evidently it is equally true of "big" women.

An anticlimactic irony resides in the way the distribution of family forces at the close of the first act has been reversed. Then it was Lady Britomart who found herself virtually deserted as Barbara and the others went off to the drawing room for a religious service with Undershaft, leaving only Stephen to side with his mother. That prompted her tearful protest about "the injustice of a woman's lot," which required her to rear the children by doing "all the unpleasant things," only to have their father come and steal their affection as soon as her work was finished (93–94). But both mother and daughter rebound from defeat and sally forth with flying colors in the end. Barbara takes a stance that is, in effect, the mirror image of her brother's: having achieved independence from her father, she is free to lean dependently on her mother.

"What do you want Barbara?" we well may ask with Lady Britomart. "I want a house in the village to live in with Dolly," she replies, "[*Dragging at the skirt*] Come and tell me which one to take" (185). Before sending Pentheus to Cithaeron, Dionysos informs him, "I shall lead you safely there; someone else shall bring you back." Bemused into misreading the true circumstances, Pentheus divines that the "someone else" will be his mother, which the god confirms: "You will be carried home . . . cradled in your mother's arms" (*Bacchae* 965–66, 968–69, trans. Arrowsmith). In *Major Barbara*, after Undershaft has similarly led his daughter to her visionary heights on his hilltop, she puts herself in her mother's hands for the return trip down to the village to select a home. The two women do not look upon their concerns of the moment as falling within the province of Undershaft or, for that matter, of his successor.

For Barbara, so much of whose time has been spent standing in the streets discussing "the holiest and greatest things" with her people, the domestic realm of hearth and home is unfamiliar territory, and she has much to learn. As the Preface to *Man and Superman* instructs, "When it comes to sex relations, . . . the woman of genius [does not share] the common woman's overwhelming specialization" (2:511). Ostensibly more elemental impulses of the Life Force are stirring within her. The nutrition passage, recall, tells us that "marriage means children" and that for women to give priority to children is "the law of Nature." Very natural then is it for Barbara to turn with implicit trust to one who, as the mother of children, "has shared in the divine travail, and with care and labor and suffering renewed the harvest of eternal life," even though "the honor and divinity of her work have been jealously hidden from her by Man," as Shaw says of Dona Ana.[54] Since the new life's work of this play's heroine is to be built on the foundation of her marriage, the immediate and pressing need is to establish a base for these ventures.

The unusual manner in which Barbara makes her entreaty—like a young girl importuning an indulgent parent to gratify a childish craving—contributes to its intriguing suggestiveness. What she wants is a house to live in with "Dolly"—her "dear little Dolly boy," as she has just called him. Do we not have here a veiled punning allusion to *A Doll's House*, the Ibsen drama that so impressed Shaw, which he commented on so frequently in his writings? In his 1890 sequel to Walter Besant's sequel to this Ibsen play, "Still After the Doll's House," Shaw has Nora say, "the man must walk out of the doll's house as well as the woman" (*The Black Girl in Search of God*, 237). This idea found further employment in *Candida*, as he more than once disclosed. As early as 1895 he wrote about that play, "and so the happy ending is in sight, but only after the complete upset of Ibsen's Doll's House, and the revelation of the husband as the doll and the managing woman as his sovereign owner."[55] He reiterated this analysis in the program for the 1937 production of *Candida* at the Globe Theatre in London, attributing its surprise to "turning the tables on A Doll's House," and showing "irresistibly that domestically [the husband] is the pet and the doll, and that it is his wife who runs the establishment" (Author's Note to *Candida*, 1:599). Once more, in 1944, Shaw called the play a "counterblast to Ibsen's Doll's House, showing that in the real typical doll's house it is the man who is the doll."[56] It is not at all strange then to find that in *Major Barbara* he is toying again with the *Candida* variation on the *Doll's House* idea, particularly in view of the recurrence of other favorite themes in more than one play.

The final speeches of Dionysos in the *Bacchae*, including the lines that have been lost (compare *Bacchae*, ed. Dodds, 234–35), are filled with prophecy for the house of Cadmus. Shaw is far less specific: he leaves us with enigmatic hints about what lies in store for the house of Undershaft. As early as his first private conversation with the head of the house, Adolphus confessed: "I don't like marriage: I feel intensely afraid of it; and I don't know what I shall do with Barbara or what she will do with me" (118). Notwithstanding these feelings, he was determined to marry her. Hence Bill Walker's dismal warning brought him no more than momentary hesitation. If he is to become the Dolly in the house that his bride and her magisterial mother are about to select for him, some degree of turbulence may be expected in the domestic life of the next Andrew Undershaft's family. But then they have plenty of precedent: there are Barbara's estranged parents, and Lady Britomart leaves no doubt from the start that furious quarrels marked the marriages of all the Undershaft precursors. But then, the prospect of hazard, even the marital variety, is not amiss in this drama of explosive potentiality.

To quote the *Major Barbara* Preface once more, "where there is danger there is hope" (40). The danger need not prove insuperable, however, for a couple united in their commitment to loftier loves and dreams than those of the hearth. Accordingly, the last word in the play is Undershaft's admonitory summons to the practical decisions and demanding work ahead: "Six o'clock tomorrow morning, Euripides." A new day is dawning and it beckons a surrogate for the creator of the *Bacchae*—a final intimation that Hellenic contributions are bound to be implicated in his program for the future. The summons, continuing the jousting over working hours, yields as corollary a parting clue that the agon between the old and the new Undershaft is by no means over. "The rest the event will show," as Dionysos says (*Bacchae* 976, trans. Winnington-Ingram).

The *Bacchae* and *Major Barbara*

The state of affairs at the conclusion of Shaw's play is far removed from the tragic outcome of its Euripidean counterpart. The *Bacchae* issues in catastrophic ruin and misery, relieved only by the enlightened shared sympathy of the surviving victims. *Major Barbara* ends on a rising tide of hope for the future. Even so, there remain some correlative points worth remarking on and appending to the general parallels between the two dramas already discussed. "If there is anyone who scorns the gods, let him look upon this man's fate—and believe in them" (*Bacchae* 1325–26, trans. Winnington-Ingram); this is the moral that Cadmus draws. The fate of Barbara, raising her from a passion and *sparagmos* of the spirit, conveys an analogous lesson in the temporal sphere: the crying need to recognize the existence and potency of the masters and purveyors of worldly power.

By resolving to die with the colors, Barbara is committed unto death. Death in both works is an unfailing test of conviction—as witness Pentheus, facing slaughter, alarmed into confessing the error of his ways (*Bacchae* 1120–21). Indeed, death is a corrective of judgments or purposes (1102–3). Each of the plays gravitates between the poles of life and death, but the one strikingly reverses the course of the other. In the *Bacchae* the way to death lies through the tree of life; in *Major Barbara* "the way of life lies through the factory of death" (184). The "unveiling of an eternal light in the Valley of The Shadow" likewise introduces a divinely inspired life and will into a locale portentous of devastation and death. It contemplates the virtual converse of the apocalyptic vision in the *Bacchae*; there the appearance of supernal light in the peaceful glades on Mount Cithaeron serves as the harbinger of divinely inspired bloodshed and disaster.

Both the modern and the ancient drama depict the interplay of mighty forces, the contention of custom and morality with the resources of nature, and the effort to ascertain and achieve the right relationship with the daemonic powers of the world, so real and so intrusive in the governance of human life. Equally under scrutiny in *Major Barbara* are the inclusive, ultimate issues that Sutherland finds in the *Bacchae*—"the relation of rational man to the irrational divine, reason itself to mysticism, the struggle of civilization against both barbarism and the natural powers, of the city against humanity, of the masculine against the feminine" (91). The two plays probe the scope and limits of wisdom, the uses and peril of power. They are alike in underscoring the urgency of wedding genuine wisdom with power if we are to master the forces of irrationality and destruction that threaten civilized life. In its own fashion each explores the dynamics of personal and political authority, as well as the shaping of individual and social identity and purpose. Evident further in both is a profound concern with "the great vital dogmas of honor, liberty, courage, the kinship of all life, faith that the unknown is greater than the known and is only the As Yet Unknown, and resolution to find a manly highway to it," to quote from the next preface to a play Shaw wrote after *Major Barbara* (Preface on Doctors, *The Doctor's Dilemma*, 3:317).

The revelatory insights in the two dramas emanate from the tensions of kinship and collision between the human and the divine. In the *Bacchae*, the stricken survivors are confirmed in a mortal dignity and moral humanity that distinguishes them from the pitiless indifference of deity and nature. In *Major Barbara* identity and awareness of reality are equivalently won in the crucible of necessity. But with Shaw the perspective is teleological, the emphasis is on human foresight and forethought, and the motive force is an insatiable evolutionary appetite for perfection. His object is to alert us to the vision that "it is godlike to be wise" and that "everybody, by the deepest law of the Life Force, desires to be godlike"; or as couched in the amphibolous language of the god Ra, "the spirit of man is the will of the gods."[57] The true destiny of such a spirit is to become a worthy citizen of the perfect city of God, which only its own zealous endeavor, in willing concert with that of kindred spirits, can create.[58] By Shaw's exacting standards, as by those of his greatest Greek forbears, the measure of man is inevitably cosmic.

Appendix

BERNARD SHAW: THE ARTIST AS PHILOSOPHER

"I sing, not arms and the hero, but the philosophic man," proclaims Don Juan in the philosophical act of *Man and Superman,* the play Bernard Shaw subtitles as "a Comedy and a Philosophy" (2:664, 489). In the Epistle Dedicatory to this drama Shaw confesses "what I have always wanted is a pit of philosophers; and this is a play for such a pit" (2:518). The devotion to philosophic concerns so unequivocally asserted here persists as a dominant theme in his dramatic writings. Shaw consciously and proudly donned the mantle of the philosophical poet, singing to philosophers and about philosophers from his dramatic scores.

So large does this aspect loom in his work that to at least one analyst of his playwriting, Martin Ellehauge, he seems to be more philosopher than artist. "The philosophic character of Shaw's dramatic work is its chief distinguishing trait," Ellehauge writes, and he reports even more extreme views that have been held concerning the disparity between philosophic and artistic elements in Shaw (*The Position of Bernard Shaw,* 379). For some tastes the dramatist evidently does not "sing" enough, and sacrifices art to philosophy. The passage of time has brought at least a partial reversal of such judgments. Already a number of the Shavian dramas exhibit a capacity for longevity exceeding that of their creator. They may even go on to rival the length of days he envisaged for his Ancients, those amazing long-livers of *Back to Methuselah.* Yet it does not appear that such powers of survival have been purchased at the expense of art or dramatic skill and invention.

Certainly Shaw took the "singing" of his philosophy seriously. He regarded himself as an "artist-philosopher" and contended that "the artist-philosophers are the only sort of artists I take quite seriously" (Ep. Ded. *Man and Superman,* 2:519). Not the least among his accomplishments, moreover, has been the demonstration that—formalistic aesthetic doctrines to the contrary notwithstanding—a considerable amount of philosophical content may be so skillfully incorporated in a drama as to enhance, rather than to impair, its dramatic interest. He fully exploited the drama, and comedy, of ideas. His work includes dramatic philosophy as well as philosophical drama. And, if it is essential to consider his philosophy in understanding his dramatic art, it would also appear to be wise to keep in mind his artistic function when examining his philosophy.

Numerous problems attend this philosophy. Perhaps some of these may prove less perplexing if the "artistic" qualification be kept constantly in mind in dealing with Shaw the philosopher. For he is a philosopher with a mission—a moral and religious mission—and art is for him its means of implementation. To consider his ends merely, ignoring their integral and essential connection with the means he employed, is to misunderstand his artistic function, if not his actual meaning. His speculation, however metaphysical, reconnoiters for changes in a factual world. "The philosopher," he tells us, "is Nature's pilot" (*Man and Superman*, 2:685). And when Shaw contemplates a universal, he recognizes that it may look different from opposing points of view; in other words, he contemplates it dramatically. A case can be made for the fact that his best philosophy is in his plays, not his prefaces. For there he puts his philosophy to work in human situations—however fanciful—and the working is the important thing.

In *Man and Superman* Don Juan describes the philosophic man as "he who seeks in contemplation to discover the inner will of the world, in invention to discover the means of fulfilling that will, and in action to do that will by the so-discovered means" (2:664). Treatments of Shaw as a philosopher often tend to concentrate on his "contemplation to discover the inner will of the world"; but this, we may see, is but one-third of his conception of the philosopher. To suggest that the phrase, "in invention to discover the means of fulfilling that will," is descriptive of Shaw's specifically dramatic activity, may seem to expand its meaning somewhat; yet it does cast a light upon his artistic-philosophic function. Similarly, "in action to do that will by the so-discovered means" completes the moral task he has set for himself. But this, too, is an essential aspect of his artistic activity. In other words, the philosopher—that is, the artist-philosopher—is not just a thinker; he is an inventor and doer as well. Consequently it is a mistake to give undue priority to Shaw's speculative inquiry in considering his philosophy, especially if this means neglecting his aesthetic and moral concerns, since in his work all three coalesce. It may prove fruitful, therefore, to consider some of the ways in which these moral and aesthetic interests qualify and clarify Shaw's philosophy.

The philosophy itself affords abundant evidence that Shaw's mind ranged widely over the works of thinkers and writers in many fields, affording him a rich and diversified philosophical ancestry. Jacques Barzun has pointed out that he "treasured up wisdom wherever it could be picked up, always with scrupulous acknowledgment." Studies of his thought, however, usually stress nineteenth-century influences. Indeed, as Barzun adds, he possessed that century "entire" ("Bernard Shaw in Twilight," 172). And Ellehauge traces in considerable detail the connections between Shaw's views and those of various literary and philosophical figures of his time.[1] The most direct and decisive roles in the development of his vitalistic metaphysics were probably played by Schopenhauer, Nietzsche, and Butler—though Shaw declared himself "rather an impostor as a pundit in the philosophy of Schopenhauer & Nietzsche" and noted that he does not care for Nietzsche "except when he is perfectly original" (*Bernard Shaw: Collected Letters 1898–1910*, ed. Laurence, 553–54).[2] He drew upon their common conception of a fundamentally irrational but creative will that realizes itself in the evolutionary development of human beings and the universe. Shaw's particular version of this evolutionary voluntarism took a teleological turn. For, with Butler, he turned to Lamarck in vehement reaction against the mechanistic determinism of the Darwinian, or natural selection, interpretation of evolution.

Probably because of the understandable preoccupation with these features of his philosophy and their origins in nineteenth-century intellectual movements, insufficient attention has been paid to the impact made on his thinking by earlier philosophers. Yet evidence abounds that Shaw was readily conversant with most of the history of philosophy. The Preface to *Back to Methuselah* (5:269) finds him tracing the idea of evolution back to Empedocles among the pre-Socratics (although he was evidently unaware of the earlier anticipations of evolutionary theory by Anaximander in the sixth century B.C.E.). More significantly, he allies himself in the same preface with the "great tradition" in philosophy when he informs us that philosophers from Plato to Leibnitz have viewed the universe "as one idea behind all its physically apprehensible transformations" (5:282). Other preface passages disclose his familiarity with the philosophies of Descartes and Spinoza, among the Continental Rationalists, as well as with that of the British skeptic David Hume.

On various occasions he partook of the philosophy of Immanuel Kant. The latter's categorical imperative, for example, is employed in the Preface to *Major Barbara*. Undershaft's conduct, we are told, stands the Kantian test of universal applicability, but Peter Shirley's does not (3:27). *The Quintessence of Ibsenism* contains this Kantian line: "Now to treat a person as a means instead of an end is to deny that person's right to live" (*Major Critical Essays*, 37). But mention of Kant is not confined to ethical contexts, for there are both implicit and explicit references to the metaphysical criticism of the *Critique of Pure Reason*. The Kantian antinomies must have supplied the groundwork for the contention, in *Back to Methuselah,* that the ultimate problem of existence is insoluble and unthinkable on causation lines (5:286). They also appear to underlie Shaw's argument with Father Addis in the same place. Again, he maintains in the Preface to *Androcles and the Lion* that he is engaged in a "criticism (in the Kantian sense) of an established body of belief" (4:565). The same preface also includes an allusion to Kant's two wonders—the starry heavens above and the moral law within us (4:468).

But even when we restrict our view to Shaw's intellectual indebtedness within the nineteenth century, it is surprising to note that comparatively little consideration has been given to the extent of Hegelian influence upon him. Yet Hegel dominated much of the philosophical thought of that century. It would seem unlikely that Shaw would have been impervious to so prominent and pervasive a force in his intellectual environment.[3] If in no other way, he would have encountered that monumental thinker in his studies of Karl Marx, who among other things owed to Hegel the whole apparatus of the dialectical account of historical development. In the Hegelian Idealism an Absolute Spirit progressively realizes itself in the course of the history of human civilization by the dialectical process of synthesizing or reconciling opposing standpoints (which Hegel called "contradictory"). Marx rejected the idealism but he did appropriate the dialectic to support his mechanical economic determinism. Shaw, in turn, repudiated the Marxian dialectic as another of the determinisms he found so unsatisfactory, while accepting the Marxian moral criticism of the bourgeoisie (for example, Pref. *Back to Methuselah*, 5:313–14). From this it might be presumed that he would be no more hospitable to Hegel, at least so far as the dialectic is concerned.

Nevertheless, a philosophy like Hegel's in treating nature and human civilization as the progressive evolutionary realization of absolute mind in the universe does bear some resemblance to the Shavian conception of a creative Life Force evolving higher forms of Life. This resemblance is at the least sufficient to have warranted the dramatist's sympathetic interest in Hegel. What is more, the Hegelian metaphysics, positing a Reason that is suprarational from the human point of view, is a form of romanticism spiritually akin to the romantic intuitionism of Schopenhauer, in which Shaw's philosophy is rooted. Both philosophies seek a certainty beyond that afforded by the rationalism of the Enlightenment. Furthermore, the Hegelian dialectic, purporting to synthesize science and poetry in what Josiah Royce called a "logic of passion," would certainly have attractive features for Shaw (*The Spirit of Modern Philosophy*, 190–227). Beyond this affinity between the two doctrines, the Hegelian philosophy offered a rich vein that the philosophical playwright could mine with profit. For Hegel's knowledge of the history of human civilization was prodigious, and his work contains many insights not necessarily dependent on his philosophical system. Moreover, Shaw's major interest was not in establishing a metaphysics but in utilizing the contributions that a philosophy might make to human betterment.

Indeed, critical examination of his writings does reveal that Shaw was far from immune to Hegelian doctrines and ideas. For instance, the Preface to *Androcles and the Lion* observes that the authors of the gospels could embrace contradictory views without apparent intellectual discomfort: "We can provisionally entertain half a dozen contradictory versions of an event if we feel either that it does not greatly matter, or that there is a category attainable in which the contradictions are reconciled" (4:477). What is noteworthy here, apart from the logically imprecise employment of the term "contradictory," is the latter part of the sentence. For this certainly sounds Hegelian whether or not Hegel is its actual source. Another passing remark along similar lines turns up in the Preface to *The Shewing-Up of Blanco Posnet*: "And since every interest has its opposition, all these influences had created hostile bodies by the operation of the mere impulse to contradict them" (3:680). Indeed, as Eric Bentley has remarked, "Shaw, as much as Marx or Hegel but after his own fashion, sees life as the interaction of opposites" (*Bernard Shaw*, 199).

But even more compelling Hegelian intimations are to be found in Shaw. One such is the passage in the Preface to the Plays Pleasant in which the playwright explains his attempt in *Candida* to distill the quintessential drama from pre-Raphaelitism. To do this, he declares, "it must be shewn at its best in conflict with the first broken, nervous, stumbling attempts to formulate its own revolt against itself as it develops into something higher. A coherent explanation of any such revolt, addressed intelligibly and prosaically to the intellect, can only come when the work is done, and indeed *done with:* that is to say, when the development, accomplished, admitted, and assimilated, is a story of yesterday. Long before any such understanding can be reached, the eyes of men begin to turn towards the distant light of the new age" (1:373–74). The first sentence quoted is inescapably a restatement of the Hegelian dialectic; the remaining lines echo Hegel's thought in *Philosophy of Right* that "Minerva's owl begins its flight only in the gathering dusk" (*A History of Political Theory,* 639). It is Hegel's view that clear knowledge of a historical movement comes only when it is completed or dying away.

Another instance appears in *The Quintessence of Ibsenism,* with the announcement that in Ibsen, as in the nineteenth century, "the way to Communism lies through the most resolute and uncompromising Individualism. James Mill, with an inhuman conceit and pedantry . . . educated John Stuart Mill to be the arch individualist of his time, with the result that John Stuart Mill became a Socialist a quarter of a century before the rest of his set moved in that direction" (*Major Critical Essays,* 102). No wonder that William Irvine, in another connection, sees Shaw more as Hegelian dialectician than as a gradualist in his attitude toward social change (*Universe of G.B.S.,* 367).

Still more conclusive, however, is the explicit endorsement of Hegelian ideas in two other passages. Again in *The Quintessence of Ibsenism* Shaw refers disparagingly to "our fathers, unversed in the Hegelian dialectic," who could not conceive that two propositions that negate each other are really the same (20 n. 1).[4] And in the Preface to *Heartbreak House,* he subscribes to a thought expressed by the German philosopher in his *Philosophy of History.* "Alas!" he sighs, "Hegel was right when he said that we learn from history that men never learn anything from history" (5:55). These instances should suffice to suggest that further inquiry into Hegelian aspects of Shaw would prove rewarding. At the same time the mere recognition of the presence of a Hegelian strain in the dramatist in itself contributes to a better understanding of his philosophic approach, or more accurately, attack.

To illustrate: Shaw's patent inconsistencies have disturbed those who have attempted to derive a unified philosophy from his manifold and diverse writings. Ellehauge's judgment may be taken as representative: "Shaw's attempt at amalgamating the different, mutually antagonistic, creeds he is handling: rationalism, naturalism, vitalism, the contrasting theories of Mill, Darwin, Butler, Schopenhauer, and Nietzsche, and shaping the product into an original Shavian creed, must be characterized as an essential failure. His acute perception, his felicity of phrasing, his lucidity of illustration, his happy deduction of inferences, which are so strikingly evident in isolated cases, fail him in the larger survey. His imaginative power seems insufficient to joint the details he has plucked out into a cohesive whole" (373; compare *Universe of G.B.S.*, 318–19).

Bentley, too, records numerous examples of Shaw's seeming indifference to logical contradiction in his polemical statements. His explanation is that Shaw is uttering half-truths, ignoring the familiar half of the truth in order to jolt us into attention to the half that we have obscured (96). Now in the Hegelian conception, opposing standpoints—indeed all positions—are partially true and partially false, approximating to the full truth only as they are progressively synthesized in a more inclusive totality. Thus, what Bentley calls "half-truths" could have been regarded by Shaw as Hegelian antitheses whose very opposition is conducive to greater truth. A reexamination of Shavian polemics from this viewpoint might prove illuminating. It is not to be expected, however, that this interpretation, any more than Bentley's, will remove the logical difficulties in Shaw's position. For, as with Hegel, a reliable criterion is still lacking by which to discriminate the relatively true from the relatively false in the opposing claims to truth. Logically considered, a half-truth may also be half false. At the least, ambiguities beset the Hegelian methodology. But logical questions aside, this methodology could suggest a highly useful approach for a playwright interested, as Shaw was, in the interplay of conflicting points of view.

Barzun has also directed attention to this interest as a romantic element in Shaw:

The quality of drama, of many-sidedness, of antithesis, in Shaw's thought is of the highest and best romantic strain: witness his fusion of scientific skepticism with religious faith, of individualism with the sense of collective discipline, of the primacy of the will with the use of reason, of a taste for heresy with a taste for legalism—dialectical oppositions which are the mainspring of his intellectual energy as well as the source of the misunderstandings he has suffered. Taken piecemeal, his opinions are easily misfiled; but there can be no doubt that Shaw himself belongs to the neo-romantic revolt against mid-century materialism, realism, and determinism, *not* to the revolt against the generation preceding these. (172)

This romanticism takes a distinctively dramatic turn as his playwright's imagination encompasses the polarities of diverse points of view. Shaw recognizes in this receptiveness to the antithetical a foundation for a viable community solidarity and fellowship. Hence his perceptive affirmation that "men who know their opponents and understand their case, quite commonly respect and like them, and always learn something from them" (Pref. *Misalliance,* 4:45). Wherefore, also, his assumption of "the fullest responsibility" for the opinions of all his characters, unpleasant as well as pleasant: "They are all right from their several points of view; and their points of view are, for the dramatic moment, mine also. This may puzzle the people who believe that there is such a thing as an absolutely right point of view, usually their own. . . . Nobody who agrees with them can possibly be a dramatist, or indeed anything else that turns upon a knowledge of mankind" (Ep. Ded. *Man and Superman,* 2:517).[5]

His romanticism, imbued with this concern for the dramatic alternatives, renders intelligible, suggestive, and stimulating much that would have to be abandoned as confusingly inconsistent when taken as literal and technical philosophy. Shaw must be granted his poetic margin for error, just as criticism of Shaw must be free to brand particular opinions and fancies as false and wrong when they are so. Hence, some of his strictures on science, including his attacks on vaccination and vivisection, are defensible only on the grounds proffered by J. D. Bernal, namely, that they represent a healthy kind of social and moral criticism of scientific activities ("Shaw the Scientist," 120–38). But we must, as Bernal does, still distinguish between the values in Shaw's moral criticisms and the erroneous judgments that his moral zeal at times produces. This is especially necessary since these judgments often seem to be supported by an inadequate conception of scientific methodology. The Preface to *Back to Methuselah,* as a case in point, abounds in instances of loose terminological usage (for example, the term "habit" applied to death, 5:273) and exhibits relatively little concern for criteria of verifiability.

Still, pointing out his errors need not blind us to what he is achieving;

nor should we expect of him that which is not his to give. Systematic metaphysics and veridical, authenticated science are not the provinces in which his major contributions are to be found, whatever coruscating light he may at times thrust into these areas. The efforts of C.E.M. Joad to cramp Shaw into a circumscribed philosophical mold illustrate the frustrations of the process. Joad, setting out as Shaw's philosophical disciple, has recorded his progressive defection in his book, *Shaw*.[6] This work starts out as a tribute and ends as a repudiation. It records a crestfallen retreat from a venerating hero-worship, nurturing a hopeful illusion of infallibility, to a fairly complete abandonment of all but a vestigial residue of the total Shavian structure. This fall from grace, rather pathetically attributed to a fundamental difference in bodily temperament, is plaintively presumed to be an ascent toward truth.

The record of this process of transformation, which runs the gamut from the rejection of anti-vivisectionism to the espousal of the doctrine of original sin, includes an expanded version of an earlier essay analyzing Shaw's philosophy of creative evolution. In this analysis, it may be noted in passing, Joad attributes the comparative neglect of the philosophical aspect of Shaw's work to the fact that Bergson in *Creative Evolution* and S. Alexander in *Space, Time, and Deity* presented in more orthodox philosophical form somewhat divergent interpretations of the same creative evolution philosophy (Joad, *Shaw*, 172–206). This explanation is hardly convincing, even when one grants Joad's admission that his own effort to provide such a philosophical setting for Shaw in his *Matter, Life and Value* was not very successful (198). His own attempt to portray the playwright in conventional philosophical guise distorts and limits Shaw. It also reinforces the view defended here, that Shaw's philosophical significance is inseparable from his art.[7]

Studies like those of Joad and Ellehauge have their uses in suggesting the philosophical orientation of the plays, even though they may go astray on specific points. But they are definitely misleading to the extent that they take the part for the whole, or even for the most important part of the whole. Ellehauge's acknowledgment that he finds it difficult to determine how far Shaw is serious is a revealing symptom that something is awry. The Shavian sense of humor presents a genuine stumbling block to overly solemn research into his thought. Nor is the obstacle to be surmounted by affirming, as Ellehauge does, that our comic writer is more serious than he appears (372). This point will be returned to later.

On the constructive side, Joad does make one suggestive comparison that, when properly expanded and qualified, provides access to certain singular facets of the playwright's philosophy. Discussing possible changes in Shaw's thinking as a result of reading Plato's *Republic*, Joad remarks on the striking affinity between these two writers:

> Both are fundamentally rationalist; both dislike enthusiasm; both are distrustful of poetry and romance; both are temperamentally unsympathetic to the common man; both are revolted by the vulgarity of his tastes and wearied by his incorrigible irrationality. It is because his reason is the slave of appetite and desire, because its conclusions are distorted by his wishes that, Plato urges—and Shaw is presently found to be agreeing with him—the common man is incapable of "true philosophy," that is to say, of seeing things as they are and of valuing them as they should be valued. There is a natural fastidiousness in both Shaw and Plato which renders them incapable either of forgetting or forgiving the "earthiness" of common men. I cannot think of any writer outside the ranks of the religious orders who has been less indulgent to common frailties and failings. . . . Each implies even if he does not explicitly assert, that, if the common man is the best that can be contrived in the way of humanity, we may as well despair of our species; each, therefore, has his own recipe for superseding the common man. (149–50)

Such a comparison does not, of course, exhaust the distinctive quality of either man. It is, moreover, exclusively concerned with their common dislikes, whereas the attitude of each toward what he looks down on is determined largely by what he looks up and forward to. There are, in addition, significant differences in the thinking of the two men at a number of crucial junctures. For example, Plato's pursuit of exact knowledge led to his preoccupation with logical, methodological, and mathematical issues quite alien to Shavian interests. Not only are their metaphysical outlooks distinct, as Joad notes (152), but on specific subjects, such as education and censorship, their doctrines move in different directions.

The parallel is nevertheless enlightening as far as it may be pursued. There are innumerable references to Plato, direct and indirect, especially in the Shavian prefaces. The spiritual kinship of the two thinkers manifests itself on many occasions and in many connections. To cite but a few of the resemblances on positive grounds, as contrasted with Joad's essentially negative linkage, there are first of all the more obvious correspondences between Shaw's treatment of a number of problems in human relations, and that to be found in the *Republic*. Plato was disturbed by the disrupting effect of the family and of property in political life. He saw in marriage and family life on the one hand, and in private wealth on the other, hindrances to good citizenship and rival interests to the necessary harmony and unity of the community. So he unhesitatingly urged their abolition. Compare Shaw's summary, in the Preface to *Androcles and the Lion,* of two of the four doctrines of Jesus that he believes are confirmed by modern social science: "Get rid of property by throwing it into the common stock. Dissociate your work entirely from money payments." And as regards marriage, "Get rid of your family entanglements. Every mother you meet is as much your mother as the woman who bore you" (4:516–17). His reasoning, particularly about marriage as providing a rival and distracting interest is unquestionably in the Platonic spirit. That Plato envisaged his communism and the establishment of the state as one big family only for his guardian class does not materially affect the similarity, since this class was to be open to all who possessed the requisite capabilities. It is to be further observed in this connection that Shaw refuses to place Jesus, as portrayed in Matthew, above Plato as a moralist (4:493).

Shaw also includes a Platonic argument in his case for equality of income. "Society," he asserts, "is not only divided but actually destroyed in all directions by inequality of income between classes" (4:528–29). This was Plato's principal objection to inequality of wealth, that "indeed any city, however small, is in fact divided into two, one the city of the poor, the other of the rich; these are at war with one another" (*Republic* 422e–423a, trans. Jowett).

Although Shaw does not urge Plato's peremptory abolition of marriage, in the Preface to *Getting Married* he does canvass a number of radical alternatives to the conventional monogamy prevailing in Western civilization. Plato, moreover, certainly would have subscribed to the Shavian revolt against marriage, directed "against its sentimentality, its romance, its Amorism, even against its enervating happiness" (Pref. *Getting Married,* 3:476). For the happiness Shaw is continually attacking is generally construed in hedonistic or individualistic terms, much as the Utilitarians conceived it, and the Utilitarians had their Hellenic precursors.[8]

Both writers, it may be added, were critics of the position of women as they found it. In both cases the support given to women is decidedly not on sentimental grounds. Plato objected to the fact that full use was not being made of all the human potential in the community. Shaw objects to the treatment of human beings as property and champions the economic independence of women (Pref. *Getting Married*, 3:499–501). Plato, however, would not have argued as Shaw does that "we must finally adapt our institutions to human nature" without imposing stringent rational controls (3:543). But there is a Platonic, as well as Schopenhauerian, spirit in Shaw's warning against the unwholesome illusions arising from the glorification of sex, "an instinctive function which clouds the reason and upsets the judgment more than all the other instincts put together"; and against the failure to recognize that "its great natural purpose so completely transcends the personal interests of any individual" (3:498).

Political proposals reflecting a Platonic slant are also to be detected in John Tanner's *Revolutionist's Handbook*. Bentley argues that the views therein proposed should not be attributed to Shaw without due qualification as to their provisional character. But his reasons for refusing to credit Tanner's doctrines to Shaw are hardly compelling. These reasons are that Tanner is given an appearance exactly like that of Shaw's political antagonist, H. M. Hyndman; that he is not a heroic, or even an effective man; that Shaw has made him an ineffectual chatterbox (79). But do considerations of appearance and characterization invalidate the views that Tanner supports? Shaw's preoccupation with these matters was dramatic—and comic. It is unlikely that he would try to undermine the credibility of the *Handbook* ideas in the theater, where the playgoers would not ordinarily encounter them anyway. As for Tanner, it is clear from the Epistle Dedicatory that he is identified with Don Juan and is taken seriously as hero by his author, which is all that matters on this point. Moreover, the views expressed in the *Handbook* are not discrepant with what Shaw says in this play and elsewhere. Nor is there any substantial reason for believing that he dashed them off merely as an experimental exercise in order to present ideas that differ essentially from his other statements of opinion. Indeed, in a later reference to this work in the Preface to *Back to Methuselah* he makes no qualifying distinction whatsoever between the *Handbook* appendix and preface as his additions to the published text of the play (5:338).

Conspicuously Platonic themes appearing in this *Handbook* include the earnest contemplation of a eugenic program of mating, distinct from marriage, to help breed the Superman (2:744–45); comments critical of democracy, modified somewhat by the call for a "Democracy of Supermen" (755); and an explicit concurrence in a Platonic judgment. "The democratic politician," we learn, "remains exactly as Plato described him" (768). These ideas are echoed in the Preface to *Getting Married* along with a Plato-like insistence on the need for government by the expert (478–80). Once more the *Republic* is cited: "Plato long ago pointed out the importance of being governed by men with sufficient sense of responsibility and comprehension of public duties to be very reluctant to undertake the work of governing" (3:490).

On occasion after occasion Shaw pays homage to the Greek philosopher. Thus he explains that it is in Plato's sense, not Zola's, that he employs the term "realist" in *The Quintessence of Ibsenism* (30). Again, in the Notes to *Caesar and Cleopatra,* he concludes that the world of men presents a less dignified appearance sixty-seven generations after Plato than it did in the latter's *Republic* (2:295).

The most important Platonic parallels in Shaw, however, are to be found in his aesthetics. Joad maintains that Plato held a twofold attitude toward art (191–92). He first regarded it with suspicion for arousing the emotional and irrational part of the soul. Later, in the *Phaedrus* and *Symposium,* he represented it as a medium for revealing the form of Beauty, thereby providing a window through which a glimpse of reality is granted us. This interpretation assumes that the two conceptions are unrelated in Plato. That assumption is erroneous, as more careful analysis of the later works would show. Plato was always suspicious of the emotional enticements of art. He praises art only when it is allied with philosophy in the pursuit of the Form of Beauty, which intellectually viewed is Truth, and morally considered is the Good. In other words, for Plato the only kind of artist to be tolerated is an artist-philosopher. In the *Laws* he as much as says that he is such a one, whose work should be taken as a standard for all admissible dramatic compositions (*Laws* 817).

Joad believes that Shaw moved from greater to less confidence in art, the opposite to Plato's movement as he conceives it (192–93). But Bentley is certainly more correct in maintaining that, like Plato's, Shaw's warnings against the dangers of sensuousness in art are but the negative side of a philosophy that places great stress on the arts (119ff.). If the Ancients in the last play of *Back to Methuselah* echo Platonic sentiments about art—comparing it with toys and dolls, judging it as providing a mirror and image instead of the reality, which reality, once possessed, the inadequate reflection may be abandoned—it is nevertheless worth noting at the same time that Shaw does not by any means abandon his own artistic endeavors. Indeed, he attaches added significance to them in the Preface to that work. Act III of *Man and Superman* he had previously called, in its Epistle Dedicatory, "a Shavio-Socratic dialogue" (2:503), but in the Preface to *Back to Methuselah* he is undertaking to be "an iconographer of the religion of my time, fulfilling my natural function as an artist" (5:337). Moreover, just as Plato always warned that his myths were only something like the truth, so also does Shaw distinguish between legend and truth, warning us not to confuse dogmas with legend, parable, and drama, "the natural vehicles of dogma" (5:328). Accordingly, to regard *Back to Methuselah* as literal Shavian dogma is to ignore its author's counsel and to forget its dramatic nature.

In the aesthetic discussion at the end of the Epistle Dedicatory to *Man and Superman,* content is held to assure the splendidness of form even though the writer's assertions inevitably are disproved and lose their credibility. Designating light and heat as the two vital qualities of literature, Shaw admits that he can go wrong, with incendiary possibilities. This is not very Platonic, but in the Preface to *Back to Methuselah* he is back once more with Plato in an essentially representational aesthetics. Even music, he says, "must represent something" (5:334). Great artistic movements are now said to wait upon great religious movements and he commends artist-prophets rather than artist-philosophers (5:333).

Another resemblance to Plato helps bring Shaw into revealing comparison with the former's master, Socrates, whom Shaw jocularly represents as having been invented by Plato as dramatist (2:519). In the *Phaedo,* the Platonic Socrates tells of his disappointment with the doctrines of Anaxagoras, which appeared to employ mind as an explanatory principle but actually accounted for phenomena in material and mechanical terms. What Socrates was seeking was an explanation of the universe in terms of purpose. Hence he would reject an explanation that attributed his being in prison to having a body, muscles, bones, and the like. He is there, rather, because the Athenians have sentenced him, and because he has agreed that it is right to remain even though his bones and muscles would be more disposed to run away and escape his imminent death (*Phaedo* 98c–99a). This teleological outlook is reflected in Plato's later criticism of philosophers who taught that the phenomena of the universe are caused "not . . . by the agency of mind, or any god, or art, but . . . by nature and chance" (*Laws* 889b, trans. Taylor).

It is precisely in this spirit that Shaw reiterates Butler's accusation that Darwin had "banished mind from the universe" (Pref. *Heartbreak House,* 5:20, Pref. *Back to Methuselah,* 5:300, Post. *Back to Methuselah,*

5:696). He insists that the world "did not look like a pure accident: it presented evidences of design in every direction. There was mind and purpose behind it" (Pref. *Back to Methuselah*, 5:288). This provides direction and meaning to human life: "This is the true joy in life, the being used for a purpose recognized by yourself as a mighty one; the being thoroughly worn out before you are thrown on the scrap heap; the being a force of Nature instead of a feverish selfish little clod of ailments and grievances complaining that the world will not devote itself to making you happy" (Ep. Ded. *Man and Superman*, 2:523).

Socrates's defense of his philosophic life in the *Apology* affords further striking parallels. One of the charges brought against him is not unlike that frequently leveled against Shaw, namely, that he made the worse argument appear the better. Though not as modestly as Socrates, Shaw too examined the views of the politicians, poets, artisans—those who laid claim to some knowledge or wisdom—and found them wanting: witness Don Juan's dissatisfaction with the doctors of medicine, the doctors of divinity, the politician, and the artist (*Man and Superman*, 2:664; cf. *Apology* 21–23). Socrates, moreover, held that human beings never do wrong voluntarily, but only through ignorance, believing thus that their motives are basically good. Although Shaw's account of human evil is more complex than this, it shares much in common with Socrates's conception. For example, he discerns an intrinsic connection between the notions of human goodness, freedom, and equality. "It is quite useless," he warns in the *Major Barbara* Preface, "to declare that all men are born free if you deny that they are born good" (3:48). And in the Preface to *Back to Methuselah* he speaks of the "instinctive righteousness" of the humble and argues that his redistillation of "the eternal spirit of religion" stresses the Protestant pursuit of the inner light that every man must see with his own eyes (5:325). A deeply religious Socrates was unjustly charged with atheism. Shaw, likewise religious, was prompted to frequent incursions against theological dogmas, which undoubtedly would have invited martyrdom in a harsher era (for example, Pref. *Androcles and the Lion*).[9]

Socrates's mission was to spend his life, according to Plato's account, "in searching for wisdom, and in examining myself and others. . . . I spend my whole life in going about and persuading you all to give your first and greatest care to the improvement of your souls." He is a sort of gadfly "constantly alighting upon you at every point to rouse, persuade, and reproach each of you all day long." For him "an unexamined life is not worth living" (*Apology* 29a, 30ab, 38a; trans. Church). Shaw's dedication is similar; and a large part of his tribute to the philosophic man is in this spirit. The Shavian credo is enunciated by Don Juan: "I tell you that as long as I can conceive something better than myself I cannot be easy unless I am striving to bring it into existence or clearing the way for it. That is the law of my life" (2:679–80). Shaw's moral passion, like that of Don Juan and John Tanner, is Socratic.

When Socrates says, "Rightly or wrongly, men have made up their minds that in some way Socrates is different from the multitude of men" (*Apology* 34e–35a, trans. Church); when he proposes as an alternative to the death penalty that he be set up at public expense in the prytaneum (public hall) as being more deserving of that honor than the winners of Olympic games; when he is surprised that the majority of those who voted against him was so small; and when he suggests that the way for the Athenians to avoid criticism is not to suppress their critics but to improve their lives—his demeanor, as well as his humor, could well be described as Shavian (*Apology* 34–39).

If there are also significant points of difference between the two individuals—as in Socrates's refusal to accept money for his teaching, in his consequent poverty, and in his understandably greater preoccupation with intimations of immortality—these similarities nevertheless outweigh them. It is possible to cite additional instances of correspondence, such as those to be found in the *Phaedo*, where Socrates is represented as putting some of Aesop's fables into verse, and supporting a Pythagorean-like view of the body as a prison of the soul. The body, he holds, distracts the soul from truth and knowledge, so that the soul should find its ultimate release from the body in death, a consummation devoutly to be wished (*Phaedo* 65–68). Dissatisfaction with the body comparable to that expressed in this latter doctrine, whether Socratic or Platonic, is voiced by the Ancients in "As Far as Thought Can Reach" of the *Back to Methuselah* cycle (5:564–631).

Again, in the *Crito* Socrates refuses to escape from prison because in so doing he would be subverting the laws upon which government must rest (*Crito* 51–54). Similarly, in the *Major Barbara* Preface, Shaw has argued surprisingly enough that there is considerable danger in attacks against current law, morality, respectability, and legal property; because if the ordinary man is led to repudiate the laws and institutions he knows, he will end by repudiating the very conception of law and the groundwork of institutions upon which society rests. Indeed, the justification he offers for his own revolutionary writing (quoted already in "Shaw's *Republic*," above) is that "our laws make law impossible; our liberties destroy all freedom; our property is organized robbery; our morality is an impudent hypocrisy; our wisdom is administered by inexperienced or malexperienced dupes, our power wielded by cowards and weaklings, and our honor false in all its points" (3:59). Finally, there is the express statement in the Preface to *Androcles and the Lion* that our hope lies in the Socratic man (4:568).

If, then, there is so much that is Socratic about Shaw, is there not a striking difference in their fates? In the *Apology* Socrates sadly prophesies, "There is no man who will preserve his life for long, either in Athens or elsewhere, if he firmly opposes the multitude, and tries to prevent the commission of much injustice and illegality in the state" (*Apology* 31e, trans. Church). Shaw was not unaware of this peril and may be presumed to have benefited from the experience of Socrates, as of other martyrs, including Saint Joan. It is not surprising to discover him pairing Joan and Socrates in the Preface to *Saint Joan,* comparing the martyrdoms of the young woman and the old man. He concludes that Socrates lasted so much longer because he was a "man of argument, operating slowly and peacefully on men's minds, whereas Joan was a woman of action, operating with impetuous violence on their bodies." Both had their terrifying ability combined with a benevolence, frankness, and personal modesty, which made hatred of them so unreasonable that they did not comprehend its extent. For, he argues, "it is always hard for superior wits to understand the fury roused by their exposures of the stupidities of comparative dullards." Socrates's accuser is really indistinguishable from a twentieth-century Londoner who would likewise dislike being shown up as an idiot "every time Socrates opened his mouth" (Pref. *Saint Joan,* 6:16; cf. *Getting Married,* 3:473). This account is not quite satisfactory, since the Socrates of the *Apology* did recognize that his condemnation would be due to "prejudice and resentment of the multitude which have been the destruction of many good men before me, and I think will be so again. There is no prospect that I shall be the last victim" (*Apology* 28a, trans. Church). There can be little doubt that he knew why he was on trial, and what it meant.

But if Socrates did nothing that effectively prevented his martyrdom, Shaw surely did. As always, he tells us just what this was. In the Postscript to *Back to Methuselah,* which is in many ways more revealing than the Preface, he writes: "A classic author has to consider how far he dare go; for though he is writing for the enlightenment of mankind he may not be willing to venture as far as martyrdom for its sake. Descartes burnt one of his books to escape being burnt for having written it. Galileo had to deny what he believed to escape the same fate" (5:692). Fear, not of the truth, but of undermining all morality and religion in the people by questioning any of it is, he explains, the reason for this intolerance by church and state. Thus some of his books have been banned and placed on the index, and there are those who would have burned him if they had the power. The moral he draws from all this is "that heretical teaching must be made irresistibly attractive by fine art if the heretics are not to starve or burn. I have to make my heresies pleasing as plays to extract the necessary shillings from those to whom they are so intensely irritating" (5:695).

But if this is the case, the fine art cannot, if successful, be taken as mere sugar coating to the pill, even though Shaw at times appears so to regard it, thereby supplying ammunition to his critics. Art when effective transforms its material, and this holds true of Shaw's better efforts. *Saint Joan* is a better play than *Back to Methuselah* just because in the former the art controls the philosophy, not the reverse. There is every indication that Shaw himself saw philosophic significance in the work of the dramatist as artist, recognizing in drama more than just a convenient vehicle for propagating philosophical or religious doctrines. "The truth is," he wrote in defense of the theater, "that dramatic invention is the first effort of man to become intellectually conscious. No frontier can be marked between drama and history or religion, or between acting and conduct" (Pref. *Plays Pleasant*, 1:378). In the *Androcles and the Lion* Preface he remarks that "we must not forget that the best dramatic art is the operation of a divinatory instinct for the truth" (4:504–5). As dramatic critic he had already advanced the thesis that plays "must all, if they are to be anything more than the merest tissue of stage effects, have a philosophy, even if it be no more than an unconscious expression of the author's temperament. Your great dramatist philosophizes quite openly: his lines become famous as aphorisms, and serve in the intercourse of philosophers as words serve in the intercourse of ordinary mortals" ("Nietzsche in English," *The Drama Observed*, 2:570–71).

His own devotion to philosophy went even further, and deeper. Laying proud claim to the title of philosopher, he disavows the detached role of speculative onlooker. For him there is no knowing without doing, no insight without involvement, no understanding without participation. Tilting at closet philosophers and aestheticians, Shaw, in the manner of a Plato, submits his own practice as a paradigm of philosophical deportment:

> To make my readers realize what a philosopher is, I can only say that *I* am a philosopher. If you ask incredulously, "How then, are your articles so interesting?" I reply that there is nothing so interesting as philosophy, provided its materials are not spurious. For instance, take my own materials—humanity and the fine arts. Any studious, timorously ambitious bookworm can run away from the world with a few shelvesful of history, essays, descriptions, and criticisms, and having pieced an illusory humanity and art out of the effects produced by his library on his imagination, build some silly systematization of his worthless ideas over the abyss of his own nescience. Such a philosopher is as dull and dry as you please: it is he who brings his profession into disrepute, especially when he talks much about art, and so persuades people to read him. Without having looked at more than fifty pictures in his life, or made up his mind on the smallest point about one of the fifty, he will audaciously take it upon himself to explain the development of painting from Zeuxis and Apelles to Raphael and Michael Angelo. As to the way he will go on about music, of which he always has an awe-stricken conceit, it spoils my temper to think of it. ("Nietzsche in English," 567–68)

His own mode of exposure is graphically contrasted:

> Now, the right way to go to work—strange as it may appear—is to look at pictures until you have acquired the power of seeing them. . . . [Then] you will, if you have a wise eye, be able to see what is actually in a picture, and not what you think is in it. Similarly, if you listen critically to music every day for a number of years, you will, if you have a wise ear, acquire the power of hearing music. And so on with all the arts. When we come to humanity it is still the same: only by intercourse with men and women can we learn anything about it. This involves an active life, not a contemplative one; for unless you do something in the world, you can have no real business to transact with men; and unless you love and are loved, you can have no intimate relations with them. And you must transact business, wirepull politics, discuss religion, give and receive hate, love, and friendship with all sorts of people before you can acquire the sense of humanity. If you are to acquire the

sense sufficiently to be a philosopher, you must do all these things unconditionally. ("Nietzsche in English," 568)

But intellectual and perceptual discernment is for Shaw propaedeutic to the recognition of the need for change and instrumental to its effectuation. As philosopher he does not cease to be reformer and rebel. He does not hesitate to censure the good in the interests of the better. But above all, the artistic perspective remains central. It permeates, even defines, his pragmatism—sensitive to the materials of experience, he is eager to reconstruct them according to their potentialities and his lights.

Therefore, if there is considerable philosophy in his art, there is also a pervasive art in his philosophy. It is this that makes it possible for a man with the mission of a moral prophet to present, when the occasion demands, a spirited defense of immorality (Pref. *Blanco Posnet*, 3:698–99). Particularly when this occurs as part of a statement with the practical political (as well as theatrical) objective of deriding British censorship, its intent is unquestionably dramatic, designed to disturb an audience. Shaw took delight in such paradoxes and exploited them to the full. In the role of devil's advocate, or even devil's disciple, he could win attention for critical or unpopular ideas by shocking or otherwise irritating his readers. "The plain working truth is that it is not only good for people to be shocked occasionally, but absolutely necessary to the progress of society that they should be shocked pretty often" (*Quintessence of Ibsenism*, 122).

A frontal attack on morality could thus further a moral purpose. The "morality" that is attacked is strictly conventional morality, but the ambiguity further highlights the rebellious nonconformity in the assault. For it was not with scientific objectivity, intellectual detachment, nor judicial impartiality that Shaw examined life and conduct, but rather with the zeal of a critic and publicist gifted with dramatic imagination. His standards in art criticism were those of the reformer, not the judge; the same kind of standards prevailed in his social and political assessments. Always the gadfly, he knew how to astound the conservative, agitate the smug, and galvanize the inert among his contemporaries; nor did he hesitate to make artful use of this skill. As moralist, as philosopher, he remained dramatic artist, able to render incandescent the point of view of the opposition. He is always more than just a moralist, or philosopher, or even religious prophet writing plays. He is rather a playwright concerned with, and about, morality, philosophy, and religion as these actuate human life and intercourse.

There is an important additional factor implicated in Shaw's avoidance of martyrdom that is at the same time a vital and distinctive feature of his dramatic art: his sense of humor. Its function he elucidates in accounting for the revolutionary impact of his writing. "The explanation," he tells us, "is to be found in what I believe to be a general law of the evolution of ideas. 'Every jest is an earnest in the womb of time,' says Peter Keegan in *John Bull's Other Island*. 'There's many a true word spoken in jest,' says the first villager you engage in philosophic discussion. All very serious revolutionary propositions begin as huge jokes. Otherwise they would be stamped out by the lynching of their first exponents. *Even these exponents themselves have revelations broken to them mysteriously through their sense of humor*" (*Quintessence of Ibsenism*, 126–27; my italics).[10]

He was fully cognizant of the fact that his comic imagination could commandeer his philosophic vision and lend its color to his moral criticism. Moreover, the energy that might have been expended in castigating him and granting him his "just martyrdom" was diverted into the laughter that turneth away wrath.[11] Elsewhere Shaw decries the "rank Satanism" that has made the Christian church "the Church where you must not laugh," so that "it is giving way to that older and greater Church to which I belong: the Church where the oftener you laugh the better, because by laughter only can you destroy evil without malice, and affirm goodfellowship without mawkishness" ("The Author's Apology," *The Drama Observed*, 3:1134). It is significant that he found positive as well as negative value in humor, and that it played so integral and definitive a role in his philosophic and moral mission.

It would seem, therefore, that any attempt to understand Shaw as philosopher or as moral or religious prophet that fails to heed the transmutations effected by his dramatic art and, more specifically, by his comic perception and penetration, is bound to miss his unique quality and significance. It is not enough to say that he is serious beneath the laughter, for if the laughter makes an important difference, which it does, it cannot be so cavalierly dismissed. The same holds true of his dramatic art in general. It provided for the fruits of his philosophic imagination a local habitation and a sustaining environment in which they might be scrutinized. Above all, it brought them to creative fulfillment in an enduringly delightful form. Accordingly, the judgment seems warranted that, whatever their author's intent, his dramas are of greater ultimate worth than his prefaces, and his art of more lasting value than his philosophy. This does not mean that his prefaces do not contribute greatly to the understanding of his plays—although they are by no means proper substitutes for such understanding. Nor does it mean that the dramas are not vitally affected by his philosophy and by strong philosophical influences, such as those suggested here. Nor does it mean that these dramas are not instruments of the moral mission of the playwright—although this exhausts neither their function nor meaning. It does mean that the most rewarding orientation for interpreting and evaluating these works is essentially aesthetic. Attention needs to be focused on the ways in which his art informs and organizes the philosophic and moral materials.

This need not blind us, of course, to the merits of Shaw's philosophic insights and moral proddings, even though critical items in his creed are unacceptable and the philosophy as a system, vulnerable. He himself offers his explicit philosophy, at the last, with proper modesty and tentativeness.[12] Moreover, whatever its shortcomings, it is always scintillating and bristling with challenges to mind and heart. Shaw's eclectic mind could draw on many sources and appropriate these to his uses with telling effect. Always he provides the necessary antidote to intellectual and moral complacency, and the constantly needed spur to human improvement. But his art is more than just a setting for these. It is an alembic that leaves no thought untouched. It has its own intrinsic charms—a sparkling, felicitous style, a wit keen and effulgent, a humor sympathetic and satirical, and a dazzling array of dialectical and theatrical pyrotechnics. These are delineated with adroit craftsmanship by a virtuoso playwright. Although he could set ideas and issues singing and dancing in the theater, his characters live as more than personifications of points of view. Furthermore, they lose no luster on the stage platform, their proper habitat, since their creator was above all a consummate showman and a master of theater art.

As artist, Shaw set out to illustrate and demonstrate in his dramas both the frailties of human beings and the failings of society, which impede human development. But he did not stop with this. He went on to suggest to us that we have great potentialities, and a pressing need for improvement. Through his dramatic and comic vision he would goad and stimulate us to find what is godlike within us, and thereby to become as gods. Like their author, the principal figures in his plays are subtle and artful. When the Roman captain in Act II of *Androcles and the Lion* asks Lavinia, "What is God?" she replies as equivocally as an oracle of old: "When we know that, Captain, we shall be gods ourselves" (4:625). Shavian acumen should not be underestimated in contemplating such Shavian enigmas. Are we not being challenged to detect beneath the surface "mysticism" a deeper second meaning? Is not Shaw saying, with Lavinia, that man is potentially divine? Does not the same hold true of Peter Keegan's "mystic" dream of a heaven "in which all life is human and all humanity divine" (2:1021)? A religion of humanity palpably pervades the plays and the theater functions as church; but the creed is aesthetically conceived and artistically elaborated. What is shown is "a vision in the magic glass of his artwork; so that you may catch his presentiment and make what you can of it" (Pref. *Plays Pleasant*, 1:374). Even the latter phrase offers a double challenge.

With Shaw, then, philosophy, religion, and morality are not superimposed on his art, but serve to enrich it. Best of all, they are conceived in terms of dynamic antitheses with dramatic reverberations, all held in a luminous comic suspension. Reason frolics, as antic punctuates argument, and jest illumines judgment. In his artistic pursuit of supermen, Shaw elevates the human race. He treats mankind not only as beings capable of thought and of moral responsibility, but of laughter as well. He shows the entertainment of ideas to be compatible with the entertainment of audiences. In his work, philosophy is allied with comedy, "the wisest and most exquisite of the arts," in the critical scrutiny of mankind ("Meredith on Comedy," *The Drama Observed*, 3:809).

Notes

Introduction

1. The quotations are from Shaw's letter to Louis Calvert, November 29, 1905, reprinted in *Shaw on Theatre*, ed. E. J. West, 109; Shaw's letter of August 12, 1905, quoted in *Bernard Shaw's Letters to Granville Barker*, ed. C. B. Purdom, 50; "To Audiences at *Major Barbara*" and "Mr. Trench's Dramatic Values," both in *Shaw on Theatre*, 121 and 114, respectively.

2. Shaw's postcard of August 8, 1906, Elizabeth Robins Papers, Fales Library and Special Collections, New York University; quoted by permission of the Society of Authors and courtesy of Fales Library. For an account of how extensively Shaw revised his drama in light of Gilbert Murray's criticism, see my article, "'In More Ways Than One': *Major Barbara*'s Debt to Gilbert Murray," which illustrates how unsettled the drama was for Shaw himself.

3. Preface to *Major Barbara*, 3:15–23. All references to Shaw's plays and their prefaces are to *The Bodley Head Bernard Shaw: Collected Plays and Their Prefaces*, 7 vols., ed. Dan H. Laurence. Page references to *Major Barbara,* in volume 3 of this work, are cited parenthetically in the text without the volume number; all other Shaw plays and prefaces are cited by both volume and page number. Following the scholarly sources, I have retained Shaw's idiosyncratic spelling and stylistic preferences.

4. For examples of these varied critical responses, see Irvine, *The Universe of G.B.S.*, 259–60; Arthur H. Nethercot, *Men and Supermen: The Shavian Portrait Gallery*, 65; Julian B. Kaye, *Bernard Shaw and the Nineteenth-Century Tradition*, esp. 45, 145; and Joseph Frank, "Major Barbara—Shaw's 'Divine Comedy,'" 61–74.

5. Disagreeing with this judgment are Edith Hall and Fiona Macintosh, in *Greek Tragedy and the British Theatre 1660–1914*, who imply that virtually all of Shaw's subsequent playwriting was under the impact of Murray's classicism (492).

6. Among those who have discerned similarities between the two writers are C.E.M. Joad, Archibald Henderson, Max Beerbohm, Edmund Wilson, William Irvine, Eric Bentley, Arthur Nethercot, and more recently Martin Puchner in his *The Drama of Ideas*. A number of Platonic-Shavian parallels are delineated in the appendix, "The Artist as Philosopher," below.

7. See "The Sanity of Art," in *Major Critical Essays*, 311. Compare John Ferguson in *Moral Values in the Ancient World*: "When the Delphic Oracle replied to Chaerophon

that Socrates was the wisest man in Greece, Socrates, who, like Bernard Shaw, put a bold face before the world and was humble at heart, was genuinely puzzled" (139). I. M. Crombie too says of one of Socrates' criticisms of Homer in the *Republic* that it "reminds one a little of G. B. Shaw sticking pins into Shakespeare" (*An Examination of Plato's Doctrines*, 1:90).

8. Comment on a Van Wyck Brook remark that "Bernard Shaw read Plato at fifty," one of Shaw's many responses to queries from Thomas Demetrius O'Bolger (a prospective biographer) throughout 1915 and 1916 at Houghton Library, Harvard University; quoted by permission in Albert, "Shaw's *Republic*," 83. The Wegg to whom Shaw refers is distinguishable as Silas Wegg in Charles Dickens's *Our Mutual Friend*.

9. Leon Hugo's *Bernard Shaw: Playwright and Preacher* (1971) offers an interpretation of *Major Barbara* in terms of Euripides and his *Bacchae*, especially "the Euripides of Gilbert Murray" and his translation of the play (147–60). In my judgment, his analysis is deficient in its exclusive reliance on the Murray path to the *Bacchae* and Euripides, as well as in some of his specific claims. Hugo's keystone premise—that the *Bacchae* was "the direct cause and inspiration of *Major Barbara*"—and his recognition of "so insistent an echo of the *Bacchae*" in Shaw's play sound like magnifications of Dodds's 1929 comment on the relationship between the two works, although Dodds is nowhere mentioned. To gain credibility the causal hypothesis needs more substantial evidence than the author adduces. As it stands it amounts essentially to a conjecture based primarily on Murray's Euripidean scholarship and his friendship with Shaw. Not even Murray's direct influence on the revision of the original Derry version of *Major Barbara*—of which surprisingly Hugo makes no mention—is cited in behalf of what remains an unconvincing case.

10. The first Shaw critic to exhibit a clear grasp of the importance of this relationship was Louis Crompton in several pregnant paragraphs of his chapter on *Major Barbara* in *Shaw the Dramatist* (1969), 113–15. This is not to say that Dionysianism in *Major Barbara* had been wholly ignored. It had been discussed, for example, by Alick West in lively fashion in his *A Good Man Fallen Among Fabians* (1950), 136–40, and again briefly by William Irvine in a short article, "*Major Barbara*," in *The Shavian* (1956), in essentially Nietzschean terms. Later critics finding Bacchic elements in *Major Barbara* include Elizabeth T. Forter in her introduction to the Crofts Classic edition of *Major Barbara* (1971), xv–xvi, xx; Raymond S. Nelson in his article, "Responses to Poverty in *Major Barbara*" (1971), 341–44; Margery Morgan in *The Shavian Playground: An Exploration of the Art of George Bernard Shaw* (1972), 134–57, esp. 138–44; and A. M. Gibbs, *The Art and Mind of Shaw: Essays in Criticism* (1983), 155–58. This listing does not presume to be exhaustive.

11. *The Bacchae*, trans. Gilbert Murray, in *Athenian Drama III: Euripides*, ix–x; Dodds, introduction to *Gilbert Murray: An Unfinished Autobiography*, ed. Jean Smith and Arnold Toynbee, 16–17.

12. Quotations are taken from the following translations of the play: *The Bacchae*, trans. William Arrowsmith, in *Euripides V: The Complete Greek Tragedies*, ed. David Grene and Richard Lattimore, 141–220; *Bacchae*, trans. Henry Birkhead, in *Ten Greek Plays in Contemporary Translations*, ed. L. R. Lind, 325–63; *The Bacchantes* in *The Plays of Euripides*, trans. Edward Coleridge, 2:87–129; *The Bacchae*, trans. Neil Curry, in *The Great Playwrights*, ed. Eric Bentley, 1:227–68; *The Bacchantes* in *Ten Plays by Euripides*, trans. Moses Hadas and John McLean, 279–312; *The Bacchae*, trans. with a commentary

by Geoffrey S. Kirk; *The Bacchae*, in F. L. Lucas, *Greek Tragedy and Comedy*, 306–42; *The Bacchanals*, trans. H[enry] H[art] Milman, in *The Plays of Euripides in English*, 2:1–37; *The Bacchae*, trans. Gilbert Murray, in *Athenian Drama III: Euripides*, 77–177; *The Bacchae of Euripides*, trans. Donald Sutherland; *Euripides: The Bacchae and Other Plays*, trans. Philip Vellacott, 181–228; *The Bacchae*, trans. Minos Volanakis, in *Euripides*, ed. Robert W. Corrigan, 165–224; *The Bacchanals*, in *Euripides*, trans. Arthur S. Way, 3:1–123. In addition, translated lines have been quoted from the commentaries in the *Bacchae* editions of E. R. Dodds and of John Edwin Sandys (*The Bacchae of Euripides*, trans. and ed. Sandys, rev. ed.), from the renderings accompanying Winnington-Ingram's running commentary on the play in *Euripides and Dionysus*, and from among selected passages translated by the following authors: D. J. Conacher, *Euripidean Drama*; G.M.A. Grube, *The Drama of Euripides*; Thomas Rosenmeyer, *The Masks of Tragedy*; John Ferguson, *A Companion to Greek Tragedy*; André-Jean Festugière, *Personal Religion Among the Greeks*; W.K.C. Guthrie, *Greeks and Their Gods*, chap. 6: "Dionysos"; Richard Lattimore, *The Poetry of Greek Tragedy*; and William Chase Greene, *Moira: Fate, Good, and Evil in Greek Thought*.

13. Dionysos's role in the Eleusinian mysteries is outlined in Xavier Riu, *Dionysism and Comedy*, 107–11, 134–40.

Part 1. Shaw's *Republic*

1. The nature and extent of this indebtedness is explored in my essay, "'In More Ways Than One': *Major Barbara*'s Debt to Gilbert Murray." As noted in the introduction, this phrase becomes "in more ways than the way from Athens" in the published screen version (*"Major Barbara": A Screen Version*, v).

2. Shaw referred to the play similarly in two letters, both written on July 21, 1905. One was addressed to J. E. Vedrenne, Granville Barker's partner in management of the Court Theatre: "I think I shall call the play 'Major Barbara'; but keep this to yourself until I have finally settled the title. I shall describe it as 'A Discussion in Three Long Acts.'" ("From Old Letters, Newfound Shaviana," *Boston Evening Transcript*, December 28, 1929). The other letter was sent to the actress Eleanor Robson: "Please tell G. T. [George Tyler, her manager] that the play is to be announced as 'A Discussion in Three Long Acts,' and that it is going to be more wildly eccentric than anything that he could ever have imagined or dreaded" (Belmont, *The Fabric of Memory*, 40–41). The original production script bears this subtitle, which was dropped when the play was published in 1907.

3. Plato holds that "reflection is provoked when perception yields a contradictory impression, presenting two opposite qualities with equal clearness, no matter whether the object be distant or close at hand. When there is no such contradiction, we are not encouraged to reflect" (*Republic* 523c).

4. Quoted in the introduction to the *Republic of Plato*, trans. Cornford, xviii, xxv. L. A. Post translates the end of the passage "except through some miraculous plan accompanied by good luck" (*Plato: The Collected Dialogues*, ed. Hamilton and Cairns, 1576). This language is equally applicable to *Major Barbara*. By an odd coincidence the play itself was "made . . . possible by a very delicate combination of circumstances & chances & interests," according to Shaw in a letter of August 21, 1905 (Belmont, *The Fabric of Memory*, 44).

5. Kingsley Martin has claimed of Shaw: "He was probably the very best dialectician who has ever written in the English language" ("Shaw—The Man, the Socialist," 30). Holbrook Jackson has claimed, "Above all he has demonstrated the dramatic possibilities of discussion, and by so doing linked up the literary drama with Platonic dialogue" (*The Eighteen Nineties*, 202). Margery M. Morgan alludes to *Major Barbara* as Platonic and dialectical in *A Drama of Political Man* (113, 145, and 317 n. 23).

6. For more on Shaw's relation to these dialectical thinkers, see the appendix below.

7. Compare the words of the Devil in *Man and Superman*: "Englishmen never will be slaves: they are free to do whatever the Government and public opinion allow them to do" (2:648).

8. A. E. Taylor has gone so far as to liken Thrasymachus to Shaw himself: "The fact is that Thrasymachus, like Mr. Shaw or Mr. Chesterton, has the journalist's trick of facile exaggeration" (*Plato: The Man and His Work*, 269).

9. Since both "major" and "Barbara" have technical connotations in traditional logic, I have previously suggested the possibility of a syllogistic basis for the title of the play in my article, "The Mood of Barbara," 8.

10. Taylor views the *Republic* similarly, holding that "politics is founded on ethics, not ethics on politics" (*Plato: The Man and His Work*, 265). The insistence that we must reform society before we can reform ourselves recurs in Shaw's writings. See, e.g., Pref. *Misalliance*, 4:93; *Doctors' Delusions, Crude Criminology, and Sham Education*, 314; Pref. *Back to Methuselah*, 5:312.

11. See also George H. Sabine, *A History of Political Theory*: "The good man must be a good citizen; a good man could hardly exist except in a good state; and it would be idle to discuss what was good for the man without considering also what was good for the city" (40).

12. According to Sir Ernest Barker, "Plato may touch upon economic questions; but he always regards them as moral questions, affecting the life of man as a member of a moral society" (*Greek Political Theory*, 170). Compare Shaw: "Every economic problem will be found to rest on a moral problem: you cannot get away from it" ("Life, Literature, and Political Economy," *Clare Market Review* [January 1906]; reprinted in *Shaw Review* 8 no. 3, 108).

13. For an analysis of the Shaw play in these terms see Albert, "The Price of Salvation: Moral Economics in *Major Barbara*."

14. As Cornford remarks of Plato: "His problem is not to build a Utopia in the air, but to discover the least changes which would radically cure the distempers of Athens" (*Republic of Plato*, 59). Barker, too, contends that "the defects of the actual showed him what to seek in an ideal; and in this sense his critique of the actual controls and determines his construction of the ideal" (*Greek Political Theory*, 172 n. 2).

15. Shaw writes, "The Communism of Christ, of Plato, and of the great religious orders, all take equality in material subsistence for granted as the first condition of establishing the Kingdom of Heaven on earth" (*The Intelligent Woman's Guide to Socialism and Capitalism*, 94). Compare the comment of Taylor: "Presumably the reason why Socrates could not look for justice in the community of farmers, but has to wait for the 'luxurious city' to come into existence and be reformed, is precisely that the members of the first society would hardly be alive to the fact that they have souls at all; they could not

feel the need for a daily supply of any bread but that which perishes; they have no 'social problem'" (*Plato: The Man and His Work*, 274).

16. In a footnote Cornford quotes *Phaedo* 66c: "All wars are made for the sake of getting money."

17. Many years later Shaw identified this moral passion with a "natural sense of honor" in *Everybody's Political What's What?*, 65.

18. See also *Republic of Plato*, 475–76, and Cornford's commentary, 301–2. For discussion of this aspect of Plato's psychology see G.M.A. Grube, *Plato's Thought*, 135–36, and E. R. Dodds, *Greeks and the Irrational*, 213.

19. "Undershaft . . . strikes the deepest note in the play as Barbara sounds the highest" ("To Audiences at *Major Barbara*," in *Shaw on Theatre*, 120–21).

20. See, e.g., Nettleship, *Lectures*, 149, and *Republic of Plato*, trans. Cornford, 119.

21. We revisit *sophrosyne* as it pertains to Undershaft in Part 1 of "Shaw's *Bacchae*," below.

22. See *Sophist* 230b, where Plato recommends reflection by dialectical cross-examination as the way to eradicate *amathia*, the conceit of wisdom in those stupidly unaware of their ignorance.

23. See also *Sophist* 229c: "When a person supposes that he knows and does not know; this appears to be the great source of all the errors of the intellect" (trans. Cornford, *Plato: The Collected Dialogues*, 972).

24. Shaw's own parable *Heartbreak House* (1919) ties in even more closely with this Platonic passage.

25. The association of Undershaft's munitions works with hell may parallel a connection between Plato's cave and Hades. Cornford suggests that the idea of the cave probably came "from mysteries held in caves or dark chambers representing the underworld, through which the candidates for initiation were led to the revelation of sacred objects in a blaze of light" (*Republic of Plato*, 227). He also finds an internal suggestion that "the Cave is comparable with Hades" (230 n. 2). Margery M. Morgan also discovers Plato's cave in Part 4, Act III of *Back to Methuselah* (see "'Back to Methuselah': The Poet and the City," in *Essays and Studies*, ed. Sisson and Byrne, 95–96; reprinted in *G. B. Shaw: A Collection of Critical Essays*, ed. R. J. Kaufmann, 140).

26. Cornford's translation is "the turning about of the soul from a day that is like night to the veritable day" (237).

27. "LADY BRITOMART. Stuff! A man cant make cannons any the better for being his own cousin instead of his proper self" (165). The name Cusins may thus betoken his origins. The name also suggests a flexibility in familial relationships appropriate not only to a Platonic guardian, but to the man who is to "become" Andrew Undershaft, as I argue below.

28. The further relevance of this quote from Father Keegan is treated in "Shaw's *Bacchae*," part 4, below.

29. One "must either share the world's guilt or go to another planet. He must save the world's honor if he is to save his own" (Pref. *Major Barbara*, 36). "We shall never have real moral responsibility until everyone knows that his deeds are irrevocable, and that his life depends on his usefulness" (ibid., 61). "The problem being to make heroes out of cowards, we paper apostles and artist-magicians have succeeded only in giving cowards

all the sensations of heroes whilst they tolerate every abomination, accept every plunder, and submit to every oppression" (ibid., 39).

30. Some indication of what Shaw meant by this phrase is to be found in an article by Patrick G. Hagan Jr. and Joseph O. Baylen, "Shaw, W. T. Stead, and the 'International Peace Crusade,' 1898–1899," 60–61. The authors report Stead's account in his weekly paper, *War Against War* (February 3, 1899), of a speech by Shaw in which the playwright insisted that "it was not armaments or ironclads that fought but men," and favored "an international tribunal to which public opinion would force nations to bring their quarrels." According to Stead, Shaw also hoped for a time when combined armaments of the most advanced nations would be used to prevent nations from fighting, compelling them instead to bring their disputes to the international tribunal, anticipating the League of Nations and the United Nations. In his Preface to *Heartbreak House*, Shaw adverted to his playwriting itself as a mode of warring against war in explaining his avoidance of writing war plays during World War I: "You cannot make war on war and on your neighbor at the same time. War cannot bear the terrible castigation of comedy, the ruthless light of laughter that glares on the stage" (5:57). We revisit the "war on war" theme in part 4 of "Shaw's *Bacchae*," below.

31. So described by Shaw in a letter to Gilbert Murray, October 7, 1905, reprinted in *Gilbert Murray: An Unfinished Autobiography*, ed. Jean Smith and Arnold Toynbee, 156–57.

32. See also Cassirer, *The Myth of the State*, 75–76, on the limited mystical tendencies in Plato.

33. "The natural property of a wing is to raise that which is heavy and carry it aloft to the region where the gods dwell; and more than any other bodily part it shares in the divine nature" (*Phaedrus* 246de, trans. Hackforth, *Collected Dialogues*, 493). See also *Theaetetus* 176ab on flight from this world to the divine.

34. On the homology between soul, state, and cosmos, see also Friedländer, *Plato*, 189.

Chapter 1. The Drama of Nutrition

1. Donald Sutherland deals briefly with the theoretical problem that Euripides's mixture of tragedy and comedy poses in the critical essay accompanying his translation of the *Bacchae* ("'At Least the Most Tragic': The Composition of *The Bacchae*," *The Bacchae of Euripides*, 110–12). On "the Euripidean fusion and contrast of comic and tragic effects" exemplified in the *Bacchae*, see also Arrowsmith, "A Greek Theater of Ideas," 17–18.

2. The interpretive controversy around *Major Barbara* has been noted in the introduction, above. Concerning the *Bacchae*, "that most puzzling of all Greek plays," Allardyce Nicoll has gone so far as to say: "No one will ever be able to say what this strange drama intends" (*World Drama*, 85). On the variety of divergent interpretations of the *Bacchae* see R. P. Winnington-Ingram, *Euripides and Dionysus*, 4–6; G.M.A. Grube, *Drama of Euripides*, 398–99; Euripides, *Bacchae*, ed. Dodds, xlff.; and on specific points, D. J. Conacher, *Euripidean Drama*, 56–72.

3. The principal character in the *Bacchae* is Pentheus according to Philip W. Harsh (*Handbook of Classical Drama*, 245) and Conacher (*Euripidean Drama*, 59–60; but, cf. 342). Grube is convinced that it is Dionysos (*Drama of Euripides*, 398–99, 104 n. 1), as is Paul Decharme (*Euripides and the Spirit of His Dramas*, 270). Arrowsmith, on the other hand, finds in the *Bacchae*, as in Euripidean dramatic structure generally, a "persistent

avoidance of the single hero in favor of the *agon* of two chief characters" ("The Criticism of Greek Tragedy," 37). Walter Kaufmann, in his *Tragedy and Philosophy*, reminds us of the Hegelian character of such an approach (239n.). Although most interpreters of *Major Barbara* take Undershaft to be Shaw's "hero" (see Pref. *Major Barbara*, 27) a strong case can be made for Barbara's centrality, and an even stronger one that it is essential to treat the Undershaft-Barbara-Cusins trinity as basic instead of focusing on any one of them as the single main character; this is dealt with in part 4, below.

4. Winnington-Ingram, in particular has pointed out that the *Bacchae* can "carry effect at different levels of approach" (*Euripides and Dionysus*, 6), and proceeds to examine such levels in the play; see also T.B.L. Webster, *The Tragedies of Euripides*, 270, 276. Hazel Barnes has approached Euripides's *Hippolytus* in similar fashion in *Hippolytus in Drama and Myth*, 72ff. In the case of *Major Barbara*, among the earliest to recognize the "depths within depths" of meaning and irony in the play was William Irvine in his article "Major Barbara," 47.

5. Shaw, letter to Vedrenne, July 4, 1905, in *Bernard Shaw: Collected Letters 1898–1910*, 2:535. Archibald Henderson, "Is Shaw a Dramatist?" 260. See also Albert, "Barbara's Progress," 88.

6. Passages of Euripides's *Bacchae* are cited parenthetically in the text by line number rather than page number; the translator is also indicated. A list of English translations used appears in the introduction, above.

7. W.K.C. Guthrie, *A History of Greek Philosophy*, 1:318, 26–28, and 2:253. "The word *daimon* also includes 'god,' and 'god' can also be used indefinitely or collectively to denote 'power,'" observes Martin P. Nilsson, *A History of Greek Religion*, 171. See also "Daimon," in *Oxford Classical Dictionary*, 2nd ed.: "*Daimon* appears to correspond to the supernatural power, the mana, not as a general conception but in its special manifestations, and always with the overtones of a personal agent."

8. Murray, *Five Stages of Greek Religion*, 3rd ed., 146–48, 152–53; cf. Charles Seltman, *The Twelve Olympians*, 173, and H. J. Rose, *Handbook of Greek Mythology*, 155. On the kinship of men with gods, see also Sir James G. Frazer, *The Golden Bough*, 1:374–77, 390–91, and Guthrie, *In the Beginning*, 88, 141 n 10. The opposing Greek idea, stressing the barrier between man and god (discussed by Murray in *Rise of the Greek Epic*, 139–40), stems from a different Greek religious tradition, as Guthrie explains in *Greeks and Their Gods*, 113–15 and 256–57. See also Rosenmeyer, *Masks of Tragedy*, 108.

9. Grube, *Drama of Euripides*, 42, 47; Gilbert Norwood, *Greek Tragedy*, 284. The presentation of a deity in human form on the stage in the *Bacchae* prompts L. A. Post to remark that both in ancient and modern times "human beings have been recognized or advertised as gods," adding that "a man who can inspire his followers with fanatical devotion has the power for good or evil that the Greeks recognized as divine" (*From Homer to Menander*, 152).

10. For example, in Pref. to *Androcles and the Lion*, 4:505; *Religious Speeches*, 49; Pref. *On the Rocks*, 6:620; Pref. *The Black Girl in Search of God, and Some Lesser Tales*, 22.

11. "Modern Religion" (November 13, 1919), reprinted in *The Religious Speeches of Bernard Shaw*, 77 (cf. 19, 35): Pref. *Androcles and the Lion*, 4:530. See the discussion of Godhead in "The Perfect Wagnerite," in which life is described as organizing itself into "rare persons who may by comparison be called gods" (*Major Critical Essays*, 174), and *The Black Girl in Search of God*, 79–80.

12. Rosenmeyer observes: "In the *Bacchae* Dionysus, in spite of his presence on stage, or perhaps because of it, is largely a symbol; the entity weighed in the scale is not a god, but men, as in all great tragedy. The precariousness of human greatness is here shown from a special angle: the god-likeness of man. . . . But this shows us that the concern of the poet is with man" (*Masks of Tragedy*, 112). Winnington-Ingram similarly holds to the principle that the true Dionysos of Euripides's play is revealed in its human characters (*Euripides and Dionysus*, 29–30).

13. Dodds, introduction to *Bacchae*, xii, quoting Plutarch, *Isis and Osiris*, 35:365a. The present and subsequent treatment of Dionysos and his cult draws primarily on Dodds's excellent introduction and commentary, along with valuable accounts in the following works: Lewis Richard Farnell, *The Cults of the Greek States*, chaps. 4–7; Erwin Rohde, *Psyche*, chaps. 8–9; Guthrie, *Greeks and Their Gods*, chap. 6; Nilsson, *A History of Greek Religion*, 32–33, 205–10, and *Minoan-Mycenaean Religion and Its Survival in Greek Religion*, 564–76; and Frazer, *Golden Bough*, vol. 7, chap. 1. See also Seltman, *Twelve Olympians*, chap. 8; Cornford, *From Religion to Philosophy*, 111–14; Albin Lesky, *Greek Tragedy*, 39–46; Jane Harrison, *Prolegomena to the Study of Greek Religion*, chap. 8; Walter F. Otto, *Dionysus: Myth and Cult*; and the *Bacchae* commentaries of Winnington-Ingram, Kirk, and Murray.

14. See Grube, *Drama of Euripides*, 46–47 and 419; *Bacchae*, ed. Dodds, xlv; Winnington-Ingram, *Euripides and Dionysus*, 16; H.D.F. Kitto, *Greek Tragedy*, 378.

15. Dodds cites classical instances in which these two great nature-powers were associated in popular thought and in literary and artistic works (*Bacchae*, 123). On the correspondences of the two gods, especially in their *Hippolytus* and *Bacchae* roles, see also Webster, *Tragedies of Euripides*, 270, 276; *Bacchae*, trans. Kirk, 1 and 58–59; Philip Harsh, *Handbook of Classical Drama*, 239.

16. See the related thought of Dodds about the *Bacchae*: "Euripides confronts us here with an irruption into normal life of the mystery behind life" ("Euripides the Irrationalist," 102). Murray uses the name "Life Spirit" for Dionysos in *The Classical Tradition in Poetry*, 64.

17. The connection between *Major Barbara* and this passage has also been noted, and briefly discussed, by Robert J. Jordan in "Theme and Character in *Major Barbara*," 471–73.

18. On the resemblance between Lady Britomart and Ann Whitefield, see St. John Ervine, *Bernard Shaw*, 400.

19. On *physis* and *nomos* see, e.g., Guthrie, *A History of Greek Philosophy*, 3:21–22, chap. 4 and 201–2; and Greene, *Moira*, 223–32, 236–40, appendix 31 (bibliography), and passim. On their role in Euripides, see Dodds, *Greeks and the Irrational*, 182–88; Murray, *Euripides and His Age*, 31–32; and on *nomos* in the Bacchae, see Conacher, *Euripidean Drama*, 76–77.

20. Stanley Weintraub first called attention to Stow's account in "'Shaw's *Divine Comedy*': Addendum," 22. Knape, from "knap" (O.E. "cnaep") is a hillock, hill summit, of rising ground, presumably that on which the maypole was erected. See Gerald Cobb, *The Old Churches of London*, 28. This historical association of the Undershaft cognomen with the idea of elevation makes it particularly fitting that the realm of its bearer, the final setting of *Major Barbara*, should be situated in hilly terrain.

21. Stow, Survey of London, 130–31; *The Parish Church of St. Andrew Undershaft* (Ramsgate, England: The Church Publishers, n.d.), an informational pamphlet available at the church itself, 4; William Kent, ed., *An Encyclopedia of London*, 118. Stow reports

that the church was almost entirely rebuilt between 1520 and 1532, most of the rebuilding being undertaken by Stephen Jennings, Lord Mayor of London in 1508, until his death in 1524. Two Sir Stephens, the one a pillar of the church, the other a sermonizing champion of religious orthodoxy, could conceivably have contributed something to the portrait of Stephen Undershaft; but the name at least of this character in the play appears to have had a different provenance. For in a list of the dramatis personae at the beginning of the *Major Barbara* manuscripts he bears the maternal cognomen Stevenage (British Library Add. MS. 50616B, fol. 3; *"Major Barbara": A Facsimile of the Holograph Manuscript*, ed. Dukore, 2), afterward changed to Stephen. Stevenage is Shaw's fictional substitute for Stanley, the family name of the Countess of Carlisle, the original of Lady Britomart. See Albert, "'In More Ways Than One,'" 124, and "From *Murray's Mother-in-Law* to *Major Barbara*." The surrogate character of the Stevenage name casts doubt on Margery Morgan's assumption of its derivation (as well as Stephen's) from that of the first Christian martyr, Saint Stephen (*The Shavian Playground*, 154 n. 2). There is no reason to believe that Shaw sought to connect either the Stevenages or their Stanley originals with the early martyr. The fictional familial name he undoubtedly appropriated from the English city of Stevenage. The case may be a bit different with Stephen himself, however, for it is true—although unmentioned by Morgan—that Shaw did regard the martyred namesake in like manner as a young, misguided bore (see Pref. *Androcles and the Lion*, 4:546).

22. See Frazer, *The Golden Bough*, 2:45–58, on the beneficent powers of tree-spirits; on May Day and maypoles, 2:59–71; on embodiments of the tree-spirit, 2:71–96; and on its relation to death and corn, 4:251–54. On Dionysos as a divinity of vegetation, and of tree life in particular, see Farnell, *Cults*, 5:118–19; Frazer, 7:3–4; Plutarch, *Quaestiones Conviviales*, book 3; Guthrie, *Greeks and Their Gods*, 62; *Bacchae*, ed. Dodds, 80–81. Dodds points to the tree in the *Bacchae* as itself "an agent and embodiment" of Dionysos (209).

23. Nilsson believes the Dionysian *thyrsos* itself was a May bough. See also Farnell, *Cults*, 5:240ff. and plate 33; Frazer, *Golden Bough*, 7:3; Sir Arthur Pickard-Cambridge, *Dithyramb Tragedy and Comedy*, 38; Webster, *Everyday Life in Classical Athens*, 87–88; *The Bacchae of Euripides*, trans. Sandys, cii.

24. Bather, "The Problem of the *Bacchae*"; George Thomson, *Aeschylus and Athens*, 134–43. See also *Bacchae*, ed. Dodds, xxvii–xxxiii.

25. See Winnington-Ingram, *Euripides and Dionysus*, 34–35; *Bacchae*, ed. Dodds, 82; and Rosenmeyer, *Masks of Tragedy*, 139–40. Note Dodds's translation of lines 1157–58: "And [Pentheus] received the blessed wand of magic, which was death unfailing" (220); Kirk interprets these lines similarly, as showing Pentheus's death guaranteed in his taking "the fennel rod, Hades's pledge, in its thyrsus-shape" (*Bacchae* 119). On some of the other properties of the *thyrsos* in the *Bacchae*, see *Bacchae*, ed. Dodds, 145; *Bacchae of Euripides*, trans. Sandys, 172 n. 553; and on the association of weapons with Dionysos, Jack Lindsay, *The Clashing Rocks*, 166.

26. The Euripidean foundling appears in his *Ion* and a number of lost plays. See Richard Lattimore, *Story Patterns in Greek Tragedy*, 9 and 74 n. 21. For Shaw's proud confession of his theatrical atavism see "The Play of Ideas," in *The Drama Observed*, ed. Dukore, 4:1527: "I was, and still am, the most old fashioned playwright outside China and Japan. But I know my business both historically and by practice as playwright and producer." See also what follows about the vital need for critical study of historical survivals.

27. Murray, "Euripides' Tragedies of 415 B.C.," 136; see also *Euripides and His Age*, 66–67.

28. Lattimore, *Poetry of Greek Tragedy*, 128; see also Guthrie, *Greeks and Their Gods*, 153. Shaw alludes elsewhere to this myth of Semele and Zeus, whom he called by his Roman name, Jupiter. See, e.g., Pref. *The Dark Lady*, 4:288; *The Black Girl in Search of God*, 79.

29. "Law is too narrow a translation for the Greek *nomos*, which includes customs such as religious beliefs, and 'believes in' is in fact the verb derived from *nomos*" (Webster, *Tragedies of Euripides*, 23). What is being contrasted, as Nilsson explains, is "natural necessity and the work of man" (*A History of Greek Religion*, 268–69). Dodds gives some indication of the variety of positions that could be represented within the framework of this historic antithesis (*Greeks and the Irrational*, 182–83). See also Guthrie, *A History of Greek Philosophy*, where attention is directed to passages in Euripides on bastardy "which insist that the bastard is by nature the equal of the legitimate, and only inferior by *nomos*, or in name" (3:154).

30. Kirk specifically relates the killing of Pentheus to the mistaken identity theme (*Bacchae*, 15). Both Forter, xxvii, and Daniel Leary, in "Dialectical Action in *Major Barbara*," 55, single out Undershaft's turning to Cusins as his son as foretokening their eventual relationship. But what significance are we then to attach to his having already greeted Lomax in this fashion, and to his subsequent taking of Sarah to be Barbara: That his future relations with the Lomaxes will be special in some way? Hardly. Or that like Barbara's "father" in the Salvation Army he too "has a great many children" (88)? Plainly all we have here is Shaw milking the comic potential of the situation to the utmost, allowing the long-absent father to make every mistake possible in identifying his own children.

31. Helen North, *Sophrosyne*, 82; see also 79. She points out that *sophrosyne* has a variety of nuances in Euripides, who makes "self-control" its normal meaning for the first time in Greek literature. Most commonly it signified "control of passion, appetite or emotion" (75–76). But among its senses is soundness of mind, or sanity, in contrast to *mania* or madness, 21, 77, 90). In his briefer survey of Greek and Roman conceptions of this cardinal virtue, John Ferguson, in *Moral Values*, judges it to be far more characteristic of the British than of the Greek way of life (32–40). On the other hand, Bruno Snell, in *Discovery of the Mind*, defining *sophronein* as "healthy thinking," offers a fascinating account of *sophronein* in terms of human health, as a kind of moral measure requiring both intellect and proper emotional functioning. It is the knowledge that governs our health, well-being, and happiness, as well as "an appreciation of organic nature with a bent toward the practical. In its own domain it has a function similar to the calculation of profit. . . . In the case of *sophrosyne* also knowledge is the court of appeal before which morality must render its account" (162; see also 184). As an approximation of the meaning of the Greek term, Murray, in his *Five Stages of Greek Religion*, suggests "temperance, gentleness, the spirit that in any trouble thinks and is patient, that saves and not destroys" (188; see also his *Rise of the Greek Epic*, 26). In Shaw's view, self-control "is nothing but a highly developed vital sense, dominating and regulating the mere appetites," a "supreme sense" distinguishing those fittest to survive ("The Greatest of These Is Self-Control," Pref. *Back to Methuselah*, 5:309).

32. See also *Bacchae*, ed. Dodds, xiv; Winnington-Ingram, *Euripides and Dionysus*, 161–63; *Bacchae*, trans. Kirk, 8–11.

33. William Hamilton Nelson, *Blood and Fire: General William Booth*, 156; cf. Richard

Collier, *General Next to God*, 74. The Salvation Army itself was organized "to carry the blood of Christ and the fire of the Holy Ghost into every corner of the world." Quoted from the *Christian Mission Magazine* in St. John Ervine, *God's Soldier: General William Booth*, 1:407. Bramwell Booth cites the verse, "He shall baptize you with the Holy Ghost and with fire" (Matt. 3:11, Luke 3:16) as superseding other enjoined baptisms (*Echoes and Memories*, 195 n. 1). The yellow star replaced a blazing sun, the emblem on an earlier flag. The sun was removed to avoid offending the Parsees of India, to whom it was a sacred symbol. Originally General Booth contemplated a flag showing a flaming sword transfixing the world, a device that would have had no difficulty winning Undershaft's approval. Weintraub explores the relation between Booth and Shaw in his "Bernard Shaw in Darkest England: G.B.S. and the Salvation Army's General William Booth."

34. See also Bramwell Booth, *These Fifty Years*, 205. On the Corybantes see Ivan M. Linforth "Corybantic Rites in Plato"; Dodds, *Greeks and the Irrational*, 77–79 and 96 n. 90; Guthrie, *Greeks and Their Gods*, 154.

35. See Albert, "'In More Ways than One,'" 127; also Murray's discussion of Bacchic and Orphic mysteries in his *A History of Ancient Greek Literature*, 62–68, and in the introductory note to his *Bacchae* translation, *Athenian Drama III: Euripides*, 166–67. Later Cornford, referring to the fictional portrait of Murray as Cusins, satirically related the Salvation Army to the ecstatic Greek cults: "In one of Mr. Shaw's plays there is a professor of Greek who, in moments of enthusiasm, quotes his own translation of Euripides. He can be identified with a personal friend of the author, well known for his pacific and rationalist opinions, who after the war became a member of the League of Nations Assembly. Some centuries hence critics may argue, on the strength of *Major Barbara*, that this gentleman had a past lamentably inconsistent with his ostensible character. Before the war he had been the director of an armament firm and, earlier still, the adherent of an unconventional religious organization, frequenting the lower quarters of the town for the purpose of indulging in corybantic rites" (quoted from an unpublished Cornford lecture by W.K.C. Guthrie in his *A History of Greek Philosophy*, 3:362). In a note Guthrie adds, "it is a curious coincidence that A. Diès (in *Autor de P[laton]*, Paris, 1927, 160) speaks of A. E. Taylor presenting Socrates as 'le général d'une antique Armée du Salut.'" Quoted in Albert, "From *Murray's Mother-in-Law* to *Major Barbara*," 59.

36. See Nilsson, *A History of Greek Religion*, 205; Rohde, *Psyche*, 259–60; Farnell, *Cults*, 5:16l; Guthrie, *Greeks and Their Gods*, 149, and *A History of Greek Philosophy*, 1:231; Murray, *Five Stages of Greek Religion*, 144. In the words of Rohde: "Enthusiasm and ecstasy are invariably the means" (290). In Greek mythology the Corybantes, or Korybantes, were originally attendant daimons of the Phrygian goddess Cybele (frequently identified with Rhea), who served this ecstatic cult with ritual dancing, mysteries, and magical cures, including the cathartic healing of madness. The Greek verb *korybantian*, formed from their name, came to denote a state of divine possession or enthusiasm, marked by excited and unusual behavior. See H. J. Rose, *Handbook of Greek Mythology*, 170–71; Linforth, "Corybantic Rites in Plato."

37. Farnell, *Cults*, 5:159–60; Winnington-Ingram, *Euripides and Dionysus*, 155. See also Guthrie, *Greeks and Their Gods*, 147–48; *Bacchae*, ed. Dodds, 83 n. 115 and 86 n. 2; *Bacchae*, trans. Kirk, 30 n. 56, 35 nn. 78–82.

38. "I will join the army of my Bacchae" (trans. Volanakis); "in their path myself shall be, and maniac armies battled after me!" (trans. Murray). The Greek word is *stratelatein*,

to lead an army into the field. This particular threat is not carried out, but the Bacchae give evidence within the play that they are fighters in a very literal sense. "Maenads form a contingent in the army of Dionysus during his campaign in India" ("Maenads," in *Oxford Classical Dictionary*, 2nd ed.).

39. Hugh Tredennick translates: "Many bear the emblems, but the devotees are few" (*The Last Days of Socrates*). Dodds's commentary on the *Bacchae* takes the proverb to mean that "many perform the ritual but few experience identification" (83 n. 115).

40. Among those translators equating tambourine with tympanon are Grube, 401, Kirk, 31 n. 58f., and "Music," in *Oxford Classical Dictionary*, 2nd ed. Linforth names the Phrygian reed pipe, drums, tambourines, and cymbals as the instruments used to arouse the participants' emotions in Corybantic rites ("Corybantic Rites in Plato," 156). In this *Bacchae* stanza Euripides syncretically identifies the Couretes of Rhea, mother of the Cretan Zeus, with the demonic Corybantes of Cybele and intermingles them with the Satyrs, attendants of Dionysos. See Guthrie, *Greeks and Their Gods*, 154–57; *Bacchae*, ed. Dodds, 76–77 and 84; *Bacchae*, trans. Kirk, 78–82 and 31, 35, 39; Winnington-Ingram, *Euripides and Dionysus*, 36.

41. Anthony Baines, *Woodwind Instruments and Their History*, 3rd ed., 195, 198–201; Karl Geiringer, *Musical Instruments*, 42–43; Warren D. Anderson, *Ethos and Education in Greek Music*, 8–10, 213–14 n. 11, and passim; "Music," *Oxford Classical Dictionary*, 2d ed. For a discussion of the emotional effects of the *aulos* see Linforth, "Corybantic Rites in Plato," 125–26, 133–34, 156.

42. The authors report that one method used to ensure continuity of sound was to affix a reservoir of air and force it through the pipe. On the attributes of the *aulos* see also Baines, *Woodwind Instruments*, 36; Willi Apel, "Early History of the Organ," 200; "Aulos," *Grove Dictionary of Music and Musicians*, 5th ed.; James MacGillivray, "The Cylindrical Reed Pipe from Antiquity to the 20th Century," 218–19.

43. "I believe that a taste for brass instruments is hereditary. My father destroyed his domestic peace by immoderate indulgence in the trombone; my uncle played the ophicleide" (*London Music in 1888–89*, 76). See also Preface to *Immaturity*: "every Shaw of that generation seemed able to play any wind instrument at sight" (xxv, cf. xii).

44. Shaw commented on these two compositions in the course of an 1890 article on Sir Arthur Sullivan, *How to Become a Musical Critic*, 189–93: "He furtively set Cox and Box to music in 1869, and then, overcome with remorse, produced 'Onward, Christian Soldiers' and over three dozen hymns besides. As the remorse mellowed, he composed a group of songs—Let me Dream Again, Thou'rt Passing Hence, Sweethearts, and My Dearest Heart—all of the very best in their *genre*, such as it is" (191). A year later Shaw referred to the early Sullivan as "a sentimental and ecclesiastical composer," whose name in 1875 suggested such works as those just mentioned (*Music in London 1890–94*, 1:226–27). More suggestive of the attitude toward Sullivan's hymn reflected in *Major Barbara* is that exhibited in a passage in the 1898 Preface to the Plays Pleasant in which Shaw recognizes a community of vital religion underlying the beliefs of the clergymen of the Guild of St. Matthew, the nonconformist Dr. Clifford, and his own: "There is only one religion, though there are a hundred versions of it. We all had the same thing to say; and though some of us cleared our throats to say it by singing revolutionary lyrics and republican hymns, we thought nothing of singing them to the music of Sullivan's Onward Christian Soldiers or Haydn's God Preserve the Emperor" (1:372–73). Later "Onward Christian

Soldiers" turns up anachronistically in *Androcles and the Lion,* with the Captain commanding that the words be altered to "Throw them to the Lions" (4:592). For a detailed study of Shaw's reviews of Sullivan's music, giving favorable and unfavorable response as it evolved over the years, see Jeff S. Dailey, "George Bernard Shaw's Criticism of Gilbert and Sullivan." I am grateful to Dailey for providing me with his study; though his views and mine as conveyed here are similar, they were arrived at independently.

45. Compare the respective translations of Guthrie and Kirk:

On ye Bacchae, on ye Bacchae,
Bringing with you
Bromios, yea Dionysos,
Who is god and son of god,
From the mountains of Phrygia
To the broad highways of Hellas—Bromios!
(*Greeks and Their Gods,* 151)

Onward bacchants, onward bacchants,
bringing Dionysus,
Bromios, god and child of a god,
down from Phrygian mountains
into Hellas' broad-trodden streets
Bromios the roaring one!
(*Bacchae,* trans. Kirk, 35–36)

46. James and Albert Morehead, eds., *101 Favorite Hymns,* 114–15.

47. T. Zielinski's analysis, as discussed and endorsed by Dodds (*Bacchae,* 71–72). See also Winnington-Ingram, *Euripides and Dionysus,* 33–37, and *Bacchae,* trans. Kirk, 32–33.

Chapter 2. The Drama of Resistance

1. The three main Athenian festivals honoring Dionysos took place during these months. See Rohde, *Psyche,* 309–10 n. 31; *Bacchae,* ed. Dodds, 110; Nilsson, *A History of Greek Religion,* 208; and Farnell, *Cults,* 5:198, who specifically identifies two of the months as December and January.

2. "Greek plays require the open air," Shaw wrote, commenting on a production of the *Bacchae* (letter of November 15, 1908, *Bernard Shaw's Letters to Granville Barker,* ed. C. B. Purdom, 139). He also recounts helping Lillah McCarthy with the part of Dionysos by playing Pentheus with "superb realism" in a scene with her.

3. See also Plato, *Ion* 534a; *Bacchae,* ed. Dodds, 163–64. Milk and honey, along with wine, "are the good gifts that mark the coming of Dionysus," as Guthrie puts it (*Orpheus and Greek Religion,* 179).

4. Euripides is here advancing a doctrine of Prodicus the Sophist, a man younger than himself, by whom he is thought to have been influenced. Prodicus taught that men came to regard natural phenomena as gods, so that bread was called Demeter and wine Dionysos. See *Bacchae,* ed. Dodds, 104–5; Guthrie, *A History of Greek Philosophy,* 3:241–42; Jaeger, *Theology of the Early Greek Philosophers,* 179, 249 n. 29; Webster, *Tragedies of Euripides,* 22.

5. The allusion presumably is to the Theodaisia, a winter festival honoring Dionysos. See *Bacchae,* ed. Dodds, 120; Winnington-Ingram, *Euripides and Dionysus,* 61 n. 2; and Farnell, *Cults,* 5:120, 198.

6. Comparably, Arrowsmith finds in Euripides a "fragmentation" of major characters, with the old single tragic hero "diffused over several characters." Euripidean plays, he points out, typically present paired antagonists who "function like obsessional fragments of a whole human soul" representing both cultural conflicts and "the new incompleteness of the human psyche" ("A Greek Theater of Ideas," 15).

7. *Bacchae,* ed. Dodds, xxvii–xxviii, and note on xliv, citing *Bacchae* lines 45–46. In marked contrast, Arrowsmith concludes that "Euripides has taken elaborate pains to show in Pentheus the proud iconoclastic innovator, rebelling against tradition" (intro. *Bacchae,* 148; cf. Conacher, *Euripidean Drama,* 76–77). Such contradictory estimations of Pentheus are not unusual among commentators on this play. The weight of evidence would seem to favor viewing Pentheus as an essentially conservative figure resisting new religious forces in the community, even though these also make an appeal to tradition. More recently, Richard Seaford has argued that Pentheus does not represent the order or interests of the polis, but the dangers of an introverted, self-destructive ruling household to the otherwise healthy communality of the polis, represented by Dionysos (*Bacchae,* trans. Seaford, 47, 49).

8. See Albert, "The Price of Salvation." Sutherland has remarked the use of money references, financial metaphors, and related value suggestions in the *Bacchae,* but takes these to be far less meaningful than he justifiably might (128–29).

9. As Jaeger indicates in *Theology of the Early Greek Philosophers,* the philosopher Heraclitus expressed a very similar idea. Compare Murray, *Euripides and His Age,* 39, and his lecture, "Greek and English Tragedy: A Contrast," 15.

10. In the same vein is Jaeger's observation that "the early Greeks never conceived anything like the personal conscience of modern times," in *Paideia,* 1:9, also 326, 419 n. 23, 429 n. 30.

11. "It is not far from 'conscience,'" says Guthrie of *aidos* in *A History of Greek Philosophy,* 3:66. Lattimore writes in *Story Patterns:* "As *aidos* is the inner feeling whose presence prevents outrageous action, so her sister *nemesis* would be the public conscience, the feeling of others against the wrongdoers" (85–86 n. 44). See the explanation of Dodds, *Greeks and the Irrational:* "The sanction of *aidos* is *nemesis,* public disapproval" (26 n. 109); also Ferguson, *Moral Values,* 12–13; Jaeger, *Paideia,* 1:7, 59, 419 n. 15; Greene, *Moira,* 18–22, 245.

12. See Democritus, frag. 264, on *aidos:* "One should feel shame before oneself no less than before others, and behave no more wickedly if no one is going to know about it than if everyone is" (trans. Guthrie, *A History of Greek Philosophy,* 2:350; frags. 84 and 244 are similar, 2:494). Frag. 45 also happens to fit Bill's state: "He who does wrong is more unhappy than he who suffers it" (2:490). On *nemesis* as a goddess see Farnell, *Cults,* 2:487–98; Lattimore, *Story Patterns,* 24; Ferguson, *Moral Values,* 13. Like Britomartis, the Cretan mother goddess, Nemesis was associated, sometimes identified, with Artemis. See Murray, *Rise of the Greek Epic,* 82 n. 1; Guthrie, *Greeks and Their Gods,* 105; Persson, *Religion of Greece,* 128, and Nilsson, *Minoan-Mycenaean Religion,* 510. Barbara, the Nemesis in Shaw's play, is of course also closely related to a Britomart[is].

13. Murray defines a suppliant as "any man or woman who formally casts away all means of self-defense and throws himself upon your mercy," which to some extent Jenny Hill does (*Rise of the Greek Epic,* 85–86).

14. Lindsay, *The Clashing Rocks,* gives this definition: "*Hybris* is the overweening insolence, arrogance, self-conceit, which makes a man go too far, transgress limits, fling himself into an untenable or unbalanced position" (350). See Lattimore, *Story Patterns,* 22–25, 80–87, Rosenmeyer, *Masks of Tragedy,* 139–40, and *Bacchae of Euripides,* trans. Sutherland, 114–15.

15. That a Bill Walker is to be found in every walk of life—hence is a type of

Everyman—Shaw stresses not once, but twice, in the play's Preface: "There are millions of Bill Walkers in all classes of society today" (45); "Take a common English character like that of Bill Walker. We meet Bill everywhere: on the judicial bench, on the episcopal bench, in the Privy Council, at the War Office and Admiralty, as well as in the Old Bailey dock or in the ranks of casual unskilled labor" (46–47).

16. See *Bacchae*, trans. Kirk, 55–56. On the significance Greeks attached to names and wordplay, see *Bacchae of Euripides*, trans. Sandys, 154–55, and Guthrie, *A History of Greek Philosophy*, 1:86, 425 n. 5, 446 n. 1, 475 n. 2, 2:474, 3:206ff., 215.

17. This theme, it may be added, extends to the nonappearing Mog Habbijam. Upon receiving Bill's answer to the question, "Whats her name?" Barbara tells him of Mog's conversion and the transformation, internal and external, it has wrought: "her soul saved, and her face clean and her hair washed," along with "a new look in her eyes" (108). The name "Mog" itself may be a shortened form of "moggy," a slang epithet of the time for a badly or untidily dressed woman.

18. See also Arrowsmith's introduction to *Bacchae*, 146–47, and *Bacchae*, trans. Kirk, 14–15, on the underlying resemblances between the rivals contrasted in the play. Though unmentioned by any of these critics, the relationship suggests G.W.F. Hegel's identity of opposites.

19. As Winnington-Ingram puts it, "the true, the essential Dionysus is sitting close at hand, biding his time" (*Euripides and Dionysus*, 9). See *Bacchae*, ed. Dodds, 114 nn. 343–44, on the psychological response of Pentheus.

20. The Greek phrase, *sympeplegmetha xenoi*, means I am entangled or at grips with the stranger, but the metaphor, as Dodds explains (*Bacchae*, 174 nn. 800–8o1), is from wrestling. Arrowsmith's translation of *Bacchae* 491, "You wrestle well—when it comes to words," seems an additional instance, but though the figure involved is gymnastic, no specific reference to wrestling appears in the Greek. Other sample translations are, "He spars, at least in words" (Sutherland); "athletic . . . in his words" (Birkhead); "a pretty fencer—with words!" (Hadas and McLean), and "not untrained in argument" (Kirk).

21. See *Bacchae*, ed. Dodds, 142. On the *Bacchae* chorus as a dramatic character see also Kitto: "It is no ideal spectator but an actor; . . . it presents always one of the spiritual forces at work in the play. It . . . is as much part of the action as any chorus in the whole of Greek Tragedy" (*Greek Tragedy*, 380); and Kirk, "The Lydian Women . . . are a stronger element in the drama . . . than almost any other chorus we know" (*Bacchae*, 2). See also Lattimore, *Poetry of Greek Tragedy*, 137–38; Lesky, *History of Greek Literature*, 2nd ed., 402; Decharme, *Euripides*, 299; Ferguson, *A Companion to Greek Tragedy*, 20, 242.

22. See Dodds, "Euripides the Irrationalist": "Euripides confronts us here with an irruption into normal life of the mystery beyond life" (102).

23. See *Bacchae*, ed. Dodds, 123 nn. 402–16; *Bacchae*, trans. Kirk, 58–59 nn. 402–16; Grube, *Drama of Euripides*, 406.

24. Murray, "The Bacchae in Relation to Certain Currents of Thought in the Fifth Century," the introductory essay to his verse translations in *Athenian Drama III: Euripides* (1902), lxiv; reprinted with minor revisions in Murray, *Essays and Addresses*, 56–87. On the democratic character of Dionysos see also *Bacchae*, ed. Dodds, 127–28 nn. 421–23, and Winnington-Ingram, *Euripides and Dionysus*, 66.

25. In this passage and the one quoted below I follow Murray's version in *Athenian*

Drama III: Euripides, first published in 1902, and subsequent editions, 126. In the separate edition under the title, *Euripides: The Bacchae* (London: George Allen and Unwin) first published in 1904, there is a comma after "see" in the first line, not used by Shaw, and the initial capital for each "Will" has been reduced to lowercase. These two editions are cited hereafter as *Euripides* and *The Bacchae* respectively.

26. Although most printed editions of the play have "his" spaced for emphasis, as does the first printing of the Standard Edition, it is not so spaced in the original Derry manuscript, nor in later printings of the Standard Edition or the Bodley Head edition of Shaw's plays.

27. The ending may be compared with that in some other translations: "But I call blessed the man whose life is happy day by day" (Hadas and McLean); "but him whose life day by day is happy do I count blessed" (Kirk); "He who loves each day / For the happiness each day offers / Him I call blessed" (Volkanis); "But the truly happy man / Is he who best enjoys / each passing day" (Curry).

28. *Bacchae*, ed. Dodds, 190 nn. 902–11, and the eudaemonism of the drama, 128 nn. 424–26 and 191 nn. 910–11. See the analyses by Kirk (based on Dodds), 99 nn. 902–11; Sutherland, 126–28; Winnington-Ingram, 114 n. 1.

29. Corroboration of Shaw's familiarity with this Murray essay can be found in Bernard Shaw, *The Road to Equality: Ten Unpublished Lectures and Essays, 1884–1918*, ed. Louis Crompton, 183. In a lecture presumably given in December 1910, Shaw reports that Murray originally presented what later became the preface to his *Bacchae* translation as a "remarkable paper" to the Fabian Society. The reading of the paper must have taken place prior to the book's publication late in 1902. Correspondence between the two men in that year also reveals Shaw urging his friend to spend no more time improving the book but to publish it at once, and later acknowledging receipt of a copy. That Shaw was a continuing reader of Murray's writings is evident: in a 1913 lecture he recommended to his audience the professor of Greek's newly published "very remarkable book," *Euripides and His Age*, and discussed some of its contents (Allan Chappelow, *Shaw—"The Chucker-Out,"* 149). With respect to Murray's treatment of Dionysos, see *Euripides and His Age*: "We have in the *Bacchae* . . . a heartfelt glorification of 'Dionysus.' No doubt it is Dionysus in some private sense of the Poet's own" (122).

30. *Bacchae*, ed. Dodds, 183; cf. 117, 198; *Bacchae*, trans. Kirk, 96 nn. 877–81. On the universalizing tendency in Greek choruses see Cornford, *Thucydides Mythistoricus*: "But in the choral odes the action is lifted out of time and place on to the plane of the universal" (144). In *Euripides and His Age*, Murray, citing Cornford, writes: "When the stage is empty and the Choral Odes begin, we have no longer the particular acts and places and persons but something universal and eternal. The body, as it were, is gone and the essence remains" (152). Compare also Sutherland: "It is probably statistically true that most of the formulated general thought in Greek tragedy occurs in the choruses" (*Bacchae of Euripides*, 125).

31. Murray, *Athenian Drama III: Euripides*, xli, lxi–lxii; see also *Euripides and His Age*, 69, 126. Dodds builds on Murray's interpretation in his *Bacchae*, 188 nn. 882–87.

32. *Bacchae*, ed. Dodds, 189 nn. 893–94; cf. Winnington-Ingram, *Euripides and Dionysus*, 111. See also Murray, *Euripides and His Age*, 124.

33. See, e.g., Shaw's definition of the Life Force in *Sixteen Self Sketches* as "a mysterious

drive towards greater power over our circumstances and deeper understanding of Nature" (78). Like Cusins, Shaw said of himself, "I have more or less swallowed all the formulas, I have been in all the churches, studied all the religions with a great deal of sympathy" ("The Religion of the British Empire," reprinted in *The Religious Speeches of Bernard Shaw*, 5–6).

34. *Bacchae*, ed. Dodds, 190 nn. 895–96; Plato, *Laws* 890. Compare Winnington-Ingram, *Euripides and Dionysus*, 111–13; Webster, *Tragedies of Euripides*, 273–74. See also Guthrie, *A History of Greek Philosophy*, vol. 3, chap. 4, esp. 113–14, where Dodds is cited on this point.

35. Lattimore, *Poetry of Greek Tragedy*, 142. Compare Kirk's version: "For it is light expense to believe that *this* possesses power, whatever it is that constitutes divinity; and that what is held lawful over length of time exists forever and by Nature." The idea that it "costs little" or is "inexpensive" to subscribe to the religious doctrines proposed in this antistrophe Shaw undoubtedly would have found delectable, but unfortunately Murray's wording gave him no inkling of it.

36. Grube, *Drama of Euripides*, 14. In assaying the liberties taken by Murray and others our judgments need to be tempered by these cautionary words of Guthrie: "The choruses of the *Bacchae* are even more untranslatable than most Greek poetry, and no one who can read them will wish to look at a translation" (*Greeks and Their Gods*, 150).

37. Murray, *Athenian Drama III: Euripides*, 173–74 (*Bacchae*, 88). Dodds, in his *Bacchae*, assesses the textual evidence without mentioning Murray (187 nn. 877–81).

38. Grube, *Drama of Euripides*, 14; Rosenmeyer, *Masks of Tragedy*, 136. Grube modifies the language of his translation somewhat on p. 415 of his book.

39. The first four of these translations are in rhymed versions. Lattimore's is from *Poetry of Greek Tragedy*, 141. The Coleridge translation of this line is identical with that of Hadas and McLean, and Winnington-Ingram's is virtually the same: "That which is fair is ever dear." Rosenmeyer reports the phrasing given here as "the academic formulation of the last line which in the Greek consists of only four words (*Masks of Tragedy*, 136).

40. Grube, *Drama of Euripides*, 15 n. 2. For an examination of the relative merits of divergent readings of the Greek text of the refrain see also *Bacchae*, ed. Dodds, 187–88. Friedländer, in his *Plato*, suggests the French *beau, beauté* as closest in meaning to the richness of the word *kalon*, rejecting the English "noble, honorable" (2:302 n. 22). In contrast, Winnington-Ingram writes: "The word *kalos* is constantly used in the plays of Euripides of the standards of honour and fair dealing which are accepted by the characters, and often with a controversial note" (*Euripides and Dionysus*, 108 n. 3). Guthrie endorses Seltman's interpretation of this ambiguous word in the latter's *Approach to Greek Art*: "Beautiful is a misrendering of *kalos*. We can perhaps get nearest to the meaning by using Fine and Fineness, for these may be employed in most of the senses of the Greek words. To say that for the Greeks Beauty and Goodness were one and the same is an error. But put it, that to the Greeks Fineness automatically included excellence, because what is fine must be fitted to its purpose and therefore good, and we are on the right track. Fineness could become the ultimate Value by which all other Values could be measured" (*Approach to Greek Art*, 29; cf. Guthrie, *A History of Greek Philosophy*, 3:170).

41. *Bacchae*, ed. Dodds, 186–87 nn. 877–81; *Bacchae*, trans. Kirk, 34 nn. 72–77, 96–97 nn. 877–81.

42. See *Bacchae*, ed. Dodds, 186–87 nn. 877–81. On *philos* see Crombie, *Examination of Plato's Doctrines*, 1:20, 2:474; Friedländer, *Plato*, 2:95; Taylor, *Plato*, 65n. Additional variations in the last line of the refrain are suggested by translations of the proverb in *Lysis* 216c, e.g.: "The beautiful is friendly" (trans. Wright); "the beautiful is the friend" (trans. Jowett); "what is beautiful is loved" (Friedländer, *Plato*, 2:98).

43. It is quite possible that the shift from "Hate" to "Fate" was inadvertent. The original manuscript of *Major Barbara* shows that Shaw retained "Hate" when he first inserted the Murray passage into the play (British Library Add. MS 50616C, fol. 36, reproduced in *"Major Barbara": A Facsimile*, ed. Dukore, 115). But inspection of two different copies of the first typescript of the work suggests that a mistake was made in typing. For the copy filed with the Lord Chamberlain reads "Fate." On the other hand, in the copy used as prompt script for the first production (in Houghton Library, Harvard University), the first letter of the word has been obliterated and an "H" printed by hand corrects it. The correction is not in Shaw's hand, however, and appears to have been made in rehearsal. The word is "Fate" again in the first published edition of the play. Since the book was probably printed from a typescript other than the prompt copy, it is understandable that it would record the first typescript reading. But then Shaw could have changed or authorized the change back to "Hate" at any later date had he so desired. Michael von Albrecht deals only with the textual aspect of the problem in "Fate or Hate? A Textual Problem in Shaw's *Major Barbara*."

44. Dodds, "Euripides the Irrationalist," 101–2. Murray, in *Euripides and His Age*, offers a very similar "literal" translation of *Bacchae* 1006–7: "But the other things . . . are great and shining" (127); cf. Greene, *Moira*, 214, and Dodds, *Greeks and the Irrational*, 187. The text and sense of the *Bacchae* is uncertain at this point, and there is considerable disagreement about the attitude expressed toward "wisdom" with which this "other" is contrasted. See Dodds on *Bacchae* lines 1005–7, 204–5; Winnington-Ingram, *Euripides and Dionysus*, 124, 125; *Bacchae*, trans. Kirk, 108 nn. 1005f.; Conacher, *Euripidean Drama*, 65–66; and Lattimore, *Poetry of Greek Tragedy*, 144. Lattimore inclines toward Murray's view that wisdom as such is not rejected in these lines; Kirk sees it being paid no more than lip service. Conacher finds the passage consistent with the attitude toward "cleverness" indicated throughout the play: that it may be good or evil, depending on its application.

45. Compare Lavinia in *Androcles and the Lion*: "Religion is such a great thing that when I meet really religious people we are friends at once no matter what name we give to the divine will that made us and moves us" (4:597).

46. Shaw letter to Louis Calvert, November 27, 1905, quoted in Albert, "Shaw's Advice to the Players of *Major Barbara*," 9.

47. See *Bacchae*, ed. Dodds, 83 n. 115, 87–88 nn. 144–50; Farnell, *Cults*, 5:153, 196. In *Back to Methuselah*, Zoo speaks of handing on the torch of civilization from generation to generation: "But every time that torch is handed on, it dies down to the tiniest spark; and the man who gets it can rekindle it only by his own light" (5:518).

48. In 1915, during World War I, Shaw wrote to Maxim Gorky that in a world gone mad it was necessary to view madness as sanity, sanity being merely the madness that happens to be acceptable to the world (Weintraub, *Journey to Heartbreak*, 138). The madness motif also pervades *Heartbreak House*.

49. See Dodds, *Greeks and the Irrational*, chap. 3: "The Blessings of Madness"; Rohde, *Psyche*, 255; R. Hackforth, introduction to *Plato's Phaedrus*, 14.

50. See James Adam, *Religious Teachers of Greece*, 315; *Bacchae*, ed. Dodds, 109 nn. 298–310; Farnell, *Cults*, 5:162; North, *Sophrosyne*, 177–78.

51. See Plato on the philosopher "exalted above human interests" who "is rebuked by the world as a madman, for the world cannot see that he is possessed by divine inspiration" (*Phaedrus* 249d, trans. Cornford in his *Principium Sapientiae*, 81).

52. Adam, *Religious Teachers of Greece*, 315. See Winnington-Ingram, *Euripides and Dionysus*, 91, on the role of sex in the *Bacchae*.

53. On the relation of poetic madness to the Muses see Cornford, *Principium Sapientiae*, 76–79. As both lover and poet Cusins also conforms to the conjunction in Shakespeare's *A Midsummer Night's Dream*, 5.l.4–17, where we are told: "The lunatic, the lover and the poet / Are of imagination all compact" (lines 7–8). On the relation of this passage to Plato's *Phaedrus* see William A. Nitze, "'A Midsummer Night's Dream,' V, 1, 4–17," 495–97.

54. See Linforth, "Telestic Madness in Plato, *Phaedrus* 244de," 163–72, esp. 170–72; Dodds, *Greeks and the Irrational*, 76–78; Cornford, *Principium Sapientiae*, 74–75.

55. Crombie, *An Examination of Plato's Doctrines*, 1:185n. Compare: "an inspired deviation from established customs" (trans. Cary, *Bohn's Classical Library*, vol. 1); "a divine release of the soul from the yoke of custom and convention" (trans. Jowett).

56. See *Bacchae*, ed. Dodds, 127–28 nn. 421–23, 129–30 nn. 430–33. "It has rightly been remarked," writes Antony Andrewes in *The Greeks*, "that Apollo always moved in the best society, whereas Dionysus was much more the god of the common man" (237). Compare Dodds, *Greeks and the Irrational*, 76. In the Preface to *Androcles and the Lion*, Shaw comparably cites Matthew's report of Jesus's declaration "that the common multitude were the salt of the earth and the light of the world" (4:487).

57. On stichomythia and *antilabe* in the *Bacchae* see the commentaries by Dodds, xxxviii, 93, 157–58, 178, 179, 194, 196, 230; Sutherland, 97; and Kirk, 45–46 nn. 191–99.

58. Lillian B. Lawler, *The Dance in Ancient Greece*, 11, 83, 84–85, 123, and passim. Discussing dancing in the Greek theater, Ferguson writes that the terms defining the positions of choral members in the orchestra "were borrowed from military strategy, and one movement was a marching movement in rectangular formation" (*A Companion to Greek Tragedy*, 21).

59. Shaw's model for Lord Saxmundham may have been the prominent actor Sir Squire Bancroft, who offered to donate a substantial sum to the so-called Darkest England scheme of General William Booth, the founder of the Salvation Army. According to Harold Begbie's biography of Booth, in 1890 the actor sent a letter to the *Times*: "I know nothing of General Booth's scheme in detail, but it seems to me to be so noble in its object that something really serious and thorough should be done to aid it. I read that the large sum of £100,000 will be necessary to insure an actual trial, and without the smallest pretence to hang on to even the skirts of philanthropy, I beg to say that, if 99 other men will do the same for the cause, I will give General Booth £1,000 towards it" (*Life of General William Booth*, 2:112). Still another Booth biographer, St. John Ervine—incidentally also a biographer of Shaw—adds that in February 1891 Bancroft "withdrew the condition and gave the money without proviso of any sort" when hostile and offensive

personal criticism of Booth began (*God's Soldier,* 2:716; see also Begbie, *Life of General William Booth,* 2:129, and Squire Bancroft, *The Bancrofts: Recollections of Sixty Years,* 331). Stanley Weintraub's article, "Bernard Shaw in Darkest England," mentions this donation to Booth's scheme (51), but does not identify Squire Bancroft as the donor.

60. See *The Bacchae* 435–40, 622, 636, 1084–85; *Bacchae,* ed. Dodds, xliv, 120 nn. 389–92, 213 nn. 1084–85; Farnell *Cults,* 5:162–63, 256; *Bacchae,* trans. Kirk, 114 nn. 1084f.

61. Especially at *Bacchae* 686–88, where the herdsman-messenger refutes Pentheus's accusations of drunkenness against the maenads. See also *Bacchae,* ed. Dodds, xiii; Winnington-Ingram, *Euripides and Dionysus,* 49; *Bacchae,* trans. Kirk, 4–5 and 49 nn. 260–62; Grube, *Drama of Euripides,* 403, 412. Greene, *Moira,* rightly observes that "the *Bacchae* is neither a teetotalist tract nor an invitation to intoxication" (216 n. 193); see also Guthrie, *Greeks and Their Gods,* 149.

62. See Shaw on John Barleycorn: drawing on Frazer's *Golden Bough* he develops the religious implications of the "primitive logic" that "led the first men who conceived God as capable of incarnation to believe that they could acquire a spark of his divinity by eating his flesh and drinking his blood" (Pref. *Androcles and the Lion,* 4:473–74).

63. "The Illusions of War," as reported in the *Christian Commonwealth,* November 3, 1915, 63, col. 2. I am indebted to Stanley Weintraub for calling my attention to this speech; see his *Journey to Heartbreak,* 125. In his account of the same speech, Chappelow quotes Shaw as saying, "We are in a condition of illusion. We are like the Bacchantes in Euripides's play; and the awakening will be just as terrible" (*Shaw—"The Chucker-Out,"* 361). These sentences do not appear in the *Christian Commonwealth* report of the speech.

64. Letter of November 18, 1905, quoted in Albert, "Shaw's Advice to the Players," 7. This version of the passage in the letter varies slightly in punctuation from that in *Shaw on Theatre,* ed. West, 108.

65. *Bacchae,* ed. Dodds, 165–66 n. 725; Guthrie, *Greeks and Their Gods,* 288; *Bacchae,* trans. Kirk, 83 n. 725. On Dionysos as a god of joy, see Dodds, *Greeks and the Irrational,* 76. Concerning the handling of *thyrsoi* and the Bacchic carriage of the head, see *Bacchae,* ed. Dodds, 82 n. 113, 185 nn. 862–65, and *Greeks and the Irrational,* 273–74. That Shaw was very much alive to the exciting quality and dramatic potential of the Bacchic cry is suggested in a sportive article he penned in 1924, reporting his first visit to a baseball game— a London exhibition game between the Chicago "Sioux" and the New York "Apaches," as he dubbed the White Sox and the Giants. Impressed by the scope baseball gives "for the higher human faculties of rhetoric, irony, and eloquent emotional appeal," he explains: "Even those players who had no gift of eloquence expressed their souls in dithyrambic cries like the Greek Evoe! which sounded to me like Attaboy! I confess that I am not enough of a Greek scholar to translate Attaboy, but it is a very stimulating ejaculation." ("This Baseball Madness," *Evening Standard,* November 4, 1924, 7:1; the article appeared earlier as "Shaw, at His First Baseball Game, Pans Both Teams Hard," in the *World* [New York], October 29, 1924).

66. Diapason is a musical term derived from the Greek *dia pason,* an abbreviated form of *he dia pason chordon symphonia,* the concord through all the notes of the scale. It denotes, among other things, the interval and consonance of an octave, a harmonious combination of notes, the entire compass or range of a voice or instrument, a rule or scale used by musical instrument makers in tuning, and is the name of the two

principal foundation stops in an organ. In a review in *Music in London* 1890–94, Shaw found the violinist Joachim "bothered by the change of diapason from Germany to England" (3:156). Here in the play the term is probably used in the figurative sense of a resounding outburst of harmonious sound. Elsewhere in *Music in London* 1890–94, Shaw alludes to Hector Berlioz's characterization of the trombone as "Olympian" (1:17). In this treatise Berlioz not only speaks of its "Olympian voice," but also describes it as an "epic" instrument of nobleness and grandeur," possessing "all the deep and powerful accents of high musical poetry,—from the religious accent, calm and imposing, to the wild clamours of the orgy." It is possible for a composer "to make it by turn . . . raise a hymn of glory, break forth into frantic cries, or sound its dread flourish to awaken the dead or to doom the living" (Berlioz, *A Treatise on Modern Instrumentation and Orchestration*, 173, 156).

67. Undershaft's way with a trombone is very much like Shaw's own father's. In *Music in London 1890–94* Shaw relates how his father joined company with other local amateur musicians in public performances. "In fact," he added, "my father not only played his trombone part, but actually composed it as he went along, being an indifferent reader-at-sight but an expert at what used to be known as 'vamping'" (2:9). The draft manuscript of O'Bolger's proposed Shaw biography expands on this account: "His natural instrument was the trombone: . . . He was one of a band (a brass band) of gentlemen who gave concerts weekly on the Dodder; but even there the good man was a first-class fraud, for he only vamped by ear pretending to read his notes the while, though he did not know one from the other . . . All the Shaw family . . . had in their blood a kind of sforzanda [*sic*] bark that admirably pleased and expressed their temperament" (MS Eng 1046.10, pages II–2 and II–3, Houghton Library, Harvard University; quoted by permission of the Society of Authors and courtesy of Houghton Library).

68. Another occasion on which Shaw aligned trombone and trumpet is suggestive here. When discussing a facsimile of a Roman buccina on display at an exhibition, he expressed a strong desire to hear it, having been told that "it sounds like four trombones rolled into one. Such a description makes my ears water; for I love an apocalyptic trumpet blast." An apocalyptic trumpet blast is precisely what the Joel allusion signals in the play.

69. Kirk construes these *Bacchae* lines as referring to the god rather than to his human celebrant (42 n. 145 and 38–39 n. 115). But see Winnington-Ingram, *Euripides and Dionysus*, 37 n. 3; *Bacchae*, ed. Dodds, 87–88, notes on lines 136, 141, and 144–50; and T. K. Oesterreich: "If the worshippers had not been changed into Dionysos the transference to them of the god's name would be inexplicable" (*Possession: Demoniacal and Other*, 339).

70. Oesterreich writes: "It is very interesting to note that the word *enthousiasmos* in itself already means possession" (*Possession*, 348).

71. In his *Helen*, Euripides described the sound of the *aulos* with the term used here for the tympanon: *barubromon*, "deep-toned, deep or loud thundering" or "rumbling." *Helen* 1349–52 reads: Aphrodite "took the deep-toned flute and was pleased with the echoing music" (trans. Warner), or "The goddess smiled and drew into her hands the deep sounding flute in delight with its music" (trans. Lattimore). So in Shaw's drama, Undershaft's trombone adds its thundering sonority to the ecstatic rumble of the drum.

72. "Corybantic Rites in Plato," 139. See also *Bacchae*, ed. Dodds, 83 n. 115.

73. Daniel J. Leary has remarked on the stichomythic rhythm of these lines in "Dialectical Action in *Major Barbara*," 52.

74. For related comments by Shaw see also the *Revolutionist's Handbook* in *Man and Superman*, 2:742; Pref. to *Androcles and the Lion*, 4:556; Pref. to *Back to Methuselah*, 5:281–82, 296. Since, as he wrote in a letter to Eleanor Robson Belmont (*The Fabric of Memory*, 50), he could affirm quite comfortably: "I believe in the Holy Ghost, the Catholic Church, the Communion of Saints, and the Life Everlasting" (Joad, *Shaw*, 144).

75. *Bacchae*, ed. Dodds, 66 n. 24; *Bacchae of Euripides*, trans. Sandys, 93 n. 24. Sandys describes it as a *joyous* shout, generally of *women* calling on the gods. R. Y. Tyrrell, in *The Bacchae of Euripides*, calls it "a cry of triumph and worship" (3 n. 24), and Kirk, a "shriek of ecstasy" (28 n. 24f.). On other Dionysian ritual cries in the *Bacchae*—"*euoi*" or "*evoe*" (141), "*Io Bacchae*" (577), and "*alalagé*" (593)—see the translations by Kirk, 42, 74, 75; Dodds, 151 nn. 591–93; and Guthrie, *Greeks and Their Gods*, 288. It may be of some interest in this connection to note that the Salvation Army named its newspaper the *War Cry*.

76. Lisë Pedersen explores the implications of these lines of Shaw's drama in connection with *The Merchant of Venice* in "Ducats and Daughters in *The Merchant of Venice* and *Major Barbara*."

77. Barbara's tragedy conforms closely to Aristotle's conception of the tragic *pathos* in *Poetics* 1452b10–13, especially in Gerald Else's interpretation of it as the suffering of a painful or destructive act (*pathos*) involving *philoi*, "dear ones," in the sense of close blood-relatives. See Else, *Aristotle's Poetics: The Argument*, 349–51, 356–58, 414–15, and *passim*. Apposite to her too is Murray's comment on the ancient tragic hero in his *Classical Tradition in Poetry*: "The Greek hero, when he suffers, almost always suffers in order to save others" (65).

78. Anthony S. Abbott, in his *Shaw and Christianity*, finds the irony in Bill's remark to be that it is aimed at Barbara, "the only member of the Army who does not deserve his reproach" (131). But this is plainly one more instance of Shaw's insistence that guilt is indivisible and shared. It was Major Barbara who represented the Army in her dealings with Bill, and she must realize that as long as she is one of its "officers" she is deeply implicated in its deeds. What *is* ironical is the peripeteia in the Barbara-Bill moral relationship. See Conacher on the *Bacchae*: "It is through Cadmus, the least guilty member of his family, that the dramatist expresses most fully an awareness of the family's collective guilt (1249–50, 1297, 1302ff.)" (*Euripidean Drama*, 71).

79. Euripides used these terminal lines in his *Alcestis, Andromache, Helen,* and (in slightly modified form) in *Medea* as well. The same Euripidean words were chosen by Bramwell Booth, son of William Booth and his successor as general of the Salvation Army, as epigraph to his book, *These Fifty Years*, in this unidentified translation: "That which is looked for is not performed, and God takes unlikely paths as He walks with men."

Chapter 3. The Drama of Heaven and Hell

1. No mention is made of Cusins's apparel, but since he has no further occasion to change clothing during the remainder of the play, it is evident he too no longer wears the uniform. This inference from the internal evidence is confirmed in a note Shaw wrote

to Esmé Percy in 1927, quoted in Albert, "More Shaw Advice to the Players of *Major Barbara*," 73.

2. See *Bacchae*, ed. Dodds, 181 nn. 854–55; also 191–92. Ernest Crawley, whom Dodds cites, writes that the vestment imposes a divine super-personality on the human wearer: "The dress is a material link between his person and the supernatural," inspiring him. "This idea is implicit in every form of dress. Dress is a social body-surface, and even in sexual dress, military uniform, professional and official dress the idea that the dress has the properties of the state inherent in it is often quite explicit" (*Dress, Drinks and Drums,* 163). For variant views of the connection between costume and identity in the *Bacchae,* see the commentaries by Arrowsmith, 147, and Kirk, 93–94 nn. 857–60.

3. "Warrior Saint" is what Shaw calls Joan in Pref. *Saint Joan,* 6:14.

4. Kurt Tetzeli von Rosador, in "The Natural History of *Major Barbara,*" views Barbara's second-act heartbreak as "the Shavian metaphor for the insight gained into reality" (146). It is difficult to see how this particular interpretation can stand up to scrutiny. For one thing, Barbara's main insights emerge during the third act when her heart, or spirit, is undergoing restoration. It is also worth noting that the person Barbara accuses of breaking her heart is Cusins, not her father; yet it is the latter who is most instrumental in educating her, as the author rightly emphasizes. More crucially, heartbreak to Shaw is no such cognitive phenomenon; this is apparent from the way he has Ellie Dunn define it in *Heartbreak House:* "It is a curious sensation: the sort of pain that goes mercifully beyond our powers of feeling. When your heart is broken your boats are burned: nothing matters any more. It is the end of happiness and the beginning of peace" (5:140).

5. Farnell, *Cults,* 5:120. See also Rohde, *Psyche,* 287 and 308 n. 2; *Bacchae,* ed. Dodds, xvi; Dodds, *Greeks and the Irrational,* 273.

6. Farnell, *Cults,* 5:128–32. On the lower-world associations of Dionysos, see ibid., 101, 118, 120, 178–85, 193; Rohde, 285; Benn, *Philosophy of Greece,* 67; Pickard-Cambridge, *Dithyramb Tragedy and Comedy,* 7, 103, 130; Guthrie, *Greeks and Their Gods,* 203, *Bacchae,* trans. Kirk, 5; "Dionysus," in *Oxford Classical Dictionary,* 2nd ed. On the relation between Hades and hell see Nilsson, *Greek Folk Religion,* 115–20.

7. Heraclitus, frag. 15, trans. Guthrie, *A History of Greek Philosophy,* 1:475; see also 463, 476. Hades, as death, is referred to twice in the *Bacchae* (857, 1157). On Dionysos as multinomical see Sophocles, *Antigone* 1115; Farnell, *Cults,* 5:94; Murray, *Athenian Drama III: Euripides,* 166. Some of the numerous names are given in Ovid, *Metamorphoses* 4:11–17.

8. *Bacchae* 179, 186, 200, 203, 266–71, 310–12, 332, 395, 427–29, 480, 641, 655, 824, 839, 877, 897, 1005, 1151, 1190. See also the commentaries by Dodds, 92 n. 179 and 121 n. 395; Winnington-Ingram, 162–63, 167–70 and passim; Arrowsmith, 144–46; Conacher, 73–77; Grube, 406; and Kirk, 45 n. 179 and passim.

9. See Pref. *The Apple Cart:* "Money talks: money prints: money broadcasts: money reigns" (6:253). As early as 1891, Shaw had asserted in "The Impossibilities of Anarchism" that "everywhere, from the Parliament which wields the irresistible coercive forces of the bludgeon, bayonet, machine gun, dynamite shell, prison, and scaffold, down to the pettiest centre of shabby-genteel social pretension, the rich pay the piper and call the tune. Naturally, they use their power to steal more money to continue paying the piper and thus all society becomes a huge conspiracy and hypocrisy" (*Essays in Fabian Socialism,* 97).

10. The psychological tendencies that work to Undershaft's advantage Shaw had

described in "'The Impossibilities of Anarchism'": "One is almost tempted in this country to declare that the poorer the man the greater the snob, until you get down to those who are so oppressed that they have not enough self-respect even for snobbery. . . . The moment you rise into the higher atmosphere of a pound a week, you find that envy, ostentation, tedious and insincere ceremony, love of petty titles, precedences and dignities, and all the detestable fruits of inequality of condition, flourish as rankly among those who lose as among those who gain by it" (*Essays in Fabian Socialism*, 81). Later, in response to a question posed by a periodical dedicated to "Egoistic Philosophy" Shaw wrote: "'There is no war between exploiters and exploited. The whole people cordially consent to and approve of inequality, privilege, peerage, and monopoly because they all have (or think they have) a chance in the lottery. The exploiting system could no more stand to-day without an overwhelming concensus [*sic*] of opinion in its favor—especially among the working classes—than Monte Carlo could stand if people were not willing to lose money there" (*Eagle and the Serpent* 4 [September 1, 1898], 62; repeated in a longer letter, *Eagle and the Serpent* 18, n.d. [ca. 1902], 69). See also "Tolstoy on Art" (1898) in Shaw's *Pen Portraits and Reviews*, 256.

11. See *Bacchae* 75 nn. 72–75, 72, 902, 904, 911, and passim, ed. Dodds. On *eudaimon* and *eudaimonia* see also Snell, *Discovery of the Mind*, 158, Winnington-Ingram, *Euripides and Dionysus*, 156, and Greene, *Moira*, 324.

12. See, e.g., *Bacchae* 101–4, 920–22, 1107, 1159; *Bacchae*, ed. Dodds, xviii, xx, and 131 n. 436. According to Rosenmeyer, in this play Euripides is dramatizing questions raised by man's dual nature as both beast and god (131), issuing in a very depressing moral: "Between the realm of the beasts from which man is born, and the realm of the gods presided over by the great beast of heaven, civilized existence and human existence are a minute enclave, hard-pressed and short-lived and utterly without hope" (151).

13. Letter of July 28, 1940, to Pascal, in *Bernard Shaw and Gabriel Pascal*, ed. Dukore, 94–95. Most of these lines, with minor variations, were actually incorporated in the film *Major Barbara* (1941), directed by Pascal, starring Wendy Hiller, Rex Harrison, and Robert Morley; see Donald P. Costello, *The Serpent's Eye: Shaw and the Cinema*, 102–3. Nevertheless Shaw did not see fit to use this addition to the speech in the printed cinematic version of the play, *Major Barbara: A Screen Version*, 131. See also Shaw's letter of November 10, 1942, to Ellen Pollock in which he indicates that Undershaft's effectiveness comes from suggesting to Barbara that Bill's conversion has been deeper even than those of Todger and Mog (quoted in Albert, "More Shaw Advice to the Players of *Major Barbara*," 76). In the Preface to *Major Barbara*, Shaw wrote: "But Bill may not be lost for all that. He is still in the grip of the facts and of his own conscience, and may find his taste for blackguardism permanently spoiled. Still I cannot guarantee that happy ending" (49).

14. The ellipsis is in Dodd's translation. Gilbert Murray translates: "I know not what thou sayest; but my will / clears, and some change cometh, I know not how." Dodds (230) and Winnington-Ingram (*Euripides and Dionysus*, 141) quote Ulrich von Wilamowitz: "She speaks very slowly and simply: we shudder as we watch her beginning a new life." "From that moment she has a new light," says Shaw of Barbara in his letter to Ellen Pollock (Albert, "More Shaw Advice to the Players of *Major Barbara*," 77).

15. See Murray's letter of October 10, 1908, to Lillah McCarthy, quoted in her book *Myself and My Friends*, 293–94. Rosenmeyer has also suggested that "in writing this play

Euripides seems to come close to creating the medieval mystery play" (*Euripides and His Age*, 109). F. L. Lucas similarly finds the *Bacchae* "recalling at moments a medieval mystery, at moments a religious revival, at moments a witches' sabbath" (*Greek Tragedy and Comedy*, 306).

16. Forter has examined the bearing of the legend of Saint Barbara on *Major Barbara* in her introduction to the Crofts Classic edition, esp. xviii–xxi. Sutherland proposes as stage set for the *Bacchae* a representation of "the outer fortification walls and outer gate of the palace complex"; this would match in part the "emplacement of concrete . . . and a parapet which suggests a fortification" of the Act III, scene 2 setting of *Major Barbara* (75–76).

17. Productions of the play, failing to understand the significance of this dummy-kicking episode, often misguidedly excise it from performances.

18. Shaw wrote in his 1898 letter to the *Eagle and Serpent*, "If the average man wishes to be a slave, the able man can do nothing for him but be a master to him, however strongly he may disapprove of slavery and wish for the society of freemen." But years later, when quoting again the words of William Morris on slavery, he appended the comment that "if we give irresponsible power over us to any man he will abuse it" (*Ethical Principles of Social Reconstruction*, a paper read before the Aristotelian Society, London, April 23, 1917; reprinted in *Platform and Pulpit*, ed. Laurence, 100).

19. Farnell reports that the mysterious early lines of a fragmentary Dionysiac hymn appear to attribute the institution of the trieteric festivals to the fact that the god "had been cut into three parts" (*Cults of the Greek States*, 5:177). A comparable Dionysian trichotomy clearly takes place figuratively in *Major Barbara*.

20. See *Bacchae*, ed. Dodds, 79 n. 99; Farnell, *Cults*, 5:447; Greene, *Moira*, 16 and passim; Nilsson, *A History of Greek Religion*, 167–72; Rose, *Handbook of Greek Mythology*, 24. Dodds points out that in Homer claims to status arising from family or social relationships are included in a person's *moira* (*Greeks and the Irrational*, 8).

21. The events of Act I occur in the evening; those of Act II the following morning (the Salvation Army meeting that afternoon and Cusins's intoxicating night with Undershaft filling the interval between the second and third acts); Act III occupies the afternoon of the next day. In the first scene of the last act Lady Britomart mistakenly reminds Stephen that it was "last night" when she told him about the Undershaft tradition (148). Bernard Dukore first called my attention to this oversight by Shaw.

22. Concerning *phronein*, see Conacher, *Euripidean Drama*, 74, Winnington-Ingram, *Euripides and Dionysus*, 42, 62.

23. Those who blithely identify the doctrines of Undershaft with the views of Shaw should consider the substantial evidence to the contrary. At least twice Shaw endorsed on his own account the dictum of the German socialist Ferdinand Lassalle (d. 1864): "The sword is never right" (see "The New Politics" [1889] in *Road to Equality*, 60, and "Common Sense about the War" [1914] in *What Shaw Really Wrote about the War*, 73). Patent evidence of Shaw's distance from Undershaft's position is presented in his letters to O'Bolger, quoted below, and in a letter to Tighe Hopkins in 1889: "If I were a watchmaker I should consider myself bound to make a watch for any fellow citizen who ordered it, without going into his political or social opinions. But if somebody ordered an infernal machine apparatus from me, I should feel equally bound to find out what it was wanted

for before I consented to make it" (*Bernard Shaw: Collected Letters 1874–1897*, 1:223). See also Donald Brook's interview with Shaw in *Writers' Gallery*: Brook asks, "Should private armament manufacturers be allowed to continue in the business?" G.B.S. replies: "State armaments should of course be a State monopoly; but private manufacture of weapons for sport and self-defence need not be outlawed" (139). Ftatateeta asks in *Caesar and Cleopatra*: "Who shall stay the sword in the hand of a fool, if the high gods put it there?" (*Three Plays for Puritans*, 2:179).

24. *Bacchae*, ed. Dodds, 82 n. 113. Sandys equates *thyrsos* and sword (ciii).

25. "Unashamed" resembles the words of Achilles in a surviving fragment from the Achilles trilogy of Aeschylus, as interpreted by Snell in *Scenes from Greek Drama*: "'I am not ashamed' means: I do not care what you think. I shall stand by what I have done, by my convictions, and shall carry it through against your resistance" (8). Snell goes on to describe this Achilles as "the first to become a man from whom one can expect genuine decisions, a man who really stands by his word and deed, without letting himself be led by *aidos*, shame before his own people, and earthly reputation" (21). But such a characterization by no means fits the typical *anaides*, the person above shame. See E. M. Blaiklock, *The Male Characters of Euripides*, 105–6, on Odysseus as *anaides* in Euripides's *Hecuba* (with a reference to *Bacchae* 269), and Dodds, *Greeks and the Irrational*, 187–88, on the Euripidean treatment of characters who repudiate shame. See also Arthur W. H. Adkins, *Merit and Responsibility: A Study in Greek Values*, 43–46.

26. On *aidos* see also Ferguson, *Moral Values*, 14; Lionel Pearson, *Popular Ethics in Ancient Greece*, 18, 26.

27. *Armatura fidei*, "armor of faith," appears in the prayer of Thomas Aquinas for Thanksgiving after Mass: "And I pray that this holy communion . . . may bring about my pardon and salvation, encompassing me with the armour of faith and the shield of a good will" (*The Missal in Latin and English*, 754). I do not know if Shaw was familiar with this prayer, but there are indications that he was acquainted with the writings of Thomas and held them in some esteem. On one occasion he counseled Archibald Henderson, his biographer: "You should read St. Thomas Aquinas: he will cure you of the notion that theology is a penitential disease." Everyone, he adds, rates "the heavenly doctors—the saints—. . . as happier, more enviable people" than the voluptuaries: "Who would not rather be Aquinas than Don Juan?" ("George Bernard Shaw Self-Revealed," 436).

28. In particular, *arkus*, a hunter's net (*Bacchae* 231, 451, 870), *brochos*, a noose for hanging or strangling (615, 619, 1022, 1173), *bolos*, a casting-net (848), *diktuon*, a hunting or fishing net (1206), *horkane*, a snare, trap, or pitfall (611), *aporia lelemmenos*, "trapped past escaping" (1102, ed. Dodds). In the latter phrase *aporia* means not knowing which way to turn. Murray renders *brochos*, noose, as "snare" (1022). For a concise summary of the hunt imagery and reversal of hunter and hunted in the *Bacchae*, see trans. Kirk, 13–14. The thought that Pentheus may catch ("trap" in Murray's version) or be caught appears in one line, at 960.

29. Rosenmeyer sees the hunt as a symbol of "the futility of organized, circumscribed life," all worldly activity appearing to be hunt and escape from "the vantage point of the larger reality" of Being. "Hunting and being hunted are the physical and psychological manifestations of Appearance, the monotonous jolts of the process of generation and decay." Between appearance and reality there is "a perpetual pull" with lasting victory going

to neither (*Masks of Tragedy*, 140–41). The *Major Barbara* passage may correspondingly be construed as pointing both to societal appearances and to the reality underlying them. Interestingly, Cusins begins it with a warning to Barbara about Undershaft's metaphysics.

30. Compare: "I have more authority than you" (trans. Hadas and McLean).

31. In the Preface to *Farfetched Fables*, as elsewhere, Shaw described himself also as "an instrument of the Life Force" (7:386), but then in his philosophy the Life Force operates through all living beings. J. L. Wisenthal argues on the basis of the dialogue in a cancelled draft of the passage that Undershaft really means by his "will" statement the will of society, but wants Barbara to think that he means the will of God ("The Underside of Undershaft: A Wagnerian Motif in *Major Barbara*," 61–62, reiterated in his *The Marriage of Contraries: Bernard Shaw's Middle Plays*, 231 n. 14). But abandoned lines by themselves are a quicksand support for interpretation, especially when, as in this case, they yield conclusions contradictory to what Shaw himself asserted, after due reflection, in his Preface. "A will of which I am a part," however, needs to be read in still another way as well: as an allusion to the famous couplet (lines 1336–37) in Goethe's *Faust*, part 1, of which Shaw took more than passing note. In *The Intelligent Woman's Guide to Socialism and Capitalism*, he wrote, "When Faust asked Mephistopheles what he was, Mephistopheles answered that he was part of a power that was always willing evil and always doing good" (300). In January 1896, over thirty years earlier, in comparing the average normal man with a villain, Shaw remarked that "we sometimes find it hard to avoid the cynical suspicion that the balance of social advantage is on the side of gifted villainy, since we see the able villain, Mephistopheles-like, doing a huge amount of good in order to win the power to do a little darling evil, out of which he is as likely as not to be cheated in the end" ("New Year Dramas" [1896], *Drama Observed*, ed. Dukore, 2:488). Although Shaw eschewed villainy in his playwriting, the language of Undershaft's enigmatic utterance suggests that a similar process of ethical equilibration has entered into the conception of this Mephistophelean character.

32. Years later Shaw wrote approvingly of Nietzsche, who in "thinking out the great central truth of the Will to Power" concluded "that the final objective of this Will was power over self, and that the seekers after power over others and material possessions were on a false scent" (Pref. *Back to Methuselah*, Standard Edition, lii). (This edition contains a section entitled "A Sample of Lamarko-Shavian Invective," lii–liii, that is omitted from the Bodley Head edition [cf. 5:309].)

33. The capital letters and hyphens at the end were a 1930 addition, appearing for the first time in the *Standard Edition of the Works of Bernard Shaw*, 2:xxii.

34. In his 1942 letter to Ellen Pollock, Shaw insisted that Barbara "must do just nothing" during this long period of silence ("More Shaw Advice," 76). See, ibid., the comment of Mrs. Patrick Campbell on this scene, from *Bernard Shaw and Mrs. Patrick Campbell: Their Correspondence*, ed. Alan Dent, 273.

35. *Bacchae*, ed. Dodds, 172; also xxviii. For the other views mentioned see the translations by Sandys, lxii, and Kirk, 17 (infatuation); Grube, 415, and Harsh, 242–43 (drunkenness, intoxication); Sutherland, 117 (madness induced by the god), Conacher, 67–68 (maddening by the god, building on tendencies in Pentheus's psychological nature); Arrowsmith, 147 (loss of identity); Rosenmeyer, 147 (personality change and death); Lesky, in *History of Greek Literature*, describes Pentheus as "oddly benumbed" (399). Among

those who consider Pentheus to be hypnotized or mesmerized are Way and Birkhead in their translations, E. M. Blailock, *The Male Characters of Euripides*, 227, Guthrie, *Greeks and Their Gods*, 167, and Greene, *Moira*, 215. Winnington-Ingram takes it to be "a process comparable to hypnotism" (160). Norwood espoused the magic influence of hypnotism in the *Riddle of the Bacchae*, 106, but abandons it in his *Essays on Euripidean Drama* for an explanation in terms of "glamour," defined as a sort of hallucinatory enchantment (57–66). Ferguson leaves it that Dionysos somehow "asserts his spiritual power over the mortal" as alternative to "hypnotic suggestion in the narrower sense" (*A Companion to Greek Tragedy*, 476). Murray's views appear in his *History of Ancient Greek Literature*, 271, and in his *Bacchae* translation, nn. 810ff.

36. Ferguson detects in the *Bacchae* an important thematic interest in the human hand, especially in the hands of the maenads. Able to wound and to soothe, the hand is "the instrument of good or evil" (*A Companion to Greek Tragedy*, 467; see also 471–83, citing *Bacchae* 25, 343, 736, 738, 745, 880 [repeated at 900], 973, 1109, 1136, 1209, 1236, 1245, 1318, to which we can add 513, 615, 1053, 1071, 1128, 1164, 1207, 1240, 1280, and 1286). Hands function comparably in *Major Barbara* but also in wider and more varied ways. For example, Bill Walker raises his hands against others and comes to rue it; Cusins replicates the uplifted hand invoked by the *Bacchae* chorus; Barbara spotlights the bad blood on her father's hands; two mottos of the Armorer's creed summon hand to sword; in the play's action not only are hands shaken in conventional greeting and to bind impellent agreements, but hands are also held in hands; more than once hands support heads bowed in dejection; both Peter and Bill receive friendly touches of Barbara's hand; and Barbara deplores the escape of the soul of Bill she had in her hand. The most arresting instances are those that articulate the undercurrent motif of power and its utilization to improve or endanger human life and civilization.

37. Much critical controversy has raged over this episode. Fortunately it is for the most part irrelevant to our concerns here. A convenient guide to some of the pertinent critical discussions may be found in Conacher, *Euripidean Drama*, 66 n. 14.

38. *Bacchae*, ed. Dodds, 147–48; on Dionysos as "Master of the Lightning," xxxii, 151, 213, and trans. Kirk, 114 nn. 1082f.

39. Winnington-Ingram, *Euripides and Dionysus*, 83, 84–86. In a note on 55 he calls attention to Euripides's arresting use of the *ano kato* expression four times in the play to describe the effects of explosive outbursts of force. See also Grube, *Drama of Euripides*, 412, and Conacher, *Euripidean Drama*, 65–66. Kitto reminds us that "natural forces are ruthless and insensitive" (*Greek Tragedy*, 379).

40. Compare Gilbey in *Fanny's First Play*: "all of a sudden everything is turned upside down" (4:415), and Aubrey on the earthquake effect suffered by institutions in *Too True to Be Good* (6:478).

41. On the literal significance of the latter phrase see Albert, "'Letters of Fire Against the Sky,'" 83–85. Earlier in the second act Snobby told Rummy of his intention to pretend seeing "somebody struck by lightnin'" (98).

42. Farnell, *Cults*, 5:135, 139–40; see also Herbert J. Muller, *Spirit of Tragedy*, 122.

43. The inclusion of respectability among Undershaft's seven deadly sins is in itself not surprising, but poses something of a puzzle, coming as it does just a few speeches after he has told his daughter that, along with cleanliness, respectability requires no

justification. So regarded it would be a self-justifying *virtue*, rather than something "sinful" or onerous. Perhaps the resolution of the seeming contradiction is that respectability, like such other "sins" as food and children, is double-edged, its very value the source of troublesome concern.

44. Dodds, *Greeks and the Irrational*, 76, 273; Farnell, *Cults*, 5:120. Kirk, 66, is skeptical of Dodds's further suggestion (*Bacchae*, 139) that there is an allusion to this title of the god at *Bacchae* 498; but Kirk himself calls attention to the god's power to release from bondage at 79 nn. 651–53.

45. Orestes, in Euripides's *Electra* (line 376), says much the same thing—that poverty is a condition of sickness, a teacher of evil.

46. Compare T. H. Huxley, "Social Diseases and Worse Remedies," in his *Evolution and Ethics and Other Essays*: "The moral nature in us asks for no more than is compatible with the general good; the nonmoral nature proclaims and acts upon that fine old Scottish family motto, 'Thou shalt starve ere I want'" (211). Stuart Baker mentions this connection with Huxley in his erudite study, *Bernard Shaw's Remarkable Religion* (140, 247–48 n. 5).

47. See, e.g., Barker, *Greek Political Theory*, esp. 64–77, 83–85. According to the political orator Antiphon, "Men draw life from the things that are advantageous to them: they incur death from the things that are disadvantageous to them" (96). Part of Barker's restatement of Antiphon's argument sounds quite Undershaftian: "The law . . . declares things not to be advantageous which by nature, really are advantageous: it declares for instance, a theft by a starving man not to be advantageous, whereas really such a theft is advantageous, since it helps the man to live" (84n.) Barker criticizes the argument for ignoring the individual's membership in society and his inevitable involvement in what is socially advantageous and disadvantageous. For Callicles's view, see Plato, *Gorgias* 483a–484c. Compare Eteocles in Euripides's *Phoenician Women*: "If one must do a wrong, it's best to do it pursuing power—otherwise, let's have virtue" (524–25, trans. Wyckoff).

48. Notes to *Caesar and Cleopatra*, 2:303; much that Shaw says about Caesar fits Undershaft as well. This is the very insight that provoked Cusins to salute the "unselfishness" of Bodger and Undershaft back in West Ham (134).

49. Other instances occur in "Ethical Principles of Social Reconstruction," in *Platform and Pulpit*, 101, and in "What Is to Be Done with the Doctors?," *English Review* (December 1917): 500, reprinted in *Doctors' Delusions* (1932), 18.

50. Italics added. Unpublished letter of April 24, 1919, at Houghton Library, Harvard University, bMS 1046.9 (28), quotation on first and second page of letter. Quoted by permission of the Society of Authors and courtesy of Houghton Library.

51. Shaw letter to O'Bolger, August 7, 1919, in *Bernard Shaw: Collected Letters 1911–1925*, 3:628–30. Shaw modified part of this long letter for "Biographers' Blunders Corrected" in *Sixteen Self Sketches* (86–91). The paternalistic Sir William Hesketh Lever, of Lever Brothers (subsequently Unilever), like Undershaft, built a model factory community called Port Sunlight for his workers. Sir William, who became Lord Leverhulme in 1917, is one of a number of possible prototypes of Andrew Undershaft.

52. Shaw letter to O'Bolger, October 9, 1919, at Houghton Library, Harvard University, bMS 1046.9 (37), quotation on last page of letter. Quoted by permission of the Society

of Authors and courtesy of Houghton Library. Much of this letter to O'Bolger appears in *Bernard Shaw: Collected Letters 1911–1925*, ed. Laurence, 3:634–37, but not the passage quoted here. Charles Berst has discerningly diagnosed and discussed the problem of relating Undershaft's gospel to Shavian doctrine in his *Bernard Shaw and the Art of the Drama*, chap. 6, esp. 154–65.

53. Although it was Murray who first suggested the lever figure to Shaw for *Major Barbara* (see Albert, "'In More Ways Than One,'" 127–28, 131), the word does not appear in his own rhymed version of these lines in the *Bacchae*: "rend the stone with crow / And trident; make one wreck of high and low."

54. Etymologically *andreia* means "manliness." One of the four cardinal virtues, it is the characteristic virtue of the auxiliary class in Plato's *Republic* (429a–430c), to which women were fully eligible (452–56c). See Ferguson, *Moral Values*, 40–42, and North, *Sophrosyne*, 97, 170–73, and passim.

55. A summary of Huxley's social philosophy by Sir Ernest Barker reads: "Nature knows no morals and no moral standard. . . . Nature, again, knows no rights that *ought* to be: her 'rights' are simply the powers which each of her creatures actually uses for its assertion of itself in struggle. . . . Her 'laws' are simply statements of cruel facts: her rights are simply brutal powers" (*Political Thought in England 1848 to 1914*, 115–16). Barker also quotes from this passage in his *Greek Political Theory*, 73n.

56. "Virtue without Power is empty; but Power without Virtue, without ideas, is blind," is the Kantian comment of Charles Frankel on this Shaw play ("Efficient Power and Inefficient Virtue," 22).

57. "Shaw's Rehearsal Notes" (Denham, September 12, 1940) addressed to Gabriel Pascal during the filming of *Major Barbara*, in *Bernard Shaw and Gabriel Pascal*, ed. Dukore, 104.

58. Compare Tarleton in Shaw's *Misalliance*, who calls his wife "Chickabiddy" throughout the play.

59. "Shaw's Rehearsal Notes," in *Bernard Shaw and Gabriel Pascal*, ed. Dukore, 104. The omission of Sarah may have been an oversight. In the initial draft of *Major Barbara* she is included, being called "a ninny." Interestingly, "Sophist" was the original epithet for Cusins but this was cancelled in favor of "Jesuit" (British Library Add. MS 50616E, reproduced in "*Major Barbara*": *A Facsimile*, ed. Dukore, 211).

Chapter 4. The Drama of Transfiguration

1. Compare *Bacchae*, ed. Dodds, 179–80 nn. 843 and 845–46, and Kirk's translation, 92 nn. 843–46. Dodds believes that Pentheus is only pretending to postpone his decision, but offers no reasons for this opinion.

2. On *eros* see Ferguson, *Moral Values*, chap. 5, and on its role in Euripides, 79–83; Dodds, *Greeks and the Irrational*, 41, 218, 231. On *pothos* see *Bacchae* 414; Ferguson, *Moral Values*, 61 and 93–94; and *Bacchae*, ed. Dodds, 126–27 n. 414. On both see Cornford, *Thucydides Mythistoricus*, 215; Plato, *Cratylus* 420a; and Aristotle, *Nicomachean Ethics*, book 9, 1167a6.

3. "Chesterton on Shaw," *Nation* (August 25, 1909), reprinted in *Pen Portraits and Reviews*, 84. Some of Shaw's observations on tragedy throw further light on his thinking

about pity: "As to pity and terror, if people's souls could only be set right by pity and terror, then the sooner the human race comes to an end the better. You cannot pity unless you have misfortunes to pity. That is the reason, by the way, why I am not a philanthropist, why I do not like philanthropists: because they love suffering of all kinds. They are never happy unless someone else is unhappy, so they can exercise their philanthropy. I do not want there to be any more pity in the world, because I do not want there to be anything to pity; and I want there to be no more terror because I do not want people to have anything to fear" ("Bernard Shaw Talks about Actors and Acting" [1928], in *Drama Observed*, ed. Dukore, 4:1421).

4. On the use and development of the term *philanthropia* in ancient Greece and its retention of a feeling of condescension, see Snell, *Discovery of the Mind*, 250–52, and Ferguson, *Moral Values*, chap. 6, esp. 102–9, 114.

5. Winnington-Ingram, *Euripides and Dionysus*, 28; Aristotle likewise took the great gulf between man and a god to preclude the possibility of *philia* (*Nicomachean Ethics*, book 8, 1159a). Consider also the general pertinence to Undershaft of Herbert J. Muller's comment about Dionysos: "There is no more love, pity, or justice in him than there is in nature. No wise man can be simply for Dionysus, or simply against him" (*Spirit of Tragedy*, 124–25).

6. *What Shaw Really Wrote about the War*, ed. Wisenthal and O'Leary, 193. The hero of Sophocles's *Ajax* arrives at the same conclusion: "For I have learned today to hate a foe / So far, that he may yet become a friend / And so far I resolve to serve a friend / Remembering he may yet become a foe" (678–82; trans. Kitto in *Form and Meaning in Drama*, 190). This prudential approach to friend and enemy is traceable to Bias of Priene, one of the seven wise men of early Greece, whose advice Aristotle alludes to: "They treat their friends as probable future enemies and their enemies as probable future friends" (*Rhetoric* 1389b24–25, trans. W. Rhys Roberts). See also Plutarch, "How to Profit by One's Enemies," *Moralia*, vol. 2, esp. 87d–88b, 89c–e, 92c, f. Compare Shaw's own practice as described to playwright Arthur W. Pinero: "My policy is to pick up my recruits on the battlefield, carefully choosing those who have hit me hardest" (letter of March 21, 1910, in *Bernard Shaw: Collected Letters 1898–1910*, ed. Laurence, 2:910).

7. Arrowsmith, *A Greek Theater of Ideas*, 9. See also Snell's earlier discussion of these contrasting Euripidean notions in *Poetry and Society*, esp. 82–85.

8. British Library Add MS. 50616E, reproduced in *"Major Barbara": A Facsimile*, ed. Dukore, 227.

9. Shaw letters of January 24, 1899, and June 10, 1907, in *Bernard Shaw: Collected Letters 1898–1910*, 2:73, 693; *What I Really Wrote about the War*, 6. See also the 1911 Shaw interview in Bernstein, *Celebrities of Our Time*, 105, and Chappelow, *Shaw—"The Chucker-Out,"* 359.

10. Stephen coincidentally uses the English equivalent of one of Teiresias's phrases, *meg' ergon* (*Bacchae* 267), a colloquial expression meaning "a big undertaking," Dodds explains (*Bacchae*, 103 nn. 266–69). Teiresias, however, employs it negatively: "no remarkable achievement" (trans. Arrowsmith); "no great feat" (trans. Winnington-Ingram), "no great task" (trans. Kirk).

11. See Winnington-Ingram, *Euripides and Dionysus*, 26–29, 81, and *Bacchae*, ed. Dodds, 110 nn. 306–9. In particular an alliance was established between Dionysos and

Apollo. See Guthrie, *Greeks and Their Gods,* 174, 178, 199–202, and Rohde, *Psyche,* chap. 9, esp. 287–91; Murray, *Athenian Drama III: Euripides,* 166 (*Bacchae,* 81).

12. Shaw letter of October 7, 1905, reprinted in "'In More Ways Than One,'" 126.

13. Maurice Valency, *The Cart and the Trumpet: The Plays of Bernard Shaw,* 255; Charles Berst, *Bernard Shaw and the Art of the Drama,* 172–73. Robert Jordan, in "Theme and Character in *Major Barbara,*" has taken some tentative steps toward answering the allegations of "weakness" in Cusins, though he is more concessive than necessary (478–79). J. L. Wisenthal does essentially the same in *Marriage of Contraries,* detailing a number of strengths of Cusins (76–81)—unfortunately forcing them into the mold of his delimiting thesis in the process—only to back away from the logic of his evidence on 233 n. 27.

14. Compare Shaw's comment in "The Impossibilities of Anarchism": "Every institution, . . . religious, political, financial, judicial, and so on, is corrupted by the fact that the men in it either belong to the propertied class themselves or must sell themselves to it in order to live. All the purchasing power that is left to buy men's souls with after their bodies are fed is in the hands of the rich" (*Essays in Fabian Socialism,* 97).

15. For a helpful treatment of this theme, see Dukore, "The Undershaft Maxims." When Shaw first rewrote the third act, he added to Cusins's earlier line about selling his soul "for reality and for power" the phrase "or [?] for the republic," but cancelled it (British Library, Add. MS 50616A, reproduced in "*Major Barbara*": *A Facsimile,* ed. Dukore, 314). On Shaw's distrust of the professions see also "The Impossibilities of Anarchism," in *Essays in Fabian Socialism,* 97; *Drama Observed,* ed. Dukore, 2:593–96; Pref. to *The Doctor's Dilemma,* 3:237, and Sir Patrick's line in that play: "All professions are conspiracies against the laity" (3:351).

16. Cusins may be presumed to embody a Shavian answer to the peril in modern civilization described more precisely by Shaw during World War I. In *Common Sense About the War* he warned: "The one danger before us that nothing can avert but a general raising of human character through the deliberate cultivation and endowment of democratic virtue without consideration of property and class, is the danger created by inventing weapons capable of destroying civilization faster than we produce men who can be trusted to use them wisely" (*What Shaw Really Wrote about the War,* 72). It ought to be obvious that Cusins typifies those who can be so trusted, whereas Undershaft does not.

17. In a 1912 speech in which he equated evil with imperfection, Shaw argued that "the tiger is not purposely the enemy of man; it is an attempt to improve on the oyster" (*Religious Speeches of Bernard Shaw,* 49).

18. Compare the earlier description by the chorus: "The Bacchic One . . . lifting high the blazing flame of the pine torch, . . . lets it stream from his wand (i.e., the flame trails behind him as he runs)" (*Bacchae,* ed. Dodds, 145–47). See *Bacchae,* ed. Dodds, 87–88 nn. 144–50, and trans. Kirk, 42 n. 145.

19. Festugière, *Personal Religion Among the Greeks,* 25. Olympus, the dwelling place of the gods, also represents the northern limit of the Greek world, as Dodds points out (*Bacchae,* 123 nn. 402–16). At *Bacchae* 1090–93 the mountain maenads are described as flying with the speed of doves. At 748–50 they "move like birds lifted by their flight" (trans. Kirk). Barbara's more immediate inspiration is biblical, to be sure, namely, Psalms 55:6, "And I said, Oh that I had wings like a dove! for then would I fly away, and be at rest."

20. Similar is the wish of the chorus in the *Hippolytus* "that Zeus might change me to a winged bird and set me among the feathered flocks. I would rise and fly"; and the question Artemis asks Theseus in the same play: "Or will you take wings, and choosing the life of a bird instead of man keep your feet from destruction's path in which they tread?" (733–35; 1291–94, trans. David Grene). Compare Euripides, *Helen* 1478–90, *Heracles* 1157–58, *Ion* 1238, and *Andromache* 862. On the escape theme as well as the longing for wings and heavenward flight, see *Bacchae*, ed. Dodds, 122–23 nn. 402–16; Murray, *Euripides and His Age*, 153–55; Festugière, *Personal Religion among the Greeks*, 25–26; Lattimore, *Poetry of Greek Tragedy*, 117–19; Euripides, *Hippolytus*, ed. Barrett, 299 nn. 732–34 and 397–98 nn. 1290–93; Webster, *Everyday Life in Classical Athens*, 155–56; Barlow, *Imagery of Euripides*, 38–41. Compare Orinthia in *The Apple Cart*: "When I leave the earth and soar up to the regions which are my real eternal home, you can follow me" (6:345).

21. Barbara's words are echoed in Cornford's account of Dionysian religious belief: "The religion holds fast to the sympathetic principle that all life is one" (*From Religion to Philosophy*, 112). The unity affirmed is that of all living creatures, whereas Barbara's dictum implies that good and bad are inextricably mingled in human life. Nevertheless, her thought is compatible with the irrepressible moral mixture that Dionysianism manifests. Shaw himself put an equivalently broad construction on Barbara's pronouncement in an address he delivered soon after the premiere of the play: "Life, Literature, and Political Economy" (December 13, 1905), reprinted in the *Shaw Review*, 108. In it he criticized attempts to isolate life's problems—especially economic ones—from their moral and religious matrix.

22. Dodds, *Greeks and the Irrational*, 76. Barlow, too, commenting on *Bacchae* 402–16 and 430–32, refers to Aphrodite and Dionysos as "the two Gods who alone can make all people equal" (*Imagery of Euripides*, 41).

23. Shaw himself calls it "her final confession of faith" in his 1942 letter to Ellen Pollock ("More Shaw Advice," 77). Interestingly, he once described his own *Man and Superman* as developing "into a thesis play, which is always a Confession of Faith or a Confession of Doubt on the author's part" (Henderson, "George Bernard Shaw Self-Revealed," 439).

24. *Sophia*, as sound judgment, and *phronein* and its cognates—"suggesting soundness, sanity, balance; a right, a salutary attitude towards things" (Winnington-Ingram, *Euripides and Dionysus*, 42)—are repeatedly used in the *Bacchae*, along with *sophos* and *sophia* in dealing with intelligence, knowledge and wisdom. See Conacher, *Euripidean Drama*, 73–76. "There is competition throughout the play for the right to claim this quality," says Winnington-Ingram of *phronein* (42); see also 61n., 62n., and passim. Compare Ferguson, *A Companion to Greek Tragedy*, 471, and *Bacchae*, trans. Arrowsmith, 144–46.

25. Barbara is neither the first nor the last of Shaw's heroines to undergo such deification. In Act III of *Man and Superman*, the Devil tells Doña Ana that she is going to have an apotheosis (2:689). In *Back to Methuselah* Mrs. Lutestring is described as having "the walk of a goddess," and in greeting her Confucius speaks of being "honored by her celestial presence"; soon thereafter the Archbishop remarks on her "transfiguration" from a parlor maid to an angel (5:465, 470). Orinthia in *The Apple Cart* repeatedly refers to herself as a divinity: "*I* tread the plains of Heaven"; "It is what I am, not what I do, that you must worship in me"; "Nothing can derogate from my dignity: it is divine" (6:340,

343). Compare, as a male instance, Shaw's explanation that Marchbanks at the end of *Candida* is "really a god going back to his heaven" (written to James Huneker in 1904; reprinted by Huneker in "The Truth about Candida," *Metropolitan Magazine* 20 [August 1904]: 635, and in the Shaw chapter of his *Iconoclasts*, 255). Anyone disposed to dismiss such language as mere hyperbole should consider how happily it comports with Shaw's religious beliefs, and how reasonable it is to expect such beliefs to find expression in the workings of his dramatic imagination.

26. *Five Stages of Greek Religion*, 154, 152; Murray cites Pliny, *Natural History* 2:7, 18. Compare "The Stoic Philosophy" in Murray, *Essays and Addresses*, 99.

27. See, e.g., *Bacchae*, ed. Dodds, 133–34 nn. 453–59, and Rosenmeyer, *Masks of Tragedy*, 130.

28. "Modern Religion I" (April 3, 1912), in *Religious Speeches of Bernard Shaw*, 42; "Some Necessary Repairs to Religion" (November 29, 1906), reported in the *New York Times* (November 30, 1906), and reprinted in the *Independent Shavian* 10, no. 1 (Fall 1971): 2. The latter lecture is mentioned in, but omitted from, *Religious Speeches of Bernard Shaw*, xix; it is also dated one week late. See *Independent Shavian* 10, no. 2 (Winter 1971–72): 14.

29. "The Life Force," 1. This and subsequent quotations are from the manuscript at the Harry Ransom Humanities Research Center, University of Texas at Austin. Quoted by permission of the Society of Authors and the Ransom Center.

30. "The New Theology," in *Religious Speeches of Bernard Shaw*, 18–19; see also 35, 49, 77–78; on "God's work," see 6–7. According to Don Juan in *Man and Superman*, what is now called "God's work" will be given other names in the future (2:659). In the "Parents and Children" section of the Preface to *Misalliance* Shaw asserts that the goal of evolution "can only be a being that cannot be improved upon (Pref. *Misalliance*, 4:16). Compare Lavinia in *Androcles and the Lion*: "I'll strive for the coming of the God who is not yet" (4:634).

31. Albert, "Shaw's Advice to the Players," 8. For another Shavian treatment of the problem, see "The Infancy of God" in *Shaw on Religion*, esp. 139–42.

32. See the reply of the black girl to the conjurer, who told her to "'make a link between Godhood and Manhood, some god must become man.' 'Or some woman become God' said the black girl. 'That would be far better, because the god who condescends to be human degrades himself; but the woman who becomes God exalts herself'" (*The Black Girl in Search of God*, 73).

33. Shaw, "To Audiences at Major Barbara," in *Shaw on Theatre*, 121; Conacher, *Euripidean Drama*, 63, also 72. Recognition of the spiritual insufficiency of bread did not, of course, diminish Shaw's insistence on according it priority as the necessary condition for more exalted values: "Man shall not live by bread alone; but he cannot live without bread; so bread has to come first, even though the things that come later be higher things. We must serve Mammon diligently and intelligently before we serve God, as anyone may prove by trying to substitute prayers for meals" ("The Simple Truth about Socialism" [1910] in *The Road to Equality*, 169). He had made essentially the same case in a private communication ten years earlier: "Man may have his opinion as to the relative importance of feeding his body and nourishing his soul, but he is allowed by Nature to have no opinion whatever as to the need for feeding the body before the soul can think of

anything but the body's hunger. That need is a fact beyond all opinion" (letter to R. Ellis Roberts, February 7, 1900, in *Bernard Shaw: Collected Letters 1898–1910*, 2:146).

34. British Library Add. MS 50733, fol. 736. Used by permission of the Society of Authors. See Albert, "Shaw's Advice to the Players," 11; also, on 8, Shaw's reference to the "aristocratic pride" exhibited in this speech of Barbara's in his letter to Annie Russell, November 20, 1905. In the peroration of a 1911 lecture on Socialism, Shaw proposed a religious ideal that is a virtual restatement and elaboration of Barbara's conception of divine indebtedness: "A man should be able to say: 'By the labour of my prime I have paid back the debt of my education . . . and I have done something more than that. I shall die, not in my country's debt, but when I die my country shall be in my debt. I shall have produced more than I have consumed.' . . . And there is something beyond that. If there is another life to come, if any man conceives that when this life is at an end that he will then go into the presence of God, who will ask him to give an account of his life, then he would not approach that God crawling and asking for forgiveness for sins, and admitting he had lived in a wicked and horrible way. He would hold up his head even before God and say: 'When I was in your world I did your work in the world. I did more than your work in the world; I left the world in my debt. You are in my debt. Now give me my reward!'" (reprinted from *Staffordshire Sentinel* [February 16, 1911], by Chappelow in *Shaw—"The Chucker-Out*," 128–29).

35. Dukore adduces reasons in support of his conjecture that what the next Undershaft will write upon the wall will be a slogan similar to the desire he expressed to Barbara: "I want a power simple enough for common men to use, yet strong enough to force the intellectual oligarchy to use its genius for the general good" ("The Undershaft Maxims," 99). Wisely, Dukore did not assay the task of reducing this sentiment to the succinct, aphoristic form of the antecedent inscriptions. I suspect the attempt might overtax the ingenuity even of the former Adolphus Cusins. Quite apart from this and other difficulties that this choice would entail, the "way of life" proposition seems distinctly preferable as a credible motto for the new Undershaft-to-be on both dramatic and philosophic grounds. Dramatically it comes as the culminating truth Cusins learns; philosophically it is the most universal and thematically fundamental principle he announces, encompassing all his other statements about power.

36. Morgan, *The Shavian Playground*, has also called attention to Barbara's "spiritual death and resurrection" (144–45).

37. Sutherland suggests that "the doctrine of the Trinity has made a multiple god a familiar mystery," and calls Dionysos "many aspects in a single deity," though the *Bacchae* exploits his kindly and deadly extremes. On the multiformity of the god, see *Bacchae* 477, 1388; also *Bacchae*, trans. Kirk, 4, and Winnington-Ingram, *Euripides and Dionysus*, 75, 149.

38. British Library Add. MS 50616E, fol. 10; reproduced in *"Major Barbara": A Facsimile*, ed. Dukore, 199.

39. On the value of physical destruction see also *What Shaw Really Wrote About the War*, 207–8.

40. "Ethical Principles of Social Reconstruction," in *Platform and Pulpit*, 109.

41. Dukore has kindly acknowledged my having called his attention years ago to this relationship between the locales of *Major Barbara* and the *Man and Superman*

definitions (*Shaw's Theater*, 104, 246 n. 12). In the interim, however, my own thinking on this aspect of Shaw's eschatology in *Major Barbara* has undergone some revision along lines partially indicated in the present discussion.

42. Program note for the Royal Court Theatre production, June 1907, reprinted in Archibald Henderson, *George Bernard Shaw: His Life and Works*, 369–70n.; also in the *Bodley Head Bernard Shaw*, 2:800–801. The idea of free and open transit between heaven and hell, making the destination a matter of deliberate and responsible choice of ends, receives further elaboration in *Man and Superman* (esp. 2:646–49). The reference to sainthood in the "Don Juan in Hell" program note is an invitation to consider how closely Barbara fits Shaw's laudatory description of the canonized saints of the popular religions "whose secret was their conception of themselves as the instruments and vehicles of divine power and aspiration: a conception which at moments becomes an actual expression of ecstatic possession by that power" (Pref. *Back to Methuselah*, 5:324–25).

43. Edmund Wilson, for example, wrote: "*Major Barbara* contains one of the best expositions of the capitalist point of view ever written . . . [Shaw] was gradually . . . turning into a dependable member of the British propertied classes" ("Bernard Shaw at Eighty," *The Triple Thinkers*, 170–71).

44. *Bacchae*, trans. Murray, lxv–lxviii. Fittingly, it is immediately after quoting these lines that Dodds draws the parallel between the *Bacchae* and *Major Barbara* cited at the beginning of this study, in his article "Euripides the Irrationalist" (102).

45. Albert Hall, London, October 11, 1912; reprinted in *Platform and Pulpit*, 95.

46. See commentaries by Dodds, 152 n. 608, 213 nn. 1082–83; and Kirk, 77 nn. 616ff. and 114 nn. 1082f. On light and darkness in the *Bacchae*, see Rosenmeyer, *Masks of Tragedy*, 123–24. He finds the stage illumination of the *Bacchae* to be "that of the womb. It is the darkness of birth and passion and death." For a discussion of the antithesis between light and night or darkness in Greek thought, see Jaeger, *Theology of the Early Greek Philosophers*, esp. 63–64, 68, 104.

47. See *Bacchae*, ed. Dodds, 76 nn. 72–75. Dodds translates: "O blessed is he who by happy favour knowing the sacraments of the gods, leads the life of holy service and is inwardly a member of god's company." Kirk's demurrer to the use of the word "sacrament" in this translation is to my mind ill-founded (33–34 nn. 72–77). On Bacchic identification with the god see Guthrie, *A History of Greek Philosophy*: "All who genuinely felt the divine afflatus were Bacchoi or Bacchae. They were *entheoi*, the god was in them, or from another point of view *ekstatikoi*, outside themselves" (1:231).

48. See commentaries on the *Bacchae* by Dodds, 77–78 n. 85 and Kirk, 35 n. 84.

49. See also *Bacchae* 930–31; *Bacchae*, ed. Dodds, 184–85 nn. 862–85, and his *Greeks and the Irrational*, 273–74; *Bacchae*, trans. Kirk, 95 nn. 864f.

50. Letter to Ellen Rovsing, November 8, 1916, printed in Albert, "More Shaw Advice," 72.

51. In 1895 Shaw had written that "it is only the saint who has any capacity for happiness" (*Drama Observed*, ed. Dukore, 1:314).

52. British Library Add. MS 50616E, fol. 49, reproduced in *"Major Barbara": A Facsimile*, ed. Dukore, 237; British Library Add. MS 50733, fol. 736. Used by permission of the Society of Authors.

53. Compare Joan in the Epilogue to *Saint Joan*: "But my head was in the skies; and

the glory of God was upon me" (6:195), and Charles: "You people with your heads in the sky spend all your time trying to turn the world upside down" (6:197). Compare also Pref. *Androcles and the Lion*: "The passionately religious are a people apart; . . . they would turn the world upside down" (4:467). Presumably Shaw sees the saintly as inhabitants of two worlds: at home in the heavens, they quake the earth around them—set it topsy-turvy (*ano kato*). So visualized, the saint acts from an orientation very like that of Plato's philosopher-king.

54. Shaw program note, "Don Juan in Hell," in *Bodley Head Bernard Shaw: Collected Plays*, 2:802; also in Henderson, *Shaw: Life and Works*, 371 n.

55. Every effort was made to locate a source for this quotation. If you have any information, please contact the University Press of Florida.

56. Shaw letter to *Evening Standard*, November 28, 1944, in the Bodley Head *Collected Plays*, 1:603 (the letter's date is given as November 30 in Stephen S. Stanton, ed., *A Casebook on Candida*, 158, and Archibald Henderson, *George Bernard Shaw: Man of the Century*, 544). See also the discussion in Shaw's 1913 Preface to the *Quintessence of Ibsenism*, especially: "Thus A Doll's House did not dispose of the question: it only brought on the stage the endless recriminations of idealistic marriage" (*Major Critical Essays*, 8). Shaw actually claims to have anticipated Ibsen in *The Irrational Knot* by having the novel end with Conolly walking out of the house, like Nora, in "Mr. Bernard Shaw's Works of Fiction: Reviewed by Himself" (1892), reprinted in *Selected Dramatic Writings of Bernard Shaw*, ed. Laurence, 312. Compare his letter to Charlotte Payne-Townshend, April 4, 1898, in *Bernard Shaw: Collected Letters 1898–1910*, 2:26. In this connection see John Rodenbeck, "*The Irrational Knot*: Shaw, and the Uses of Ibsen," 73–74. Margery Morgan, developing a somewhat different point in *The Shavian Playground*, has also detected the linkage between *Major Barbara* and *A Doll's House* (154 n. 1).

57. Preface on Doctors, *The Doctor's Dilemma*, 3:263; Prologue to *Caesar and Cleopatra* in *Three Plays for Puritans*, 2:164. Compare Shaw's reference to "the aspiring will of humanity towards divinity" in the Preface for Politicians to *John Bull's Other Island*, 2:868.

58. See, e.g., the warning in Pref. *Back to Methuselah* that "indifference will not guide nations through civilization to the establishment of the perfect city of God" (5:326).

Appendix

1. Among those to whom Ellehauge finds Shaw directly or indirectly indebted are: Schopenhauer, Nietzsche, John Stuart Mill, Marx, Ibsen, Samuel Butler, Lamarck, Bergson, Strindberg, Remy de Gourmont, Léon Blum, Mommsen, Wagner, Tolstoy, Chekhov, Taine, Haeckel, Feuerbach, Kierkegaard, Hauptmann, and Schnitzler (passim, esp. 356–71). Characteristically, however, in the Preface to *Major Barbara* Shaw twits his critics by claiming to be influenced less by the better-known continental thinkers than by such unfamiliar British writers as Ernest Belfort Bax, Stuart-Glennie, and Captain Wilson (3:19–21). And in the same preface he himself lengthens the roster of his intellectual creditors when he professes to be standing on the shoulders of Bentham, Dickens, Carlyle, Henry George, William Morris, Ruskin, and Kropotkin, along with the earlier Euripides, More, Montaigne, Molière, Beaumarchais, Voltaire, Rousseau, Swift, Goethe, Jesus,

and the prophets (3:39). In addition, the names of numerous other contributors to his thought, including Proudhon, Blake, Bunyan, Burke, and Shelley, recur in his prefaces.

2. In a 1912 note added to *The Quintessence of Ibsenism* Shaw evinces confidence that the "movement voiced by Schopenhauer, Wagner, Ibsen, Nietzsche and Strindberg, was a world movement and would have found expression if every one of these writers had perished in his cradle," and he discerns the persistence of this movement in "the philosophy of Bergson and the plays of Gorki, Tchekov, and the post-Ibsen English drama" (*Major Critical Essays*, 34).

3. See, e.g., Robert F. Whitman, *Shaw and the Play of Ideas*. Whitman acknowledged in a letter to me that his research was following in the footsteps of my "pioneering work in exploring the Hegelian aspects of Shaw's thinking" twenty years earlier (personal letter, June 7, 1978).

4. This remark occurs, interestingly enough, during an assessment of Schopenhauerianism in which Shaw denies that accepting Schopenhauerian metaphysics entails the endorsement of its pessimistic philosophy.

5. Shaw's critics forget this dramatic orientation when they cite as evidence of a proclivity for pragmatic sophistry his advice to Ellen Terry: "In taking your side don't trouble about its being the right side—north [*sic*] is no righter or wronger than South—but be sure that it is really yours and then back it for all you are worth" (*Ellen Terry and Bernard Shaw: A Correspondence*, ed. St. John, 136.) See also, Irvine, *Universe of G.B.S.*, 243.

6. Joad, *Shaw*, see esp. chap. 8: "Differences and Deviations," 206–40.

7. For more detailed criticism, see Bentley's *Bernard Shaw*, 77–80.

8. Shaw's insistence on the desirability of a Socrates happy or unhappy (Pref. *Androcles and the Lion*, 4:568) is reminiscent of John Stuart Mill's inconsistent preference, in his *Utilitarianism*, for a Socrates dissatisfied to a fool satisfied (*Utilitarianism, Liberty, and Representative Government*, 9).

9. Witness also his iconoclastic belligerence in the Censorship statement: "I am a specialist in immoral and heretical plays. My reputation has been gained by my persistent struggle to force the public to reconsider its morals. In particular, I regard much current morality as to economic and sexual relations as disastrously wrong; and I regard certain doctrines of the Christian religion as understood in England to-day with abhorrence. I write plays with the deliberate object of converting the nation to my opinion in these matters" (Pref. *Blanco Posnet*, 3:698).

10. The He-Ancient also counsels the Newly-Born in *Back to Methuselah*, "When a thing is funny, search it for a hidden truth" (5:613).

11. See Ep. Ded. to *Man and Superman*, where he expresses his fear that he will be "defrauded of my just martyrdom" by the compact that admits books to the canon of greatness "in consideration of abrogating their meaning" (2:525–26).

12. See Post. *Back to Methuselah*: "We must have a hypothesis as a frame of reference before we can reason; and Creative Evolution, though the best we can devize so far, is basically as hypothetical and provisional as any of the creeds" (5:701–2).

Selected Bibliography

Works by Shaw

"The Author's Apology." In *The Drama Observed*. Edited by Bernard F. Dukore, 3:1132–34. University Park: Penn State University Press, 1993.

Bernard Shaw and Gabriel Pascal. Edited by Bernard F. Dukore. Toronto: University of Toronto Press, 1996.

Bernard Shaw: Collected Letters. Edited by Dan H. Laurence. 4 vols. New York: Dodd, Mead, 1965–88.

Bernard Shaw's Letters to Granville Barker. Edited by C. B. Purdom. New York: Theatre Art Books, 1957.

The Black Girl in Search of God, and Some Lesser Tales. Definitive text edited by Dan H. Laurence. New York: Penguin, 1959.

The Bodley Head Bernard Shaw: Collected Plays and Their Prefaces. Edited by Dan H. Laurence. 7 vols. London: Max Reinhardt, 1970–74.

Doctors' Delusions, Crude Criminology, and Sham Education. Standard Edition of the Works of Bernard Shaw. London: Constable, 1950.

The Drama Observed. Edited by Bernard F. Dukore. 4 vols. University Park: Penn State University Press, 1993.

Ellen Terry and Bernard Shaw: A Correspondence. Edited by Christopher St. John. New York: Theatre Arts Books, 1949.

Essays in Fabian Socialism. London: Constable, 1932.

Everybody's Political What's What? London: Constable, 1944.

Farfetched Fables. In *Buoyant Billions, Farfetched Fables, and Shakes versus Shav*. Standard Edition of the Works of Bernard Shaw. London: Constable, 1950.

"From Old Letters, Newfound Shaviana." *Boston Evening Transcript*, December 28, 1929.

G. B. Shaw: A Collection of Critical Essays. Edited by R. J. Kaufmann. Englewood Cliffs, N.J.: Prentice-Hall, 1965.

How to Become a Musical Critic. Edited by Dan H. Laurence. New York: Hill and Wang, 1961.

Immaturity. Standard Edition of the Works of Bernard Shaw. London: Constable and Company, Limited, 1931.

The Intelligent Woman's Guide to Socialism and Capitalism. London: Constable, 1928.

The Irrational Knot. London: Constable, 1905.

"Is Shaw a Dramatist? A Debate in which George Bernard Shaw Answers His Critics." In *Authentic Utterances Selected by his Biographer, Archibald Henderson. Forum* 82, no. 5 (November 1929): 260.

"Life, Literature, and Political Economy." *Clare Market Review* (January 1906). Reprinted in *Shaw Review* 8, no. 3 (September 1965).

London Music in 1888–89 as Heard by Corno di Bassetto (Later Known as Bernard Shaw) with Some Further Autobiographical Particulars. Standard Edition of the Works of Bernard Shaw. London: Constable, 1937.

"Major Barbara": A Facsimile of the Holograph Manuscript. Edited by Bernard F. Dukore. Early Texts: Play Manuscripts in Facsimile. General editor Dan H. Laurence. 12 vols. New York: Garland, 1981.

"Major Barbara": A Screen Version. Harmondsworth, England: Penguin, 1945.

Major Critical Essays. Standard Edition of the Works of Bernard Shaw. London: Constable, 1932.

Music in London 1890–94. 3 vols. Standard Edition of the Works of Bernard Shaw. London: Constable, 1932.

"Nietzsche in English." In *The Drama Observed.* Edited by Bernard F. Dukore, 2:567–72. University Park: Penn State University Press, 1993.

Pen Portraits and Reviews. Standard Edition of the Works of Bernard Shaw. London: Constable, 1930.

Platform and Pulpit. Edited by Dan H. Laurence. New York: Hill and Wang, 1961.

Preface to *Back to Methuselah.* Standard Edition of the Works of Bernard Shaw. London: Constable, 1931.

Preface to *Three Plays by Brieux.* New York: Brentano's, 1911.

The Quintessence of Ibsenism. In *Major Critical Essays.* Standard Edition of the Works of Bernard Shaw. London: Constable, 1932.

"The Religion of the British Empire." *Christian Commonwealth,* November 29, 1906. Reprinted in *The Religious Speeches of Bernard Shaw.*

The Religious Speeches of Bernard Shaw. Edited by Warren S. Smith. University Park: Pennsylvania State University Press, 1963.

The Road to Equality: Ten Unpublished Lectures and Essays, 1884–1918. Edited by Louis Crompton, assisted by Hilayne Cavanaugh. Boston: Beacon Press, 1971.

"The Sanity of Art." In *Major Critical Essays.* Standard Edition of the Works of Bernard Shaw. London: Constable, 1932.

Selected Dramatic Writings of Bernard Shaw. Edited by Dan H. Laurence. Boston: Houghton Mifflin, Riverside Edition, 1965.

"Sham Education." In *Doctors' Delusions, Crude Criminology, and Sham Education.* Standard Edition of the Works of Bernard Shaw. London: Constable, 1932.

Shaw on Religion. Edited by Warren Sylvester Smith. London: Constable, 1967.

Shaw on Theatre. Edited by E. J. West. New York: Hill and Wang, 1959.

Sixteen Self Sketches. New York: Dodd, Mead and Company, 1949.

"Some Necessary Repairs to Religion." *Independent Shavian* 10, no. 1 (Fall 1971).

Standard Edition of the Works of Bernard Shaw. 37 vols. London: Constable, 1930–51.

What I Really Wrote about the War. New York: Brentano's, 1932.

What Shaw Really Wrote about the War. Edited by J. L. Wisenthal and Daniel O'Leary. Gainesville: University Press of Florida, 2006.

Other Works Cited

Abbott, Anthony S. *Shaw and Christianity.* New York: Seabury Press, 1965.

Ackerman, Robert. "Euripides and Professor Murray." *The Classical Journal* 81, no. 4 (April-May 1986): 329–36.

Adam, James. *Religious Teachers of Greece.* Gifford Lectures. Edinburgh: T. and T. Clark, 1909.

Adkins, Arthur W. H. *Merit and Responsibility: A Study in Greek Values.* Oxford: Clarendon Press, 1960.

Albert, Sidney P. "Barbara's Progress." In *SHAW: The Annual of Bernard Shaw Studies* 21. Edited by Gale K. Larson, 81–93. University Park: Pennsylvania State University Press, 2001.

———. "From *Murray's Mother-in-Law* to *Major Barbara:* The Outside Story." In *SHAW: The Annual of Bernard Shaw Studies* 22. Edited by Gale K. Larson and MaryAnn K. Crawford, 19–65. University Park: Pennsylvania State University Press, 2002.

———. "Gilbert Murray." In *Dictionary of Literary Biography.* Edited by Stanley Weintraub, 61–71. Vol. 10, *Modern British Dramatists, 1900–1945.* Part 2: M–Z. Detroit: Gale Research, 1982.

———. "'In More Ways Than One': *Major Barbara's* Debt to Gilbert Murray." *Educational Theatre Journal* 20 (May 1968): 123–40. Reprinted in *Bernard Shaw's Plays.* Edited by Warren S. Smith, 375–97. Norton Critical Edition. New York and London: W. W. Norton, 1970.

———. "'Letters of Fire against the Sky': Bodger's Soul and Shaw's Pub." *Shaw Review* 11, no. 3 (September 1968): 82–98.

———. "The Mood of Barbara." *The Regional* 2:1. London: New York Regional Group of Shaw Society (October 1958): 8. A slightly expanded version is reprinted in *The Independent Shavian* 32, nos. 2–3 (1994): 27–28.

———. "More Shaw Advice to the Players of *Major Barbara.*" *Theatre Survey* 11, no. 1 (May 1970): 66–85.

———. "The Price of Salvation: Moral Economics in *Major Barbara.*" *Modern Drama* 14, no. 3 (December 1971): 307–23.

———. "Shaw's Advice to the Players of *Major Barbara.*" *Theatre Survey* 10, no. 1 (May 1969): 1–17.

———. "Shaw's *Republic.*" In *SHAW: The Annual of Bernard Shaw Studies* 25. Edited by MaryAnn K. Crawford, 82–88. University Park: Pennsylvania State University Press, 2005.

Albrecht, Michael von. "Fate or Hate? A Textual Problem in Shaw's *Major Barbara.*" *Notes and Queries* 36 (1989): 196–97.

Anderson, Warren D. *Ethos and Education in Greek Music: The Evidence of Poetry and Philosophy.* Cambridge, Mass.: Harvard University Press, 1966.

Andrewes, Antony. *The Greeks.* New York: Knopf, 1967.

Apel, Willi. "Early History of the Organ." *Speculum* 23 (1948): 191–216.

Aristotle. *Rhetoric.* Translated by W. Rhys Roberts. New York: Modern Library, 1954.

Arrowsmith, William. "A Greek Theater of Ideas." In *Ideas in the Drama: Selected Papers from the English Institute.* Edited by John Gassner. New York and London: Columbia University Press, 1964.

————. "The Criticism of Greek Tragedy." *Tulane Drama Review* 3, no. 3 (March 1959): 31–57.

Baines, Anthony. *Woodwind Instruments and Their History.* 3rd edition. London: Faber and Faber, 1967.

Baker, Stuart. *Bernard Shaw's Remarkable Religion: A Faith That Fits the Facts.* Gainesville: University Press of Florida, 2002.

Bancroft, Squire. *The Bancrofts: Recollections of Sixty Years.* London: John Murray, 1909.

Barker, Sir Ernest. *Greek Political Theory: Plato and His Predecessors.* London: Methuen, 1960.

————. *Political Thought in England 1848 to 1914.* 2nd edition. London: Oxford University Press, 1947.

Barlow, Shirley A. *Imagery of Euripides: A Study in the Dramatic Use of Pictorial Language.* London: Bristol Classical, 2008.

Barnes, Hazel E. *Hippolytus in Drama and Myth: The Hippolytus of Euripides.* Translated by Donald Sutherland. Lincoln: University of Nebraska Press, 1966.

Barzun, Jacques. "Bernard Shaw in Twilight." 1943. *George Bernard Shaw: A Critical Survey.* Edited by Louis Kronenberger, 158–77. Cleveland: World Publishing Company, 1953.

————. "From Shaw to Rousseau." In *The Energies of Art: Studies of Authors Classic and Modern.* New York: Harper and Brothers, 1956.

Bather, A. G. "The Problem of the *Bacchae.*" *Journal of Hellenic Studies* 14 (1894): 244–63.

Begbie, Harold. *The Life of General William Booth: The Founder of the Salvation Army.* 2 vols. New York: Macmillan, 1920.

Belmont, Eleanor Robson. *The Fabric of Memory.* New York: Farrar, Straus, and Cudahy, 1957.

Benn, Alfred William. *The Philosophy of Greece Considered in Relation to the Character and History of Its People.* London: G. Richards, 1898.

Bentley, Eric. *Bernard Shaw.* New York: Applause, 2002.

————. *A Century of Hero-Worship.* Boston: Beacon Press, 1957.

Berlioz, Hector. *A Treatise on Modern Instrumentation and Orchestration.* Translated by Mary Cowden Clarke and Joseph Bennett. Revised edition. London: Novello, 1882.

Bernal, J. D. "Shaw the Scientist." In *G.B.S. 90.* Edited by Stephen Winsten, 120–38. London: Hutchinson, 1946.

Bernstein, Herman. *Celebrities of Our Time.* Freeport, N.Y.: Books for Libraries, 1968.

Berst, Charles. *Bernard Shaw and the Art of the Drama.* Urbana: University of Illinois Press, 1973.

Bertolini, John Anthony. *The Playwrighting Self of Bernard Shaw.* Carbondale: Southern Illinois University Press, 1991.

————. *Shaw and Other Playwrights.* University Park: Pennsylvania State University Press, 1993.

Blaiklock, E. M. *The Male Characters of Euripides.* Wellington: New Zealand University Press, 1952.

Bloom, Harold, ed. *George Bernard Shaw's "Major Barbara": Modern Critical Interpretations.* New York: Chelsea, 1988.

Booth, Bramwell. *Echoes and Memories.* London: Hadder and Stoughton, 1925.

————. *These Fifty Years.* London: Cassell, 1929.

Brook, Donald. *Writers' Gallery.* London: Rockliff, 1944.

Bunyan, John. *The Pilgrim's Progress.* Edited by Roger Sharrock. London: Penguin, 1987.

Carpenter, Charles A. *Bernard Shaw as Artist-Fabian.* Gainesville: University Press of Florida, 2009.

Cassirer, Ernst. *The Myth of the State.* Garden City, N.Y.: Doubleday Anchor, 1955.

Chappelow, Allan. *Shaw—"The Chucker-Out."* London: George Allen and Unwin, 1969.

Chesterton, Gilbert K. *Eugenics and Other Evils.* London: Cassell, 1924.

————. *George Bernard Shaw.* London: Bodley Head, 1901.

Cobb, Gerald. *The Old Churches of London.* 3rd revised edition. London: B. T. Batsford, 1948.

Colbourne, Maurice. *The Real Bernard Shaw.* New York: Dodd, Mead, 1940.

Collier, Richard. *The General Next to God: The Story of William Booth and the Salvation Army.* London: Collins, 1965.

Conacher, D. J. *Euripidean Drama: Myth, Theme, and Structure.* Toronto: University of Toronto Press, 1967.

Cornford, Francis M. *From Religion to Philosophy: A Study in the Origins of Western Speculation.* New York: Harper, 1957.

————. *Principium Sapientiae: The Origins of Greek Philosophical Thought.* Cambridge: Cambridge University Press, 1952.

————. *Thucydides Mythistoricus.* 1907. London: Routledge and Kegan Paul, 1965.

Costello, Donald P. *The Serpent's Eye: Shaw and the Cinema.* Notre Dame: University of Notre Dame Press, 1965.

Crawley, Ernest. *Dress, Drinks and Drums.* Edited by Theodore Besterman. London: Methuen, 1931.

Crombie, I. M. *An Examination of Plato's Doctrines.* New York: Humanities, 1962.

Crompton, Louis. *Shaw the Dramatist.* Lincoln: University of Nebraska Press, 1969.

Cushman, Robert E. *Therapeia: Plato's Conception of Philosophy.* Chapel Hill: University of North Carolina Press, 1958.

Dailey, Jeff S. "George Bernard Shaw's Criticism of Gilbert and Sullivan." *Opera Journal* 37, no. 2 (June 2004): 3–14.

Decharme, Paul. *Euripides and the Spirit of His Dramas.* 1906. Translated by James Loeb. Port Washington, N.Y.: Kennikat, 1968.

Dent, Alan, ed. *Bernard Shaw and Mrs. Patrick Campbell: Their Correspondence.* London: Victor Gollancz, 1952.

Dodds, E. R. "Euripides the Irrationalist." *Classical Review* 43, no. 3 (July 1929): 97–104. Reprinted in *The Ancient Concept of Progress and Other Essays on Greek Literature and Belief.* Oxford: Clarendon Press, 1973.

————. *The Greeks and the Irrational.* Boston: Beacon, 1957.

————. Introduction to *Gilbert Murray: An Unfinished Autobiography.* Edited by Jean Smith and Arnold Toynbee. London: George Allen and Unwin, 1960.

Dukore, Bernard F. *Bernard Shaw, Playwright: Aspects of Shavian Drama.* Columbia: University of Missouri Press, 1973.

————. "Dolly Finds a Father: Shaw's Dramatic Development." *Papers on Language and Literature* 24 (1988): 81–90.

———. "'Father Undershaft' and the Kids." In *SHAW: The Annual of Bernard Shaw Studies* 21. Edited by Gale K. Larson, 95–105. University Park: Pennsylvania State University Press, 2001.

———. "Shaw's 'Big Three.'" In *SHAW: The Annual of Bernard Shaw Studies* 4. Edited by Stanley Weintraub, 95–105. University Park: Pennsylvania State University Press, 1984.

———. *Shaw's Theater*. Gainesville: University of Florida Press, 2000.

———. "The Time of *Major Barbara*." *Theatre Survey* 23 (1982): 10–11.

———. "Toward an Interpretation of *Major Barbara*." *Shaw Review* 6 (1963): 62–70.

———. "The Undershaft Maxims." *Modern Drama* 9 (May 1966): 90–100. Reprinted in Zimbardo, *Twentieth Century Interpretations of* Major Barbara.

Eliot, T. S. "Euripides and Professor Murray." 1920. In *The Sacred Wood: Essays on Poetry and Criticism*. New York: Barnes and Noble, 1960.

Ellehauge, Martin. *The Position of Bernard Shaw in European Drama and Philosophy*. Copenhagen: Levin and Munksgaard, 1931.

Else, Gerald Frank. *Aristotle's Poetics: The Argument*. Cambridge, Mass.: Harvard University Press, 1957.

Ervine, St. John. *Bernard Shaw: His Life, Work and Friends*. New York: William Morrow, 1956.

———. *God's Soldier: General William Booth*. New York: Macmillan, 1935.

Euripides. *The Bacchae*. Translated by William Arrowsmith. In *The Complete Greek Tragedies: Euripides V*. Edited by David Grene and Richard Lattimore, 141–220. Chicago: University of Chicago Press, 1959.

———. *Bacchae*. Translated by Henry Birkhead. In *Ten Greek Plays in Contemporary Translations*. Edited by L. R. Lind. Boston: Houghton Mifflin, 1957.

———. *The Bacchae*. Translated by Neil Curry. In *The Great Playwrights*. Edited by Eric Bentley, 1:227–68. Garden City, N.Y.: Doubleday, 1970.

———. *Bacchae*. Edited with introduction and commentary by E. R. Dodds. 2nd edition. Oxford: Clarendon Press, 1961.

———. *The Bacchae: A Translation with Commentary*. Translated by Geoffrey S. Kirk. Englewood Cliffs, N.J.: Prentice-Hall, 1970.

———. *The Bacchae*. Translated by F. L. Lucas. In *Greek Tragedy and Comedy*, 306–42. New York: Viking, 1967.

———. *The Bacchae*. Translated by Gilbert Murray. In *Athenian Drama III: Euripides*, 77–177. New York: Longmans, 1908.

———. *The Bacchae*. Introduction, translation, and commentary by Richard Seaford. Warminster, England: Aris and Phillips, 1996.

———. *The Bacchae of Euripides*. Translated and edited by John Edwin Sandys. Revised edition. Cambridge: Cambridge University Press, 1885.

———. *The Bacchae of Euripides: A New Translation with a Critical Essay*. Translated by Donald Sutherland. Lincoln: University of Nebraska Press, 1968.

———. *The Bacchae of Euripides: A New Version*. Translated by C. K. Williams. Introduction by Martha Nussbaum. New York: Farrar, Straus and Giroux, 1990.

———. *The Bacchae and Other Plays*. Translated by Philip Vellacott, 181–228. Baltimore: Penguin, 1954.

———. *The Bacchae*. Translated by Minos Volanakis. In *Euripides*. Edited by Robert W. Corrigan, 165–224. New York: Dell-Laurel, 1965.

———. *The Bacchanals*. Translated by Arthur S. Way. In *Euripides*, 3:1–123. 4 vols. Loeb Classical Library London: W. Heinemann, 1912.

———. *The Bacchanals*. Translated by H. H. Milman. In *The Plays of Euripides in English*, 2:1–37. 2 vols. London: J. M. Dent, 1908.

———. *The Bacchantes*. In *The Plays of Euripides*. Translated by Edward Coleridge, 2:87–129. London: George Bell, 1904.

———. *The Bacchantes*. In *Ten Plays by Euripides*. Translated by Moses Hadas and John McLean, 279–312. New York: Bantam, 1960.

———. *The Helen of Euripides*. Translated by Rex Warner. London: Bodley Head, 1951.

———. *Helen*. Translated by Richmond Lattimore. *The Complete Greek Tragedies: Euripides II*, 189–260. Chicago: University of Chicago Press, 1955–59.

———. *Hippolytus*. Edited by W. D. Barrett. Oxford: Oxford University Press, 1966.

———. *Hippolytus*. Translated by David Grene. *Three Greek Tragedies in Translation*. Chicago: University of Chicago Press, 1942.

———. *Ion*. In *Euripides*. Translated by Arthur S. Way. 4 vols. Cambridge, Mass.: Harvard University Press, 1942–52.

———. *Phoenician Women*. Translated by Elizabeth Wyckoff. In *The Complete Greek Tragedies: Euripides V*. Edited by David Grene and Richmond Lattimore, 71–140. Chicago: University of Chicago Press, 1959.

Everding, Robert G. "Fusion of Character and Setting: Artistic Strategy in *Major Barbara*." In *SHAW: The Annual of Bernard Shaw Studies* 3. Edited by Daniel Leary, 103–16. University Park: Pennsylvania State University Press, 1983.

Farnell, Lewis Richard. *The Cults of the Greek States*. 5 vols. Oxford: Clarendon Press, 1909.

Ferguson, John. *A Companion to Greek Tragedy*. Austin: University of Texas Press, 1972.

———. *Moral Values in the Ancient World*. London: Methuen, 1958.

Festugière, André-Jean. *Personal Religion among the Greeks*. Berkeley and Los Angeles: University of California Press, 1960.

Forter, Elizabeth T. Introduction to *Major Barbara*. Crofts Classic Edition. New York: Appleton-Century-Crofts, 1971.

Frank, Joseph. "Major Barbara—Shaw's *Divine Comedy*." PMLA 71 (March 1956): 61–74.

Frankel, Charles. "Efficient Power and Inefficient Virtue; Bernard Shaw: *Major Barbara*." *Great Moral Dilemmas in Literature, Past and Present*. Edited by R. M. MacIver. New York: Institute for Religious and Social Studies, 1956.

Frazer, Sir James G. *The Golden Bough*. 12 vols. London: Macmillan, 1911–15.

Friedländer, Paul. *Plato: An Introduction*. Translated by Hans Meyerhoff. Bollingen Series 59. New York: Pantheon, 1958.

Fuller, B.A.G. *History of Greek Philosophy*. 3 vols. New York: H. Holt and Company, 1923–31.

Gahan, Peter. *Shaw Shadows: Rereading the Texts of Bernard Shaw*. Gainesville: University Press of Florida, 2004.

Geiringer, Karl. *Musical Instruments*. Translated by Bernard Miall. New York: Oxford University Press, 1945.

Gibbs, A. M. *The Art and Mind of Shaw: Essays in Criticism*. New York: St. Martin's, 1983.

———. *Bernard Shaw: A Life*. Gainesville: University Press of Florida, 2005.

Greene, William Chase. *Moira: Fate, Good, and Evil in Greek Thought*. New York: Harper Torchbook, 1963.

Grene, Nicholas. *Bernard Shaw: A Critical View*. London: Macmillan, 1984.

Grube, G.M.A. *The Drama of Euripides*. London: Methuen, 1961.

———. *Plato's Thought*. Boston: Beacon, 1958.

Guthrie, W.K.C. *The Greeks and Their Gods*. Boston: Beacon, 1950.

———. *A History of Greek Philosophy*. 6 vols. Cambridge: Cambridge University Press, 1962–81.

———. *In the Beginning: Some Greek Views on the Origins of Life and the Early State of Man*. London: Methuen, 1957.

———. *Orpheus and Greek Religion*. 2nd edition. New York: Norton Library, 1966.

Hagan, Patrick G., Jr., and Joseph O. Baylen. "Shaw, W. T. Stead, and the 'International Peace Crusade,' 1898–1899." *Shaw Review* 6, no. 2 (May 1963): 60–61.

Hall, Edith, and Fiona Macintosh. *Greek Tragedy and the British Theatre 1660–1914*. Oxford: Oxford University Press, 2005.

Harrison, Frank, and Joan Rimmer. *European Musical Instruments*. New York: W. W. Norton, 1964.

Harrison, Jane Ellen. *Prolegomena to the Study of Greek Religion*. 3rd edition. New York: Meridian, 1955.

———. *Themis: A Study of the Social Origins of Greek Religion*. 1927. 2nd edition. Cleveland: World, Meridian, 1962.

Harsh, Philip W. *Handbook of Classical Drama*. Stanford: Stanford University Press, 1944.

Henderson, Archibald. *George Bernard Shaw: His Life and Works*. Cincinnati: Stewart and Kidd, 1911.

———. *George Bernard Shaw: Man of the Century*. New York: Appleton-Century-Crofts, 1956.

———. "George Bernard Shaw Self-Revealed." *Fortnightly Review* 125 (April 1926): 433–42, 610–18.

Holroyd, Michael. *Bernard Shaw*. 5 vols. London: Chatto and Windus, 1988–92.

Hospers, John. *Meaning and Truth in the Arts*. Chapel Hill: University of North Carolina Press, 1946.

Hugo, Leon. *Bernard Shaw: Playwright and Preacher*. London: Methuen, 1971.

Huneker, James. *Iconoclasts*. New York: Charles Scribner's Sons, 1905.

Huxley, Thomas H. *Evolution and Ethics and Other Essays*. New York: D. Appleton, 1896.

Irvine, William. "*Major Barbara*." *The Shavian* 7 (July 1956): 43–47.

———. *The Universe of G.B.S.* New York: Whittlesey House, 1949.

Jackson, Holbrook. *The Eighteen Nineties: A Review of Art and Ideas at the Close of the Nineteenth Century*. New York: Knopf, 1922.

Jaeger, Werner. *Paideia: The Ideals of Greek Culture*. Translated by Gilbert Highet. 2nd edition. New York: Oxford University Press, 1945.

———. *The Theology of the Early Greek Philosophers*. Translated by Edward S. Robinson. Oxford: Clarendon, 1948.

Joad, C.E.M. *Shaw*. London: Victor Gollanz, 1949.

Jordan, Robert J. "Theme and Character in *Major Barbara.*" *Texas Studies in Language and Literature* 12, no. 3 (Fall 1970): 471–80.

Kaufmann, Walter. *Tragedy and Philosophy.* Garden City, N.Y.: Doubleday Anchor, 1969.

Kaye, Julian B. *Bernard Shaw and the Nineteenth-Century Tradition.* Norman: University of Oklahoma Press, 1955.

Kent, William, ed. *An Encyclopedia of London.* London: J. M. Dent, 1951.

Kerenyi, Carl. *Eleusis: Archetypal Image of Mother and Daughter.* Translated by Ralph Manheim. Bollingen Series 65. Princeton: Princeton University Press, 1967.

Kirk, G. S., and J. E. Raven. *The Presocratic Philosophers.* Cambridge: Cambridge University Press, 1963.

Kitto, H.D.F. *Form and Meaning in Drama.* London: Methuen, University Paperbacks, 1960.

———. *Greek Tragedy: A Literary Study.* 3rd edition. London: Methuen, 1961.

Kronenberger, Louis, ed. *George Bernard Shaw: A Critical Survey.* Cleveland: World Publishing Company, 1953.

Lattimore, Richmond. *The Poetry of Greek Tragedy.* Baltimore: Johns Hopkins Press, 1958.

———. *Story Patterns in Greek Tragedy.* Ann Arbor: University of Michigan Press, 1964.

Lawler, Lillian B. *The Dance in Ancient Greece.* Seattle: University of Washington Press, 1967.

Laurence, Dan H. *Bernard Shaw: A Bibliography.* 2 vols. Oxford: University of Oxford Press, 1983.

Leary, Daniel J. "Dialectical Action in *Major Barbara.*" *Shaw Review* 12, no. 2 (May 1969): 46–58.

Lesky, Albin. *Greek Tragedy.* Translated by H. A. Frankfort. London: Ernest Benn, 1965.

———. *History of Greek Literature.* Translated by James Willis and Cornelius de Heer. 2nd edition. New York: Thomas Y. Crowell, 1966.

Lindsay, Jack. *The Clashing Rocks: A Study of Early Greek Religion and Culture and the Origins of Drama.* London: Chapman and Hall, 1965.

Linforth, Ivan M. "Corybantic Rites in Plato." *University of California Publications in Classical Philology* 13, no. 5 (1946): 154–62.

———. "Telestic Madness in Plato, Phaedrus 244de." *University of California Publications in Classical Philology* 13, no. 6 (1946): 163–72.

MacCarthy, Desmond. *Shaw: The Plays.* 1951. Newton Abbot: David and Charles, 1973.

MacGillivray, James. "The Cylindrical Reed Pipe from Antiquity to the 20th Century." In *Music: Libraries and Instruments.* Edited by Unity Sherrington and Guy Oldham. London: Hinrichsen Edition, 1961.

Martin, Kingsley. "Shaw—The Man, the Socialist." In *Shaw and Society.* Edited by C.E.M. Joad. London: Odhams, 1953.

McCarthy, Lillah. *Myself and My Friends.* London: Thornton Butterworth, 1933.

Meisel, Martin. *Shaw and the Nineteenth-Century Theater.* New York: Limelight Editions, 1984.

Mill, John Stuart. *Utilitarianism, Liberty, and Representative Government.* London: Everyman's Library, 1944.

The Missal in Latin and English. New York: Sheed and Ward, 1949.

Morehead, James and Albert Morehead, eds. *101 Favorite Hymns*. New York: Pocket Books, 1953.

Morgan, Margery M. "'Back to Methuselah': The Poet and the City." In *Essays and Studies Collected for the English Association*. Edited by Charles Jasper Sisson and M. St. Clare Byrne. London: Murray, 1960. Reprinted in *G. B. Shaw: A Collection of Critical Essays*. Edited by R. J. Kaufmann. Englewood Cliffs, N.J.: Prentice-Hall, 1965.

———. *A Drama of Political Man: A Study in the Plays of Harley Granville Barker*. London: Sidgwick and Jackson, 1961.

———. *The Shavian Playground: An Exploration of the Art of George Bernard Shaw*. London: Methuen, 1972.

Muller, Herbert J. *The Spirit of Tragedy*. New York: Knopf, 1968.

Murray, Gilbert. *A History of Ancient Greek Literature*. 1897. New York: Frederick Ungar, 1966.

———. "The *Bacchae* in Relation to Certain Currents of Thought in the Fifth Century." Introductory essay in *Athenian Drama* III: *Euripides*. London: George Allen, 1902.

———. *Essays and Addresses*. London: George Allen and Unwin, 1921. American edition: *Tradition and Progress*. Boston and New York: Houghton Mifflin, 1922.

———. *The Classical Tradition in Poetry*. Charles Eliot Norton Lectures. London: Oxford University Press, 1927.

———. *Euripides and His Age*. London, New York, and Ontario: Oxford University Press, 1946.

———. "Euripides' Tragedies of 415 B.C.: The Deceitfulness of Life." In *Greek Studies*. Oxford: Oxford University Press, 1946.

———. *Five Stages of Greek Religion*. Garden City, N.Y.: Doubleday Anchor, 1955.

———. "Greek and English Tragedy: A Contrast." *English Literature and the Classics*. Edited by G. S. Gordon. New York: Russell and Russell, 1969.

———. *The Rise of the Greek Epic*. New York: Oxford University Press, 1960.

Mylonas, George E. *Eleusis and the Eleusinian Mysteries*. Princeton: Princeton University Press, 1961.

Nelson, Raymond S. "Responses to Poverty in *Major Barbara*." *Arizona Quarterly* 27, no. 4 (Winter 1971): 335–46.

Nelson, William Hamilton. *Blood and Fire: General William Booth*. London: Century, 1929.

Nethercot, Arthur H. "Bernard Shaw, Philosopher." *Proceedings of the Modern Language Association* 69, no. 1 (1954): 57–75.

———. *Men and Supermen: The Shavian Portrait Gallery*. Cambridge: Harvard University Press, 1954.

Nettleship, R. L. *Lectures on the "Republic" of Plato*. London: Macmillan, 1954.

Nicoll, Allardyce. *World Drama from Aeschylus to Anouilh*. New York: Harcourt, Brace, 1950.

Nilsson, Martin P. *Greek Folk Religion*. New York: Harper Torchbooks, 1961.

———. *A History of Greek Religion*. Translated by F. J. Fielden. Oxford: Oxford University Press, 1949.

———. *Minoan-Mycenaean Religion and Its Survival in Greek Religion*. 2nd revised edition. New York: Biblo and Tannen, 1971.

Nitze, William A. "'A Midsummer Night's Dream,' V, 1, 4–17." *Modern Language Review* 50, no. 4 (October 1955): 495–97.

North, Helen. *Sophrosyne: Self-Knowledge and Self-Restraint in Greek Literature.* Cornell Studies in Classical Philology 35. Ithaca: Cornell University Press, 1966.

Norwood, Gilbert. *Essays on Euripidean Drama.* Berkeley and Los Angeles: University of California Press, 1954.

———. "Euripides and Shaw: A Comparison." 1911. In *Euripides and Shaw with Other Essays.* London: Methuen, 1921.

———. *Greek Tragedy.* London: Methuen, 1948.

———. *Riddle of the Bacchae: The Last Stage of Euripides' Religious Views.* Manchester: University Press, 1908.

Oesterreich, T. K. *Possession: Demoniacal and Other.* London: Kegan Paul, Trench, Trubner, 1930.

Orage, Alfred Richard. *Friedrich Nietzsche: The Dionysian Spirit of the Age.* Chicago: A. C. McClurg, 1911.

Otto, Walter F. *Dionysus: Myth and Cult.* Translated by Robert B. Palmer. Bloomington: Indiana University Press, 1965.

Oxford Classical Dictionary. Edited by M. Cary and others with the assistance of H. J. Rose, H. P. Harvey, and A. Souter. 2nd edition. Oxford: Clarendon, 1949.

Ozy [pseud.]. "The Dramatist's Dilemma: An Interpretation of *Major Barbara.*" *Shaw Bulletin* 2, no. 4 (1958): 18–24.

———. *The War against Bernard Shaw.* New York: White Plume Publishing, 1957.

Pearson, Hesketh. *G.B.S.: A Full Length Portrait and a Postscript.* New York: Harper, 1950.

Pearson, Lionel. *Popular Ethics in Ancient Greece.* New York: W. W. Norton, 1972.

Pedersen, Lisë. "Ducats and Daughters in *The Merchant of Venice* and *Major Barbara.*" In *SHAW: The Annual of Bernard Shaw Studies* 4. Edited by Stanley Weintraub, 69–86. University Park: Pennsylvania State University Press, 1984.

Persson, Axel W. *The Religion of Greece in Prehistoric Times.* Berkeley and Los Angeles: University of California Press, 1942.

Peters, Margot. *Bernard Shaw and the Actresses.* Garden City, N.Y.: Doubleday, 1980.

Peters, Sally. *Bernard Shaw: The Ascent of the Superman.* New Haven: Yale University Press, 1996.

Pharand, Michel W. "Introduction: Dionysian Shaw." In *SHAW: The Annual of Bernard Shaw Studies* 24. Edited by Michel W. Pharand, 1–10. University Park: Pennsylvania State University Press, 2004.

Pickard-Cambridge, Sir Arthur. *Dithyramb Tragedy and Comedy.* Revised by T.B.L. Webster. 2nd edition. Oxford: Oxford University Press, 1962.

Plato. *Euthyphro, Apology, Crito.* Translated by F. J. Church. Englewood Cliffs, N.J.: Prentice-Hall, 1987.

———. *The Last Days of Socrates.* Translated by Hugh Tredennick. London: Penguin Books, 1954.

———. *Phaedo.* Translated by R. Hackforth. Cambridge: Cambridge University Press, 1955.

———. *Phaedrus.* Translated by Henry Cary. Vol. 1, *Bohn's Classical Library.* London: H. G. Bohn, 1950–55.

———. *Phaedrus.* In *The Dialogues of Plato.* Translated by B. Jowett. 5 vols. London: H. Milford, Oxford University Press, 1931.

———. *Plato: The Collected Dialogues.* Edited by Edith Hamilton and Huntington Cairns. Bollingen Series 71. New York: Pantheon, 1961.

———. *Plato's Phaedrus.* Translated by R. Hackforth. Cambridge: Cambridge University Press, 1952.

———. *The Republic of Plato.* Translated by Francis M. Cornford. New York: Oxford University Press, 1945.

———. *The Republic.* In *The Dialogues of Plato.* Translated by B. Jowett. 5 vols. London: H. Milford, Oxford University Press, 1931.

Plutarch. "How to Profit by One's Enemies." In vol. 2, *Moralia.* Translated by Frank Cole Babbitt. Loeb Classical Library. New York: G. Putnam's, 1927–28.

Post, L. A. *From Homer to Menander.* Berkeley and Los Angeles: University of California Press, 1951.

Puchner, Martin. *The Drama of Ideas: Platonic Provocations in Theater and Philosophy.* Oxford: Oxford University Press, 2010.

Rattray, R. F. *Bernard Shaw: A Chronicle and an Introduction.* London: Duckworth, 1934.

Riu, Xavier. *Dionysism and Comedy.* Lanham, Md.: Rowman and Littlefield, 1999.

Roberts, Charles. *The Radical Countess: The History of the Life of Rosalind Countess of Carlisle.* Carlisle, England: Steel Brothers Limited, 1962.

Rodenbeck, John. "*The Irrational Knot:* Shaw and the Uses of Ibsen." *Shaw Review* 12, no. 2 (May 1969): 66–76.

Rohde, Erwin. *Psyche: The Cult of Souls and Belief in Immortality among the Greeks.* Translated by W. B. Hillis. London: Kegan Paul, Trench, Trubner, 1925.

Rose, H. J. *Ancient Greek Religion.* London: Hutchinson's University Library, 1946.

———. *Handbook of Greek Mythology.* New York: E. P. Dutton, 1959.

Rosenmeyer, Thomas G. *The Masks of Tragedy.* Austin: University of Texas Press, 1963.

Royce, Josiah. *The Spirit of Modern Philosophy.* Boston: Houghton, Mifflin and Co., 1892.

Sabine, George H. *A History of Political Theory.* New York: Holt, Rinehart, and Winston, 1961.

Seltman, Charles T. *Approach to Greek Art.* London: Studio Publications, 1948.

———. *The Twelve Olympians.* New York: Thomas Y. Crowell-Apollo, 1962.

Shorey, Paul. *Platonism, Ancient and Modern.* Berkeley and Los Angeles: University of California Press, 1938.

Smith, J. Percy. "Shaw's Own Problem Play: *Major Barbara.*" *English Studies in Canada* 4, no. 4 (Winter 1978): 450–67.

Snell, Bruno. *The Discovery of the Mind: The Greek Origins of European Thought.* 1953. Translated by T. G. Rosenmeyer. New York: Harper Torchbook, 1960.

———. *Poetry and Society: The Role of Poetry in Ancient Greece.* Bloomington: Indiana University Press, 1961.

———. *Scenes from Greek Drama.* Berkeley and Los Angeles: University of California Press, 1967.

Stanton, Stephen S., ed. *A Casebook on Candida.* New York: Thomas Y. Crowell, 1962.

Stow, John. *Survey of London.* Revised edition 1603. London: J. M. Dent and Sons, 1956.

Taylor, A. E. *Plato: The Man and His Work.* New York: Meridian, 1956.

Tetzeli von Rosador, Kurt. "The Natural History of *Major Barbara*." *Modern Drama* 17, no. 2 (June 1974): 141–53.

Thomson, George. *Aeschylus and Athens: A Study in the Social Origins of Drama*. 2nd edition. London: Lawrence and Wishart, 1946.

Turco, Alfred, Jr. *Shaw's Moral Vision: The Self and Salvation*. Ithaca and London: Cornell University Press, 1976.

Tyrrell, R. Y. *The Bacchae of Euripides*. London: Longmans, Green, Reader, and Dyer, 1871.

Valency, Maurice. *The Cart and the Trumpet: The Plays of Bernard Shaw*. New York: Oxford University Press, 1973.

Vlastos, Gregory. "Equality and Justice in the Early Greek Cosmologies." *Classical Philology* 42, no. 3 (July 1947): 156–78.

Ward, Maisie. *Gilbert Keith Chesterton*. London: Sheed and Ward, 1944.

Webster, T.B.L. *Athenian Culture and Society*. Berkeley and Los Angeles: University of California Press, 1973.

———. *Everyday Life in Classical Athens*. New York: G. P. Putnam's Sons, 1969.

———. *The Tragedies of Euripides*. London: Methuen, 1967.

Weintraub, Stanley. *Bernard Shaw: A Guide to Research*. University Park: Penn State University Press, 1992.

———. "Bernard Shaw in Darkest England: G.B.S. and the Salvation Army's General William Booth." In *SHAW: The Annual of Bernard Shaw Studies* 10. Edited by Stanley Weintraub and Fred D. Crawford, 45–59. University Park: Pennsylvania State University Press, 1990.

———. *Journey to Heartbreak: The Crucible Years of Bernard Shaw 1914–1918*. New York: Weybright and Talley, 1971.

———. *Private Shaw and Public Shaw: A Dual Portrait of Lawrence of Arabia and G.B.S.* New York: Braziller, 1963.

———. "'Shaw's *Divine Comedy*': Addendum." *Shaw Bulletin* 2, no. 5 (May 1958): 21–22.

West, Alick. *A Good Man Fallen Among Fabians*. London: Lawrence and Wishart, 1950.

Whitman, Robert F. *Shaw and the Play of Ideas*. Ithaca: Cornell University Press, 1977.

Wilson, Duncan. *Gilbert Murray, OM, 1866–1957*. Oxford: Clarendon, 1987.

Wilson, Edmund. *The Triple Thinkers: Twelve Essays on Literary Subjects*. New York: Oxford University Press, 1963.

Winsten, Stephen, ed. *G.B.S. 90: Aspects of Bernard Shaw's Life and Work*. London: Hutchinson, 1946.

Winnington-Ingram, R. P. *Euripides and Dionysus: An Interpretation of the Bacchae*. Amsterdam: Adolf M. Hakkert, 1969.

Wisenthal, J. L. *The Marriage of Contraries: Bernard Shaw's Middle Plays*. Cambridge, Mass.: Harvard University Press, 1974.

———. "The Underside of Undershaft: A Wagnerian Motif in *Major Barbara*," *Shaw Review* 15, no. 2 (May 1972): 56–64.

Zimbardo, Rose A., ed. *Twentieth Century Interpretations of* Major Barbara: *A Collection of Critical Essays*. Englewood Cliffs, N.J.: Prentice-Hall, 1970.

Index

Sidney P. Albert, Professor Emeritus of Philosophy, California State University, Los Angeles, is a well-known Shaw authority specializing in *Major Barbara*, who became 97 years old in 2011. His interest in *Barbara* combines his lifelong interest in philosophy and the theater, for in addition to a 1939 Ph.D. in Philosophy from Yale University, Albert did postdoctoral study in drama and theater at Carnegie Institute of Technology (now Carnegie Mellon), Northwestern, Stanford, the University of Illinois (Champagne-Urbana), and Columbia. His focused interest in *Major Barbara* is reflected in numerous lectures and papers delivered on various aspects of the play and more than a dozen published essays. A founding member of the International Shaw Society, now on the ISS Advisory Committee, and a former member of the *Shaw Review* editorial board, he has amassed two extensive Shaw collections, one now at Brown University and the other that is seeking a permanent home. In his later years he founded and served as president of two emeriti faculty organizations, one at California State University, Los Angeles, and the other for the 19 (now 23) campus California State University system (CSU-Emeritus and Retired Faculty Association), currently a powerful influence in the state.

The Florida Bernard Shaw Series

This series was made possible by a generous grant from
the David and Rachel Howie Foundation.

EDITED BY R. F. DIETRICH